America's Problems

Social Issues and
Public Policy

Second Edition

Elliott Currie and Jerome H. Skolnick • UNIVERSITY OF CALIFORNIA, BERKELEY

Scott, Foresman/Little, Brown College Division
SCOTT, FORESMAN AND COMPANY
Glenview, Illinois   Boston   London

Library of Congress Cataloging-in-Publication Data

Currie, Elliott.
    America's problems: social issues and public policy/Elliott
Currie and Jerome H. Skolnick.—2nd ed.
    p.   cm.
    Bibliography: p.
    Includes indexes.
    ISBN 0-673-39714-9
    1. United States—Social conditions—1980-   2. United States—
Social policy—1980-   I. Skolnick, Jerome H.   II. Title.
HN65.C88   1988
306′ .0973—dc19   87-29812
                                                                   CIP

1 2 3 4 5 6 7 8 9 10 — RRC — 93 92 91 90 89 88 87

Printed in the United States of America

Acknowledgments

    "Allentown" (pp. 4–5 and 245), words and music by Billy Joel. Copyright ©
1981, 1982 by Joel Songs (BMI). All rights controlled and administered by Black-
wood Music, Inc. All rights reserved. Used by permission.
    Table 10-2: Data from "Reforming the Electric Power Industry" by Christopher
Flavin, reprinted from *State of the World 1986, A World Watch Institute Report on Progress Toward a Sustainable Society*, edited by Lester R. Brown, et al. Used by permission
of W. W. Norton & Co., Inc. Copyright © 1986 by the World Watch Institute.
    Table 10-4: Data from David Burmaster, "The New Pollution: Groundwater
Contamination" reprinted with permission of *Environment*, a publication of the
Helen Dwight Reid Educational Foundation.
    Table 12-5: Data from "Warming to the Freeze" by Leon V. Sigal in *Foreign
Policy* 48 (Fall 1982). Copyright 1982 by the Carnegie Endowment for International
Peace.

Preface

We've been gratified by the response to the first edition of *America's Problems*, and for this new edition we've made some changes that, we think, have improved the book considerably while keeping its overall character intact. In particular, we've streamlined the book, cutting down on many lengthy arguments and shortening or eliminating many tables and charts. Our aim has been to make the book less cumbersome and more accessible to students without sacrificing content or our original commitment to comprehensive and high-level discussion of contemporary social issues. We hope we've succeeded, and we deeply appreciate the comments of all those readers who gave us helpful feedback on the first edition.

We wrote this book because we felt that the United States faces both unprecedented challenges and unprecedented opportunities as we move toward the twenty-first century and that meeting those challenges will require the best and most careful analysis of social issues we can muster. We believed that students should be introduced to the complex—and often difficult—research bearing on the most important debates about social problems today, and that without that kind of exposure, they would be poorly prepared to participate in shaping American society in the future. We still share these beliefs. More than ever, we see the need for a book that can interpret the forces underlying contemporary changes in American society, and do so in a way that is accessible and interesting to students. We have tried to write a textbook for people who don't like textbooks — one that achieves depth without being stuffy and formal, that teaches without being pedantic, that is up-to-date and timely while staying in touch with the best traditions of social science.

As does our reader, *Crisis in American Institutions*, *America's Problems* assumes that particular problems must be understood in the context of broader social and economic structures and forces that shape them. Too often the literature still treats social problems in isolation from each other and from larger social processes. As a consequence, most texts on social problems, even if they have moved beyond the traditionally narrow focus on personal deviance and disorganization, seem awkwardly fragmented. They often appear to be a hodgepodge of disconnected concerns; they seldom make an effort to provide students with an overall sense of the master forces of their society and of how these forces affect social and personal life.

Our book's organization addresses these shortcomings. It covers the traditional categories within the field — from family problems to crime and poverty — but consistently focuses on them through the lens of fundamental structures and processes of American society.

Specifically, *America's Problems* is divided into two closely related parts. The first, "Systems and Structures," deals with what we regard as some of the most important of the broad structural features of American society — the contours of the private-profit economy in America and its changing role in the *world* economic order, and the historically pervasive inequalities of class, race, and sex. The second part, "Impacts and Institutions," considers several areas of social concern — the family, the workplace, health and illness, environment and energy, crime, and national defense — in the light of the discussion in Part I. Finally, we conclude with a chapter, "Strategies for Social Policy," which casts a look at some prospects for the future based on what has gone before. We believe that a discussion of social problems should not be static; though it cannot predict the future, it should offer some guide to understanding developments on the leading edge of social action and social policy.

The book's organization, then, stresses the linkages in American society between public and private, social and personal, structure and symptom. In addition, two emphases further distinguish *America's Problems* from other texts in the field.

First, though we do not grind axes or indulge in narrow polemic, *America's Problems* (like *Crisis in American Institutions*) does not pretend to be value-neutral. Its approach consistently stresses the values of democracy, equality, and personal fulfillment. In an age in which these values are under persistent attack, we feel this is a vital part of our task as social scientists and as educators.

Second, though we stress the *social* nature of social problems — the idea that personal problems are deeply influenced by larger social processes — we view people not as passive objects of social forces but as active participants who shape those processes as well as being shaped by them.

In emphasizing these themes, we affirm what we feel is the most powerful and valuable tradition in social problems writing. It is the tradition of C. Wright Mills' insistence on the value of the "sociological imagination," and the tradition of E. A. Ross' conception of a "civic sociology" that not only analyzes and describes social issues but helps prepare students for a more aware and more principled participation in public life.

A book of this size and scope is necessarily a collective enterprise, whose quality depends enormously on the effort and dedication of the many people who help create it. Rod Watanabe, Chief of Staff at the Center for the Study of Law and Society, helped see the project through from beginning to end with his customary skill and patience. Susan Senger's skills, insight, and good spirits were indispensable in helping us turn out a finished manuscript under very demanding time constraints. Much of the original work on the manuscript was ably done by Christina Miller, Ingrid Barclay, and Margo Cisneros. We were also blessed with an unusually capable group of researchers: special thanks to Jennifer Hammett, Michael Peltz, and Laurie Rubinow for their initiative and creativity. We would like to thank the reviewers for their comments on the manuscript: Robert Ross, Clark University; Edward Ponczek, Harper College; John Mahoney, University of Richmond; Bernadette Tarallo, University of California at Davis; and David Linewebber. We greatly appreciate, as well, the careful and skillful production work on successive editions by Ron Newcomer and Scott Huler and their coworkers.

Finally, a project of this kind makes heavy demands, both direct and subtle, on family and friends who have to endure the book's intrusion into their lives. Once again, we are especially grateful to Rachael Peltz and Arlene Skolnick for the good advice, indispensable personal support, and consistent encouragement that ultimately made this book possible.

Elliott Currie
Jerome H. Skolnick
Center for the Study of Law and Society
Berkeley, California

Contents

Part I: Systems and Structures

**Chapter 4:
Social
Inequality I:
Wealth and
Poverty
96**

Contents **ix**

1

Introduction: Thinking about Social Problems

Almost thirty years ago, a well-known American sociologist, C. Wright Mills, wrote that "ours is a time of uneasiness and indifference." Despite unparalleled prosperity, Americans were suffering from the vague feeling that all was "somehow not right" (1959, p. 11). Today, many of us might be inclined to say the same thing. Just as in the 1950s, when Mills wrote those troubled words, American society presents a complicated picture. It is — on the whole — a prosperous and powerful society. But it is also full of disturbing contradictions.

It is a society of enormous wealth — and growing poverty. It is a society that creates astonishing technological wonders — and frightening toxic wastes. It is a society that produces millions of jobs — and condemns millions to unemployment. It is a society of booming cities and swelling ranks of the homeless, of fervent expressions of national optimism and widespread retreat into drugs and alcohol.

Changing Problems, Old Solutions

Most of these contradictions are not new: They have been with us for a long time. What is new is that many of them are growing sharper as we move toward the twenty-first century. Moreover, American society

1

The war in Southeast Asia led many to question America's military role.

is changing rapidly and often dramatically, and there is a growing sense that our traditional ways of coping with society's ills are no longer adequate for the task. Three changes in particular have forced us to rethink many of our traditional assumptions about social problems: limited economic expansion, the crisis of the welfare state, and the failure of technological solutions.

Limited Economic Expansion

For the first time in American history, we are faced with truly limited economic prospects; not just a period of slower-than-normal growth, or a temporary downturn in the economy, but the closing-off of economic options we had come to take for granted — and on which we had based a whole way of life.

America began as a frontier society, with what seemed like limitless lands and natural resources. The pattern that originated with the constant expansion of the American frontier continued, especially after World War II, as American businesses expanded overseas in search of new resources and new markets. Only recently have we begun to understand how much of our peculiarly American brand of prosperity has depended on this capacity for expansion, first throughout the country and then throughout the world. That expansion was not, of course, entirely a blessing — either for Americans or for the rest of the world. But it did allow us to postpone reckoning with some fundamental issues: the limits of natural resources, the distribution of income and wealth, and the need for guiding and coordinating the economy.

As the political theorist Alan Wolfe has written, "economic growth offered a smooth and potentially harmonious future," leading to "a whole new approach to government, one that would not so much exercise political power to make choices as it would manage expansion and empire to avoid choice" (1981, p. 10). But it's clear that this approach to the "management" of America's problems is running out of time. For a variety of reasons, we are no longer able to roam the rest of the planet at will, mining its human and natural resources to fuel the engines of economic growth. Some of the reasons are political, some economic, and some ecological.

On the political level, the most obvious example is the oil-producing countries' seizure of greater control over the most crucial resource of all for the energy-guzzling economies of the industrial world — an event that has had far-reaching consequences for every industrialized country. But, more generally, the "underdeveloped" countries' assertion of greater control over their own destinies is one of the key political facts of our time. Many countries that were once considered passive objects of American policy are now charting a much more independent course.

At the same time, American dominance has been challenged on the economic level — first, by other industrial countries, especially Japan and several Western European countries, which, after starting from rock bottom at the end of World War II, are now often "winning" in competition with the United States in many industries, and now also by a number of Third World countries, such as South Korea, Taiwan, and Singapore. The terms of international economic competition have shifted — and there is no indication that they will shift back.

Even more fundamentally, we have discovered that economic growth is limited by what the authors of the Global 2000 report, a major study of world ecological trends, call the "carrying capacity of the planet." "If present trends continue," that report argues, "the world in 2000 will be more crowded, more polluted, less stable ecolog-

Figure 1-1
Feiffer cartoon

ically, and more vulnerable to disruption. . . . Barring revolutionary advances in technology, life for most people on earth will be more precarious in 2000 than it is now — unless the nations of the world act decisively to alter current trends" (Council on Environmental Quality, 1982, p. 10). The mounting problems of toxic wastes and the continued pollution of air and water supplies are warnings that American affluence has been too often based on a heedless disregard of the limits of the natural environment. And they are only the most obvious symptoms of the tension between our style of economic growth and the integrity of the natural ecology on which growth ultimately depends.

These economic changes have, in a dramatically brief time, altered the terms of debate about social problems in America. They have created a whole new set of questions and sharpened the urgency of more familiar ones.

Perhaps the most pressing questions concern the problems of the economy itself. The American economy has always had its ups and downs. As we'll see in Chapter 3, the consequences of economic instability have often been severe, even in the prosperous decades of the 1940s, 1950s, and 1960s. Today, however, there are new and deeper concerns. Large parts of America's former industrial heartland have been laid waste, factories bolted and shuttered, and no one can predict whether some of their stricken industries will ever recover to levels approaching those of fifteen to twenty years ago. More people were unemployed in the mid-1980s than at any time since the 1930s — but, worse, it is unclear whether even renewed economic growth will put all of the unemployed back to work in an age of sophisticated robots and computer-guided machinery.

The economic crises of the 1970s and 1980s have cast a shadow on the future prospects of entire generations of Americans. Even a college education no longer guarantees a rewarding job or the kind of living standards that were often taken for granted in earlier years (though not by *everyone*, as Figure 1-1 suggests).

One of the benefits of the age of economic expansion, for many Americans, was the belief in the possibility of getting ahead, of moving up the social and economic ladder. To be sure, the realistic chances for upward mobility were always much more limited than Americans often assumed, especially for minorities and women. But though America was never the land of unrestricted opportunity many of us were taught it was, there is reason to fear that, with the shrinking prospects for growth, it may become even less so in the future. A popular song from the early 1980s, Billy Joel's "Allentown," captured the mood of this change in expectations:

> Every child had a pretty good shot
> To get at least as far as their old man got;
> But something happened on the way to that place;
> They threw an American flag in our face.

Copyright © 1981, 1982 by Billy Joel Songs (BMI)

The impact of limited growth has been especially harsh for minorities and the poor. An expanding economy could find some room for those with talent or luck to rise. It could lift some of the poor out of poverty and open some doors for minorities and women, all without greatly hurting anyone else's chances. As we'll see in later chapters, most of the recent successes in the struggle for equality, such as the reduction of poverty and the narrowing of disparities in income and jobs for minorities, took place in the expansionary 1960s; they slowed, stopped, or even reversed thereafter. More than thirty years after the birth of the Civil Rights movement, America's ghettos and barrios are still impoverished, still volatile, their residents often trapped in what some describe as a permanent underclass.

The Crisis of the Welfare State

Just as an expanding economy opened up expectations for the good life for many Americans, so too it made possible a spurt of generosity toward the less fortunate. A bigger economic "pie" all around meant that Americans could engage in what the economist Robert Reich called a "peculiarly low-cost form of charity" (1985, p. 72). Today the public mood has changed; we see that change in efforts to reduce social spending for the disadvantaged, in criticism of equal-opportunity programs, and, more generally, in the attack on the basic principles of what has come to be called the welfare state.

Given the current concern with the dangers of "big government," it is easy to forget that the package of government policies and programs that make up the welfare state is fairly new to the United States. Until the 1930s, the American economy was mainly run on the principles of laissez-faire: the idea that an economy powered by the drive for private profit and free from government intervention would produce constantly rising levels of prosperity while preserving political freedom and social choice. (That some intervention by government to aid private interests has always been a part of our history, as we'll see in Chapter 2, did not detract much from the intensity of this belief.) Then came the Great Depression, which brought growing acceptance of the idea that the private-profit economy would work much better with certain kinds of government intervention — indeed, that it might not work at all if left to its own devices.

That idea led to two profound developments in American social policy. One was a commitment by government to accept at least a minimal role in managing the economy, in order to avoid the possibility of another severe depression. The other was a commitment to a system of public services and benefits that would provide a basic cushion for those most at risk in the private-profit economy: the old, the sick, the involuntarily unemployed.

These commitments grew during the 1960s with the coming of what President Lyndon Johnson called the Great Society. Social programs for the poor, the elderly, the sick, and the disabled were created or expanded; job training, compensatory education, and urban development programs were launched with high hopes. This was never as big a commitment as some of its critics believe. The development of social programs in America was slow and, as we shall see, never went as far as it did in many other industrial societies. Still, by the 1970s, many people were arguing that the welfare state had become too large, government's role too great, the principle of entitlement to social benefits too lenient.

The reasons for these criticisms are not hard to find. At first glance, the legacy of these developments isn't impressive: a "mixed" economy prone to periodic stagnation and declining productivity growth; a public welfare system that is both costly and degrading to its recipients; an "urban renewal" program that blasted inner cities into craters and destroyed more low-income housing than it built; a public school system that turns out illiterates and threatens us with what a national commission in 1983 called a "tide of mediocrity" (National Commission on Excellence in Education, 1983, p. 2). The positive results of other social programs on which we once placed great hopes also are sometimes hard to see at first glance, and some of the improvements seem disappointingly small even on hard analysis.

The criticism of the welfare state's tendency to "throw money at problems" exaggerates the amount of money we *did* spend, and some of the "failure" of social programs is the result of their not being taken seriously from the start. Moreover, as we shall see, some programs have been extremely successful. But the ineffectiveness and high cost of *some* programs, coupled with the financial pinch of a faltering economy, led many people to lose faith in the government as a provider of solutions to social problems.

A third trend underlying our current sense of uncertainty is the failure of modern science and technology to deliver what we (somewhat naively) expected from them. The tendency to believe that a technical solution can ultimately be found for virtually every social problem (from drug addiction to cancer to international tensions) has been particularly strong in the United States, a country that has traditionally prided itself on its technical know-how. Like economic growth, technological progress has often served as a substitute for hard choices about social priorities; but it, too, is no longer capable of performing this role as it once did.

The Failure of Technological Solutions

Energy is a good example. In the 1950s and 1960s, the apparent promise of unlimited energy supplies through splitting the atom was one reason for America's heedless approach to energy conservation and for our failure to develop effective social policies governing energy use. But today questions of both safety and economics have crippled the promise of nuclear power; the devastating Soviet nuclear accident at Chernobyl in 1986 only accelerated already strong skepticism about the long-term potential of nuclear energy. What was once regarded as a quick-fix solution to the world's energy problems now seems more like a costly and dangerous albatross around society's neck.

Likewise, Americans have often looked to technology as a cure-all for problems of disease and, indeed, some medical technologies *have* worked wonders in the fight against illness. But other technologies are increasingly implicated in *causing* disease, particularly cancer and other diseases associated with exposure to industrial chemicals in the workplace and the environment.

Similarly, sophisticated microelectronic technologies promise to increase economic productivity and, perhaps, to eliminate some of the most menial and stifling work. But they also threaten us with massive unemployment and the destruction of the economic base of entire communities, paradoxically impoverishing American society as they enrich it.

Finally, there is frightening evidence that technologies we once accepted, enthusiastically and unreflectively, as the engines of our unprecedented economic growth, are also deeply harmful to the natural environment. Acid rain, contaminated groundwater, and the enormous problem of toxic waste signal the end of an age in which we could take the economic benefits of productive technology for granted while ignoring its social and environmental costs.

New energy technology continues to raise as many questions as it answers.

The problem is not that technology in general is harmful in some abstract sense, as critics have sometimes argued. It is that technological innovation without some means of controlling its pace and evaluating its larger costs has not only failed to solve America's problems but has often fostered new — and even more threatening — ones.

Changing Perspectives on Social Problems

All of these trends have changed the way we think about social problems — and the policies we create to deal with them. In the 1960s, we launched a wave of social activism on behalf of the poor, minorities, women, and the environment. We developed innovative programs to treat juvenile delinquents outside of the prisons, to ensure safer workplaces, to offer quality preschool education to poor children and preventive health care for their parents. Legislation like the Civil Rights Act of 1964 and the Occupational Health and Safety Act of 1970 created new rights for minorities, women, and workers. All of these efforts were rooted in the belief that much could be done about our most glaring social problems — if we had the will to do it. And most also rested on the conviction that government should bear some responsibility (though not all of the responsibility) for overcoming these problems.

At the same time, the growing women's movement was challenging traditional roles of men and women at home and on the job. And the bitter war in Southeast Asia led many people to develop serious doubts about the wisdom of America's approach to foreign policy — especially our reliance on military power to strengthen our influence around the world.

But the multiple crises of the 1970s brought these views and the policies that flowed from them into question. In their place a very different perspective began to dominate American social thought and policy. In contrast to the mood of the 1960s, many Americans in the 1970s strongly criticized what they regarded as the excessive role of government in American life, suggesting that government intervention might have caused — or at least aggravated — many of the problems it was designed to solve. Some began to argue, for example, that programs for the poor actually *caused* poverty — along with a host of other problems, including rising crime, family breakup, drug addiction, and illegitimacy — by removing the incentive to work and weakening the bonds of low-income families (Murray, 1984). By the early 1980s, it had become almost an article of faith among many observers that "the troubling behavior and conditions of the disadvantaged is due to the social programs on which many are dependent" (Mead, 1982, p. 22).

Beyond this, many argued that the growth of the welfare state had encouraged a general atmosphere of permissiveness and self-indulgence, which could be held responsible for much of America's recent troubles. A 1980 article in *Time*, for example, pinned much of the blame for America's economic troubles on the indulgent attitudes that American prosperity itself had created:

> Capitalism created the affluent society, but the more prosperity the public enjoyed, the more it wanted. If hard work, talent and savings no longer provided the affluence, the public demanded it from government. . . . In short, people today ask things from capitalism that no system can deliver. (*Time*, 1980, p. 44)

An editorial in *Fortune* similarly attributed America's ills to "the fact that Americans want just about everything, without considering or fully understanding the cost." The big question for social policy, the editorial declared, involved whether American democracy could "restrain the excessive demands made on the society" and slow "the drift toward the welfare state and egalitarianism" (Grunwald, 1981, p. 72).

Many critics complained about an insidious decline of traditional moral standards, which they held responsible for aggravating social problems ranging from the erosion of authority and stability in the family (Kramer, 1983) to rising crime rates (Wilson, 1983) to the weakening of America's military and economic position in the international arena (Podhoretz, 1980). From this perspective, the decline of American power and influence in the world was only partly explained by the increasing aggression of the Soviet Union and the growth of anti-American sentiments and actions, especially in the Third World; another part of the explanation was a "failure of nerve" within American society itself (Steinfels, 1980, p. 78) — a failure that led Americans to play down the foreign threats to American security and the need to build up our military capacity in the face of a hostile, malevolent world. Similarly, the rise in crime rates was due to our leniency with criminals; the erosion of the family to the weakening of discipline by parents and teachers and the challenge to traditional family roles caused by the growing employment of women outside the home.

New Realities, New Doubts

Given the fears and frustrations that have accompanied American life in recent years, the popularity of these views was understandable. Many found this vision compelling in its simplicity, its ability to offer what seem to be clear and direct solutions in an age when social, economic, and political forces seem both deeply threatening and often incomprehensible. And its appeal to the simpler virtues of a less complex society of unfettered markets, traditional families, and American "strength" resonates with basic values that lie deep within the American cultural tradition: individual liberty, self-reliance, mistrust of government power.

It is not surprising, then, that these views have had a powerful impact on social policy in the United States — particularly in altering the role of government. As we'll see, they did not reduce government's role so much as shift it. This strategy calls for reducing government spending — for social programs, but not for defense. It calls for curtailing government regulation of business — but often has no qualms in calling for more government regulation of our private lives. Accordingly, we increased spending on defense, cut spending for domestic social programs, increased the severity of punishment for criminals, toughened the schools' attitudes toward troublesome students. But by now, these policies have been pursued for many years, and the problems they proposed to attack are still with us. Despite considerable success in reducing government regulation and taxation of business, the state of the economy remains precarious and uncertain; and even when the economy appeared to be undergoing a "recovery," unemployment was stuck at disturbingly high levels. Despite deep cuts in the social programs that were said to be the main cause of poverty and social pathology, there were many *more*, not fewer, Americans below the poverty line in the 1980s than in the early 1970s. Despite an unprecedented shift of government spending toward the military, there were no signs of either an improvement in America's national security in a still-threatening world or in the quality and efficiency of America's huge but clumsy military. And though a record number of Americans were behind bars, crime was still terribly high — and, as of this writing, was rising.

As a result, America's thinking about social problems is once again in ferment. There is a clear sense that old answers — and even some not-so-old ones — are no longer very helpful, but there is no strong consensus around *new* ones. Instead, there is a deep and wide-ranging debate about the roots of America's problems — and about what kinds of social policies we should create in response to them.

Our Perspective

Our purpose in this book is to provide some of the tools you will need to become effective participants in this debate. The chapters that follow are short on definitive answers, long on describing what we feel are some of the most important *questions* and some of the best ways of going about *looking* for the answers.

In pursuit of that goal, we have emphasized bringing the most recent, most sophisticated social scientific research to bear on the issues raised in contemporary debates over social problems. We also explain how to interpret and understand some of the common statistics and data sources on which so much of these debates depend, such as crime and unemployment rates and measures of poverty and the distribution of income. These are crucial tools for analyzing social issues, and understanding how to use them is a necessary first step in thinking about social problems, regardless of the moral or political questions they raise.

Nevertheless, we want to make some of our own assumptions and preconceptions clear at the beginning. All books about social problems rest, in part, on deeply felt personal values. Some of those values reflect broad social and political convictions, which frequently translate into decisions about what constitutes a "social problem" in the first place. Others involve the authors' sense of the "possible" — their visceral feelings about how much society's ills can usefully be addressed by social action.

Values and Biases

In the past, as we noted in an earlier book (Skolnick and Currie, 1985), social scientists often tried to avoid confronting the judgments that lay behind their own approaches to the study of social problems. They frequently made a sharp (and misleading) distinction between a "scientific" versus a "value-laden" approach to society and spent a good deal of effort trying to convince readers that they were offering an "objective" or "value-free" perspective. The fallacy in such a position was pointed out many years ago by the Swedish social scientist Gunnar Myrdal, with a directness that is hard to improve upon. "Every study of a social problem," Myrdal wrote, "however limited in scope, is and must be determined by valuations. A 'disinterested' social science has never existed and, for logical reasons, can never exist." But, Myrdal argued, the values that underlay most social science were "generally hidden," left "implicit and vague" (1969, p. 54).

For Myrdal, as for us, there is an important difference between values, in this sense, and the personal or political biases that often distort social research and analysis. *Values* are both inevitable and necessary; a social science *without* any values or moral foundations would be not only incomprehensible but — if it could exist — morally repugnant. *Biases,* on the other hand, are the result of values that are unacknowledged and left to work their way into the analysis of social issues by the back door. As Myrdal contended, the only way to avoid such biases, and to achieve the kind of objectivity that *is* possible in social science, is to "expose the valuations to full light" and to make them "conscious, specific, and explicit" (1969, pp. 55–56).

Especially since the authors have somewhat different backgrounds and views, it would be too much to try to lay out our own values in great detail. But some of our more general shared assumptions are reasonably well expressed by the goals that two political theorists have described as those of what they call the social welfare state: "Equality, freedom, democracy, solidarity, security, and economic efficiency" (Furniss and Tilton, 1979, p. 28).

We also believe that American society has enough economic, technological, and intellectual resources to do a better job of achieving these goals than it has done so far. Most of the social problems we face as we move toward the close of the twentieth century are not the result of human nature or fate or inevitable economic or technological processes. More often than not, they involve choices that we make — or fail to make — about our priorities as a society. We think that a common thread running through many of America's problems is that we've historically been a society that has taken too little responsibility for the well-being of individuals, families, and communities. Like most Americans, we appreciate the value of individual initiative and enterprise. But we also believe that society as a whole bears an important responsibility for the common good. Unlike some others, we don't think that simply unleashing the forces of the private economy — the "market" — is necessarily conducive to the values we share; and we believe those forces must be balanced by an active and compassionate government. These are broad values, and there is plenty of room for argument about how best to put them into practice in the form of specific social policies. But as you'll see, these themes run through and unify the book as a whole; and we will return to discuss some of their implications in our concluding chapter.

Social Theory and Social Policy

We are less clear about what to call ourselves, which may disappoint some who care about political or academic labels. Both of us tend to be somewhat distrustful of such labels; those looking for the name of our "theoretical system" won't find it here. But some clues about our inclinations toward both social action and social science are relevant. Both of us have been participants in a number of activist causes for many years. Both of us also tend to be a little impatient with the abstractions of what C. Wright Mills called "grand theory" and to look early on for the more concrete, practical implications of social theories.

This leaning helps explain why *America's Problems*, unlike some other books on social problems, is so strongly concerned with issues of social *policy*. Contrary to some recent thinking, we believe that the tools of social science ought to help inform decisions about social policy; even more importantly, we also believe it's *possible* for social science to do so. Nowadays, it has become fashionable in some quarters to denigrate the use of the tools of reason and analysis to affect the course of social life. We don't share that pessimism or the self-serving quietude it encourages. We think that much can be done to build a society that is more equal, more supportive, more respectful of personal liberties and differences, less insecure, less dangerous. At the same time, we believe that doing so will require the best intellectual efforts we can muster and the most skillful use of the intellectual tools available to us.

Disciplines and Boundaries

For us, this means using tools from whatever academic disciplines will help. Both of us were trained as sociologists, but we regard that training as a starting point, and we tend to be impatient with the somewhat artificial boundaries of traditional academic disciplines. *America's Problems* draws on the methods and findings of political scientists, social psychologists, specialists in public health and environmental science, and many others. And it pays particular attention to economic issues, traditionally the territory of professional economists.

But though we draw on many different disciplines, two basic sociological themes underlie the approach we've taken throughout this book. The first is what we would call the *importance of the social* in thinking about social problems. The other is the importance of connecting, in C. Wright Mills's phrase, "private troubles" with "public issues." What do these mean?

The Importance of the Social

By the importance of the social, we mean that we will not be able to understand social problems if we see them as simply the result of millions of individual choices. Mills put it this way in describing the quality he termed the *sociological imagination:*

> The first fruit of the sociological imagination is the idea that the individual can understand his own experience and gauge his own fate only by locating himself within his period, that he can know his own chances in life only by becoming aware of those of all individuals in his circumstances. In many ways it is a terrible lesson — in many ways a magnificent one. (Mills, 1959, p. 5)

Taking a social view of social problems means that we begin with the recognition that, as individuals, we are enmeshed in a complex network of social and economic relations that limit our range of choices and shape fundamentally our prospects for health or illness, wealth or poverty, happiness or misery. Moreover, that network is not a world of timeless abstractions but a concrete society with its own peculiar history, its own unique way of organizing the production and allocation of goods and services, and its own priorities about the use of natural and human resources. Living in America is not the same as living in China or Nigeria; living in the corporate America of the late twentieth century is not the same as living in the society of small

The threat of nuclear accident hovers in the background of American life.

entrepreneurs that was nineteenth-century America. The social critic Paul Goodman (1970, p. x) once wrote of these surrounding social and technological conditions that "the way they lay out the streets is the way we must walk" — a metaphor that is particularly appropriate in an age that often seems to regard humans as if they were small computing machines, calculating their courses of action in isolation from community, history, or tradition.

Further, within that social, economic, and historical framework, we do not confront the world as an assortment of individual atoms. Instead, we are sorted into specific groups according to our income, our racial and ethnic background, our sex, religion, age, and so forth. And which groups we are in profoundly affects nearly everything else about our lives, shaping our experience of the society around us.

Both these points can be illustrated by an example: the meaning of unemployment. To many economists, whether an individual has a job or not is simply a matter of a transaction in the labor market, a result of individual choices by employers on the one hand and potential employees on the other. To some politicians, many taxpayers, and some of those fortunate enough to have a job, it is a matter of individual merit or motivation: "People who really want to work can always find a job." Both perspectives, of course, may have a kernel of truth in them. But neither tells us why *some* societies, *some* regions, or *some* groups have much greater unemployment than others.

The idea that social problems must be understood within a specific socioeconomic and group context has an important corollary: that social problems are also political and ethical problems. They are not the inevitable result of blind social forces. Instead, they often reflect painful conflicts between competing groups. Decisions about what we should consider social problems at all — much less how we should deal with them once we have defined them as problems — involve often bitter and sometimes deadly struggles over social resources.

What the American sociologist Willard Waller said more than 40 years ago remains true: Very often, social problems "are not solved because people do not want to solve them" (1936, p. 928). What Waller meant is that a social problem that injures some people may have considerable *benefits* for others. Unemployment is a problem for those who lose their jobs — and for their families and communities — but not necessarily for employers, who may benefit because the scarcity of work brings a widespread fear of joblessness that allows them to maintain low wages, inadequate benefits, and poor working conditions for those still on the job.

As the economist Robert Lekachman put it:

> The brutal fact is that unemployment . . . confers many benefits upon the prosperous and truly affluent. If everyone were employed, extraordinarily high wages would have to be paid to toilers in restaurant kitchens, laundries, filling stations, and other unpleasant work environments. Whenever decent employment at living wages is available, it is exceedingly difficult to coax young men and women into our volunteer armed services. . . . Unemployment calms unions and moderates wage demands. Threats to shut down or shift mills and assembly plants coerce workers into acceptance of wage freezes or actual wage cuts and unfavorable revisions of work rules. When men and women fear for their jobs, they work harder and gripe less. (Lekachman, 1982, p. 200)

This same point is illustrated, even more straightforwardly, in the candid remarks of the president of a large grocery-store chain who said, "We cannot run good stores when unemployment by government standards is below 5 percent. . . . Productivity even for you and me is better when two or three people are waiting at the door for our jobs" (Davis, 1980, p. 11).

Social problems, then, are often problems for some groups and not for others; and even when they are universally considered to be problems, they are often the by-product of social and economic processes that are difficult to change precisely because some groups have a stake in maintaining them. Few people really profit from street crime; but to the extent that street crime is a reflection of unemployment, the unequal distribution of income, and the disruption of families and communities by economic shifts, it is a by-product of social arrangements that are not only profitable for some groups but are an integral part of our traditional pattern of economic development.

Our first principle in looking at social problems, then, is that they cannot be understood outside the specific social and economic structures in which they occur — and that they are unlikely to be effectively addressed without confronting those structures.

The second principle is closely related. It is that the analysis of social problems should help to bridge the gap between what Mills called "private troubles and public issues." In other words, it should help people understand the connections between their personal anxieties, fears, and frustrations and the social forces that often give rise to them — between their hopes for themselves and their families and the obstacles in the larger society that may frustrate them.

Private and Public: Bridging the Gap

Think about unemployment once again. The loss of a job often results in feelings of inadequacy and self-blame, in family conflicts, in nagging fears about the future. Too often, our society and culture reinforce those feelings by defining unemployment as a problem of individual failure or bad luck. One of the most important tasks of social science is to allow us to look beyond that narrowly personal level by illuminating the connections between the private tragedy of unemployment and the economic forces that predictably throw millions of Americans out of work each year. By connecting our private problems to the influence of social forces outside ourselves, social science can demonstrate that individuals are not alone in confronting the problems that trouble their lives — and, by extension, that they are not powerless to change them.

A Look Ahead

These themes guide the chapters that follow. *America's Problems* is divided into two related parts. The first deals with some of the most fundamental aspects of American society — basic structures and values that profoundly shape specific social problems and also influence our social and political policies toward them. Chapters 2 and 3 focus on our economy and how it is changing; Chapters 4 and 6, on the social inequalities that run through American life.

Chapter 2 sketches the contours of the American economic system, with particular emphasis on the growth of large private corporations and the corresponding growth of government. As we've seen, many people believe that most of America's social problems can be traced to the size and influence of government; this chapter sorts out the balance between government, business, and labor in America.

This analysis provides the background for our discussion, in Chapter 3, of some recent problems in the American economy and some common explanations for them. We don't pretend that a single chapter can substitute for a long and careful study of economic problems. Our aim is the more modest one of sorting through some of the current debates about our economic troubles in order to separate rhetoric from reality.

The following three chapters (4, 5, and 6) address the continuing inequalities of class, race, and gender in the United States. All three chapters share a common theme. During the 1970s, some social scientists began to argue that these inequalities were on the verge of disappearing from American life. Others argued that government antidiscrimination and antipoverty programs had "gone too far" in trying to eliminate social inequalities and that social stability and economic growth had suffered as a result. These chapters offer evidence on the continuing patterns of disadvantage by race, class, and gender. In all three chapters, we focus primarily on the broad material aspects of inequality: jobs, income, wealth, and the risk of poverty.

The chapters in Part II view several specific problems through the lenses provided by the larger issues addressed in Part I. We focus on six areas: the family, work, health, energy and the environment, crime and justice, and national security. Without applying the straitjacket of a rigid theoretical system, we emphasize the ways in which the specific troubles of particular institutions are linked with the broader issues of inequality and the distinctive pattern of our economic priorities.

Our concluding chapter, "Strategies for Social Policy," draws together some of the themes raised throughout the book, not simply to summarize what we've said before but to help provide understanding of some of the possibilities for the American future — and some of the hard social choices we will face in the coming years.

Summary

This chapter has described some of the trends in thinking about social problems in America in recent years, examined some social changes that may underlie those trends, and outlined our own approach to the study of social problems.

Public attitudes about social problems have changed significantly in the past several years. This shift is partly the result of several trends that have changed American society in fundamental ways. These include new limits on economic expansion, the apparent inability of the welfare state and technical innovation to cope with American social problems, and the tendency for technology to generate new problems of its own.

These trends helped pave the way for widespread criticism of government intervention, of "excessive" concern for social equality, and of the "neglect" of America's international military role. But the resulting social policies proved no better at resolving America's problems. And so the debates over the nature and solution of those problems continue.

Our own perspective emphasizes that the values that guide an approach to social problems should be made explicit. We believe that the study of social problems cannot provide all the answers but should give students the tools to provide their own; that those tools can and should be drawn from a variety of academic disciplines; and that an effective approach to America's problems should emphasize their *social* nature and stress the connections between personal experience and larger social forces.

For Further Reading

Burnham, Walter Dean. *The Current Crisis in American Politics*. New York: Oxford University Press, 1983.

Mills, C. Wright. *The Sociological Imagination*. New York: Oxford University Press, 1959.

Palmer, John, ed. *Perspectives on the Reagan Years*. Washington, D.C.: Urban Institute Press, 1986.

Reich, Robert. "The New Public Philosophy." *Atlantic*, May 1985.

Skolnick, Jerome H., and Elliott Currie. *Crisis in American Institutions*, 7th ed. Boston: Little, Brown, 1987.

Steinfels, Peter. *The Neoconservatives*. New York: Simon and Schuster, 1980.

Part I

Systems and Structures

2

Economy and Society: Business, Government, and Labor

Much of the debate over America's social problems revolves, in one way or another, around the relations between business and government, between the private sector and the public sector, between the welfare state and the system of free enterprise. The intensity of this debate is a reflection of important changes in American life during the past few decades.

The ideal of the free enterprise system — in which many small independent entrepreneurs use hard work and initiative to compete in a market system largely free of interference by government — is deeply embedded in our culture. We often contrast that idealized system with others based on "planning" or "government control" or what some economists call the principle of "command": It is a system in which individuals, in the economist Milton Friedman's (1980) phrase, are "free to choose," subject only to the discipline of the market itself. In many ways, this is an appealing vision and, with qualifications that we'll describe later, one that bears some resemblance to the America of the past.

But, aside from occasional bursts of nostalgia, it is generally understood that this vision, in its pure form, no longer corresponds to American reality. Even the hardiest believers in the free enterprise ideal acknowledge that private enterprise in the United States is no longer adequately described as a collection of small individual or family businesses: The reality of General Motors does not fit comfortably in a vision based on the corner grocery store. And, especially since the Great Depression and World War II, the government has taken on a crucial, and complex, role in American economic and social life.

To an important extent, current controversies over economic issues (and many other social problems as well) are about the balance that has resulted from these changes. Many believe that the growth of government has gotten out of hand, threatening to overpower a fragile, besieged private enterprise system. They feel that economic and social life in America are increasingly dictated by distant bureaucrats rather than by the natural and beneficial choices of the free market. The growth of government has, in this view, been responsible for most of the problems of the American economy in recent years, including loss of international competitiveness, slow growth, and unemployment. Milton Friedman put it this way: "There is nothing wrong with the American economy that a dose of good government wouldn't cure. By that, I mean a dose of smaller government" (quoted in *U.S. News and World Report*, 1983, p. 67). And the president of the United States told a responsive audience in 1983 that many of America's problems were due to the fact that "government has intervened in areas where it is neither competent, nor needed, nor wanted by the mass of Americans" (quoted in *San Francisco Chronicle*, May 10, 1983).

Controversy over the balance between government and private interests shapes almost every aspect of public policy in the United States today, whether the specific issue is regulation of business, the distribution of income, the problems of the welfare system, the best ways of dealing with race or sex discrimination, or a host of others. In this chapter we will try to put this controversy in perspective. We begin with a profile of the dimensions of private power in America, focusing on the size and concentration of economic resources in our large corporations. We then consider the corresponding trends in the government's size and role in the economy, especially in comparison with the role of the public sector in other industrial societies. We also take a look at organized labor, often considered an equal partner with business in the American economy. Finally, we look briefly at some of the ways in which government and business have historically been *interconnected* in the United States. As we'll see, the relations between private business and government are more complex than many people assume, and the balance between them looks considerably different than much conventional wisdom suggests.

The Dimensions of
Private Power

It takes only a few statistics to show how far we have come from the
society of small independent producers envisioned by the traditional
conception of free enterprise. Let's consider, first of all, the sheer size
of the largest American corporations and how much they have grown
in recent years.

Corporate size is measured in several ways — usually by the dollar
volume of sales in a given year, the dollar value of total assets, or the
number of employees. The different measures give somewhat different pictures of corporate size and influence, but all show that big
business in America is *very* big indeed. Each year the business magazine *Fortune* publishes a list of the 500 largest industrial corporations
in the United States. (This list doesn't include companies mainly
involved in banking or retail sales, for example — only manufacturing.) In 1986 the Fortune 500 had combined sales of over $1.7 *trillion*
(*Fortune*, 1987, p. 359). When the list was first published (for 1954),
the corporation at the bottom had roughly $50 million in sales; by
1986 the bottom company had sales of $420 million.

As Figure 2-1 shows, several of the largest American corporations
have sales that rank them among the world's largest economies. In
1984, only the United States, the Soviet Union, Japan, and West
Germany had gross national products larger than the combined sales
of the top ten American industrial corporations.

By the late 1970s, the two largest American industrial corporations,
Exxon and General Motors, together had greater sales (even adjusted
for inflation) than *all manufacturing corporations combined* at the turn of
the century (Mueller, 1977, p. 444).

The trends in numbers of people employed by the largest corporations are somewhat different. A substantial part of the American
labor force is employed by the biggest firms; in 1984, the top 785
American corporations employed about 21 million workers — or
roughly 1 in 5 people in the employed civilian labor force (*Forbes*,
1985, p. 231). Today General Motors alone employs more people
than the entire population of San Francisco; more people work for
Sears, Roebuck than live in St. Louis. But the *growth* in the number of
people working for the biggest corporations has been much less
dramatic than the growth in size (or in profits). After a period of
substantial growth in the mid-to-late 1960s, employment in the largest
industrial corporations leveled off, and it declined in the early 1980s

Figure 2-1

Corporate sales and gross national products, 1984

* The ten largest industrial corporations in 1984 were Exxon, General Motors, Mobil, Ford, Texaco, IBM, duPont, AT&T, General Electric, and Standard Oil of Indiana.

Source: Corporate sales from *Fortune*, April 29, 1985, p. 266; GNP estimates from U.S. Central Intelligence Agency, *World Factbook 1986.*

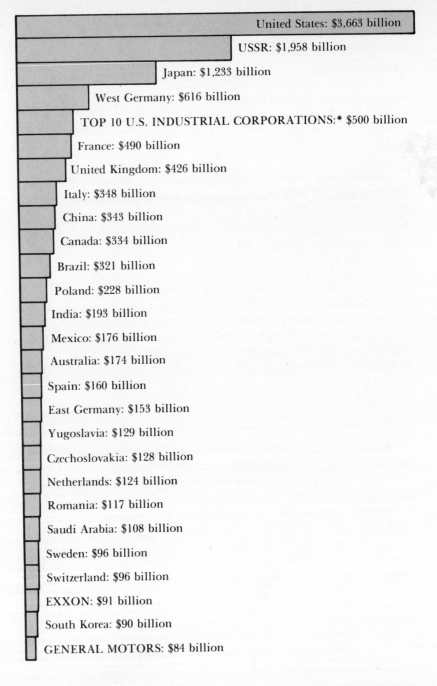

United States: $3,663 billion

USSR: $1,958 billion

Japan: $1,233 billion

West Germany: $616 billion

TOP 10 U.S. INDUSTRIAL CORPORATIONS:* $500 billion

France: $490 billion

United Kingdom: $426 billion

Italy: $348 billion

China: $343 billion

Canada: $334 billion

Brazil: $321 billion

Poland: $228 billion

India: $193 billion

Mexico: $176 billion

Australia: $174 billion

Spain: $160 billion

East Germany: $153 billion

Yugoslavia: $129 billion

Czechoslovakia: $128 billion

Netherlands: $124 billion

Romania: $117 billion

Saudi Arabia: $108 billion

Sweden: $96 billion

Switzerland: $96 billion

EXXON: $91 billion

South Korea: $90 billion

GENERAL MOTORS: $84 billion

(*Fortune*, 1983, p. 227). (As we'll see in Chapter 8, this has some disturbing implications for the future of work in America.)

But it is not simply the *size* of America's giant corporations that is at issue. What has most concerned observers of the American economic system since before the turn of the century is the problem of economic *concentration* — the degree to which a relatively small number of corporations control a disproportionate share of the country's economic resources.

The concentration of corporate power is not a new trend. It was already well on its way (and, by some measures, may even have reached a peak) in the last years of the nineteenth century, which saw the rise of giant corporate "trusts" in banking, railroads, steel, and many other industries (Herman, 1981, pp. 191–193). This growing concentration led to the creation of our system of antitrust laws, designed to curb some of the more glaring excesses of private power. But, despite those laws, corporate concentration increased substantially by the 1930s, causing President Franklin D. Roosevelt to declare:

> Among us today, a concentration of private power without equal in history is growing. This concentration is seriously impairing the economic effectiveness of private enterprise as a way of providing employment for labor and capital and as a way of assuring a more equitable distribution of income and earnings among the people of the nation as a whole. (U.S. Congress, House Committee on Small Business, 1979, p. 37)

Roosevelt was right about the growth of private power. Economic concentration *has* increased in the years since he sounded that alarm. At the end of the Great Depression, in 1941, the largest 100 manufacturing firms held just over 39 percent of all manufacturing assets; 43 years later, as Table 2-1 shows, their share had risen to about 49 percent.

Measuring Economic Concentration

Corporation ranking	1950	1960	1970	1980	1984
100 largest	39.7	46.4	48.5	46.7	48.9
200 largest	47.7	56.3	60.4	59.7	60.7

* Prior to 1970, excludes newspapers. Data prior to 1974 not strictly comparable with later years.
Source: Statistical Abstract of the United States, 1986 (Washington, D.C.: Government Printing Office, 1986), p. 524.

Table 2-1
Largest manufacturing corporations* — percent share of assets held, 1950–1984

This table and our preceding discussion are based on a measure of economic power called the *aggregate concentration ratio* — the share of total corporate assets (or, sometimes, total sales, output, profits, or employment) held by a small number of companies. As Table 2-1 shows, the largest 200 manufacturing firms — which represent less than one-tenth of 1 percent of all such firms in the United States — held *three-fifths* of all manufacturing assets in 1984. Moreover, this share increased markedly — by about one-fourth — during the 1950s and 1960s, though it apparently reached a plateau thereafter.

The usefulness of aggregate concentration ratios in measuring economic power has been the subject of considerable debate. One issue is that simply describing the shares of economic activity that a small group of companies hold at any given point doesn't tell us whether those companies are the *same* ones over the years. Obviously, if the top 50, 100, or 200 corporations are entirely different ones every few years, our assessment of the significance of economic concentration would be different than if the same corporations dominated the economy year after year. Although there has been considerable movement in and out of the ranks of the top corporations, the amount of stability is striking. Of the 50 largest companies in 1982, half were among the 50 largest 25 years earlier; only 9 were not among the 200 largest 25 years before (U.S. Bureau of the Census, 1986, p. 7-4).

Though the aggregate concentration ratio clearly gives us a rough portrait of the overall distribution of private economic power, if we want to know how much of an industry — or the sale of some particular product — is dominated by a small group of companies, we need to use a measure that economists call *market concentration.* (Table 2-2).

Market concentration is a measure of the amount of sales in a given industry or product category (rather than in the economy as a whole) accounted for by a small number of companies. We can grasp the meaning of this measure if we think about the way a small number of corporations influences the daily morning routine most of us follow. The alarm clock you wearily turn off in the morning was probably made by one of the four companies that produce 84 percent of all clocks and watches sold in the United States. Four companies make 90 percent of the linoleum you walk on as you go to open the kitchen refrigerator, which in turn was almost certainly bought from one of the four companies that sell 82 percent of American refrigerators. If you have cereal for breakfast, it is highly likely that it comes from one of the four corporations that produce four-fifths of breakfast cereals. Four companies provide two-thirds of the coffee you may drink, and another four sell two-thirds of the sugar you may put in it.

If you smoke a cigarette with your coffee, there is an 88 percent chance that it was made by one of four tobacco companies. And the

Product and year	Share of sales accounted for by 4 largest American companies (percentages)
Passenger cars	
1982	99+
1954	98
Razors and razor blades	
1982	99
1954	97
Light bulbs	
1982	91
1958	90
Cigarettes	
1982	90
1958	80
Electronic calculators	
1982	90
1972	68
Radios	
1982	77
1963	51
Televisions	
1982	67
1958	55
Roasted coffee	
1982	66
1958	46
Records and tapes	
1982	58
1963	68
Computers	
1982	44
1972	75
Semiconductors	
1982	36
1958	46
Books	
1982	16
1958	16
Wood furniture	
1982	14
1972	14

Table 2-2
Some examples of market concentration

Source: Adapted from U.S. Bureau of the Census, *1982 Census of Manufactures: Concentration Ratios in Manufacturing* (Washington, D.C.: Government Printing Office, 1986), table 9.

car you drive (if it is American made), as well as over nine out of ten other cars produced by American manufacturers, was made by one of four companies, as are three-quarters of the tires they ride upon.

Is market concentration increasing? Again, the question has been the subject of considerable debate. The answer is made more difficult by the lack of good data for earlier years and the practical difficulties of defining changing products and industries with sufficient precision to make reliable comparisons possible. On the whole, the evidence is that the *average* degree of concentration has increased in American industry since World War II, though there is some dispute over its magnitude. But such an average may obscure more than it reveals, since it conceals important differences between different industries. Note in Table 2-2 how different the production of many goods has become from the classical image of a market system made up of many small entrepreneurs. At the top of the scale, a few products — cars, cigarettes, calculators — are, for all practical purposes, produced entirely by four (or fewer) companies. (The table even minimizes the degree of concentration in these markets, by presenting the data only in terms of four companies; sometimes a huge market share is held by just one or two.) Many of these highly concentrated industries have been so for some time, at least since the 1950s or early 1960s. Others have shown very rapid increases in concentration in recent years: calculators, refrigerators and freezers, radios, and TVs, among others. At the same time, other industries (notably the computer industry) have become less concentrated. And some important industries are not highly concentrated by this measure, including furniture and book publishing.

All of this suggests that the American economy is best understood as containing two somewhat distinct sectors, one highly concentrated and the other characterized by a large number of smaller firms where no one producer controls a very large share of the market.

Mergers and Takeovers

The statistics may actually understate the degree of economic concentration, however, because of the rapid pace of takeovers and mergers of large businesses in recent years. Epecially during the 1960s, this often involved companies buying up other firms in unrelated industries, creating what are often called conglomerate corporations. The usual measures of market concentration cannot adequately encompass the various activities of a conglomerate like Gulf and Western, for example — which, as one observer noted during the 1970s, "owns Madison Square Garden, grows sugar cane in the Dominican Republic, produces movies for Paramount Pictures, publishes books under Simon and Schuster, makes cigars, weaves clothing, manufactures pulp, rolls steel and lends money, to name a few of its businesses" (Pertschuk, 1980, p. 362).

More recently, corporate mergers and acquisitions have tended to involve companies in the same or similar industries, but the pace has if anything increased — reducing the number of competitors in a given industry and creating fewer, and bigger, giant corporate entities. Between 1981 and 1986 there were almost eight thousand mergers or acquisitions that involved companies worth over a million dollars, adding up to more than half a trillion dollars worth of "deals." The acquisition of RCA by General Electric alone cost over $6 billion (Gilpin, 1986, p. 26).

**The "Beer Wars": A
Closeup of Economic
Concentration**

Beer is the most popular alcoholic beverage in the United States and an integral part of the American economy — an $11 billion a year industry in 1982. Americans consume about 24 gallons of beer annually per capita, a total of almost 180 million barrels in 1985.

Serious beer drinkers are aware that beer has changed in the past several years. There are fewer independent brands to choose from, though there are many new labels and new kinds of brew, such as the light beers. To many drinkers, the different beers seem to taste more and more alike. And beer, like nearly everything else, costs more than it used to.

Behind these changes lies a drastic reorganization of the beer industry that has had even deeper consequences for those who work in the industry itself. The beer business, once a classic example of a small, family-based enterprise, has become an arena in which a handful of giant, aggressive corporations are battling tooth and nail for shares of the national beer market. In the process thousands of independent businesses have been wiped out, along with tens of thousands of good, skilled jobs and a good part of the economic base of many communities. The beer industry, in short, is a kind of microcosm of the wider trend toward concentration in the American economy, and it tells us a lot about the social impact of that trend.

The beer industry in the United States grew during the nineteenth century, largely through the efforts of European (especially German) immigrants who brought with them long-established, sometimes centuries-old brewing skills. The small breweries they built catered mainly to local markets, and they took great pride in producing a small (by current standards) number of barrels of high-quality, distinctive beer. In 1880, there were 2,741 independent breweries in the United States.

But the industry began to change rapidly by the early part of this century. By 1935 there were 750 brewers; by 1967, 125; and by 1979, only 40. Concentration of the industry is continuing so rapidly that some beer industry experts expect as few as 5 or 6 large brewers to survive within the next few years. In 1986 the two largest brewers alone, Anheuser-Busch and Miller, were estimated to share about 60 percent of the market — up from 43 percent just eight years earlier.

(continued)

What caused this transformation?

Concentration in the beer industry escalated after world War II. Before then, most brewers sold their beer locally, or at most regionally. A handful were so-called national brewers: Anheuser-Busch (makers of Budweiser and Michelob), Schlitz, Pabst, and Miller. During the 1950s, these national companies began moving aggressively to conquer local and regional beer markets, followed by some of the larger and more powerful regional brewers (like Coors, Falstaff, and Lone Star).

The results of this competition were savage. From the 1940s to the early 1960s, an average of 16 beer firms each year went out of business; about 9 closed down each year in the 1960s and early 1970s. Close to 90 others were bought out by bigger brewers from 1958 to 1975.

The big brewers were able to wipe out the smaller, localized ones partly because they could afford to build much bigger and more cost-effective breweries. They could also lower labor costs by building new, highly automated breweries and by building them mainly in the South, where labor costs were low, rather than in the highly unionized Midwest and Northeast, where most of the industry had traditionally been located. In the old Schlitz main brewery in Milwaukee, the brewhouse (the heart of the beermaking operation) employed 24 workers per shift. The company's new brewhouses in its automated southern plants (now owned by the Stroh corporation, which bought Schlitz in 1982) are run by only *two* workers.

The new cost-effective breweries also require enormous capital investment that the smaller firms could not manage. As late as 1960 there were 229 working breweries in the United States; by 1984, just 96.

The biggest brewers were also able to outspend their competitors on advertising and promotion. Like so many of today's consumer products, there are really very few noticeable differences among different brands of beer. What makes growth in market shares possible is the ability to sell the beer's *image* — to develop what in the corporate world is called brand-name capital. Big brewers, to gain a greater share of the market or avoid losing what they have, must make their brand names so well known that customers reach for their beer almost automatically. The main way of accomplishing this is through massive ad campaigns (beer, wine, and liquor adds account for about 8 percent of all magazine advertising); another is to develop new ways of packaging beer. These strategies require enormous amounts of money. As far back as 1946, the beer industry was already spending $50 million a year on advertising; by 1977, largely because of the mushrooming use of costly TV advertising, the top five companies alone spent about a quarter of a *billion* dollars on advertising. Obviously, only the largest corporations can afford to compete at this level.

The most striking example of these trends has been the battle by what is now the number two brewer in the country, Miller, for dominance in the industry. Always one of the major national brewers, Miller began an ambitious effort to become number one in the early 1970s, after it was purchased by the Philip Morris Company, makers of Marlboro cigarettes and Virginia Slims. (Philip Morris bought Miller from another giant conglomerate, the agribusiness corporation W. R. Grace.)

Philip Morris changed the terms on which the "wars" among the beer companies were fought. Through aggressive marketing and a promotion of its cigarettes (the "Marlboro Man," "You've Come a Long Way, Baby"), it had built an empire with assets, in 1977, of more than $4 billion; it sold 160 brands of cigarettes in 170 countries. It had also begun to diversify into several, other industries and real estate ventures. As a huge conglomerate, Philip Morris could afford to sink enormous resources into its Miller subsidiary for promotion and new plant capacity. It launched the trend to light beers with an ad campaign for its Lite brand, costing hundreds of millions of dollars. It attacked the market for high-priced premium beers by buying the right to use the name and label of Lowenbrau, the old, established German beer, in the United States. (American beer drinkers can no longer buy the real Lowenbrau in this country; Miller's variety is another beer altogether, made through a different — and cheaper — process, though costing the same.) To launch its Lowenbrau against other competitors' premium beers, Miller spent more than $11 million on ads in 1977 alone — this for a beer that, by 1982, accounted for less than 1 percent of the country's beer sales.

The strategy of flooding the market with massive advertising worked well for Miller. During the mid-1970s, the company's share of the beer market grew by 30 percent a year; by 1982, Miller controlled 22 percent of the domestic beer market. (Miller's rapid rise stalled in the mid-1980s, when its High Life brand sagged in competition with other "premium" beers.)

Obviously, only a company backed by massive corporate assets could have pulled off this kind of victory in the beer wars. Miller itself actually lost hundreds of millions of dollars during the first years of its campaign because of its huge expenditures, but it had a virtually inexhaustible fund of cash in its parent corporation.

The rapid concentration of the brewing industry has led to great profits for the winners in the battle of the beers. During the mid-1970s, corporate profit rates were six times as high for beer companies with more than $50 million in assets than for those with less. But what about the *costs*? Some argue that concentration has brought greater efficiency to brewing, resulting in many benefits to the consumer. And it is true that brewing has become, in bare economic terms, more cost-effective. But these potential benefits have *not* been passed on to the consumer.

Beer is considerably more expensive today than it was before the surge in industry concentration during the 1970s. And, in-creasingly, the price you pay for a six-pack has little to do with what it actually costs to produce it. The light beers, to take the most obvious example, generally cost the consumer more than regular beers, though they cost less to make; premium beers cost roughly 10 percent more than regular beers at the store, but they cost the same to produce.

What the consumer pays for is the price of the packaging and advertising that go into creating the beer's brand image. In 1977, about 35 percent of the wholesale price of a bottle of Lowenbrau went to pay for advertising designed to convince consumers that Lowenbrau was still a special beer, despite the fact that it was no longer imported.

There have been larger *social* costs as well. Growing concentration has been accompanied by declining jobs, as smaller, labor-intensive breweries are replaced by the big, automated ones. Between 1965 and 1982, the number of brewery industry workers in the United States dropped from about 60,000 to 43,000 — though production went *up* from 108 to 194 million barrels. These jobs have traditionally been highly skilled and well paid. The workers who lose them are typically middle-aged or older, with few other job prospects. (In the mid-1970s, workers at one New York brewery, Rheingold, which had been passed through several conglomerate owners, including Chock-Full-O-Nuts coffee, chained themselves to their machines to protest the closing of their plant.)

The rapid destruction of so many of the smaller breweries has brought substantial economic problems for many communities, especially in the Northeast and Midwest. In a deeper sense, the rapid shakeout of the industry has sped the decline of a whole way of life. This was summed up in the testimony of a brewery association official before a Senate committee investigating the changes in the industry:

> Brewers are a wonderful lot. A brewery was a family affair; small salaries and dividends

(continued)

have always been the rule. Profits were poured back into making the brewery a better place in which to brew their fine beer. Brewers take pride in their product; if product trouble ensues, it is a matter of real and sustained grief, and to witness, as I have, the demise of small brewers — my friends — has not been an easy thing to face. The very thought of ending a family brewery was a source of grief. Fathers and grandfathers before them had always been able to keep the brewery going. What is the matter with me that I cannot do as well? (U.S. Congress, Senate, Committee on the Judiciary, 1978, p. 72)

Sources: Beverage Industry, 1982; *Business Week*, 1977; Fogarty, 1985; Hall, 1986; Keithan, 1979; Maslow, 1979; Morrison, 1982; *Newsweek*, 1978; *Statistical Abstract of the United States*, 1986, pp. 553, 759; *Time*, 1979; U.S. Congress. Senate, Committee on the Judiciary, 1978, p. 72.

The Corporate Network

The rapid growth of mergers and acquisitions is only one reason why the American economy is even more concentrated than the official statistics suggest. Another reason is that a variety of interconnections bind the largest corporations together in crucial ways. As Edward Herman has noted, "Corporate power depends not only on the resources and market control of individual companies, but also on the extent to which companies coordinate their behavior and activities" (1981, p. 194). Studies of American industry have come to different conclusions about the significance of these connections in influencing business decisions and overriding competition between corporations. But no one doubts that corporations are linked together in many ways, including everything from the common schooling, background, and club membership of corporate executives (Domhoff, 1974, 1985) to informal discussions over drinks or on the golf course to more formal, institutional links between firms.

Among the latter, probably the most important is the *interlocking directorate* — the somewhat cumbersome term for the tendency for large corporations to have the same people sit on their boards of directors. In a *direct interlock*, a single director sits on the boards of two supposedly separate corporations. In an *indirect interlock*, two corporations' directors meet through sitting on the board of a third corporation. Direct interlocks, in particular, tend to create close working ties, mutual interest, and channels of communications that bind corporations together in ways that cast doubt on the conventional picture of independent, competitive enterprises.

A 1978 Senate study of interlocks among the largest 130 American corporations (which together controlled over a trillion dollars in assets) found the following (U.S. Congress, Senate, Committee on Government Affairs, 1978, p. 457):

- The 130 corporations shared a total of 530 direct and more than 12,000 indirect interlocks.

- The top 13 corporations alone had 249 direct and over 5,500 indirect interlocks with other corporations. AT&T alone interlocked with 93 of the 130 top corporations.
- Indirect interlocks often took place between companies that were, formally, competitors. For example, both AT&T and IBM — officially heavy competitors in communications equipment — had directors who sat together on the board of Citicorp, a bank that lent to both companies and was a customer of their products.

An International Economy

One further limitation of the usual measures of economic concentration deserves mention: The measures do not encompass either the growing role since World War II of American corporations overseas or, the other side of the coin, the increasing role of foreign corporations in the American economy. These two developments (both of which will be treated in more detail in Chapter 3) distort the conventional measures of corporate power, in opposite directions.

Thus, our usual measures of corporate shares in the domestic economy ignore the fact that a substantial number of corporations now do much of their business in foreign countries. Between 1970 and 1984 alone, American private investment in foreign countries grew from about $76 billion to about $233 billion (*Economic Report of the President*, 1986, p. 281). A growing number of the largest American corporations (and many smaller ones as well) now draw much of their income from foreign sales, and foreign workers are a substantial fraction of their total work force. The Ford Motor Company is still headquartered in Michigan, but it builds Fords and Ford components in countries as diverse as Brazil, West Germany, and Spain, and it supplies the livelihoods of thousands of workers in those countries. In 1980, fully 55 percent of Ford's worldwide production took place in foreign countries: 30 percent of General Motors' employees are foreign (United Nations, 1983, pp. 41, 203). Understanding only the domestic role of these corporations, therefore, obscures the influence they exert throughout the world's economy. Cadillac's newest luxury model offers an illustration:

> There has never been anything like it. Cadillac's spanking new Allante is a $50,000 two-passenger luxury car made on two continents with parts from eight nations. Stamped, welded, and painted, the finished auto body is shipped thrice-weekly by specially configured jumbo jet from Turin, Italy, to Detroit's Metropolitan Airport. Uniquely modi-

fied trucks haul it to the brand-new GM Detroit-Hamtramck Assembly Plant, where the engine, transmission, and suspensions are added. (Williams, 1986, p. 70)

At the same time, however, as a glance along any American street reveals, the same measures of corporate power also ignore the growing role of foreign businesses in the American economy. As Japanese cars (to take only one of the more obvious examples) gained an increasing share of the American auto market by the 1970s, measures of the American auto companies' share of domestic production obviously became less useful guides to the shape of the automobile market as a whole in this country. Increasingly, consumers in the past few decades have been faced with fewer choices among American-made cars, and the signs are that this trend may increase. On the other hand, consumers gained many more choices among Japanese, German, French, Italian, Swedish, and Korean cars; and a similar process has taken place in many other industries. In assessing the concentration of private power in the American economy, therefore, it's important to keep in mind that our economy is not a closed, impermeable system but increasingly part of a constantly shifting balance of resources and power in a *world* economic system.

The Two Economies

The other side of the increasing power of the largest corporations is the relatively shrinking share of economic activity accounted for by *small* businesses. In focusing on the growth of the large corporation, we have so far ignored the other end of what the economist John Kenneth Galbraith (1973) has called a "bimodal" economy. This sector contains millions of small businesses, each often with only a handful of employees.

The lopsided character of business enterprise in America becomes apparent when we look at tax returns. Almost 3 million corporations filed income tax returns with the Internal Revenue Service in 1982. Of them, 99 percent had assets of less than $10 million; just 3,000, or 0.1 percent, had assets of over $250 million. But those 3,000 brought in three-quarters of the total profits while the bottom 99 percent brought in just over one-tenth (*Statistical Abstract of the United States*, 1986, p. 526).

Students of American industry have developed a variety of terms for this split between (in Galbraith's phrase) the "planning" and the "market" sector. Some distinguish between the "monopoly" and the

Jack Spratt/Picture Group, Inc.

Fredrik D. Bodin/Picture Group, Inc.

The image of the small business no longer fits the reality of America's corporate economy. America's urban skylines reflect the dominance of the large corporation.

"competitive" sector, or more simply, between "primary" and "secondary" sectors of the economy. But whatever terms are used, the trend is the same. The traditional conception of free enterprise — the competition of many small, independent businesses — applies to only *part* of our economy. The other part is, more and more, a center of concentrated power that bears virtually no resemblance to the idealized conception of small enterprise. This division has many consequences, some of which we'll examine in later chapters. The nature and quality of work, for example, as well as the level of earnings on the job, vary considerably between these sectors of the economy. So, too, do the risks of unemployment and poverty. And the different distribution of minorities and women in the two sectors has much to do with their differing life chances, as we'll see in Chapters 5 and 6.

The displacement of much small-scale production by large corporate enterprise, as the political scientist Charles Lindblom put it, "constitutes a revolution" — a revolution "never much agitated, never even much resisted," and for which "no flags were raised" — but one that has "transformed our lives" (1977, p. 95). What are the consequences of this growth of private power for American life? We will be addressing that question, in one way or another, throughout many of the chapters of this book. But first we need to look at two other aspects of the distribution of economic power in America. For it is not size or concentration alone that defines the contours of corporate power in American life, or that distinguishes the United States from other industrial societies, many of which have as great or greater levels of concentration among a few giant firms. Even more important is the question of how that power stacks up against two other,

The Two Economies   **37**

potentially counterbalancing sources of social and economic influence: government and labor. As we've noted, there has been much criticism of the overpowering effects of "big government" on the economy and society as a whole in recent years, and a similar criticism of the overbearing role of "big labor." To round out our preliminary picture of the basic institutions of the American economy, therefore, let's look at some key facts about the relative place of government and labor in the American system.

How Big Is "Big Government"?

In an article ominously titled "Big Government: Democracy's Deadly Creation," the economist Allan Meltzer (1980) put forward a view of the role of government in the American economy that many people share. "Whether measured by the share of income taken by taxes or by the portion of the labor force employed," Meltzer said, "government has grown relentlessly." Is this an accurate assessment?

It is certainly true that the government plays a much greater role in the economy than it did in the past. But both the *size* and the *functions* of government in the American economy turn out to be considerably different, on close examination, than many assume.

Trends in Government Employment   Let's consider first the trends in government *employment*. At first glance, the government appears as a very large employer, indeed; in 1984 government at all levels (federal, state, and local) employed over 16 million people — 15 percent of all Americans employed in the civilian labor force (*Statistical Abstract of the United States*, 1986, p. xiii). Two facts, however, qualify this picture.

First, the overwhelming majority of government employees work for state and local government. Less than one in five works for the federal government. The conception of the federal government as a giant, overpowering bureaucracy seems less compelling in light of the fact that it employs about one-fifth as many people as the Fortune 500 manufacturing corporations. Measured by number of employees, the biggest "bureaucracy" in the United States in the mid-1980s was the Department of Defense, with about 1 million civilian employees. But next in line was General Motors, with three-quarters of a million. And several other private corporations, including Sears, Roebuck, Ford, and IBM, are bigger bureaucracies than any federal agency other than Defense and the Post Office. About twice as many people work for K-Mart as for the Department of Health and Human Services (*Forbes*, 1985, p. 231; *Statistical Abstract of the United States*, 1986, p. 325).

Second, we need to examine the kind of work most government employees actually *do*. Again, the conventional image is one of legions of faceless bureaucrats wielding inordinate power over economic decisions. But the reality is quite different. At the federal level, government employment is overwhelmingly dominated by civilian employees of the Department of Defense, who constituted more than 1 million (more than a third) of the 2.9 million federal workers in 1984. Adding together the Defense Department workers with the next largest category by far, the 682,000 postal workers, accounts for well over half of all federal civilian employment. Another roughly 250,000 work in health care. In state and local government, the work force is dominated by teachers and health-care workers: More than half of local government employees work in education.

Still another perspective on the growth of government-as-employer is provided by the trend of government employment over time. Viewed in raw figures, this growth has been substantial. Government employment more than doubled between 1955 and 1984. But, once again, the overall trend masks crucial distinctions. *Federal* government employment has grown relatively little since the 1950s and has declined significantly as a proportion of the American work force. In 1960 the federal government employed almost 4 percent of American workers; by 1985 it employed less than 3 percent (*Statistical Abstract of the United States*, 1987, p. 309).

One result is that the state and local government (and especially the latter) have taken a growing share of all government employment. Though it's often said that the growth of the federal government has meant that more and more power is concentrated in distant, unresponsive bureaucracies, the actual trend is in the opposite direction, at least in the case of government employment. The federal presence in American life has been increasingly overshadowed by the growth of more *localized* levels of government. In 1955, 68 percent of government workers were employed at the state and local levels; by 1984, 82 percent were. And even there the rise in government employment peaked during the late 1960s (see Table 2-3).

So far we have ignored an important qualifying factor — the growth in the American population. Statistics on the growth of government seem more impressive than they really are if they are taken out of the context of a growing population whose needs the government must serve. In fact, when measured against the growth of the population as a whole, federal government employment has *fallen* substantially since 1950. More precisely, most of the post–World War II era can be divided into two periods: between 1950 and 1970, when

Most of the growth in government employment has been in education and health care.

per capita federal employment remained virtually unchanged, and after 1970, when it fell considerably. Thus, in 1950 there were 71 civilians for each civilian employed by the federal government; in 1984, there were 80 (*Statistical Abstract of the United States*, 1986, pp. xiii, 5).

Government Spending and Taxes

Government employment, however, is just one of many indicators of the government's size and influence. The levels of taxing and spending by government are others.

The "relentless" growth in government's share of income through taxation is often cited, along with the growth in employment, as a sign that the government has taken an ominously increasing role in American life. No one likes taxes and there is plenty of room for debate over whether our tax dollars are being wisely used. But is it true that the tax burden is especially severe in the United States — and that the tax bite is getting bigger all the time? One of the most common ways of measuring the significance of the government tax burden is to

Table 2-3
Trends in government employment, 1950–1984

Level of government	1950	1960	1970	1980	1985
Employees (in thousands)					
Total	**6,402**	**8,808**	**13,028**	**16,213**	**16,690**
Federal (civilian)	2,117	2,421	2,881	2,898	3,021
State and local	4,285	6,387	10,147	13,315	13,669
Percent of total	67	73	78	82	82

Source: Adapted from *Statistical Abstract of the United States, 1982–83* (Washington, D.C.: Government Printing Office, 1983), p. 303; 1987, p. 280.

	Years	
Country	1970	1984
United States	30.1	29.0
Austria	35.7	42.0
Canada	32.0	33.7
Denmark	40.4	48.0
France	35.6	45.5
Italy	27.9	41.2
Japan	19.7	27.4
Netherlands	39.9	45.5
Norway	39.2	46.4
Spain	17.2	28.4
Sweden	40.7	50.5
Switzerland	23.8	32.2
United Kingdom	37.5	38.5
West Germany	32.8	37.7

Source: Statistical Abstract of the United States, 1982–83 (Washington, D.C.: Government Printing Office, 1983), p. 870; 1987, p. 828.

Table 2-4
Tax revenues as percent of gross domestic product, 1970 and 1984

view it as a proportion of economic activity as a whole. Table 2-4 presents the level of national and local taxes as well as Social Security contributions for the United States and a number of other countries.

Two things are immediately apparent. First, taxes as a proportion of the gross domestic product (the GDP is the value of all goods and services produced by the domestic economy in a given year; it is the same as the gross national product, but minus goods and services produced abroad) have remained remarkably stable in the United States in recent years: There was *no* significant increase (even a slight decline) in the government's role, measured in this way, during the 1970s and early 1980s. Second, even more strikingly, the relative level of taxes is *greater* in almost every country represented than in the United States. Indeed, Table 2-4 shows that every advanced industrial society except Japan gathers a higher share of taxes than the United States; only the less developed European countries (like Spain) tax less. In some cases (Denmark, France, the Netherlands, Norway, and Sweden), the tax burden is at least 50 percent higher than in the United States. Moreover, Japan, the major exception to this rule, turns out on closer inspection to be less an exception than it seems at first, since — like many other countries in the table — its tax burden as a proportion of its gross domestic product has increased rapidly in recent years, while that of the United States has stabilized.

What is true of taxes — the government's main source of income — is also true of government *spending*. As Figure 2-2 demonstrates, the United States falls, once again, near the very *bottom* of the advanced industrial societies in the proportion of economic activity accounted for by public spending. As with taxes, Japan is the only comparable country on the list with a lower proportion of government outlays. Though the figure doesn't show this, the only reason our government expenditures are slightly higher than Japan's is our much higher spending on *defense;* we spend more than six times as much of our national product on defense as the Japanese. When it comes to spending on *nondefense* programs, the United States' proportion is even smaller than Japan's. (The same point, of course, should also be kept in mind in understanding Japan's lower taxes.)

Public and Private Enterprise

Even these rather dramatic comparisons, however, don't adequately express the differences between the government's role in the United States and in most other advanced societies. It is not merely the *amount* of government spending that differs among industrial societies, but also the *kind* of government spending. In most other advanced industrial countries, the government takes a far more active, productive role in the overall economy than it does in the United States. In many countries substantial sectors of the economy are owned and operated as *public* enterprises rather than as private ones. These public enterprises range from coal and steel (in several European countries) to automobiles (such as Germany's Volkswagen and Italy's Alfa Romeo) to a substantial part of oil, gas, and other energy production (as in Italy). In a number of countries, a good part of the banking industry is publicly owned as well, as are many national airlines and railway systems. (In the United States, probably the best-known example is the major public utility, the Tennessee Valley Authority, TVA.) As this implies, many of these public enterprises are very large, are integral to the national economy, and, in fact, are major contenders on the list of the most important *world* enterprises. Italy's public energy conglomerate, ENI, was the world's tenth largest industrial corporation in 1985 (outside the United States); Compagnie Francaise des Petroles, the French public oil company, was nineteenth (*Forbes*, 1986, p. 176).

The *importance* of public enterprise in other countries is suggested by Table 2-5, which is based on a recent analysis from the Organization for Economic Cooperation and Development (OECD). It shows the shares of overall investment and national employment accounted for by public enterprises in various countries.

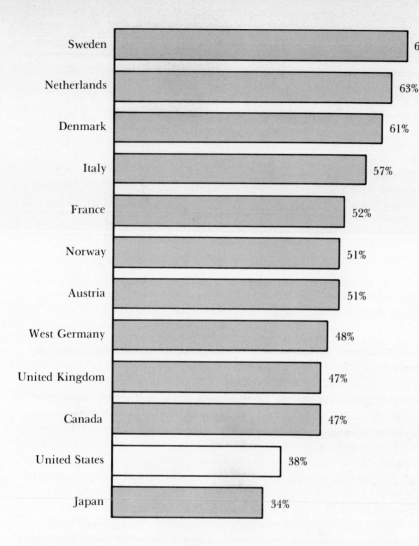

Sweden	66%
Netherlands	63%
Denmark	61%
Italy	57%
France	52%
Norway	51%
Austria	51%
West Germany	48%
United Kingdom	47%
Canada	47%
United States	38%
Japan	34%

Figure 2-2
Government expenditures as a percentage of gross domestic product, selected countries, 1983

Source: Data from Organization for Economic Cooperation and Development, *OECD Economic Outlook,* Paris, May 1986, p. 181. Reprinted with permission.

Once again, the differences are striking. It is not just that the United States has a smaller sector of public enterprise; it isn't even in the same ball park as the others. The foreign countries with comparatively low levels of public-sector enterprise invest close to three times what we do in such enterprises, and the difference in shares of employment is often even greater. Countries like Sweden and West Germany employ almost 1 in 12 of their labor force in public enterprises, and Austria almost 1 in 8. In the United States, the figure is 1 in *60.*

These sharp differences in both the size and the function of the public sector help illustrate, once more, how thoroughly *private* the

Table 2-5
Share of public
enterprises in total
investment and
employment,
1975–1978/9

Country	Investment	Employment
Austria	5.3	12.4
Belgium	3.3	5.2
Canada	3.7	4.5
France	2.5	4.4
Italy	3.3	6.4
Japan	3.8	NA
Norway	6.5	4.2
Sweden	3.5	8.0
United Kingdom	3.5	8.2
United States	*0.9*	*1.6*
West Germany	2.7	7.9

Note: NA means not available.
Source: Leila Pathirane and Derek W. Blades, "Defining and Measuring the
Public Sector: Some International Comparisons," *Review of Income and Wealth*, series
28, no. 3, September 1982, pp. 268–273. Reprinted with permission of the
International Association for Research in Income and Wealth and the authors.

American economy is in comparison to the economies of other countries. This is true not only of government employment, revenue, and
spending in general but, perhaps even more decisively, of control
over economic *investment*. In the United States, where not only virtually all industrial production but also virtually all banking and
finance are under *private* auspices, decisions about what kinds of
investment should be undertaken and financed, more than in most
comparable societies, are overwhelmingly made by private actors
for private purposes. (Some European countries — especially England — have recently turned a number of public companies over to
private ownership, but the general picture remains the same.)

This difference goes beyond the somewhat clumsy categories of
"capitalism" versus "socialism": None of the countries we've just compared with the United States is socialist since, in all of them, *most*
production still remains in private hands — though some are gov-
erned by Socialist political parties. All of this variation in the role of
the public sector is within the spectrum of the world's "mixed" economies. Chapter 3 touches on some of the ways in which government's
role in these other countries has affected the growth and performance of their economies in recent years. For now, it's important to
stress that a strong role for government in the economy doesn't
necessarily translate into the grim, totalitarian rigidities often associated with some of the countries of Eastern Europe. In varying degrees, it is a fundamental development common to most of the
world's advanced industrial nations.

How Big Is "Big Labor"?

"Big labor" is frequently classified with "big business" and "big government" as the third member of a three-cornered system of shared power in America. Both economists and the general public often describe labor unions as monopolies that fight toe-to-toe with big business on equal terms — or even with an unfair advantage. Partly because of this belief, the public takes a dim view of labor unions, which usually rank low in opinion polls measuring our support for various institutions. Labor is increasingly seen — along with government and business — as another powerful, distant, and unresponsive bureaucracy.

But the reality of labor's current position in the United States is quite different. To begin with, unions enroll a relatively small — and declining — proportion of the American labor force. Union membership constituted a little less than 25 percent of the total labor force in 1955; by 1984 it was less than 19 percent. In some states, especially in the South, the proportion of workers in unions is considerably smaller, below 10 percent, for example, in North and South Carolina, Florida, and Mississippi (*Statistical Abstract of the United States*, 1987, p. 408). The labor movement has had great difficulty organizing workers in many of the fast growing parts of the economy, such as the data processing and computer industries, fast-food restaurants and other retail sales industries, and banking and finance. Of about 36 million new jobs added to the American economy during the 1960s and 1970s, only about 2 million were organized by unions (Chernow, 1981, p. 20).

At the same time, the unions' traditional base of strength in the blue-collar manufacturing industries has eroded badly. Although the labor movement made significant membership gains in some service industries (like health care) and in state and local government during the 1970s and 1980s, it lost over a million members in manufacturing industries. The United States steelworkers of America alone lost over 400,000 members between 1975 and 1985 (*Statistical Abstract of the United States*, 1987, p. 408). Recession-level unemployment, automation, and the movement of production jobs overseas or to nonunion areas have all taken their toll on union membership in these industries.

But declining membership is only one facet of labor's present difficult position. Unions have been relatively unsuccessful in winning the right to represent workers through elections in recent years. In 1934, unions won 94 percent of those representation elections; they won 61 percent of them in 1966, but just 45 percent in 1979. And the threat of a strike as a weapon in the struggle with employers has been weakened in a number of ways in addition to the loss of membership and representation.

For one thing, automation in many industries has meant that, in a pinch, companies can often keep up close to their usual level of production with only supervisory employees on the job. And this is likely to become an even more telling problem for unions as workplace automation becomes still more sophisticated; as an article in *Fortune* put it, "Robots don't strike" (Meyer, 1981, p. 67). Further, the rise of the conglomerate corporation has also hurt unions' ability to pose a threat to management since, in order to keep up with a company's diversification, labor must coordinate different unions across a variety of industries. The increasingly multinational char-

Overseas production has weakened the position of American labor.

J. P. Laffont/Sygma

acter of many American corporations has also weakened labor's position. A company that does half of its production overseas can easily shift even more of it abroad in the event of labor problems at home, and labor has not yet been able to create the international organizations that could match the corporations' mobility. As the president of the AFL-CIO put it recently, "Capital is mobile and labor is not. Capital has no flag and no country. Labor is locked not just into its country, but its community" (quoted in Kuttner, 1984, p. 25).

The result of these trends is that, as *Fortune* declared in 1981, "a historic shift appears to be looming in the balance of power between labor and management" (Meyer, 1981, p. 66). Although one business writer argues that unions are "fading into the background of American public life" (Freedman, 1985), that is surely too stark a prediction. Unions have made important gains in some industries and have won innovative settlements in others (Kuttner, 1984). But it's true that labor's power is shifting relative to that of business. And what makes this shift especially troubling for labor is that unions have *traditionally* occupied a distinctly subordinate position in relation to business in the United States, as compared with most other advanced industrial countries. Some of that disparity is revealed by membership figures; while less than 20 percent of the American labor force is unionized, the proportion is about 40 percent in West Germany and Spain, 45 percent in Italy, 50 percent in Great Britain, and an astonishing 90 percent in Sweden (Hayward, 1980, p. 4). These differences translate into a much greater political role for labor in most European counties — a role that has profoundly affected life in those countries in many ways: tougher occupational health and safety laws, more generous and more easily available social welfare benefits, regulations governing plant closings and retraining policies, and much more. In the United States, business's discretion to lay off workers, to shut down factories and stores, and to determine workers' exposure to toxic chemicals and other hazards — to name only a few key issues of labor policy — is much greater than it is in most industrial societies. And if "big labor" shrinks further, this imbalance could become even more telling.

Government Support for Private Enterprise

Though the public sector of the American economy is relatively small *by comparison* with that of other countries, the government's role in economic life in the United States is by no means insignificant. On the contrary, government intervention in the service of economic goals has been an important feature of America's development since well before the Civil War. And that intervention has not necessarily been hostile to business interests; on the contrary, government support has been actively — and successfully — sought by private enterprise from the country's beginnings (Herman, 1981, chap. 5).

The great system of canals that opened up settlement beyond the East Coast in the early nineteenth century was largely underwritten by public funds; as much as 80 percent of the investment came from the government (DuBoff, 1980, p. 397). In the later part of the century, the government provided extensive support for the development of the railroads that made possible both America's westward expansion and the post–Civil War industrial revolution. Private railroad companies received grants of valuable land (often bearing coal, copper, and other mineral wealth) totaling more than 180 million acres. Other subsidies and tax exemptions, from local and state as well as the federal government, brought public support to the private railroad industry to an estimated $1.3 billion during the nineteenth century. Similarly, following World War II, the federal government provided a bonanza to private business by selling more than $15 billion worth of war-related assets to private industry at less than a third of their cost (Shepherd and Wilcox, 1979, p. 568).

Today, that tradition of government aid has blossomed into a complex, often confusing array of publicly funded supports for private enterprise. In Chapter 4 we will consider how they affect the distribution of income and wealth in the United States. But it is helpful to look at them briefly now as well, for this network of subsidies and protections should profoundly affect the way we think about the relations between business and government. Taken together, it amounts to what may be called a hidden welfare system for private business. The subsidies and protections include:

- *Bailouts:* Subsidies and loans to enable failing companies to remain afloat are the most obvious examples of government support of private business. The largest and best known of these, the $1.2 billion federal loan to stave off the collapse of the Chrysler Corporation in the early 1980s, is only the most striking example of government's frequent commitment to providing a "safety net" for corporations in trouble.

- *Direct subsidies:* Another relatively straightforward part of the system of public assistance to business is the payment of direct subsidies to certain key industries. Two of the most important consumers of public funds have been the energy industries and agriculture. As we'll see in Chapter 10, the private energy industry has benefited from an estimated $250 *billion* in direct government subsidies since the end of World War I, of which half has gone to the oil industry alone. The much younger nuclear power industry, by the mid-1970s, accounted for about 8 percent of that historical total and is now dependent on federal subsidies for its economic survival. The federal government has paid for most of the research that built the industry, has helped pay for the construction of nuclear power plants, and has subsidized the cost of insurance against nuclear accidents.

Federal subsidies to agriculture, many dating from the Great Depression, amounted to about $70 million a *day* in 1986 (*New York Times*, December 26, 1986). A number of crops are protected by "target" prices, meaning that government will pay farmers the difference between the price their crop brings on the market and a preestablished price. The government also supports agricultural prices by buying surplus farm products (including sugar, cotton, and wheat) that would otherwise be unsold on the market (U.S. Congressional Budget Office, 1984).

• *Trade restrictions:* Despite much rhetorical support for the idea of "free trade," many industries have sought — and won — extensive government protection against competition from foreign producers. American-made liquors, motorcycles, clothing, machinery, sporting goods, musical instruments, and appliances, among other products, are protected by import tariffs that artificially raise the prices of foreign goods for American consumers. (Government protection, for example, helped keep Harley-Davidson's motorcycles alive in the face of the onslaught from Honda, Yamaha, and Suzuki.) Foreign-built ships are restricted from operating in certain American waters. The steel industry is protected by a system of so-called trigger pricing that automatically regulates the cost of imported steel. The value of these government-enforced restrictions has ranged from about 5 percent to close to 50 percent of the cost of the particular product.

• *Tax expenditures:* In addition to outright subsidies and payments, the government also supports private industry through exemptions from taxes. As Chapter 4 shows, such tax expenditures are widespread throughout the American economy, and some benefit individuals and groups other than private businesses. But they have historically provided staggering benefits to business. In 1986 the federal government gave the oil industry tax credits for exploration and depletion amounting to over $1.8 billion. Tax credits for business investment generally amounted to more than $25 billion; the Accelerated Cost Recovery System, which the U.S. Congressional Budget Office describes as being like an interest-free loan to business, cost the government an estimated $23 billion in 1986 (*Statistical*

Abstract of the United States, 1987, p. 297). Some of these tax expenditures, including the investment tax credit, were modified or eliminated (at least temporarily) by the federal tax reforms of 1986. But many remain in place.

- *Shields against competition:* We've already seen that government trade restrictions help protect many American industries against foreign competition. The risks of *domestic* competition are also cushioned by the government in a variety of ways. The most important example is defense production. Military production is a giant sector of the American economy, supplying a significant proportion of the total sales of a number of the largest American corporations as well as many smaller ones. But the bulk of defense contracting is done in ways that bear no resemblance to the model of free enterprise. Government defense planners typically establish close working relations with a small number of familiar, established companies; there is little genuinely competitive bidding for military contracts. One comprehensive review estimates that about two-thirds of military purchases "occur under conditions with virtually no competition at all" (Shepherd and Wilcox, 1979, p. 559).

- *Absorbing "externalities":* A more subtle kind of government aid for private business may be the most important of all, though its dollar costs are virtually impossible to measure. Many of the social and environmental problems that are created in the course of doing business are enormously costly — but they do not appear as costs on the balance sheets of private industry. In economists' language, these costs are called *externalities*. But the fact that they are "external" to the firms themselves doesn't mean that no one ultimately pays for them. In both direct and subtle ways, they are typically paid by the public — and they are often criticized, somewhat paradoxically, as burdensome costs of "big government." Two examples are industrial pollution and unemployment caused by layoffs or business shutdowns. In both cases private business decisions create conditions that demand a response; in both cases much of the response — the disposal of toxic wastes, the payment of public assistance benefits — falls on the shoulders of government agencies and is paid for by the general public through taxes.

You may or may not believe these public supports for business are justified, but the important point is that they are an integral part of our economic system. Private industry is aided and cushioned by a complex system of publicly funded "welfare," which substantially diminishes the risks of private enterprise and spreads the true costs of doing business throughout society as a whole. Whether the cost involved is that of drilling an oil well, cleaning up a toxic chemical spill, or paying for the inefficiency of a new weapons system, business relies

Would America be better off without Chrysler?

It's a fair question.

You've heard from all the pundits, the instant experts, and the vested interests. They all have their favorite version of what's wrong with Chrysler.

Now we'd like to set the record straight.

We've made our share of mistakes in a tough competitive business. And we're willing to accept responsibility for them.

But to turn our back on 140 thousand of our own employees would be irresponsibility.

To close the doors in 52 American communities in which Chrysler is a major factor of the local economy would be irresponsibility.

To deny employment to the 150 thousand people who work for the dealers who sell Chrysler products would be irresponsibility.

To curtail the income of the hundreds of thousands who supply goods and services to Chrysler would be irresponsibility.

Would America be better off with a Big 2 instead of a Big 3?

When it comes to competition, more is better than less.

A Big 3 means you have more choices. More products, more innovations of which Chrysler has delivered its fair share, and then some, over the years.

Example: Chrysler was first with a solid state electronic ignition system as standard equipment.

But the Big 3 or the Big 2 has its real meaning only in terms of people. People who have jobs. People who pay taxes to America and to the communities in which they live. A Congressional Budget Office study shows that people with jobs at Chrysler, or jobs that depend on Chrysler, contribute 11 billion dollars each year in tax revenues to our country. Without those jobs they would be collecting 2 billion dollars instead in unemployment benefits.

So you'd have to say that a Big 3 contributes a lot more to the health of the American economy than a Big 2.

Is Chrysler building gas guzzlers?

A lot of people who should know better have been peddling this myth.

The fact is that Chrysler has the best average gas mileage of the Big 3.

Chrysler has more models rated 25 miles per gallon or better than GM, Ford, Datsun, Toyota or even Honda.

We also have one of the industry's most proven 6-cylinder engines in the efficient Chrysler Slant 6. The Slant 6 is standard in all our current compact and mid-size cars. Even in many of our full-size cars as well.

And Chrysler's percentage of small car sales to big cars is the best of the Big 3 by far—not the worst —as some would have you believe.

Over 87 percent of the cars Chrysler builds are not big cars at all—they're mid-size or smaller.

So let's put to rest the myth that Chrysler is building the wrong kind of cars.

To date we've built more of the right kind of cars than anyone else.

We were in the market two years ahead of General Motors with America's first front-wheel drive small cars: the roomy and fuel-efficient Omni and Horizon.

However, we lacked the resources to build our own 4-cylinder engines. We felt it was important to get these cars to the American people in the shortest possible time, so we reached an agreement to buy up to 300 thousand engine blocks a year from Volkswagen.

As a result, our production has been limited by the availability of these engines. We apologize to all the people who have had long waits for their Omni or Horizon.

We will eliminate the engine shortage during 1980 when our new 400 million dollar engine plant starts turning out our own 4-cylinder engines.

In 1981 we will bring to market a new fleet of compact-size front-wheel drive cars including the first American front-wheel drive station wagons. This one car line alone represents a 1 billion dollar investment.

Our engineering tests project that these cars will have an average fuel economy rating of over 25 miles per gallon. Yet they will have more room inside than GM's new X cars.

In all, Chrysler will be providing about one million efficient front-wheel drive vehicles to continue its leadership in front-wheel drive.

What is Chrysler asking for—a handout?

No.

We're asking the government to help us offset the heavy cost of regulation.

This is a bad year for the automobile industry. And a worse year for Chrysler. First, gas lines flattened sales of almost all cars except the smallest. Now the country is moving rapidly toward a recession. Even GM is having difficulty moving large stocks of full-size cars.

But GM can weather the storm better than Chrysler because they can distribute the costs of regulation over a lot more cars. For example, studies indicate that Chrysler costs per car for government regulations are $200 to $300 more per car than for GM.

As a result, interest costs for Chrysler average about $125 per car, but only $10 per car for GM. Those differences alone are staggering for Chrysler.

Because of the hundreds of millions committed for new plants and new products, and the hundreds of millions invested to meet regulations, Chrysler faces a temporary shortage of funds. Chrysler has no choice but to seek temporary assistance from the heavy burden regulation places on us. We want equity restored to

the competitive system because the system is anti-competitive as it stands now.

We're not asking for a hand-out, a bail-out, or welfare. Chrysler is asking for temporary assistance for 1979 and 1980 equal to the cost of meeting government regulations for those two years.

It will not cost the taxpayer anything because Chrysler will repay the government out of future profits.

Has Chrysler done everything it can to help itself?

We have restructured all our overseas investments to generate new working capital so we can concentrate on the North American market.

We have mounted an all-out effort to get record financing for programs that will make us competitive and profitable.

We have become more efficient by eliminating duplication, cutting expenses and introducing innovative and even unconventional programs. In fact, we have reduced our costs by $500 million so far this year.

We've added top level marketing management.

We've hired the best brains in the business to improve manufacturing quality, and to put tighter controls on purchasing.

Our dealers and our suppliers have given Chrysler strong commitments of support.

Does Chrysler have a future?

You can count on it.

Seventeen million Chrysler owners can count on it.

Our 4700 Chrysler-Plymouth and Dodge dealers can count on it. Our employees can count on it. Our suppliers can count on it.

The concerned citizens of 52 communities whose livelihoods are closely tied to Chrysler can count on it.

And the *competition* can really count on it.

We have in place for 1980 and 1981 the programs, the products and the management Chrysler needs to be competitive, to sell cars, to meet our obligations, to become profitable.

We've been in business for fifty-four years, and almost all fifty-four have been profitable.

We plan to be around at least another fifty-four. You can count on it.

John Riccardo

John Riccardo
Chairman, Chrysler Corporation

Lee A. Iacocca

Lee A. Iacocca
President, Chrysler Corporation

Sometimes, corporations (like individuals) need government help to survive.

heavily, in one way or another, on that system of public welfare. And this not ony affects our understanding of the true meaning of government spending but, as we shall see, has important consequences for many aspects of American life — from the distribution of income to the state of national security.

A Privatized Economy

In the 1950s and 1960s, many social scientists believed that the world's advanced societies were coming more and more to resemble one another. Common technological and political trends, it was argued, were leading to an increasing convergence among what were variously called the "new industrial states" or the "postindustrial societies" (see, for example, Galbraith, 1967; Bell, 1971). In some ways, these predictions have been borne out. The industrial societies of Europe, North America, and Japan are all characterized by the growth of large corporate bureaucracies alongside the more traditional sectors of small enterprise and also by the increasing role of government in economic life. But, at the same time, these predictions unduly minimized the persistence of important differences among the industrial societies — particularly the balance between private and public power, and between business and labor.

In the United States, as we've seen, the private economy is no longer understandable in the terms traditionally applied to the competitive market system. Instead, it is characterized by an extraordinary concentration of economic power in a relatively few very large corporations. But this in itself is not what distinguishes the United States from other countries within the advanced capitalist world. What *is* strikingly different is the distribution of resources and power among government, business, and labor. Even among the world's mixed economies, the United States stands out as uniquely dominated by *private* power, with a relatively miniscule public sector and a relatively small, historically weak labor movement.

This contrast affects almost every aspect of American life; we'll encounter it over and over again in the following chapters. It influences our rates of poverty and shapes our distribution of income, structures our health-care system and affects our policies toward the environment. Indeed, whatever one may believe about the moral or philosophical issues involved, it is difficult to comprehend American social problems and the public policies addressing them without viewing them through the lens of the underdevelopment of *public* institutions and services in the United States, relative to other, comparable societies. This is especially important in understanding the problems of the economy itself, to which we now turn.

Summary

This chapter has described some dimensions of the institutions of business, government, and labor in America, and some of the relationships among them.

Though the American economy is often described as a system of small enterprise competing in a free market, it is increasingly dominated by a relatively small number of large, often interconnected corporations wielding great economic influence.

The American government — especially the federal government — is sometimes seen as a giant, all-powerful bureaucracy overwhelming private business. But by a variety of measures, including those of government spending, taxation, and the role of public enterprise, government has a *smaller* role in America than in almost any other advanced industrial society. The role of the *federal* government hasn't grown in recent years. The growth that *has* taken place in government in the past decade has been at the state and local level, mainly in the provision of basic services like schooling and health care. With the exception of the Department of Defense and the Postal Service, America's largest bureaucracies are private, not governmental.

Government and free enterprise are often thought to be opposing forces in American society. But the federal government provides an elaborate network of special supports and subsidies that constitute a kind of hidden welfare system for private business. That system includes bailouts of troubled corporations, public subsidies for agriculture and other industries, special tax favors, and protection against competition.

The other "partner" in the American economic system — labor — is neither as large nor as powerful as is often believed. Membership in the organized labor movement is declining and economic changes, including automation and the decline of traditional blue-collar industries, may make labor's influence even more precarious.

Because of the relatively small roles of government and labor in the American economic system, our economic and social policies are influenced to an unusually high degree (as compared to other advanced societies) by the interests of private business.

For Further Reading

Adams, Walter. *The Bigness Complex*. New York: Pantheon, 1986.

Freeman, Richard B., and James L. Medoff. *What Do Unions Do?* New York: Basic Books, 1984.

Galbraith, John Kenneth. *Economics and the Public Purpose*. Boston: Houghton Mifflin, 1973.

Herman, Edward S. *Corporate Control, Corporate Power*. 2nd ed. New York: Cambridge University Press, 1981.

Lindblom, Charles E. *Politics and Markets: The World's Political-Economic Systems*. New York: Basic Books, 1977.

3

The End of Affluence? Social Aspects of Economic Change

For many years, the threat of economic insecurity has touched almost every corner of American life. The specifics of the country's economic problems have varied; and the changes have often come with bewildering speed — as we've seen in the rapid shifts in the relative balance between the two great scourges of the modern American economy, unemployment and inflation. But beneath the confusing changes in the dry statistics on unemployment, productivity, and prices lie some very tangible realities that affect most Americans in one way or another — shrinking chances for a decent job, housing prices so high that an adequate home may seem forever out of reach, the need to take on a second job just to pay the bills, the closing of factories, and the devastating collapse of long-established businesses.

It wasn't always this way. For most of the period from World War II to the 1970s, constant economic growth was virtually taken for granted in the United States. Social theorists celebrated the arrival of what John Kenneth Galbraith (1957) called the "affluent society"; some went so far as to argue that America's prosperity was a sign that most of the fundamental economic problems of the past had been essentially solved (Bell, 1965). No one denied that America still had problems — poverty, inadequate housing, urban decay — but these were often regarded as unfortunate leftovers from the less affluent past. Unceasing economic growth would, in the economic metaphor of the time, "trickle down" to the poor and the less prosperous areas of the country; what growth failed to accomplish could be supplied by antipoverty or urban renewal programs. Even critics of American society during the 1950s and 1960s usually took its affluence for granted; they leveled most of their criticism at what they saw as America's cultural sterility and loss of meaning and purpose, not at its failure to grow and produce in material terms (see, for example, Riesman, 1955; Goodman, 1960; Marcuse, 1964).

These expectations were based on what was at least a partial reality. A unique combination of factors had put the United States in the enviable position of being the dominant economic power in the world, and that power was translated into rising standards of living at home. A 1980 article in *Business Week,* titled "The Shrinking Standard of Living," described this postwar development succinctly:

> For three decades after the end of World War II, Americans enjoyed an ever-rising standard of living; each successive year, with few exceptions, found people working less and earning more. It became not only two chickens in every pot, but two cars in every garage for most Americans, not to mention the radios, TV sets, hi-fi's, blenders, wall ovens, and trash compactors. (1980e, p. 73)

The profusion of consumer goods wasn't, of course, the only fruit of postwar economic growth. Even more important for the way most Americans lived and thought were other benefits, such as the feeling that hard work would bring economic security and the good life for one's children, if not for oneself, and the opening of possibilities for social and economic advancement for many people who had been denied them.

But the crippling recessions and mounting inflation of the 1970s ended the era of largely unbroken economic growth and jolted the country awake from the "American dream." As the *Business Week* article concluded, "The American credo that each generation can look forward to a more comfortable life than its predecessor has been shattered" (1980e, p. 72).

Today social scientists are less likely to study the problems of affluence than the causes and remedies of economic insecurity and stagnation; and politicians compete over different strategies to restore America's economic strength. Most people agree that the American economy is going through profound changes, but there's not much agreement on what the changes mean for our collective future. Some believe the changes have ominous implications for our economic security and standard of living. Others think the changes are more benign, the fears exaggerated. Even those who agree that we face some serious economic problems often disagree about the causes — and even more about the cures.

As we saw in Chapter 2, some blame the problems of the economy on too much government intervention, on greedy workers and unions, on the claims of environmentalists and the poor. These views have led to demands to limit government regulation, shift resources away from workers and toward business, and reduce spending on programs for the disadvantaged. But others argue that the economy's troubles are less the result of a dearth of resources than the result of the failure to use the material and human resources we have in effective ways. Moreover, that failure — in this view — can be traced as much to the social and economic priorities of business as to the restrictive influences of government and labor. We are, in short, in the midst of a fundamental debate about our economic priorities. In this debate there are few definitive answers; the issues will be argued for years to come.

This chapter explores some of those issues. In the first section we look at some facts about the economy's performance in recent years, examining, in particular, the changing balance of economic power and performance between the United States and a number of foreign countries and the effects of economic change on the American standard of living. Disagreements over economic policy often involve differing judgments about the social and personal costs of alternative strategies for dealing with economic problems, so another section of the chapter addresses what social scientists know about the human costs of recession and unemployment. Finally, we evaluate several popular explanations for the problems of America's economy in the light of the best evidence available to us.

How Are We Doing?

Making sense of the economy isn't easy. In recent years it has presented a baffling and contradictory picture. Part of the picture is that of a booming, dynamic, and enormously wealthy economy — the biggest and most powerful in the world — pouring out ever-increasing goods and services and generating more and more jobs and higher and higher incomes. But the other part of the picture shows an economy that is rapidly losing ground relative to those of many foreign countries, that maintains shockingly high levels of unemployment and unused productive capacity, and that has not been able to consistently translate its undoubted wealth and power into a rising standard of living for all Americans. What makes all of this so difficult

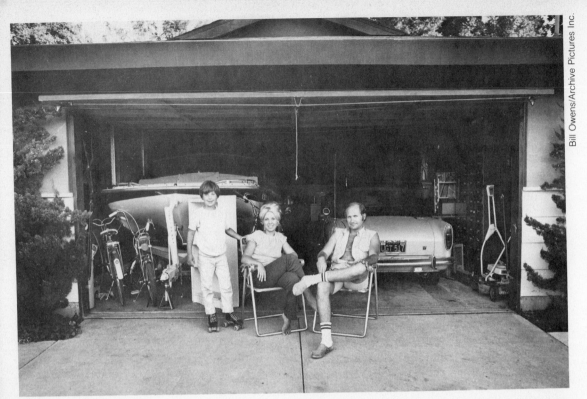

Until the 1970s, many Americans took material abundance for granted.

to understand is that both sides of the picture are accurate. Let's look at each of these issues in turn.

Growth and Competition

By any measure, the American economy is huge — and growing. But it is growing unevenly, and over the past few decades it has been generally outpaced by several foreign competitors. Ours is still the world's most powerful economy, but as a congressional report recently put it, "The United States once dominated the world economy with virtually effortless superiority. Those days are gone forever" (quoted in Behr, 1984).

Economic growth is often measured by the rate of increase in *Gross National Product* (GNP) or its close relation, *Gross Domestic Product* (GDP); these are similar measures, often used interchangeably, of the dollar value of all the goods and services the economy produces each year. (See the box near the end of this chapter for more technical definitions.) More important than sheer growth itself in its implication for the way we live is the measure of GDP *per capita* (see Table 3-1), which adjusts the growth rate to account for changes in popula-

Table 3-1
Trends in economic
growth, selected
countries

Country	Percentage growth of gross domestic product per capita, 1970—1984	Gross domestic product per capita as percentage of GDP in the United States	
		1970	1984
Norway	304	79	100
Japan	294	64	80
Austria	271	63	74
France	243	76	82
West Germany	232	83	86
Italy	225	64	65
United States	218	100	100
United Kingdom	211	74	73

Note: GDP per capita is measured here by "purchasing power parties" — that is, what it would cost to buy an equivalent amount of goods and services in different countries.

Source: Calculated from *Statistical Abstract of the United States,* 1987, p. 825.

tion and thus gives a rough indicator of how much there is to go around. By this measure, the United States has not been faring well. Since 1970 it has been outpaced by every single country in the table, with the exception of the United Kingdom, often viewed as the "sick" economy of Europe. Japan's performance is striking compared to ours, but so is Austria's, and the overall winner in the growth of per capita GDP is another European country — Norway.

Many of these countries emerged from the Second World War in ruins. All were well below our level of wealth (as measured by per capita GDP) through the 1960s. But all have rapidly gained on the United States, and some have passed it. Comparing these measures across different countries is difficult and controversial, partly because of fluctuations in the money exchange rates among countries and partly because of the difficulty of determining what money will buy (its purchasing power) in different economies. But by all measures one country — Switzerland — had passed us by the mid-1970s, and by some measures the list of countries that had passed the United States would now include Sweden, Norway, West Germany, France and Denmark. Whatever measure is used, it is undeniable that many countries have greatly narrowed the gap in recent years, despite the fact that many ran into serious economic troubles of their own in the 1970s. The well-known Japanese economic "miracle" is reflected in its rise from 64 to 79 percent of our per capita GDP (see Table 3-1 again); less well known but equally significant is Austria's rise from 63 to 74 percent or Norway's from 79 to 100 percent of our per capita GDP.

The relative stagnation of the American economy is actually understated by these figures, however. During the 1970s an extraordinary proportion of Americans entered the labor force — at a rate significantly higher than that of most other industrial countries. Other things being equal, that greater increase in people able and willing to work ought to have translated into comparatively higher output for the United States. But other things were not equal. An examination of GDP per *worker*, which can serve as a rough but revealing measure of the productive use an economy is making of its work force, reveals that other industrial countries have done better in this area. As illustrated in Table 3-2, our growth in GDP per worker was only a little over half that of Japan, and less than those of every other country on the table, including the United Kingdom.

These disparities in growth rates are paralleled by the changing position of the United States in the world economy. In the 1960s about 25 percent of all American-made goods competed with foreign-made goods; today the figure is closer to 70 percent. And though most countries have faced severe economic problems in recent years, the relative position of the United States in global economic competition has weakened.

An article in *Business Week* in 1980 declared that relative to the economies of the rest of the world, the United States was "in steep decline." We were, the author lamented, "entering the decade of the 1980s as a wounded, demoralized colossus" (1980a, p. 1). Although this statement is an exaggeration — for the United States remains the world's dominant economic power, accounting for about one-quarter of all the goods and services the world produces — the overall message is on target. Important changes in the relative success of different economies have been both a cause and a consequence of America's troubles.

Table 3-2
Growth of gross domestic product per worker, 1970–1984

Country	Percentage increase in GDP per worker
Japan	317
West Germany	233
France	233
Italy	225
United Kingdom	188
United States	*167*

Source: Calculated from *Statistical Abstract of the United States*, 1987, pp. 825, 830.

The most obvious of these changes is the increasing dependence of the American economy on imported oil — which, as we will see in Chapter 10, has had important implications for the quality of American life.

But not only has the United States become a massive importer of oil; it has also become an importer of many manufactured goods. At the beginning of the 1960s, only 4 percent of the cars Americans bought were imported. By 1981, more than 25 percent were. In 1960 we imported less than 6 percent of consumer electronic products (such as radios, TVs, stereos, and calculators); just two decades later, 45 percent of calculators and over 50 percent of other consumer electronics were imported (*Business Week*, 1980a, p. 60; Reich, 1983, pp. 44–45). As late as 1965, the United States imported around $63 million worth of semiconductors, transistors, and electronic parts. By 1984, the total was over $48 *billion* (*Statistical Abstract of the United States*, 1986, p. 816).

These shifts translate into changing shares of the world market for industrial goods—changes in favor of Japan, Western Europe, and (increasingly) some countries of the Third World. During the 1960s and 1970s, the American share of the world market for passenger cars and industrial machinery fell by about a third each; the share of agricultural machinery fell by two-fifths, and that of telecommunications equipment by half (Reich, 1983, p. 45).

The growing presence in America of Japanese cars and electronics products is by now familiar. In 1984 we imported $57 billion worth of goods from Japan (over $900 for every American family), while we shipped less than $24 billion worth in the other direction (*Statistical Abstract of the United States*, 1986, p. 812). But the increasing share of some fast-growing *Third World* countries in the world economy is even more striking. Consider the steel industry—once one of the foundations of America's international economic power. In 1950 the United States produced almost half of the world's raw steel; by 1984, it produced less than one-eighth. Japan, a country with half our population, surpassed the United States in steel production by 1980. However, from the mid-1970s to the mid-1980s, Japanese steel production dropped slightly, and American production dropped by a fourth. In the same period, Chinese steel production grew by two-thirds, and Korean production nearly tripled (*Statistical Abstract of the United States*, 1986, p. 850).

Two important consequences flow from the increasingly successful economic competition of other countries. The first is that assuring growth and prosperity in the American economy—and thus in Americans' standard of living—will henceforth be more difficult than it was in the past. The other is that the very nature of the American economy may be shifting in fundamental ways, as many kinds of industrial

The face of unemployment in the 1980s: An American worker scans the want ads.

production are increasingly being ceded to Japan, Europe, and the industrializing Third World. Given these recent trends, one observer argues, we are in danger of becoming "a nation of extractors, assemblers, and retailers—relatively poor by the standards of the industrial world" (Reich, 1983, p. 102). Not everyone agrees with that gloomy prediction (see Lawrence, 1984), but one thing is certain: The changes in the American economy have had a profound and often devastating impact on the chances of getting and keeping a good job.

Economic instability is by no means new to America; neither is high unemployment. During the Great Depression of the 1930s, up to a quarter of American workers were without a job. Since then we have achieved something close to "full employment" only during periods of war or preparation for war. But the experience of recent years is especially troubling. We are becoming accustomed to higher "normal" rates of unemployment than ever before; and whole sectors of American industry have suffered massive — and in some cases permanent — loss of jobs.

We will be considering the problem of unemployment in detail in Chapter 8, but let's look at a few general trends here. To begin with, as Figure 3-1 shows, until very recently, our levels of unemployment have been considerably higher than those of almost every other industrial society. Since the mid-1970s, several European countries have suffered rising unemployment, and some have passed the U.S. rate. But many have not. Since 1976 an American's chances of being

Deepening Recessions, Enduring Unemployment

Figure 3-1
Average unemployment rates: 1970–1985 and 1976–1985, selected countries

Source: Adapted from Organization for Economic Cooperation and Development, *OECD Economic Outlook*, May 1986, Table R-12.

Percent of labor force unemployed

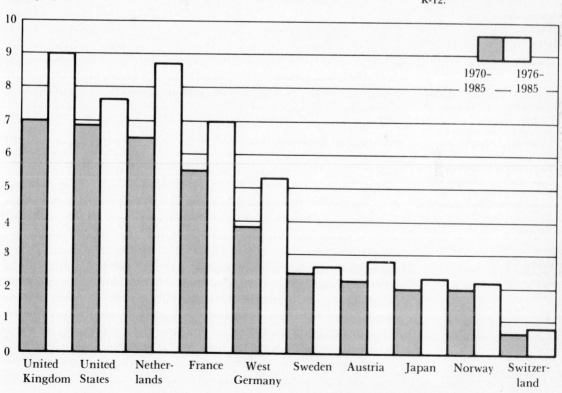

Percent

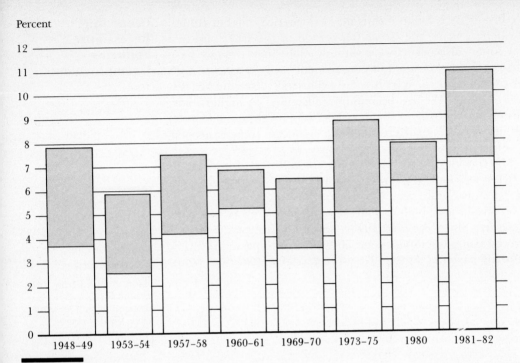

Figure 3-2
Unemployment rates during postwar recessions

Source: Michael A. Urquhart and Marillyn A. Hewson, "Unemployment Continued to Rise in 1982 as Recession Deepened," *Monthly Labor Review*, February 1983, p. 4. Reprinted with permission.
Note: The shaded area of each bar in the chart indicates the peak and trough of unemployment during each period.

unemployed have averaged around three (or more) times those of an Austrian, Swede, Norwegian, or Japanese, and twelve times that of the fortunate Swiss.

Many people point to our capacity to generate new jobs as an indicator of economic health. But our ability to create jobs has not kept up with the demand for work. And the evidence suggests that this disparity has worsened in recent years. Figure 3-2 offers one illustration. Each bar represents the level of unemployment we suffered in each of the major recessions since World War II. Note that, in general, the height of the bars has increased over time — though unevenly — indicating that the recessions have tended to become deeper, throwing more people out of work. But the worst news is depicted in the bottom, unshaded portion of the bars, which represents the *lowest* level of unemployment achieved during the recession. Since the late 1960s that level has risen like a series of steps. In other words, as each recession has ended it has left us with higher rates of joblessness than when it began. The result is that the level of unemployment we must learn to live with as "normal" has risen fairly steadily over the years. We cannot predict whether that trend will continue, but it clearly represents a massive under-use of our human resources.

What is true of jobs is also true for the extent to which the economy is using its *overall* productive capacity. For manufacturing industries, this is usually calculated by a measure called the *capacity utilization rate*. In 1982, that rate fell to less than 70 percent — its lowest level since before World War II. Even more troubling, however, is that the capacity utilization rate reached its highest level (about 91 percent) in 1966 and has never risen as high again. And though capacity utilization has risen a bit over its 1982 low point, it's still true that in the 1980s, on average, about a quarter of our industrial capacity is simply not being used.

Two further factors make these declines in employment and production especially troubling for the future. First, there is every indication that because of increasing automation, many of the job losses of the past decade will not be recovered even if the economy as a whole undergoes a healthy revival. Second, the process of what the economists Barry Bluestone and Bennett Harrison (1982) call *deindustrialization* has not been limited to the older industrial regions of the northeast and northcentral states but has been felt in the South and West as well. In the 1970s it became popular to contrast the economic troubles of the northern "Frost Belt" with the growth and prosperity of the "Sun Belt" of the South and West. But almost half of all American jobs lost as the result of the closing or relocation of plants during the 1970s were in the Sun Belt states (Bluestone and Harrison, 1982, p. 9). And in the 1980s, while some northern states (such as Massachusetts) were rapidly creating new jobs and spawning dynamic industries, some Sun Belt states (such as Texas) had plummeted into severe recession. In the 1970s, the booming state of Texas had become such a magnet for unemployed workers from the Midwest that Houston became known as the "second-largest city in Michigan"; in 1986, Texas had the nation's highest unemployment rate. It seems clear that what is happening is much more than simply another trough in the familiar economic cycle, from which we will soon recover, and much more than just the relative stagnation of some regions as opposed to others. The evidence suggests that the structure of the American economy is undergoing basic changes — in the kinds of things we will produce and in the number and kinds of workers who will be needed to produce them.

The changes in our economy are anything but abstract. They affect our lives in some very basic ways — the amount of money we have to spend, how much we can save for the future, the standard of living we

A Shrinking Standard of Living?

can realistically expect for our children. And, on the whole, the effects of the recent changes in our patterns of growth, international competitiveness, and joblessness have been troubling.

Measured by the money they made and what it could buy, Americans' standard of living increased fairly steadily until the early 1970s. But since then, that steady march toward prosperity has been bogged down — and some groups, particularly people under 30, are clearly worse off today than their counterparts were *fifteen years ago.*

The most common measure of economic well-being is *median family income.* "*Median*" means that half of American families made more, and half made less, than the average figure. As Figure 3-3 shows, median family income rose through the early 1970s, after which it dropped, then began to climb upward again in the mid-1980s — but not far enough to reach its former peaks.

The figure charts the progress of family income in what economists call *constant* dollars — that is, dollars adjusted for inflation, which tells us how much the dollars could actually buy. Measured in this way, the average American family in 1985 was making about $1,400 *less* than the average family back in 1973.

Some social scientists argue that these statistics exaggerate the losses suffered by American families. For one thing, they count income *before taxes* and therefore don't reflect possible declines in the tax burden on families — which could result in the families having the same amount or even more income, after taxes, than in the past. Some economists believe that measures of *real disposable income* (after-tax income adjusted for inflation) show that family incomes have

Figure 3-3
The stalled standard of living: Median family income, 1960–1985

Source: Data from *Statistical Abstract of the United States,* 1987, p. 436.

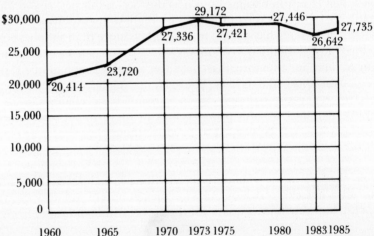

Median income, 1985 dollars

The End of Affluence? Social Aspects of Economic Change

actually increased since the early 1970s (Heilbroner and Thurow, 1981, p. 21). Others argue that the overall statistics on falling family incomes are distorted because they don't consider changes in family *size*. Families have gotten smaller, on average, since the early 1970s; thus, even if they made less money they were just as well — or better — off because there were fewer people among whom to spread the income (see Rich, 1986).

Both of these qualifications are surely important. But it's unlikely that they change the overall picture of a decline in Americans' incomes, because there are also several factors working in the opposite direction — that is, several ways in which the usual statistics *understate* the losses in family income.

First, the conventional income statistics, like most figures based on

Category	1967	1973	1984	1973–84
All Families with Children	$28,369	$32,206	$29,527	−8.3%
White	29,679	33,859	31,298	−7.6
Black	17,790	20,708	18,504	−10.6
Hispanic	N/A	23,280	21,663	−6.9
All Two-Parent Families with Children	30,139	35,493	34,379	−3.1
White	30,963	36,276	34,954	−3.6
Black	21,121	27,040	28,096	+3.9
Hispanic	—	26,247	25,777	−2.5
All Female-Headed Families with Children	14,184	14,371	13,257	−7.8
White	15,836	15,853	14,611	−7.8
Black	10,819	11,619	10,522	−9.4
Hispanic	N/A	12,175	10,560	−13.3

Table 3-3
Mean income of families with children (1984 dollars)

N/A = Not available; the Census Bureau did not begin collecting annual data on persons of Hispanic origin in the Current Population Survey until 1972.
Source: Data from Sheldon Danziger and Peter Gottschalk, U.S. Congress, Joint Economic Committee, 1986.

averages, disguise the fact that some people gained in income over these years while others lost even more than the overall statistics would suggest. On the whole, older people in the 1970s and 1980s gained in income and younger people lost. Families with children, especially minority families and those headed by women, lost substantially, as Table 3-3 shows. Note that since the early 1970s, only one category of families with children — two-parent black families — has actually gained in real (inflation-adjusted) income. All other families with children have lost in income, whether they were headed by two parents or one (Danziger and Gottschalk, 1986).

Second, the ordinary income statistics don't consider the crucial question of what a family had to *do* to make ends meet. Hidden within

---

A "Generation of Exiles"? Economic Change and the Young

In the affluent 1960s and 1970s, steady economic growth led many young Americans to "expect confidently that they would soon surpass their parents and reach out to grasp the American Dream" (Rich, 1986). But, more recently, things have turned out differently. Younger people have been hit particularly hard by the economic changes of recent years. As two economists have written, they have suffered a "drastic decline" in their ability to "pursue the conventional American Dream: a home, financial security, and education for their children" (Levy and Michel, 1986).

Between 1973 and 1984, for example, couples over 55 enjoyed an income that rose considerably faster than the cost of living, while those 35–54 slipped slightly behind and those 25–34 lost ground significantly relative to what it cost to keep up, as Figure 3-4 illustrates. *Most* of the overall slump in the standard of living in America, in fact, is accounted for by the crunch on the earnings of younger people.

The drop in income, coupled with the rising costs of housing, has meant that owning a home now takes such a big bite out of the paychecks of younger couples that home-

ownership is effectively out of reach unless they can borrow money from their parents and/or both work full time. In 1973 a typical 30-year-old man could make payments on an average house with 21 percent of his salary; twelve years later, it took 44 percent. Younger families have responded by renting instead of buying — or, if that is still too costly, by moving in with parents or moving to less expensive areas. A recent news article paints this picture of the housing scene in the suburbs of New York City:

> In increasing numbers, people in their 20s and 30s, married and earning $30,000 or more a year, are leaving the area they grew up in because they cannot afford the housing.
>
> They have become a new generation of exiles. . . .
>
> Many young people who remain are making sacrifices to do so. They are renting instead of buying. They are living with parents or in-laws. They are sharing homes with friends. They are working two and sometimes three jobs to make steep house payments. (Knudson, 1986)

the dry figures on family income lies one of the most important social changes of our time: the great increase in the number of people who have entered the labor force. The only reason average measures of family income have not shown greater declines in recent years is that more and more Americans — especially women — have gone to work.

On average, *only* those families that have been able to put two (or more) earners to work have avoided declines in their standard of living. From the 1950s to the 1970s, all kinds of families enjoyed an average rise in income. But during the 1970s, only married couples in which the wife was in the paid labor force increased their income (and then only slightly) — and even those families lost income after 1980. Single heads of families (of both sexes) saw their real incomes decline, as did married couples in which the wife did *not* work in the paid labor force. Another bit of evidence drives the same point home. If we look at what *individuals* earned during this period (instead of looking at *family* income), we discover that men who worked year-round, full time in 1984 made less money, in real terms, than in 1969, and nearly $3,000 less than in 1973. Women working full time fared a little better. But despite intense efforts to reduce discrimination in earnings, women made only about $265 more in 1984 than in 1973 (*Economic Report of the President*, 1986, p. 286). If the personal income of Americans rose at all during the 1970s and 1980s, then, it did so largely because many more hours of work were being put into creating that income.

But there is still another reason why the conventional statistics may

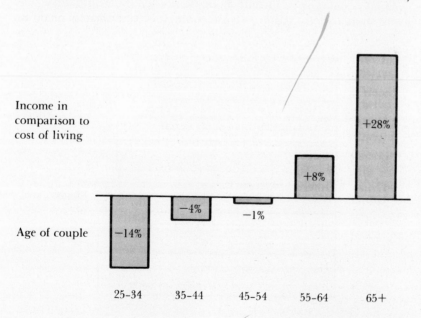

Income in comparison to cost of living

Age of couple

Figure 3-4
Hard times for the young: Married couples' income and the cost of living, by age group, 1973–1984

Source: Data from United States Bureau of the Census, as cited in Spencer Rich, "Are You Really Better Off than You Were 13 Years Ago?" *Washington Post* National Weekly Edition, September 8, 1986.

underestimate the pinch on American living standards in recent years. Even though they are adjusted for inflation — for rises in the costs of living — they don't reflect the fact that the cost of some things has risen much faster than others. This is especially true of some basic necessities, as Figure 3-5 shows. The cost of home utilities rose the fastest, but soaring medical care bills were close behind; and perhaps the most painful rise has been in the cost of owning a home. Coupled with the decline in average earnings, this has shaken the American Dream, especially for younger families (Currie, Dunn, and Fogarty, 1987). In the early 1970s, typical homeowners were spending about a quarter of their income on housing; in the mid-1980s, they were spending more than a third. Not surprisingly, the proportion of Americans who own their own homes had dropped slowly but consistently since the beginning of the 1980s, reversing a decades-long trend (Bredemier, 1986).

The tendency for the costs of housing and some other basic necessities to rise — even when inflation generally has been at fairly low levels — has amounted to a kind of hidden tax that is obscured by the conventional statistics on trends in family income. Economists have developed a measure of *discretionary income* — all income left over after paying for taxes and necessities — that helps illuminate this important, often neglected dimension of the standard of living. Discretionary income per worker fell by 16 percent between 1973 and 1979 alone (*Business Week*, 1980e, p. 73). By the mid-1980s, two-thirds of American families told the Census Bureau they had *no* discretionary income (Schreiner, 1985).

Finally, statistics on income alone do not tell the whole story. The living standard of a family — or a country — is ultimately made up

Figure 3-5
The rising cost of necessities (changes in the consumer price index, selected items, 1967–1985).

Source: Data from *Economic Report of the President* (Washington, D.C.: Government Printing Office, 1986), pp. 315–317.

Note: 1967 is used as the base year for the consumer price index; that is, it is given the index number 100.

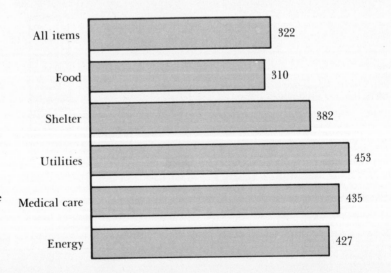

All items	322
Food	310
Shelter	382
Utilities	453
Medical care	435
Energy	427

of much more than money. It includes the risk of unemployment, the availability of public services, the quality of the natural environment, and the risks of crime and disease, among other things. We'll examine all these issues later in this book. But one attempt to put dollar values on some of these aspects of America's living standard deserves mention. According to the economist Horace Brock (1983), an accurate assessment of Americans' economic well-being in recent years would have to adjust the usual statistics of income downward by adding into the equation other measures of long-run economic prospects. These include the increased risk of being unemployed, the economic impact of the deterioration of the nation's physical capital (such as roads and bridges) and of the quality of education, and the future costs of paying for obligations for Social Security and health care. The "risk premium" for the increased chance of unemployment alone, in Brock's calculation, would have decreased the income of a full-time, married male worker in 1982 by $660. Adding up all these usually uncounted losses, Brock calculates that American workers suffered a 17 percent decline in average income between 1972 and 1982.

The Social Costs
of Economic Failure

Recession, high unemployment, and a stalled standard of living have, then, become all too common features of American life. There is considerable evidence that, whatever fluctuations may occur from year to year, the longer-term trends in the economy are deeply disturbing. We will look in a moment at some common explanations for those trends. Now we need to consider another issue — the *human impact* of recession and high unemployment on the lives of individuals and communities.*

This is not simply an abstract, academic issue. Many economists and public officials believe that the use of recession as a deliberate economic policy may be justified as a tool for fighting inflation and restoring a healthy efficiency to the economy. Indeed, encouraging (or at least tolerating) recession has been a common policy in recent years, in the United States as well as in some other countries (notably Great Britain).

*This section draws on materials originally prepared for the U.S. National Advisory Council on Economic Opportunity by Elliott Currie and published as "The Human Costs of Unemployment — 1981," in Arthur I. Blaustein, ed., *The American Promise: Equal Justice and Economic Opportunity* (New Brunswick, N.J.: Transaction Books, 1982).

Such policies have typically been justified partly on the ground that, though painful, they are a necessary "medicine" for sick economies and partly by the argument that their impact on individuals, families, and communities today is much less painful than it may have been in the past because of the growth of unemployment insurance and other benefits for those out of work (Feldstein, 1973, 1978). Similarly, it is often assumed that workers who lose their jobs through economic slowdown can always find new ones when the economy recovers. This notion of painless unemployment helps make the policies that throw great numbers of people out of work more acceptable to some people, especially when the presumably low costs of these policies are balanced against the hoped-for benefits of lower inflation and an efficient "shaking-out" of the economy. But how does this argument square with the evidence?

Not well. It may be true that unemployment is not as devastating as it was in the 1930s, but social science research backs up what many of us know already from personal experience — for most who lose their jobs, unemployment is still extremely painful. Many social and personal problems are aggravated by job loss; worse, unemployment often causes a kind of chain reaction in the lives of the jobless, a vicious cycle with harsh consequences not only for the unemployed but for society as a whole.

Economic Deprivation

Much of the argument for the relative painlessness of recession rests on the assumption that because of the benefits of the welfare state, unemployment no longer brings significant losses in income. This argument sidesteps the emotional and psychological losses that are not measurable in economic terms. But it also misreads the *economic* situation of the unemployed. We will consider this issue at greater length in Chapter 8, but a few points will help provide some perspective now.

In 1984, the average weekly unemployment benefit was $123.47 — on an annual basis, about $4,300 *less* than the federal poverty line for a family of four (*Economic Report of the President*, 1986, p. 297; *Statistical Abstract of the United States*, 1986, p. 430). Furthermore, by 1985 only about one-third of the unemployed collected unemployment benefits at all. And, in the course of the long-term recessions of the 1970s and 1980s, increasing proportions of those who *did* collect benefits exhausted them without finding new jobs.

In a special survey taken during the recession in 1976, the U.S. Bureau of Labor Statistics found that of the unemployed workers they sampled, only a little over 33 percent had received income from unemployment insurance in the previous month, only 13 percent had received food stamps, and only 12 percent had received welfare payments. As many as 5 percent of the sample reported that they had no income at all (Rosenfield, 1977, pp. 42–43). And these percentages became even smaller when Government restricted eligibility for unemployment benefits in the 1980s.

The *noneconomic* losses from high unemployment are sometimes more subtle, but they are equally well documented. The connection between job loss and mental health problems, from loss of self-esteem and depression to psychosis and suicide, is well established in social research.

Mental Illness

Some of the most influential research linking mental illness to the state of the economy has been done by the sociologist M. Harvey Brenner (1973a, b, 1976). In one study (1973b), Brenner looked at the relationship between economic cycles and the rate of admissions to psychiatric hospitals in Massachusetts from the mid-nineteenth century to the 1960s. He found that the admission rate was closely related to changes in the level of employment in manufacturing industries. In a more recent study (1976), Brenner examined mental hospital admissions from the 1940s through the 1960s and concluded that every increase in the national unemployment rate had a precisely measurable impact on the number of people undergoing psychiatric hospitalization. A 1 percentage-point increase (say, from 7 to 8 percent) in the unemployment rate, in Brenner's calculation, could be expected to raise psychiatric admissions by 3.4 percent.

Other researchers have argued that these increases may result from factors other than the stresses of unemployment. During periods of economic strain, the usual family and community resources for dealing with the mentally ill may be lost or weakened, forcing more of the burden of care onto public institutions (Catalano, Dooley, and Jackson, 1981). Likewise, a higher level of admissions to mental hospitals could simply mean that more hospital beds are being created to accommodate the mentally ill. But a 1979 study that took into account changing hospital capacities confirmed that the rate of admission to psychiatric hospitals is "decisively influenced" by the level of economomic distress (Marshall and Funch, 1979, p. 243). It seems most likely that high unemployment causes *both* an increase in the kinds of stresses that can bring on psychiatric symptoms *and* a weakening of the ability of family and community agencies to provide help.

Other studies have used interviews and psychological tests to trace the link between the loss of a job and the development of various psychological problems. One study of what happened to 80 families after the husband lost his job found that these men had much higher levels of psychiatric symptoms than a control group who were not unemployed. If and when they went back to work, the formerly

While workers worry about the loss of jobs to foreign competition . . .

unemployed men actually felt *better* than those in the control group (Liem and Rayman, 1982, pp. 118–119).

A number of studies have shown that the direct effects of unemployment on mental health are compounded by the fact that job loss often leads to other stressful crises — like divorce or having to move from a community — which in turn are often associated with greater risks of mental illness (Catalano and Dooley, 1977). In addition, recession simultaneously cuts funding for the mental health and family counseling agencies that help individuals cope with these problems.

The most drastic effect of high unemployment — and one of the best established — is its impact on the suicide rate. As one study put it, "Unemployment rates tend to be the most important and stable predictor of short- and long-term variations in suicide rates examined across time" (Vigderhous and Fishman, 1978, p. 239). According to Brenner, each 1 percent increase in the national unemployment rate raises the suicide rate by about 4 percent. He concluded that the suicide rate is so closely related to changes in unemployment levels that it is one of the most reliable indicators of the overall state of the economy (1976, p. 29).

Physical Health

Research has also established strong — and sometimes surprising — links between unemployment and the risk of disease. Brenner (1976) found that cardiovascular disease (heart disease and stroke), cirrhosis of the liver, and kidney disease were among the most frequent and devastating consequences of high rates of unemployment. The 1.4 percent increase in the national jobless rate in 1970, he calculated, was responsible for over 25,000 deaths from these diseases during the following five years. Brenner attributed the rise in deaths from liver disease to increased alcohol consumption brought on by unemployment — another example of the chain-reaction effect of joblessness.

Even more striking evidence of the pervasive effects of job loss on health has been found by researchers who tested the physical status of workers before and after they lost their jobs. In a series of studies during the 1970s, for example, Stanislav Kasl, Susan Gore, and Sidney Cobb found a number of symptoms, including high blood pressure, as well as more subtle medical indicators of physical stress (including abnormally high levels of cholesterol) among men who lost industrial jobs in the Midwest. And many of these symptoms ap-

consumers continue to purchase imported goods of all kinds.

David S. Strickler/Picture Cube

peared as soon as the men learned that their jobs were in jeopardy, even *before* they had actually lost them (Cobb, 1974; Kasl, Gore, and Cobb, 1975).

Other research shows that unemployment takes its toll very early. Because it often causes — or aggravates — poor nutrition, stress, and the abuse of alcohol, tobacco, and other drugs by expectant mothers, it leads to higher rates of mortality among newborns. Unemployment and the resulting loss of income also mean that families are less likely to receive adequate medical care — also leading to more deaths of infants and children from preventable infections and other ills (Brenner, 1973a).

Family Stress, Child Abuse, and Crime

Recent research confirms that "economic uncertainty brought on by unemployment and marginal employment is a principal reason why family relations deteriorate" (Furstenburg, 1974, p. 354). The wives of unemployed workers in the 80-family study described above were found to be significantly more depressed, anxious, and unhappy about their family relationships after their husband's job loss; a few months after that loss, their families became much less cohesive and more conflict-ridden than the families of employed workers (Liem and Rayman, 1982). A survey of unemployed workers in the Boston area in the late 1970s (Schlozman and Verba, 1978) found that unemployment benefits (which some commentators argue have eliminated the pain of unemployment) did not alleviate the family tensions that rose predictably as the length of time without work increased. As we'll see in greater detail in Chapter 7, family violence — both between husbands and wives and between parents and their children — has also been closely linked with economic insecurity.

A number of studies have also linked rising unemployment with increasing crime rates. Higher rates of unemployment have been found to be associated with substantial increases in admissions to state and federal prisons (Brenner, 1976; Yeager, 1979). The relationship between joblessness and crime, though, is complicated; we will return to it in more detail in Chapter 11.

These findings make it abundantly clear that economic policies cannot be adequately understood or evaluated in economic terms alone. We have said before, and will have many occasions to say again, that the economy is a *social* institution. What we decide to do with it — to slow it down, close factories, or shift industries from one area to another — has consequences that ripple through all the other institutions that affect the quality of our lives: the family, the local community, the agencies of social support and help.

Explaining Economic Decline

These, then, are some of the dimensions and consequences of America's economic problems. But what about the *causes*?

There has been no lack of explanations. As traditional economic policies seem less and less capable of coping with industrial decline, unemployment, and a shrinking standard of living, explanations that blame these problems on the misguided practices of the past have become increasingly popular. The ones we will consider here have much in common. They often focus on the excessive role of government in the economy or on the unfair demands and inadequate performance of American workers. Many of them, therefore, lead to policies designed to get the economy moving again by restricting the scope of government and/or tilting the balance of economic rewards more toward private business and away from workers, consumers, and concerns for environmental quality or workplace safety.

As we will see, however, these issues are rarely as simple as is often assumed. Let's consider five of the factors that are most often held to be at the root of the problems of the economy: too much government spending, excessive taxes, a shortage of capital for business, high wages, and the decline of the "work ethic."

Too Much Government Spending?

It's often argued that as government has become ever larger, its spending (especially on social programs) has drained funds from more productive private investment and put a brake on economic growth. Is this charge accurate?

We've already had a clue to one problem with this argument. If government spending in itself were a major cause of economic stagnation, we would expect economic performance to be predictably worse in countries with higher levels of government spending and better in countries where the government spends less. But, as we saw in Chapter 2, government spending in the United States is actually much *less*, proportionately, than that in almost all other advanced industrial societies — including many that have generally outperformed the United States by most economic measures for years.

In the late 1970s, West Germany's government spending (excluding defense) was 61 percent higher than American spending, but the German unemployment rate averaged only a little less than half ours (see Table 3-4). The Swedish government spent, proportionately, more than twice as much as the U.S. government did — and suffered less than a third of our level of joblessness. Measured another way — by growth in GNP per worker — the "spendthrift" German economy outperformed the American economy by more than four to one.

What Unemployment Really Costs

Everyone laments the rise of unemployment during periods of recession, yet programs to put the unemployed back to work are often condemned as too costly. This attitude carries a hidden assumption — that no substantial costs are incurred by the public as a result of government's *failure* to create jobs for the unemployed. But that assumption is misleading.

The most immediate cost of unemployment is that of lost production. When workers do not work, the economy does not produce goods and services. According to an early 1980s estimate by the U.S. Bureau of Economic Analysis, each 1 percentage-point increase in the national unemployment rate, over a year's time, reduces the gross national product by $68 billion (Bluestone and Harrison, 1982, p. 11). And this figure has increased since then.

On top of the lost production is the tax revenue lost as the income of both workers and employers declines. According to an estimate by the director of the U.S. Congressional Budget Office in 1982, each 1 percentage-point increase in unemployment costs the federal government between $20 and $30 billion in revenues per year (Rivlin, 1982, p. 3). (Note that this does not include losses in state or local revenues; a 1982 study estimated that each $10,000-per-year job lost in Massachusetts cost the state over $1,300 in lost local and state taxes [Bluestone and Harrison, 1982, p. 73]).

But this is just one side of the problem. Unemployment involves not only lost government *revenues*, but also increased government *spending*. Indeed, a substantial part of the growth in domestic government spending in recent years has been for income support for the unemployed. In 1982, each one-point rise in unemployment caused an estimated increase of $3 to $4 billion in unemployment benefits and another $1 billion for other forms of social welfare. To these expenses may be added an estimated $2 to $5 billion in interest costs resulting from higher government budget deficits (Rivlin, 1982, p. 3).

Adding up even the lower of these estimates gives $94 billion for each one-point increase in unemployment. If that cost were spread out evenly among American households, it would amount to $1,150 per household in 1981. Recall, though, that this amount is what *each* percentage-point increase in unemployment costs. In 1981, the American unemployment rate averaged 7.6 percent, or about 5 percentage points higher than the Swedish rate of 2.5 percent. Our failure to reduce unemployment to Sweden's level, therefore, cost each American household an average of about $5,750 — or about *30 percent* of the median household income in 1981. (By 1985, the figure would have been close to $7,000 per household.) In other words, the average household pays an extraordinarily high "tax" to maintain a high rate of unemployment.

And these estimates are conservative; they count only the most obvious cost of unemployment. They do not take into account the costs of higher rates of imprisonment or psychiatric hospitalization, for example, though both, as we've seen, are clearly linked to increases in unemployment. Nevertheless, adding up these figures produces estimates of the *cumulative* costs of our failure to achieve full employment that are almost too enormous to be comprehensible. One former chair of the president's Council of Economic Advisors estimated that in the years from 1953 to 1980, the failure to operate the economy at full employment cost over $8 *trillion* (in 1979 dollars) in lost production — and more than $2 trillion in lost federal, state, and local tax revenues (Keyserling, 1981, p. 227).

Country	Government spending (excluding defense) as proportion of GDP, 1978(%)	Average annual unemployment rate, 1975–81 (%)	Growth rate in GDP per worker, 1970–79 (%)
United States	26.3	7.1	0.8
Japan	28.0	2.1	4.2
France	40.1	5.6	3.4
West Germany	42.2	3.4	3.4
Netherlands	51.4	NA	3.3
Sweden	56.5	2.0	NA

Note: NA means not available.
Source: Government spending data from Ira C. Magaziner and Robert B. Reich, *Minding America's Business* (New York: Harcourt, Brace, Jovanovich, 1982), p. 43. Unemployment rates calculated from *Statistical Abstract of the United States, 1982–83* (Washington, D.C.: Government Printing Office, 1983), p. 873. GDP growth rates from Bruce R. Scott, "Can Industry Survive the Welfare State?" *Harvard Business Review* (September/October 1982, p. 78).

Table 3-4
Government spending and economic performance

The same pattern holds if we compare another measure of government's role — the size of the public sector — with economic performance. We've seen in Chapter 2 that the United States has the lowest level of public ownership of enterprises among advanced industrial societies. Austria, with one of the highest levels, achieved some of the lowest unemployment rates of any industrial society during the 1970s and 1980s, while also keeping inflation well below American levels.

The argument about the negative effects of government spending is sometimes phrased in terms of government *deficits* (the amount the government spends over what it takes in through taxes and other sources of revenue). Some argue that large deficits mean that government must borrow so much to pay its obligations that not enough funds are available for private business investment: Government's borrowing "crowds out" borrowing by the private sector, which is starved for capital as a result. More generally, an unbalanced budget is taken as a sign that a spendthrift government is wasting scarce capital that would otherwise be spent for productive investment. Balancing the budget, in this view, is a necessary first step to economic prosperity. We will look in a moment at the issue of whether American business really is starved for capital — and whether shifting more resources to the private sector will necessarily lead to productive investment. For the moment, let's focus on some general difficulties with the notion that deficits are *inherently* bad for the economy.

One of the difficulties is that, historically, no clear relationship has existed between the size of the deficit and the performance of the economy; high deficits have been coupled with strong economic growth as often as not. The United States emerged from World War II with one of the most unbalanced budgets in history as a result of massive war spending — and promptly entered a long period of unparalleled economic prosperity and growth.

The experience of other countries also casts doubt on the belief that it's necessarily bad for a government to spend more than it takes in. As with government spending in general, the excess of spending over revenues has often been *greater* in many countries that have outperformed the United States economically than they have been in the United States (*Business Week*, 1982a, p. 91). West German deficits have typically been higher than ours, and so, recently, have been the Japanese.

Why doesn't deficit spending hurt these economies? As most families and most businesses know from experience, spending more than you have is not *always* an unproductive thing to do. What counts is the *purpose* of the spending. We usually feel that borrowing money to buy or improve a house is an intelligent economic decision for a family, assuming that it's within their means to make the payments on what they borrow. Businesses borrow money from banks in order to start up, expand, or invest in new plants or equipment.

Whether the borrower is a family, a government, or a business, the real issue is whether the money borrowed is invested in productive ways. We feel one way when a family borrows to help send a child to college, another way when they ignore the child's education and borrow to buy a pleasure boat or a luxury car.

And here there *are* reasons for concern about the nature of government spending in America. But the concerns have less to do with the *amount* of government spending than with its *direction*. We will consider one aspect of this problem later, in Chapter 12, when we examine the growth and impact of government spending for defense. But the problem isn't just the balance between defense spending and other priorities. To a disturbing extent, the American economy maintains what the economist Jeff Faux (1983) called a *passive deficit*. Government has had to spend more to pay for the consequences of high unemployment, while its revenues have simultaneously been reduced by unemployment, slow growth, and public policies that have cut taxes for businesses and affluent individuals. In short, large deficits have been a *result* of the slowdown of the economy rather than a cause of it. An "active" deficit, on the other hand, would reflect more positive uses of government spending (especially direct efforts by the government to create jobs) rather than simply the costs (in income supports and lost revenues) of a stalled private economy.

Just as government spending is often blamed for the problems of the economy, so too are the taxes that make that spending possible. Critics argue that the use of the tax system to further the American quest for a more egalitarian distribution of income has deeply hurt the economy. Because corporations and wealthy individuals must pay so much to the government, it's argued, their incentive to invest and produce is weakened. In this view, economic prosperity can only be assured by keeping taxes low — at least for businesses and for those with substantial amounts of money to save and invest (Wanniski, 1979; Gilder, 1981).

We will look more closely at the effects of taxes on inequality in America in Chapter 4. But we need to point out several facts that make this a less than satisfactory explanation of the poor performance of the American economy.

For one thing, like the case against government spending, this argument runs up against a basic paradox: How can *excessive* taxes be a primary cause of America's economic problems when our taxes are much *less* heavy than those of most of our successful economic competitors? In Chapter 2 we saw that taxes are higher in almost every advanced industrial society than in the United States and that our overall tax rates as a proportion of GDP have remained stable in recent years while those of many other industrial societies (including Japan) have *increased*. Now consider how these differences affect rates of economic growth. Taxes are over 60 percent higher in the Netherlands than in the United States, but the Dutch growth rate in GDP per employed person was *four* times higher than ours during the 1970s. West German taxes take nearly 30 percent greater share of the GDP than American taxes, while the West German growth rate was also more than four times ours. The corporate tax rate in Japan is much higher than in the United States (Kirkland, 1986, p. 132); meanwhile, the Japanese growth rate per worker was more than eight times the American rate.

A second difficulty with the view that high taxes cause economic stagnation is a historical one. During the recent years of uneven economic performance, the share that corporate taxes have contributed to the government's coffers has *fallen* sharply. In 1960, corporate income taxes accounted for about 20 percent of government tax revenues; in 1970, about 17 percent; and in 1985, about 9 percent. What took up the slack in the other direction? Mainly the individual income taxes (and Social Security contributions) that all earners pay. Revenues from individual income taxes were 38 percent of total tax revenues in 1960 and almost 45 percent in 1985 (*Statistical Abstract of the United States*, 1986, p. 306). Over the years, wage earners have been paying a greater share of taxes, corporations a smaller share. The declining tax on corporate incomes should have spurred a great surge of productive investment; it did not. Similarly, extensive cuts in taxes for wealthy individuals during the early 1980s had no clearly discernible effect on economic growth or unemployment.

We have, in short, been fairly steadily *decreasing* the tax burden we place on corporations and the affluent. Why hasn't this had the hoped-for effect?

The answers are complicated, and we can only touch on them here; other aspects will be taken up in later chapters. First, it seems clear that the failure of these policies to generate productive growth and jobs involves both the reluctance of business and wealthy individuals to invest their tax savings in productive ways and the failure of the investments they *do* make to create much employment. Cutting taxes for wealthy individuals is as likely to lead to unproductive investment in luxury goods or real estate speculation as to more productive uses. And, as we'll see next, too much corporate investment has followed a similarly unproductive path in recent years. A second problem is more complicated. As we'll see in more detail in Chapter 8, in a modern, highly automated economy, even more productive, growth-generating investment will not necessarily create many new *jobs*.

A Shortage of Capital?

Without investment, of course, the economy slows down, workers lose their jobs, and families lose income. As we've seen, the criticism of excessive government spending and high business taxes is based largely on the argument that they drain funds from productive business to unproductive social uses. We've seen some of the limitations of those arguments. Now let's look more closely at the broader question: Is a shortage of business capital a compelling explanation for the recent problems of the American economy?

A *Business Week* article in 1980 described the "dilemma" of one company, Standard Oil of Ohio, which had brought in so much cash from its Alaskan oil operations that it was "swimming in money" and facing the unusual problem of finding places to "invest a mountain of cash." Unable to find ways of reinvesting more than $2.4 billion of extra cash in the oil business itself, Sohio was looking for other industries to buy into — including coal, chemicals, genetic engineering, and information processing (1980b, pp. 60–61). A similar picture appears in a 1981 San Francisco newspaper article entitled "Bay Area Firms Loaded with Cash." The cash-heavy corporations included Kaiser Steel, which held a "hoard" of over a quarter-billion dollars; Natomas Corporation, which, with hundreds of millions in cash from Indonesian oil profits, was busily "looking for natural resource properties" to buy; and Standard Oil of California, with cash reserves of

$3.4 billion. The article examined the uses to which these massive funds were put:

> Do they reinvest in new capital projects? Well, there's no big hurry when there's double-digit returns on commercial paper (18.5 percent), government securities (14–15 percent), . . . and Eurodollars (18.8 percent). Or, the companies can simply put their money in a bank in a certificate of deposit that pays 14.5–18.5 percent, depending on how long they want to tie it up.
>
> Those are safe, guaranteed returns — tough to match when compared to the uncertainties and risks of investing in a refinery, a coal mine, or a savings and loan. (Gartner, 1981)

A look at the steel industry — one of the biggest losers in international competition — illustrates the problem further. Faced with stiff competition from Japanese and European steelmakers in the 1970s, the American steel companies demanded government protection, including trade restrictions on the import of foreign steel. This protection amounted to a massive government subsidy, justified on the ground that it would help give the industry breathing room so it could modernize and meet the challenge of the more efficient foreign competitors. Instead, most of the large steel corporations began shifting their assets out of steel production and into other, more immediately profitable lines of business. Often the steel companies "disinvested" in plants and subsidiaries that were actually *profitable* ones. As an article in *Fortune* noted in 1981, the U.S. Steel Corporation, for example, sold a profitable cement division to the West Germans instead of investing in the new technology that would have made it more competitive. What did the company do with the cash it didn't invest in its steel (or cement) divisions? According to the *Fortune* article, it shopped for "selective acquisitions," including companies in transportation, chemicals, and perhaps a mortgage or credit company. Meanwhile plans to build a new, technically advanced steel plant in Ohio had been shelved "indefinitely" (Kirkland, 1981, p. 30). Another corporation, National Steel, planned to acquire three savings and loan companies with a combined value of almost $7 billion (Reich, 1983, p. 99). The steel industry also won big wage cuts from its workers during the 1980s. But, as with the government support, the resulting cost savings were only rarely translated into upgrading the efficiency of steel production itself. Meanwhile, many foreign steelmakers were systematically channeling their funds into modernization (see Zeitlin, 1985).

The steel industry is by no means the only example of this trend. One of the distinguishing features of the American economy in recent years is that many corporations have used their resources to invest in something *other* than new productive capacity. A study of more than 400 of the largest American corporations revealed that during the 1970s they invested in the expansion of only *one in seven* of the plants they owned at the beginning of the decade (Bluestone and Harrison, 1982, p. 41).

In place of expansion and modernization, a substantial part of the business done by many major corporations has involved the *acquisition* of other, already existing firms. As we saw in Chapter 2, the amounts involved ranged in the hundreds of billions of dollars during the 1980s. And these acquisitions often brought in huge sums even for the bankers and lawyers who merely *handled* them. A top executive of one of the largest investment banking firms involved in these deals — Lazard Freres — earned, by himself, an estimated $125 million in 1986, many times more than the chief executive of any American manufacturing corporation (*Investor's Daily*, June 9, 1987). On the whole, the main result of this trend has been to shift economic resources form one formal, "paper' ownership to another, without creating new jobs or productive capacity (Reich, 1983, p. 55). As Robert Reich put it, the result is the growth of a "symbolic economy" that doesn't enlarge the total economic pie, but merely rearranges its slices (1983, p. 52). It is an economy in which enormous resources of both capital and human ingenuity are devoted to complicated financial transactions that may be lucrative for some of the parties involved but that add no new goods to the economy and divert resources that could otherwise be used to upgrade our industrial capacity and efficiency.

What is the reason for this tendency to substitute paper shuffling for productive investment? Some observers trace it to a difference in the *attitudes* of American and Japanese or Western European managements (Hayes and Abernathy, 1980; Morita, 1986). According to this view, American management is inclined to aim for maximum *short-term* profit, while many European and Japanese managers emphasize *long-term* efficiency and competitiveness. Japanese businesses, for example, typically target their hoped-for profits at lower levels than their American counterparts. Where some American steel companies rapidly abandoned operations that brought in less than 20 percent profits, for example (Kirkland, 1981, p. 30), Japanese steel companies were content with profits averaging well below 10 percent. Japanese steel companies during the 1960s and 1970s shifted much more of their investment into long-term improvements in technology rather than to outside acquisitions or cheaper, "quick-fix" investments in expanding capacity using existing, less-efficient technology (Reich and Magaziner, 1982, Chapter 13). And the resulting long-term loss in the competitive position of American steel has been replicated in many other industries.

Many people also place the blame for inflation and the slowdown of the economy on excessive wages and benefits for workers. In their view, wages push up the prices of everything from energy to housing, and the rising demands of workers have cut deeply into business profits and, consequently, into business' capacity to invest and produce. Is this an accurate assessment?

Figure 3-6 illustrates one problem with this argument: Workers' earnings have *fallen*, not risen, in recent years. In 1985, the average American worker was making about $27 a week *less* (when corrected for inflation) than his or her counterpart 13 years earlier, and about the same as the average worker in 1962 (*Economic Report of the President*, 1986, p. 301). It is sometimes argued that such average figures are misleading because they ignore a number of important changes in the American work force, such as the increase in part-time workers and the growing proportion of women and youth. We will examine the impact of some of these changes in Chapter 8. But for now we should note that the slowdown in earnings has affected workers across the board. Measured by the consumer price index, the cost of living rose 168 percent between 1970 and 1984. The average weekly earnings of *full-time* workers rose just 151 percent, leaving them well behind in the race to keep up with inflation. Men who worked full time did better than women, but their earnings (which rose 165 percent) also fell behind the rise in the cost of living (*Statistical Abstract of the United States*, 1986, pp. 404, *xxiv*).

This doesn't mean that there are no overpaid workers. And wages *may* strain profits in some companies, or some industries. But using

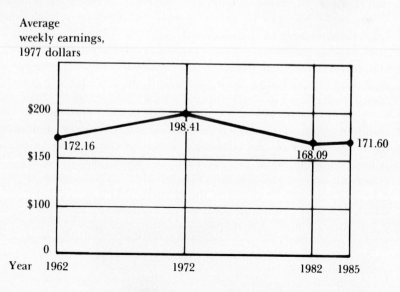

Average weekly earnings, 1977 dollars

$200

198.41

172.16

$150

168.09

171.60

$100

0

Year   1962   1972   1982   1985

Figure 3-6
American workers' wages, 1962-1985

Source: Data from *Economic Report of the President*, 1986, p. 301.

Note: Earnings figures are for private, non-agricultural industries.

rising wages as a *general* explanation of the problems of the economy as a whole doesn't fit the evidence. On average, American workers have fared poorly in recent years. And with the decline in union membership and severe cost-cutting measures by businesses, this unhappy trend seems likely to continue.

Moreover, in some of the countries that are our most effective competitors in the world economy, earnings and benefits for workers have increased faster — sometimes *much* faster — than in the United States. In the crucial manufacturing industries (where we have suffered the most from international competition), the hourly compensation of American workers (when adjusted for inflation) rose at a snail's pace from the mid-1970s to the mid-1980s. It rose eight times faster in West Germany, four times faster in Japan, and twice as fast in Sweden (*Statistical Abstract of the United States*, 1986, p. 849).

Those who blame workers' wages for inflation often ignore the role of the large corporation. We've seen that the American economy no longer fits the model of pure competitive capitalism, in which many small firms compete with one another. One result of the concentration of economic power among a smaller number of large corporations is a profound change in the ability of the normal forces of the economic market to affect the prices of goods and services.

In a genuinely competitive system, according to traditional economic theory, prices are restrained by the threat that higher prices will drive consumers into the arms of competitors. Where many sellers are vying for the consumer's allegiance, the company that raises its prices too high will price itself out of business. Where only a few corporations effectively dominate an industry, however, the situation changes. In economic language, these corporations are now able to *administer* prices — to set them with considerable independence from the pressures of the market (Case, 1981, Chapter 2).

Most often, administering prices doesn't involve actual agreements among the large corporations not to undercut one another's prices; such direct "price fixing" is illegal. Instead, the usual pattern is one of "price leadership," in which there is a tacit understanding that if one company raises its prices, the others will follow. This ensures that competition through prices is diminished in the concentrated industries. The effect on the consumer is that prices in such industries (which, as we've seen, include most of the important ones in the American economy) rarely go down and almost always *go up*, short of a really dramatic slowdown in the economy. This is one key reason why prices have often continued to rise even during recessions. Some economists estimate that the annual cost to consumers of such "monopoly pricing" may run to about 3 percent of gross national product, about $120 billion in 1985 (Scherer, 1980, p. 117).

A somewhat similar argument blames the economy's troubles on workers' *attitudes*. In the 1960s and 1970s, the argument runs, the traditional "work ethic" that animated older generations of American workers was increasingly replaced by an ethos of "rights without responsibilities," especially among *younger* workers (O'Toole, 1981). More generally, the rise of the welfare state is often said to have created "disincentives to work" (Scott, 1982) and to have encouraged workers to want "something for nothing." What is the evidence for this view?

No one would deny that the description applies in *some* cases. Everyone knows some lazy people, a few who really *do* seem to want a "free lunch." But two problems immediately arise. First, there is simply no evidence that work has ceased to be a central social value for Americans of *any* age (see Chapter 8). Second, the image of a population grown increasingly lazy as a result of the largesse of the welfare state fits badly with the fact that a greater proportion of people have gone to work in recent years than ever before in American history. What economists call the *labor-force participation rate* (the proportion of the population either at work or looking for work) rose from about 59 percent through the 1960s to an all-time high of almost 65 percent in 1985 (*Economic Report of the President*, 1986, p. 292).

The fact that more people are in the labor force, of course, doesn't mean that they are working *harder*, and critics often point to statistics on declining rates of productivity in America as evidence that the quality of workers' effort is going down. But this is a misunderstanding of what productivity, as an economic concept, actually means. The misunderstanding is not surprising, since productivity is a very tricky concept, indeed.

Economists define productivity as the level of output of some good or service per hour of work put in to produce it. It's often said that, measured in this way, productivity has been falling dramatically in the United States. This isn't the case. Between 1970 and 1984, output per hour in American industry rose by almost 20 percent. By 1984 productivity was higher than ever before in American history. But it was only a tiny fraction higher than it had been in 1977 and 1978 — and this suggests the real problem. Though productivity has generally risen, the *rate* at which it has done so has been quite low in recent years. During the first half of the 1980s, for example, output per hour increased by less than 1 percent per year, on average. The annual average in the late 1970s was 1.2 percent; in the first half of the 1970s, about 1.4 percent; and in the late 1960s, almost 2.3 percent (*Economic Report of the President*, 1986, p. 303). Something has obviously happened to the rate of productivity growth in America. But what?

Recall that the usual measure of productivity is output per hour of work. Many things can affect that ratio; how hard individual workers work is *one* of them, but it is not the only one, or even necessarily a very important one. The amount of output — production — workers can turn out in a modern, technologically advanced economy also depends on such things as the level of technology (the quality of the tools and techniques of work), the intrinsic technical difficulty of the job, the changing mix of goods and services being produced throughout the economy as a whole, the ways in which workers are trained and organized to do the work, and the other social goals we may choose to implement in the process of producing goods and services.

Some of the decline in rates of productivity, for example, reflects the *reduced pace of technological changes* that shifted workers out of what had been a low-productivity sector of the economy (agriculture) into higher-productivity manufacturing. The shift away from agriculture has been one of the most profound changes in the nature of work in America (see Chapter 8). In terms of productivity statistics, for many years it meant both rapidly rising productivity in agriculture (as fewer workers were needed for the same level of output) and an overall rise in the productivity of the economy (as a greater proportion of workers moved into manufacturing). But this transformation is now largely complete, and so it no longer pushes up our rates of productivity (Thurow, 1981a).

A similar though somewhat later change has *shifted workers from manufacturing industries*, where productivity is relatively high, to the "service" industries (including white-collar industries like finance and health care), in which productivity has traditionally been lower. There is some dispute over how much this shift has lowered overall productivity, but there is wide agreement that it bears *some* responsibility.

Productivity in some parts of the economy is declining simply because of inevitable *changes that make production more difficult and costly* in terms of workers' effort. A good example is energy; as the supply of domestic oil reserves runs down, extracting what remains has become more difficult and expensive, resulting in a lower measured output per hour worked. Recession also lowers the rate of productivity; the recent recessions have struck manufacturing industries hardest, so that the workers who have been idled are disproportionately those whose average output is the highest.

Productivity also involves the *effectiveness with which the skills and potentials of the economy's human resources are put to use.* And though it is difficult to pin down the elusive decline of the work ethic, it is increasingly clear from recent research that the ways in which we organize our human capital may have much to do with the faltering performance of the American economy, particularly when compared to other countries. Most workers in Japan, West Germany, and Scandinavia enjoy both considerably greater security of employment and much greater participation in the workplace than their American counterparts (Table 3-5).

In the United States, for example, firms are not required to provide workers any advance notice of plant shutdowns, while the European countries and Japan require from one to six months notice by law. The foreign countries listed in the table all guarantee worker benefits if a company goes out of business; the United States provides none. The European countries and Japan require companies to provide extensive leaves for illness and childbirth. Perhaps more strikingly, most of the countries other than the United States — either by law or (as in Japan) by established industry policy — provide for at least some degree of worker representation in the management of their companies.

Many other differences do not appear in the table. For example, Japanese corporations typically grant workers considerable authority to make day-to-day decisions in the workplace (Cole, 1979; Thurow, 1981a, p. 4), a practice also followed in some European countries. The Japanese system of so-called lifetime employment has become well known. In some Japanese industries, companies strive to keep workers productively employed, despite changes in technology or in the demand for particular products. To be sure, this "lifetime employment" system is not uniformly adopted throughout the Japanese economy, and in general it would be mistaken to overstate the concern of Japanese employers for the well-being of their workers (Junkerman, 1982; Kamata, 1982). But the contrast between that approach and the typical American practice, in which business firms accept little or no responsibility for the security and continuity of their workers' jobs, is an important one. The head of Japan's Sony Corporation, whose TV sets and "Walkman" stereos have overwhelmed American competition, put it this way:

> I cannot understand why there is anything good in laying off people. If management takes the risk and responsibility of hiring personnel, then it is management's ongoing responsibility to keep them employed. Once we have hired people, we try to make them understand . . . how if a recession comes the company is willing to sacrifice profit to keep them in the company. (Morita, 1986)

Many European countries also tackle the problem of job insecurity more positively than the United States, though in somewhat different ways than the Japanese. Most have extensive training and retraining programs, often government run, that help ensure that workers are not simply cut adrift by changes in technology, company relocations, or business failures. As Robert Reich noted, "Alone of all Western industrial nations the United States lacks any retraining program

Table 3-5
Rights of workers in large companies in selected industrialized countries

Rights	West Germany	France	Japan	United Kingdom	Netherlands	Sweden	United States
Average period of notice for shutdown	2–6 months by law	1–3 months by law	1 month by law; 6 months by custom	3 months by law	2–6 months by law	6 months + by law	None
Worker representation in management	⅓–½ of board members from workers	Consultation with workers' council on decisions affecting work rules	No law, but ⅔ of companies have board members who are active in unions	None	Consultation with workers' council on all major management decisions	2 members on board; consultation on all major management decisions	None
Paid leaves Sickness (not including disability insurance)	6 weeks full pay and 4 weeks 75% pay	50% of earnings up to 36 months after brief waiting period	80% of wages indefinitely	Average 50% for 6 months	80% of pay for 1 year	6 months at full pay	None
Maternity or paternity	6 months after birth and 6 weeks before birth with monthly allowance and guarantee against dismissal	4 months at 90% pay with monthly nursing allowance and guarantee against dismissal	No law, but 3 months' paid leave is widely adhered to	6 weeks at 90% salary	3 months full pay	9 months full pay shared between parents	None
Employee rights on employer insolvency	First priority is 68% average pay for 1 year to all workers	Guaranteed income maintenance allowances varying by age and seniority	Full wage for 2 years; 80% of 3 months' salary guaranteed by the state	Guaranteed 1 weekday for every year of service	80% of all wages for 6 months guaranteed, then 75% for additional time to a maximum of 2 years	90% of wages for 6 months to 2 years	None

Source: Adapted from Ira C. Magaziner and Robert B. Reich, *Minding America's Business* (New York: Law & Business, Inc./Harcourt, Brace, Jovanovich, 1982), p. 144. Reprinted with permission.

available to the majority of its labor force" (1983, p. 102). Most other advanced industrial countries also provide much higher and more easily available income supports for unemployed workers.

In the United States, programs and benefits to promote job security have traditionally been viewed as unwarranted government meddling in private matters. We have tended to believe that workers should fend for themselves if their employer moves or if they lose their jobs for any other reason. But research (O'Toole, 1981; Reich and Magaziner, 1982) suggests that this attitude has disruptive consequences for the economy. It wastes the skills of workers and makes it difficult for them to develop a long-term identification with their work or a sense of its meaning and purpose. It is precisely those countries that have invested *most* in the care and training of their human resources (such as Sweden and Japan) that have also chalked up the best economic performance in recent years.

Before leaving the question of the productivity of American workers, we need to touch on one final issue: the impact of government *regulations* on productivity. We will save most of our discussion of the impact of regulation for Chapters 9 and 10, since, as we'll see, so much of the debate about regulation centers on antipollution and health and safety measures. But the effect of such regulations on productivity raises the important issue of the limits of the concept of productivity itself as a guide for social policy. Take the Coal Mine Safety Act, passed in 1969. It's widely agreed that the passage of the act — one of the first federal efforts to enforce safety standards in an industry — caused output per hour in the coal industry to decline. Productivity in coal mining declined over 4 percent in the early 1970s. But death rates on the job were also cut by two-thirds. Which is more important — the slight drop in productivity or the substantial saving of miners' lives? Hidden in the abstract, statistical arguments about productivity (as in so many other seemingly "technical" questions of social policy) are fundamental choices about social and economic *goals*. The question, in short, is not simply how much coal we produce per hour of miners' labor, but also *how* we produce it, and with what social costs.

Conclusion: Economic Problems as Social Problems

Traditionally, the study of economic problems has been left to professional economists. One likely reason why other social scientists generally ignored the economy is simply that it seemed to work so well that its problems could safely be left to the technical experts. All this has changed because of the depth of our economic problems in recent years. The state of the economy has come to be seen (even by many economists) as an issue too important and many-faceted to be handled by the tools of economic analysis alone (Thurow, 1984). We in-

Some Economic Vocabulary

Like other social science disciplines, economics contains a language all its own, which can be mystifying and frustrating to the uninitiated. Here are a few basic definitions that may help:

Anti-trust: legislation aimed at reducing or eliminating monopoly in business. The earliest anti-trust legislation in the United States, the Sherman Antitrust Act of 1890, was designed to combat the giant combinations of companies (*trusts*) in oil, steel, and other key industries.

Business cycle: the more-or-less regular alternation in the economy from recession to expansion and back. The high periods are often called *peaks, upswings,* or *expansions;* the low points are variously called *contractions, troughs, downturns,* or some similar term. The movement out of a downturn is most often called a *recovery.*

Capital: often used to describe money available for investment, but more generally means the sum of all the funds, tools, and equipment used to produce goods and services.

Capital-intensive: an industry or production process that uses a large amount of capital relative to the amount of labor. *Labor-intensive* refers to processes that use relatively large numbers of workers in proportion to the amount of capital invested. Thus, the oil industry, with enormous plants and equipment but relatively few workers, is highly capital-intensive; restaurants are labor-intensive.

Competition: the condition in which rival sellers of goods and services vie for buyers and profits at one another's expense.

Concentration: the degree of control of an industry, a particular market, or the economy as a whole exercised by a relatively small number of firms. Concentration is measured by *concentration ratios* or *market shares.*

Conglomerate: a corporation that does business in several different markets at once. Conglomerates are typically created by the *merger* of formerly separate firms.

Constant dollars: a measure of purchasing power that adjusts the buying power of the dollar to account for inflation. It is calculated by dividing *current dollars* by some measure of changes in their value, such as the consumer price index.

Consumer price index (CPI): a measure of changes in the prices of goods and services, calculated monthly by the U.S. Bureau of Labor Statistics. It is a rough measure of changes in the cost of living and is usually presented both for all items produced and for several key items including food, energy, housing, and medical care.

Deficit: generally, an excess of debts over assets or income; in this book, used to describe an excess of government spending over government revenues.

Depression: an extreme downturn in the economy, characterized by very high unemployment and low levels of production and growth. There is no hard-and-fast line between depression and severe recession. The depression of the 1930s, ending

creasingly understand that the abstraction we call the economy is part of a larger society, and that it is deeply affected by that society's institutions — just as these institutions are themselves affected by what happens in the economy.

Much recent controversy over economic policy, as we saw in Chap-

---

only with World War II, was the worst in recent American history.

Disposable income: personal income minus taxes. Therefore it is the income available to be consumed or invested.

Gross national product (GNP): the money value of the total production of goods and services, usually measured over a year. *Gross domestic product (GDP)* is GNP minus income from investments and possessions owned *outside* the country. GNP (or GDP) *per capita* divides this sum by the population; it is often used as a very rough indicator of a country's economic well-being.

Human capital: the sum of skills, abilities, and knowledge possessed by individuals. The income individuals earn in the labor market is sometimes described as the *returns* to human capital.

Inflation: an increase in the prices of goods and services, often measured by rises in the consumer price index (see definition above).

Labor force and labor-force participation rate: the total number of people over age 14 who are either at work or unemployed but willing to work. The *labor-force participation rate* (LFPR) is the proportion of a given population in the labor force.

Market share: the proportion of sales in a particular industry, or for a particular product, enjoyed by one or more firms; a common measure of economic concentration (see definition above).

Market system: technically, the exchange relations of buying and selling goods and services for profit; loosely used to describe the economy of the United States and other countries with relatively little government intervention in the private economy compared to those with relatively more.

Mixed economy: an economy combining substantial private control of economic activity with substantial government intervention in certain areas, particularly the provision of social welfare.

Monopoly: technically, the condition in which a single firm dominates an entire market; more loosely, a condition in which a relatively small number of firms exert great influence in particular markets or in the economy as a whole. (Economists often use the more precise term *oligopoly* for the latter condition.)

Multinational corporation: a corporation that derives a substantial part of its income from producing (as opposed to merely selling) goods overseas.

Productivity: the amount of some product produced by a worker in a specific amount of time; often measured as workers' *output per hour.*

Recession: a mild version of depression; downturn in the business cycle.

Stagflation: the combination of inflation and recession or economic stagnation. Coined to describe the unprecedented coexistence of the two in the American economy during the 1970s.

Transfers or transfer payments: payments not made in return for some service performed, as opposed to *earnings;* usually used to describe government payments to the needy, such as Social Security and public assistance.

---

ter 2, concerns the nature of this relationship between the economy and the larger society — especially the institution of government. Many common explanations of the troubles of the American economy suggest, in one way or another, that efforts at social control of the economy through government intervention are the heart of the problem. But things are not so simple. The American economy is actually one of the least taxed and least regulated of advanced industrial economies; it spends among the least on government; and it has the smallest and least active public sector. It seems apparent that the decline in our economic situation relative to some other industrial countries has less to do with a general, government-induced lack of resources for private enterprise than with a pervasive misuse of the resources that are available. And this too is a social issue, not just a technical, economic one. It involves the relative value we place on the pursuit of private gain versus other social goals, on the broader social responsibilities of management, and on the care and welfare of our human and environmental resources.

So far we have only begun to touch on these issues. They will reappear again and again throughout this book. In the next three chapters we will focus on one of the most troubling aspects: the pervasive — and in some ways growing — pattern of *inequality* in the United States. As we shall see, both the benefits and the burdens of a turbulent and changing economy have been unequally distributed among different groups in America — sometimes altering and sometimes aggravating the traditional divisions of income, race, and sex.

Summary

This chapter has examined the problems of the American economy in recent years. Though the specific expression of those problems has fluctuated, there are several disturbing long-term trends: slower growth compared to earlier periods and to other industrial countries; deeper recessions, leaving ever-greater numbers of people unemployed; a stalled or even declining standard of living; and growing international competition leading to a loss of our commanding position in the world economy.

Though it is often argued that recession and unemployment are less painful than in the past, the evidence shows that they still cause increased family disruption, mental and physical illness, suicide, and crime, in addition to staggering economic costs in lost production and government revenues.

Common explanations for the economy's troubles include excessive government spending and taxation, a shortage of capital for business investment, excessive wages for American workers, and the decline of the work ethic. But none of these explanations stands up well to the evidence. Government spending is lower in the United States than in most countries with more successful economies. American taxes are among the lowest of industrial societies, and taxes on *business*, specifically, have fallen sharply. Many businesses do not lack capital to invest, but they have frequently invested what they have in unproductive ways. Workers' wages have generally *fallen* in recent years relative to the cost of living. And there is no evidence that American workers are less motivated than in the past or that poor attitudes have much to do with America's problems of productivity.

The uncertain performance of the economy, especially in comparison with other countries, may be better explained as partly the result of the misuse of human and natural resources, often resulting from the choice of short-term gains over long-term economic and social health.

For Further Reading

Blaustein, Arthur I, ed. *The American Promise: Equal Justice and Economic Opportunity.* New Brunswick, N.J.: Transaction Books, 1982.

Bluestone, Barry, and Bennett Harrison. *The Deindustrialization of America.* New York: Basic Books, 1982.

Heilbroner, Robert, and Lester Thurow. *Five Economic Challenges.* Englewood Cliffs, N.J.: Prentice-Hall, 1981.

Kuttner, Robert. *The Economic Illusion.* Boston: Houghton Mifflin, 1985.

Morita, Akio. *Made in Japan.* New York: Random House, 1986.

Reich, Robert B. *The Next American Frontier.* New York: Penguin, 1984.

Thurow, Lester. *The Zero-Sum Solution.* New York: Simon and Schuster, 1986.

4

Social Inequality I: Wealth and Poverty

The ideal of economic equality has always had an ambiguous place in American life. In principle, we hold equality to be one of the central values of a democratic society. But in practice, we tolerate enormous differences in the quality of life that Americans can hope for. We remain, in many ways, the richest country on earth; but we also allow many people to live at some of the worst levels of poverty in the developed world.

In the 1950s and 1960s, when the economy was expanding rapidly and our standard of living was generally rising, social scientists often argued that these sharp economic differences were on the verge of disappearing. The affluent society, they believed, would blunt the edges of inequality and reduce poverty to a minor problem.

But things haven't turned out quite that way. We did make some steps — often big ones — toward reducing poverty and narrowing the gap between rich and poor. We stimulated the economy to provide jobs and income, hoping they would "trickle down" to the poor. We declared war on poverty and created job programs, better schooling, and expanded benefits, such as food stamps and public health care. And these efforts made a difference. Until the early 1970s, poverty in the United States declined rapidly; until the mid-1970s, the income gap among American families experienced a similar decline — so much so that some critics began to complain that we had "gone too far," that we had achieved "too much equality" (Browning, 1976, p. 76).

But the trend didn't last. By the late 1970s it was apparent that something was wrong. Poverty wasn't falling any more; it was rising. By the middle of the 1980s an American family had a higher chance of being poor than when the war on poverty began 20 years before. And the chasm between the wealthiest and the poorest Americans was wider than it had been since World War II.

What happened? Some blame the antipoverty efforts themselves — especially the growth of welfare and other government benefits (Murray, 1985; Mead, 1986). Others look to basic changes in the American economy that have made it increasingly difficult for many Americans to earn a decent living — and to sharp reductions in government benefits for low-income people. And still others argue that what seems to be an ominous rise in poverty and inequality is more apparent than real — a reflection of changes in the family and in the proportions of young and old in American society.

In this chapter we'll examine just how much economic equality has been achieved, and how much the extremes of wealth and poverty have been affected by government policies and changes in the economy. Our focus, for now, will be on the more easily measured aspects of inequality, such as differences in income, earnings, and wealth. These are, of course, only some of the ways in which inequality makes itself felt in our lives. Inequality is not only a matter of differences in how much we earn or own but also of the differing pleasures — and dangers — of the work we do, the kind of education and health care we can expect, and much more. In fact, the pervasive effects of economic inequality are a main theme throughout this book. But, for the moment, we will concentrate on the more specific issue of inequality in the distribution of income and wealth. Has it changed? If so, what lies behind these changes — and what is the outlook for the future? Are we becoming, as some people fear, a society ever more sharply divided between the "haves" and the "have-nots"?

First, we'll consider what the evidence tells us about trends in the distribution of income and wealth in the United States — how the American "pie" has been divided since World War II. Then we'll examine the most troubling aspect of that distribution, the depth and persistence of poverty in America. This leads us into a discussion of the welfare system and how it affects poverty and inequality and, finally, to a look at some of the ways in which a lesser-known, hidden welfare system for the affluent counterbalances the effects of the better-known welfare system of the poor.

The Distribution of Income

In economic language, *income* means money from any of several different sources, including earnings, Social Security benefits, and welfare payments. Not all sources of income are counted in government statistics, however, and this has important consequences for the way income distribution is measured. For example, income from *capital gains* (income derived from the increased value of a business, stocks, or other property) is not counted in most income statistics, which means that the statistics underestimate the income of affluent people, who are more likely to be property owners. And, of course, much income is never reported (usually in order to foil the tax collector) and therefore never appears in official statistics. Poor people underreport welfare payments; blue-collar workers and professional people fail to report work done "under the table"; and wealthy people hide the extent of their unearned income. Who underreports the most is obviously hard to determine, but it's important to keep in mind that underreporting is one reason income statistics must be treated with caution.

The most common way of measuring the distribution of income is to divide the population into fifths, rank the fifths from the highest (richest) to the lowest (poorest), and determine how large a percentage of the nation's *total* personal income each fifth receives. (This approach measures income *before* taxes; we will look at the effect of taxes on income distribution shortly.) As Table 4-1 shows, income shares have remained highly unequal in the United States since World War II. The top fifth of American families has enjoyed over two-fifths of all income; the lowest fifth, only about one-twentieth.

Table 4-1
Slicing the American pie: Changes in income shares since the 1940s

Year	Lowest fifth	Second fifth	Third fifth	Fourth fifth	Top fifth	Top 5%	Index of income concentration
1947	5.0	11.9	17.0	23.1	43.0	17.5	0.376
1960	4.8	12.2	17.8	24.0	41.3	15.9	0.364
1966	5.6	12.4	17.8	23.8	40.5	15.6	0.349
1975	5.4	11.8	17.6	24.1	41.1	15.5	0.358
1985	4.6	10.9	16.9	24.2	43.5	16.7	0.383

Source: Statistical Abstract of the United States, 1986, p. 452; U.S. Bureau of the Census, Current Population Reports, Series P-60, No. 157, 1986, p. 11.

The top fifth, in other words, has consistently had about *eight times* the share of the bottom fifth.

Focusing on the top *fifth,* however, actually minimizes the concentration of income at the top, since the top fifth includes many people who aren't wealthy. (In 1985, for example, it included everyone with a family income above about $48,000 a year.) The picture is sharper if we look instead at the share of the top 5 *percent* of American families — those making more than about $78,000 in 1985. Those families received almost 17 percent of the total income in 1985 — a proportion that, again, has not changed much since World War II. Their share is more than that of the bottom two-fifths — 40 percent of the population — combined.

But a closer look reveals some distinct changes over time. The share of the bottom (poorest) fifth of the population rose during the 1960s, for instance, while that of the top fifth fell. Though the percentages are small, the shift is significant, particularly for the lowest fifth, whose income share rose by about 17 percent during that decade. This change is also expressed in the decrease in the size of the other measure in Table 4-1, the *index of income concentration.* This figure (technically called the *Gini index*) measures the overall degree of inequality among American families. The higher the value of the Gini, the greater the inequality of incomes. The Gini dropped somewhat during the early 1950s and again in the mid to later 1960s, indicating a noticeable (though hardly overwhelming) trend toward equality during those years.

Now note, however, what seems to have happened more recently. The share of the poorest fifth has fallen back below its early 1960s levels and that of the upper fifth has grown beyond its 1960s levels. And in the 1980s the Gini index shows the greatest income inequality in four decades. If these figures are to be believed, there has been a clear reversal of the trend toward greater income equality that peaked in the late 1960s. The gains lower-income people made have been turned around, and we are now a more unequal society than we were 40 years ago.

Are Income Statistics Misleading?

But like most official statistics, income statistics have been criticized as inaccurate and misleading. Some of the critics argue that they overstate income inequality; others argue that they *understate* it.

One of the most important criticisms is that the official income statistics fail to take into account changes in the broader society that may have a powerful effect on the distribution of income. In particular, it's argued the changing *age* structure of American society means that simple comparisons of income over time are misleading. Other things being equal, older people and very young people have smaller incomes than people in the prime working ages, since a much smaller proportion work for a regular salary or wage or, if they do, are either on their way out of the labor force or just getting started. In American society the aged have become a steadily larger proportion of the population. And during the 1970s there was a large influx of young people into the labor force — the children of the so-called baby boom of the 1950s — with the result of a tip in the population balance toward people in entry-level jobs, who would be expected to earn less. Both of these population changes — what social scientists call *demographic* changes — may mean that the usual measures of income make inequality seem worse than it really is (Paglin, 1975; Novak and Green, 1986).

Likewise, two-parent families are likely to have higher incomes than those headed by a single parent, especially a single woman, other things being equal. So to the extent that the proportion of single-parent families has increased, according to this argument, the income statistics will also be misleading.

We will look more carefully at both of these trends later in this chapter and again in Chapters 6 and 7. Both trends *are* important — and both tell us much about the changing patterns of inequality and poverty. But do they mean that the official figures are seriously misleading — and that there may have been a trend *toward* equality in recent years?

The most careful studies show that both the increase in family breakup and the influx of baby-boomers *have* aggravated a trend toward inequality. But they haven't made enough of a difference to explain all of that trend (Danziger and Plotnick, 1977; Harrison, Tilly, and Bluestone, 1986).

Another argument holds that the official picture is misleading because it fails to take into account a variety of benefits people at the lower end of the income scale receive. These so-called in-kind benefits (including food stamps, Medicaid, and housing subsidies) are not counted as income but have become an increasingly important part of the overall income of the poor. We'll return to this argument later in discussing the impact of the welfare system on inequality. For now, we'll note that this argument raises many other issues, some of which lead to the opposite conclusion — that the official statistics probably *underestimate* the degree of inequality in America. Once we begin looking at forms of income that are not officially counted, we also have to include many benefits that wealthy and middle-income people receive that low-income people rarely do: tax loopholes, government contracts, and income from capital gains, for example. All of these add to income inequality. For example, if all capital gains income were counted, the richest 1 percent of American households, which now receives a substantial 5 percent of official income, would receive about 11 percent (Thurow, 1980, p. 168).

How do we explain the persistence — and recent rise — in economic inequality? We've seen that part of the explanation is that there are more older and younger people in the population, and another is that there are also more single-parent families. But there's more to it than that. In the past several years there have been a number of complex social changes that have affected inequality in America — some working to increase it, some to decrease it.

Why Has Inequality Worsened?

One of the forces that has lessened inequality has been the growth of what economists call *transfer payments* — like welfare and Social Security. (They're called transfers because they transfer money from some groups to others.) There is considerable debate over just how *much* these benefits have narrowed the economic gap, but the best estimate is that the total impact of all cash transfer programs reduces the Gini index of inequality by about one-fifth from what it would be if those programs didn't exist. Though government, as we shall see, "transfers" money to the upper as well as to the lower parts of the income scale, the *main* effect of the expansion of transfer programs has been to boost the share of the bottom fifth. Without cash benefits, the bottom fifth's share of the country's total income would probably be only about 1 to 2 percent, rather than almost 5 percent (Danziger, Haveman, and Plotnick, 1981).

But if transfers tend to soften the edges of inequality, other forces have simultaneoulsy sharpened them. One is unemployment. This is because people in the lower end of the income distribution are far more likely to be unemployed than more affluent people. It's likely that a good part of the rise in inequality in the past few years reflects the high and increasingly stubborn unemployment rates we noted in Chapter 3.

But recent studies have also found growing inequality in the earnings of workers who are *employed*, year round, full time. Part of this disturbing trend, as we've seen, is the result of a greater proportion of younger workers (who tend to have lower and more unstable earnings). But the trend toward growing earnings inequality remains even when age (as well as work experience and education) is accounted for (Dooley and Gottschalk, 1982, 1985; Harrison, Tilly, and Bluestone, 1986). American workers' wages probably grew more equal until the mid-1970s, then took a sharp U-turn, and have been growing wider apart ever since (Harrison, Tilly, and Bluestone, 1986, p. 111). And, at the same time, many of the government benefits that once helped

Leonard Freed/Magnum Photos, Inc.

Extremes of wealth
and . . .

reduce inequality have been increasingly cut back. Together, these two trends have widened the gap between the affluent and the poor in the United States.

We will return to the problems of unequal earnings and declining benefits in a moment, for they are crucial to understanding America's successes and failures in the battle against poverty. But let's look first at another aspect of economic inequality in America: the unequal distribution of wealth.

The Concentration of Wealth

The gap in incomes, wide as it is, is only one aspect of economic inequality. In many ways, a more crucial one is the difference between those who own and those who do not own substantial *wealth*. Most people's income is tied to a job and/or to some form of government benefits. As we've seen, the differences in income are quite large between different groups; but even at the top, the upper fifth of

poverty persist in the United States.

income earners includes many people who would hardly be considered rich. But the ownership of wealth is another matter. Wealth, much more than income alone, divides the population between those who have the capacity to influence and control economic life and those who do not; between those who can confidently expect a life of economic security and comfort and those who cannot. And wealth is much more narrowly concentrated than income.

Accurate estimates of the concentration of wealth, however, are hard to come by. Even more than personal income, personal wealth is usually a well-guarded secret. But even the rough data we have paint a striking picture.

Table 4-2 shows some of the startling results of a recent study of wealth in America for the Joint Economic Committee of Congress. The study found that a handful of Americans — one-half of 1 percent — owned a third of the country's net assets (that is, wealth left over after any debts have been subtracted) in 1983. The study, not surprisingly, called these people the "super-rich." There were just 420,000 of them, and the *poorest* of them owned $2.5 million dollars worth of assets. Just below them, another one-half of 1 percent — the "very rich" — owned another 7 percent of the total wealth. These two

Table 4-2
The concentration
of wealth

	Number of households	Percent of net assets, 1983
Super rich	420,000	35.1
Very rich	420,000	6.7
Rich	7,553,000	29.9
Everyone else	75,000,000	28.2

Note: Assets in this study include stocks, bonds, real estate, bank accounts, IRA and Keogh accounts, trusts, business assets, insurance policies, land contracts, and miscellaneous other assets.

Source: Data from U.S. Congress, Joint Economic Committee, *The Concentration of Wealth in the United States*, Washington, D.C., U.S. Government Printing Office, 1986, p. 8.

groups, 1 percent of the population, owned over two-fifths of the country's personal wealth.

Another group — sufficiently less fortunate to be called simply, "the rich" — held another 30 percent of the wealth. Finally, there is "everyone else" — the other 90 percent of the population — who owned 28 percent of the wealth (and two-thirds of all the debt).

The inequality in wealth distribution shown by these figures is extreme, but in a way even this picture understates the financial power of those at the top. Much of the wealth held by the bottom 90 percent of Americans consists of their own homes. About two-thirds of American families own a home of their own. If we eliminated this form of wealth from the comparison, the top 1 percent would own over *half* the country's personal wealth, and the bottom 90 percent less than a fifth.

Even with homes included, the super-rich family, on average, owns well over two hundred times the wealth of the average family in the "everyone else" category. And the figure is, of course, even higher if we compare the super-rich to families farther down the income scale, most of whom have no net wealth at all — and many of whom have what is called "negative net worth," which is a polite way of saying that they're in debt up to their ears.

What about changes over time? Are the rich getting richer? Historical studies suggest that the most egalitarian period in American history, in terms of wealth concentration, was from the colonial era to shortly after the American revolution. On the whole, the concentration of wealth increased during the nineteenth and early twentieth centuries, and declined somewhat from the Depression and World War II until the 1960s. Between 1963 and 1983 (mainly after the late 1970s) the share of the "super-rich" shot up 38 percent, while that of

Figure 4-1

"Yes, son, life is unfair, but not at our level."

"everyone else" dropped by 20 percent. The average super-rich family increased its wealth by a cool $5 million during that period, while the rest of us added about $12,000 to our coffers.

It's sometimes argued that wealth — and economic power — are actually widely diffused in America because so many people own stocks. Through stock ownership, it's said, even the average citizen can own a piece of the American economy and have a voice in the affairs of even the biggest corporations. It's true that many Americans do own stock — about 42 million as of 1983, or 18 percent of the population, up from 15 percent in 1970 (*Statistical Abstract of the United States*, 1986, p. 509). But stock ownership is skewed toward the affluent, especially the "super-rich." In 1983 two-thirds of all stock owners earned over $25,000 a year, and more than a fifth earned over $50,000 — when the average income in the country was less than $15,000. Indeed, the Joint Economic Committee study shows that the vast majority of corporate stock (about 90 percent) is owned by the richest 10 percent of the population, and the 420,000 super-rich families alone own nearly half of all corporate stock in the United States. This level of concentrated ownership means more than just dollars; it means economic power (Figure 4.1). As one study concluded, the super-rich "potentially control all corporate assets" (Smith and Franklin, 1976, p. 178).

Wealth, then, is even more unequally shared than income. Whether you think this is unfair is, of course, a subjective judgment. But how we feel about the inequality of wealth is usually influenced by our beliefs about how the rich got that way. Many people believe that extremes of wealth, like very high incomes, are socially and economically valuable because they represent the fruits of qualities we all admire — hard work, careful investment, disciplined saving. And it's certainly true that great wealth does flow from these qualities — sometimes. But more often, it results from what some social scientists, with tongue in cheek, have called the "careful selection of one's parents" (Kloby, 1986, p. 5). According to the Joint Economic Committee's research, roughly two out of three wealthy Americans got most of their assets through inheritance — though they may have increased them afterward. To be sure, in every generation some people newly join the ranks of the wealthy, through skill, luck, or pluck and some children of the wealthy fall out of the ranks. But the chance that the child of wealthy parents will stay rich is probably as high as 80 percent (Brittain, 1978; Canterbury and Nosari, 1985).

The Persistence of Poverty

In 1964, the federal government formally declared a War on Poverty. For a while, we seemed to be winning that war. When it began there were 36 million Americans below the government-defined poverty line; by 1969, only 24 million. As a *proportion* of the population, the poor dropped from 19 percent in 1964 to about 12 percent by the end of the 1960s.

But the progress turned out to be short-lived. By 1979, there were almost 2 million *more* poor Americans than there were in 1969; and as the 1980s began, the poverty count took a sharp, dramatic leap upward. Between 1979 and 1985, more than 7 *million* people joined the ranks of the poor; the *rate* of poverty jumped by 20 percent (see Table 4-3 and Figure 4-2).

But these figures give only part of the picture. Things look even worse when we look beneath the statistics at the long-term trends in poverty and what they may imply about the future. We will see in Chapters 5 and 6 that poverty has always been more severe for minorities and women, and is becoming even *more* so. But several other trends also make for a more ominous pattern than the statistics show at first glance.

1. Even in the 1960s, the successes against poverty were mostly confined to *some* areas, and to *some* kinds of people, and not others; and most of those successes have been reversed in the 1980s.

Year	Number below poverty level (in thousands)			Percent below poverty level		
	All persons	65 and over	Related children under 18	All persons	65 and over	Related children under 18
1985	33,064	3,456	12,814	14.0	12.6	20.5
1979	26,072	3,682	9,993	11.7	15.2	16.0
1973	22,973	3,354	9,453	11.1	16.3	14.2
1969	24,147	4,787	9,501	12.1	25.3	13.8
1959	39,490	5,481	17,208	22.4	35.2	26.9

Source: Data from U.S. Bureau of the Census, *Current Population Reports,* Series P-60, No. 138, April, 1983, p. 7; and No. 154, August, 1986, p. 21.

Table 4-3
The growth of poverty

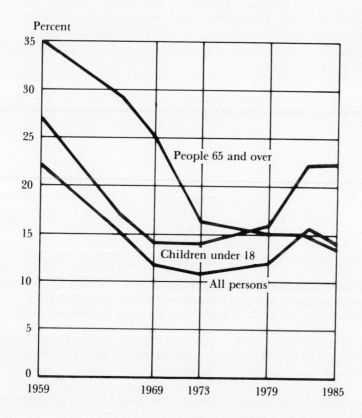

Figure 4-2
Poverty rates,
1959–1985

Source: Data from U.S. Bureau of the Census, *Current Population Reports,* Series P-60, No. 139, April 1983, and No. 154, August 1986.

2. Even more disturbingly, economic growth by itself no longer seems to have much effect in reducing poverty.

3. The official poverty figures don't adequately measure the much larger group of people whose incomes cannot support a decent standard of living — and who live precariously close to poverty.

Let's consider each issue in turn.

Rural Success, Urban Failure

Most of the successes against poverty, even in the 1960s, took place in rural areas, especially in the South. In the inner cities, especially in the Northeast and Midwest, poverty has always been more stubborn; and it has worsened sharply in recent years.

There were more poor people in the northern and western states in 1985 than in *1959*, well before the War on Poverty began. In the South, meanwhile, the number of poor decreased by about 6 million people. The South still has higher rates of poverty, but improvement there has been greater — and the recent rises in poverty much less sharp (U.S. Bureau of the Census, 1986, p. 27). Why? Part of the answer is that the Civil Rights movement in the South, along with strong economic growth, led to improvements in both jobs and welfare benefits, especially for southern blacks. At the same time, there was a massive movement to the North and West by many of the southern poor.

Executives' Earnings: Competence and Compensation at the Top

The statistics in this chapter show that the distribution of income in the United States is highly unequal. But even these statistics minimize the extreme differences between those at the *very* top of the income scale and almost everyone else.

In 1981, according to an article in *Fortune* dramatically titled "The Madness of Executive Compensation," the average compensation (including salaries, bonuses, and other cash benefits) of the chief executives of the country's 10 largest conglomerates was just over $1 million. The highest-paid executive, the author calculated, was J. Peter Grace, head of the W. R. Grace corporation, a conglomerate with interests in chemicals, food, and other industries. Grace's compensation in 1981 was about $1.8 million (Loomis, 1982, pp. 42–45).

The compensation of the 10 highest-paid conglomerate executives, if distributed directly to the poor, would have brought 3,415 families over the poverty line in that year. J. Peter Grace's compensation, by itself, could have lifted 601 American families out of poverty (calculated from U.S. Bureau of the Census, 1983a, p. 26). The inequality between what these executives receive for their work and what most other workers receive for *theirs* is startling: 100 skilled craftworkers

That exodus was primarily the result of the transformation of southern farming — and of American agriculture as a whole. And one of the effects of that transformation is crucial for understanding the nature of poverty today. As machines and chemicals replaced much of the work formerly done by the rural poor, millions of jobs were eliminated, and millions of people left for the cities. This had two results. Many of the rural poor simply changed location and became the urban poor. Also, the rural poor sometimes "escaped" from poverty by a statistical slight-of-hand. Their standard of living may have actually improved little, or even deteriorated. But by moving to areas where earnings and welfare benefits were higher, they suddenly had higher incomes — enough to bring them above the official poverty level.

The shift from southern to northern poverty, then, is closely tied to the wider change from rural to urban poverty. The poverty rate in America's inner cities was higher in the mid-1980s than in *1959* — while the rate in what the government calls "nonmetropolitan areas" was much lower. But this long-term shift makes the rural picture look better than it really is, for the decline in rural poverty has been halted. Since 1979 rural poverty has risen by more than a *third* — an even faster rate than in the central cities.

What happened? The crisis that has hit America's smaller farms — and the small towns that depend on them for business — has plunged many rural people into poverty. Some of these "new poor"

could have been hired (at average 1981 wages) or 260 youth (at the minimum wage) with J. Peter Grace's earnings (calculated from *Statistical Abstract of the United States,* 1983, pp. 400, 402).

These vast differences are usually justified by the argument that they reflect the "free market's" judgment that the skills of these executives are worth the price. But is this true? According to the article in *Fortune,* executive compensation is actually *unrelated* to performance on the job. "In the upper reaches of corporate America," the author concluded, "the market frequently does not seem to work." In a more reasonable world, corporate managers would be paid "handsomely" for top performance and "would lose out when they flopped. But to an extraordinary extent, those who flop still get paid

handsomely" (Loomis, 1982, p. 42). W. R. Grace and Company showed a "distinctly low grade" performance in 1981; the head of ITT, which performed poorly over the five years ending in 1981, earned almost twice as much as the head of Raytheon, which outperformed ITT on every measure of business performance (Loomis, 1982, pp. 42–43). In a 1986 *Fortune* survey of the "best and worst" corporations in America, other business executives ranked W. R. Grace close to the bottom in performance among a group of chemical companies.

As an interesting footnote, J. Peter Grace was appointed to head the Reagan administration's Private Sector Advisory Council on Cost Control, a body charged with the task of finding ways of reducing costs in government operations.

have left for the cities, where they have joined with the "old poor" in competition for insufficient jobs and shrinking government benefits. Others have stayed on the land — and have stayed poor. The farm crisis, along with the decline in some basic industries we described in Chapter 3, has dealt a particularly hard blow to the American heartland — the Midwest. Since 1979, poverty in the mid-western states has risen a stunning 43 percent.

Increasing Poverty of the Young

Another limitation of the success of the War on Poverty involves age rather than residence or region. Most of those who have moved out of poverty have been older people. Meanwhile, rates of poverty among children and youth have risen sharply.

Between 1969 and 1985, the number of poor people over age 65 dropped by almost a million and a half. Most of this decline resulted from improved Social Security benefits. But this didn't mean that the low-income aged achieved real comfort or security: Many still lived uncomfortably close to the poverty line. (And the Social Security system itself has become ever more precarious in the face of economic stagnation and political criticism.)

But the more drastic change is at the other end of the life cycle. Look back at Table 4-3 for a moment. There were over 3 *million* more poor children and youth in 1985 than there were in 1969. At the close of the 1960s, the youth poverty rate was less than 14 percent; by the mid-1980s it was over 20 percent. More than one American child in five is growing up in poverty.

The Declining Significance of Economic Growth

In the War on Poverty, then, it looks as though poverty has been winning. There have been some victories for the other side, but they've mainly affected certain areas (such as the South) and certain groups (such as the elderly). For children, for the people of the inner cities, and increasingly, the rural farm areas, things have been getting much worse. And perhaps even more troubling is that one of our most important tools for fighting poverty — economic growth — doesn't seem to work as well as it once did.

Our approach to poverty has always relied heavily on the idea that the fruits of an expanding economy would naturally trickle down to even the poorest people; and since the start of the 1980s that has been our *main* approach to fighting poverty. But — as the figures we've seen attest — that strategy hasn't worked. Part of the rise in poverty in this decade results from the harsh recession of the early 1980s. But even in years of economic recovery, poverty has remained naggingly high. Economic growth, even when it brings jobs and income to many people, seems increasingly to be leaving the poor behind.

When we take a closer look at the statistics on poverty, in fact, we discover an especially disturbing trend: The proportion of Americans able to earn a decent living by *working* has fallen dramatically in recent years. It is only the welfare system that has kept many of them from poverty. Without that system, the poverty count would have increased even faster than it has.

One way of looking at this is through the technical distinction between what economists call *posttransfer* and *pretransfer* poverty. Official poverty statistics measure posttransfer poverty, which includes income from cash transfer payments such as Social Security or welfare benefits, as well as earnings. Pretransfer poverty counts only the income people receive from earnings. It therefore gives a rough estimate of how well the economy enables people to make a living by working. Obviously, there will be more pretransfer than posttransfer poor at any given time.

The indications that poverty persists are everywhere.

By the official — posttransfer — measures, about one in seven Americans were poor during the mid-1980s. But the number increases to *one in four* when pretransfer poverty is measured. One in four Americans, in other words, did not get enough income from working to subsist at the poverty level. Some of these people are aged, and would not be expected to earn much, if any, money. But even among the nonaged, over one in six has earnings that, by themselves, leave them below the poverty level (Danziger and Gottschalk, 1985, p. 76).

What's especially troubling is that pretransfer poverty has increased so rapidly — by over a third since 1969. (Posttransfer poverty — poverty after welfare benefits are counted — has gone up a bad-enough 26 percent.) Let's pause to consider what this seemingly obscure, technical point means: Despite considerable growth in our economy in the past two decades, a smaller proportion of Americans are able to get by without public assistance today than 20 years ago.

Something about the way the economy has grown in recent years, then, has meant that growth by itself (even when we achieve it) seems no longer capable of altering the deeper inadequacies of work and earnings that keep people in poverty. "Trickle down," as one study put it, has "petered out" (Thornton, Agnello, and Lind, 1978). We'll shortly consider how and why this has happened. For now, we'll simply note that the declining impact of growth has important and ominous implications for the future of poverty in America.

Redrawing the Poverty Line

But there is still another reason why the official statistics may understate the dimensions of poverty. What we've said so far has assumed that the way the government now *defines* and *measures* poverty is satisfactory. But, in fact, the poverty line is one of the most criticized of official statistics. Some people believe it exaggerates the amount of poverty in the United States. Others believe that it minimizes the problem.

How does the government decide who is poor and who isn't? The poverty level is based on an estimate of the costs of a minimally adequate food budget, a so-called *thrifty food plan*, developed in the 1950s by the U.S. Department of Agriculture. The cost of a basic subsistence diet was estimated and then multiplied by three, because surveys had shown that the poor spent about a third of their income on food. Three times the cost of a minimal diet therefore would give a reasonable estimate of the cost of a minimal level of subsistence. The poverty line is adjusted for different family sizes (and for individuals). It is also adjusted each year for the rising cost of living. Beginning at

$3,000 for a family of four in 1964, the poverty level reached $10,989 by 1985.

Critics have long noted several problems with this measure. One of the most crucial is that the thrifty food plan, by the Department of Agriculture's own admission, does *not* cover the cost for a sound diet, even of the most minimal kind. So a poverty line based on it is bound to understate what it really costs to live even at the bare subsistence level (Blaustein, 1982, pp. 48–49).

Many studies have confirmed this point. One investigated the costs of what it called a "minimum adequacy budget" — what it actually cost to buy basic necessities (food, rental housing, clothing, and so on) in New Jersey. (This budget did not include any expenses for such "non-necessities" as child care, reading materials, recreation, or education.) In 1980, when the official poverty level for a four-person family was $7,450 in New Jersey, the cost of this "minimum adequacy budget" was $12,192. The official poverty level, in other words, was less than *two-thirds* of what was necessary to buy "those goods and services which the federal government defines as essential to the maintenance of adequate nutrition, housing, safety and health" (Blaustein, 1982, p. 49).

Another measure, sometimes offered as an alternative to the poverty level, is a *lower family budget* estimated each year (until recently) by the U.S. Department of Labor. As in the New Jersey study, this budget, while slightly less basic, leaves very little room for anything beyond the bare essentials. In 1981, for example, the lower budget amounted to $15,323 for a family of four. It allowed about $87 per week for food, about $235 a month for *all* housing expenses, including furnishings (it assumes that the family rents, rather than owns a home), and about $1,160 a year for all transportation, including the cost of a car and gas. In the early 1980s, the official poverty level for a family of four was only about three-fifths of the Department of Labor's lower budget. Using the lower budget as a more reasonable measure of the upper limit of poverty, as some have suggested, would more than *double* the proportion of Americans we define as "poor."

How large is that fraction? A University of Michigan study, following the economic fortunes of 5,000 American families since the late 1960s, estimated that about 25 percent of Americans can expect to fall below the official poverty line in at least one year over a nine-year period (Duncan and Morgan, 1980). Close to 60 million Americans, therefore, are now poised precariously close to the poverty line.

What this means, in less abstract terms, is that life can be very hard indeed for many people who are not "poor" by the government's measure. In 1984, for example, about 15 percent of Americans were "officially" poor. But 20 percent said there were times when they

didn't have enough money to buy food, 25 percent said they sometimes couldn't afford necessary health care for their families, and 35
percent said they worried "most" or "all of the time" that they didn't
have enough money to pay the bills (Gallup Poll, cited in *San Francisco
Chronicle*, March 19, 1984).

As with the distribution of income and wealth, the persistence (and

Equality and Progess

Traditionally, the United States has been considered to be the country in which the democratic vision of economic equality has come closest to realization. And, as we've seen, it has even been argued that the American commitment to equality has gone too far, with unfortunate consequences for economic growth and well-being. In this view, the wealthy need the lure of potential riches in order to maintain the incentive to invest in profitable enterprises. And, at the other end of the scale, coddling by the welfare state makes people too content with their lot in life, reduces their motivation for hard work, and ultimately weakens the economy as a whole (Kristol, 1979; Gilder, 1981; Scott, 1982).

But if we compare the United States with other industrial countries, we find a different picture. Most of those countries have gone further than we have in reducing inequality of incomes — *and* in many respects have outperformed the United States in the economic realm.

The shares of the wealthiest and poorest segments of the population in several countries are compared in Table 4-4. It's apparent that there is a wide variation among these countries, both in the share of income held by the relatively wealthy and, even more strikingly, in the share held by the relatively poorest people. The income share of the most affluent fifth of the population ranges from just over a third in Sweden to nearly half in France, with the United States toward the more unequal end of the scale. The share of the lowest-income fifth shows a similar but

sharper pattern. The most unequal countries are Spain and France, with the United States, Canada, and Australia not far behind. The poorest fifth of the Dutch population gets, proportionately, twice the share of income as their Spanish and French counterparts, and nearly twice the share of the poorest fifth of Americans.

Dividing the share of the richest by the share of the poorest gives a ratio of rich to poor that can serve as a shorthand guide to the income gap in these countries. In the relatively egalitarian Netherlands, the most affluent fifth receives only about four times the income of the poorest. Sweden, Norway, and Japan also rank high on income equality. Only Spain and France, among these countries, have a more unequal distribution of income than the United States.

Does the greater income equality in countries like Sweden, Holland, or Japan interfere with economic efficiency? Simply mentioning a country like Japan is enough to suggest the limits of this argument. The evidence in the table, in fact, supports the opposite conclusion: Greater equality and a stronger economy most often go hand in hand. Measured by gross national product per capita, *most* of the countries with a smaller income gap have moved ahead of the United States in economic performance. Those with similar or greater income inequality remain behind. There are exceptions: England has relatively high income equality and a smaller GNP per capita. Japan does, too, but in this case, the measure is misleading since Japan is simply moving up from further behind — and at a

recent growth) of poverty presents a striking paradox. How can there have been so little progress despite the growth of the welfare state — a welfare state that has been criticized for pushing too hard for equality and for throwing money at the poor?

To understand this paradox, we need to look more carefully at that much-maligned abstraction, the welfare state, itself.

pace that has become the envy of other industrialized countries. (The French data are somewhat misleading, too; France has an unusually large agricultural population, which tends to make its income data less directly comparable with those of other advanced countries and masks a lower spread of inequality in its urban population.)

The reasons for this positive relationship between equality and economic progress are complex. One of the most important is the amount of unemployment a society is willing to tolerate. High unemployment is part of the explanation for the very low share of in-

come earned by the lowest fifth in the United States. Full employment policies are one of the most important reasons why countries like Sweden or Japan have a more equal spread of income. At the same time, of course, full employment means that these countries are making better and more productive use of their human resources, leading to a stronger, more competitive economy.

Table 4-4
Income inequality and economic performance, selected countries

Country	Income share of lowest fifth, %	Income share of highest fifth, %	Ratio of highest fifth to lowest fifth	GNP per capita	Rank according to GNP per capita
Netherlands	9.1	36.3	4.0	$10,841	4
Sweden	7.3	35.0	4.8	12,337	2
Norway	6.6	36.9	5.6	10,860	3
Japan	7.1	41.9	5.9	8,891	8
United Kingdom	6.1	39.3	6.4	7,054	10
West Germany	6.5	46.3	7.1	12,387	1
Canada	5.2	40.5	7.8	9,257	7
Australia	4.8	40.9	8.5	8,259	9
United States	4.9	42.1	8.6	10,739	5
Spain	4.2	45.0	10.7	5,294	11
France	4.2	47.1	11.2	10,656	6

Income equality figures are for various periods in the late 1960s and early 1970s. GNP per capita is from 1979, standardized to value of American dollar. Shares of income are adjusted to account for differences in average size of households.

Source: Adapted from Malcolm Sawyer, *Income Distribution in OECD Countries* (Paris: Organization for Economic Cooperation and Development, 1976). Reprinted with permission.

Welfare: Myths and Realities

The argument that American society has become overly egalitarian centers on the welfare system. It's often said that too many able-bodied people are on welfare and that welfare benefits are so high that it is possible to live all too comfortably without working. It's also said that the growth of the welfare state has sapped the strength of the economy and contributed to the problems of low productivity and loss of competitiveness. These arguments are frequently used to support cutbacks in government spending — at least in spending for programs that benefit people with low incomes. In 1981, the incoming president argued:

> Our society's commitment to an adequate social safety net contains powerful, inherently expansionary tendencies. If left unchecked, these forces threaten eventual fiscal ruin and serious challenges to basic social values of independence and self-support. The federal government has created so many entitlements for unnecessary benefits that it is essential to begin paring them back. (Reagan, 1981)

But if an overgenerous welfare state has channeled so much money from the affluent to the poor, why has there been so little change in the distribution of income? And why has poverty remained such a stubborn problem?

"The social safety net is pitched precariously close to the ground in the United States."

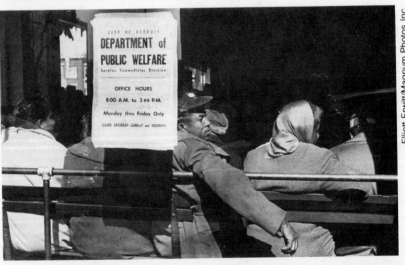

Elliott Erwitt/Magnum Photos Inc.

Part of the answer is that the image of a huge, out-of-control welfare state is misleading. In fact, the American welfare state turns out to be quite meager when compared with the welfare spending of other industrial countries. It has grown much less in recent years than is often supposed, especially in the programs that directly transfer money to the poor. In fact, those programs have often declined. It provides little more than a minimum level of subsistence for most of the people who depend on it. And the great majority of those people are not lazy shirkers or cheaters but people who, for one reason or another, are unable to work regularly enough, at high enough wages, to earn an adequate living in our present economy. Let's consider each of these points in turn.

The picture of an overgrown welfare state is usually based on the sheer amount of money the government spends on social welfare. And at first glance, this seems a very large amount, indeed. What the federal government calls *social welfare expenditures* grew from about $24 billion in 1950 to $642 billion in 1983. As a proportion of *gross national product*, the growth of social welfare appears even more striking. From just under 9 percent of GNP in 1950, it rose to 19 percent by 1982.

The Myth of the Exploding Welfare State

On the surface, this would appear to be a dramatic surge of egalitarianism. But remember the trickiness of figures on the growth of government spending. We need to probe more deeply, to ask several questions about the apparent explosion in welfare spending.

To begin with, how much of this spending is actually targeted to the poor? Much less than it first appears. Most of these funds pay for what are called *social insurance programs*, such as Social Security, unemployment insurance, retirement systems for public employees and railroad workers, and workers compensation for people injured on the job. In 1983 these programs together accounted for about 52 percent of all social welfare spending.

These programs share two characteristics. First, they are paid for (at least in part) out of special "trust funds" to which the recipients have contributed in one way or another. Second, they are for everyone, not just the poor. They do involve a great deal of money. But they are not what most people mean when they think of "welfare." Nor, certainly, is government spending for schools, which accounted for another 22 percent of social welfare spending in 1982. If these are taken out of the picture, how much is left?

At the end of the 1970s, only 13 percent of all social welfare spending went for what the government calls *public aid*, which includes, among others, the Aid to Families with Dependent Children (AFDC) program, the food stamp and Medicaid programs, and the Supplemental Security Income (SSI) program for low-income people who are aged, blind, or disabled.

That's still a lot of money. But it is a relatively small part of government spending, and it is getting smaller — despite the fact that the number of people needing assistance has gotten bigger. And the social welfare spending figures we've looked at have not been adjusted to account for the falling value of the dollar — that is, for inflation. When the shrinking buying power of the dollar is counted in, things look very different: In 1978, government spent about $364 per person on public aid; by 1982, the amount had dropped to $344 (*Statistical Abstract of the United States*, 1986, p. 356).

The shrinking of the welfare system is perhaps best illustrated by the changes in the AFDC program (see Figure 4-3). The number of people "on welfare" increased sharply in the late 1960s but reached a peak in the mid-1970s and has fallen since — by several hundred thousand. We would expect this to happen if the number of poor families and children had *also* dropped over that period. But we've seen that the opposite is true; the number of poor children has increased sharply while the availability of welfare has declined. The result is that in the five years from 1979 to 1984 the proportion of

Figure 4-3
The shrinking welfare system: Recipients of AFDC, various years

Source: Adapted from *Statistical Abstract of the United States, 1986* (Washington, D.C.: Government Printing Office, 1986), p. 379.

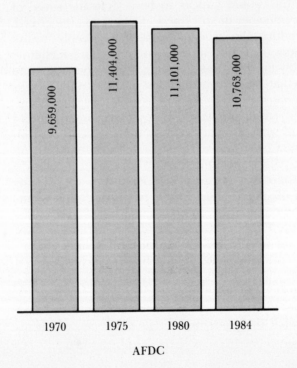

9,659,000 — 1970

11,404,000 — 1975

11,1,01,000 — 1980

10,763,000 — 1984

AFDC

poor children receiving AFDC benefits fell by 22 percent (Select Committee on Children, Youth and Families, 1985). There were nearly two million more poor children in 1984 than in 1980, but half a million *fewer* children receiving welfare (*Statistical Abstract of the United States*, 1986, p. 379).

Welfare in America, then, while still costly, isn't "exploding" — or even growing. Still, many believe that the benefits people on welfare do receive, when they get them, are too high. In this view, welfare has become so generous that the poor can now live better by going on welfare than by working. Newspapers sometimes print indignant stories about welfare mothers who own fine homes and luxury cars. Critics of the welfare system periodically announce that welfare families can accumulate startling incomes by adroitly combining different kinds of benefits. No one seriously doubts that some people manage to take advantage of the welfare system, but is this an accurate understanding of what *usually* happens?

The Myth of Lavish Welfare

The statistics show that, on the contrary, the social safety net is pitched precariously close to the ground in the United States — and, again, is getting lower all the time. Some illustrations:

- AFDC benefits vary widely across different states (see Table 4-5). But *in none of them* can welfare alone pull a family with no other earnings above the poverty line. In all but 13 states, the average welfare benefit in 1984 was less than half the poverty level for a

Top ten		Bottom ten	
State	Average monthly AFDC payment, 1984	State	Average monthly AFDC payment, 1984
Alaska	$501	Mississippi	$ 91
California	$489	Alabama	$111
Minnesota	$482	Tennessee	$120
Wisconsin	$478	South Carolina	$139
New York	$438	Texas	$142
Connecticut	$433	Arkansas	$151
Michigan	$425	Louisiana	$168
Washington	$419	Georgia	$186
Hawaii	$404	Kentucky	$188
Vermont	$400	North Carolina	$188

Source: Data from *Statistical Abstract of the United States*, 1987, p. 365.

Table 4-5
The myth of lavish welfare: Monthly AFDC payments versus the poverty line (poverty level for a family of three, 1984: $690 per month)

family of three; in 7 southern states it was less than a quarter of the poverty line (*Statistical Abstract of the United States*, 1987, p. 365).

- And, like the nation's total spending on welfare, the amounts that families on welfare actually receive have fallen sharply — partly because of government cuts in benefits, even more because of inflation. Between 1970 and 1984 the average welfare benefit for impoverished families with children fell by a *third* (House Ways and Means Committee, 1985).

- Even though most welfare recipients *can* combine more than one kind of benefit, their total benefits still usually remain very low; it is *very* difficult to live well on welfare, even in those states that provide relatively high benefits. As of 1986, combined AFDC and food stamp benefits still amounted to less than the poverty level in every state, and less than three-fourths of the poverty level in 40 states (Edelman, 1987, p. 69). And, like welfare in general, the *combined* value of food stamps and AFDC has dropped sharply — by 22 percent between 1971 and 1983 (Ellwood and Summers, 1986, p. 68).

Of course, whether you regard these benefits as too skimpy or too generous is a matter of opinion. But several facts need to be considered when you make that judgment. Welfare does *not* typically offer lavish benefits for needy people; the benefits it does offer have been shrinking for many years. And, as Figure 4-4 shows, they are quite meager by comparison with those of many other industrial societies. All of this helps explain, too, why poverty has grown in spite of the welfare state — and why the contours of economic inequality have changed so little for decades and have even shifted upward in recent years.

But here we need to look at another view of welfare and poverty that has gained considerable popularity in recent years. We've already seen that a large and growing share of the benefits the welfare state provides to the poor are "in-kind" benefits, not cash. In 1984, in-kind or noncash benefits for low-income people totaled about $98 billion, of which $46 billion went for medical care, $13 billion for food stamps, $4 billion for child nutrition programs, and about $6 billion for housing subsidies (*Statistical Abstract of the United States*, 1986, p. 357). Since these in-kind benefits are not counted as income when the government counts the number of poor people or estimates the share of income received by different groups, some have argued that the usual statistics overstate the number of poor people and the degree of inequality. A few have even argued that the growth of in-kind benefits has, for all practical purposes, abolished poverty in the United States (Anderson, 1980).

Country

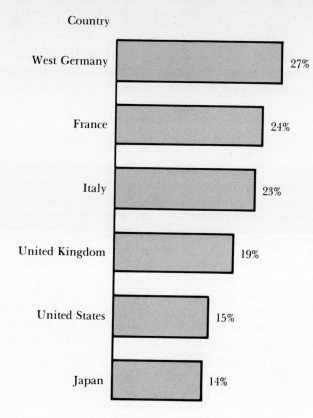

Figure 4-4
Government spending
on social welfare: Se-
lected countries, 1981

Source: Data from Organization for Economic
Cooperation and Develop-
ment, cited in Gary L.
Burtless, "Public Spending
for the Poor," in Sheldon
Danziger and Daniel Wein-
berg, eds., *Fighting Poverty:
What Works and What Doesn't,*
Cambridge: Harvard University Press, 1986, p. 46.

Note: Social welfare spending
in this figure includes government spending on income
maintenance, pensions, and
health care.

    This may seem like a very technical issue, but it has important im-
plications for the way we look at poverty and inequality, and how we
design social policies to deal with them. What should we make of it?

    The growth of in-kind benefits *is* significant — but has had less
impact on poverty than some believe. First, not all of the money the
government spends on in-kind benefits for the poor actually reaches
them. This has serious, and sometimes bizarre, consequences for the
argument about in-kind benefits and poverty. Take medical benefits,
the largest proportion of in-kind benefits for the poor. When we say
that the government spends this money "on the poor," what we really
mean is that the government reimburses doctors and hospitals for
treating the poor. The poor do not receive the money and cannot use
it as if it were money. The problem with calling such benefits income
is that, using this logic, a poor person who became seriously ill and
incurred thousands of dollars worth of government-subsidized hospital expenses would suddenly (and miraculously) be counted as no
longer poor — and might even have to be considered rich!

Subtracting the money cost of medical benefits dramatically reduces the impact of in-kind benefits on the official poverty rates. For example, in 1984 the official poverty rate, for the whole population, was a little over 14 percent. According to a Census Bureau study, if all in-kind benefits in food, housing, and medical care were added to the poor's incomes according to how much those items would cost if the poor had to buy them in the private market, the rate would drop to about 10 percent. But adding just food and housing benefits, the Census calculated, would reduce the poverty count only a little — to about 13 percent instead of 14 (*Statistical Abstract of the United States*, 1986, p. 461). Clearly, noncash benefits are important, and they have certainly contributed to the well-being of low-income people. But they have not "abolished" poverty, or even come close.

A second, more subtle problem is that these arguments, painstakingly applied to the income of the poor, aren't applied equally to the income of the affluent. But if we want to understand how various noncash benefits have affected the pattern of inequality, we must look at the noncash benefits of *all* groups, not just the poor. Some of these benefits come from private employers, like employer-paid health plans and other "fringe benefits" that are such an important part of the compensation of middle-class workers. But the non-poor also receive considerable government benefits. For example, in 1985 the government spent $56 billion on noncash benefits for poor people — but it spent $71 billion on noncash benefits for people who weren't poor. And, as we'll see in a moment, there are many other ways in which the government transfers forms of income to the affluent that do not appear in official statistics.

The Myth of the Welfare Chiselers

Most of the growth in the welfare state, then, has come about through the growth of social insurance programs. Only a fraction of government spending for social welfare has gone to public assistance programs, which have declined in recent years. And benefits to needy individuals are, on the whole, typically both low and declining.

But it isn't just the *amount* of spending that makes many people critical of the welfare system; it is the feeling that it gives money to people who don't deserve it. As one critic put it, the size of the welfare system is "less controversial than its permissive nature" (Mead, 1986, p. 14). One of the most common criticisms is that welfare supports people who really ought to be working — and in fact encourages them not to work. Since it lowers the motivation to be self-supporting, critics argue, welfare itself may be one of the main causes of poverty — and of the other social problems that go with it, such as crime, illegitimacy, and drug abuse (Murray, 1985; Mead, 1986). We'll look more closely at the links between work and welfare in Chapter 8. For now, let's just note one key problem with the argument that welfare causes poverty, and it's one we've seen already: Poverty has gone *up* the fastest in recent years, just when welfare has been going *down* (see Ellwood and Summers, 1986).

Even more important, the argument assumes that a big proportion of people on welfare could be working if they just had the motivation. But let's take a look at who actually receives welfare — and why. Are they able-bodied "chiselers" who would be at work if it weren't for society's misplaced generosity? And did the growth of welfare spending in the past signal a sudden burst of that misplaced generosity — a "permissive" response to growing demands for equality?

The reasons for the growth of the modern welfare system are complex. They involve not only changing attitudes toward welfare, but changing social needs as well. Those changing needs, in turn, are related to broad demographic shifts in American society, two of which are especially important: the rising proportion of *older* people in the population and the growth in the proportion of *families headed by women*.

The largest part of government social welfare spending goes to the aged, and their share has grown rapidly. The reasons are clear. Between 1960 and 1984, the number of people 65 and over jumped by more than 11 million, from a little more than 9 percent to almost 12 percent of the population. The number of Americans over 75 grew by nearly 7 million. By comparing the proportion of older people in the population to those in the conventional working-age range of 18 to 64, we get what is called a *support ratio*. In 1960 the support ratio stood at just over 16; that is, there were 16 people over 65 for every 100 people between the ages of 18 and 64. By 1984, there were 19 (*Statistical Abstract of the United States*, 1986, p. 362).

The rise in the proportion of older, and often (though not always) economically dependent, people is compounded by another important change in modern American society. Many more people now live alone, apart from their families and from the material support that families have often provided. This is especially true for the aged. The number of people living alone rose by almost 13 million between 1960 and 1984; about 5 million were over 65, and over 4 million of them were women (*Statistical Abstract of the United States*, 1986, p. 47).

There are, then, more people over 65, and fewer of them are supported by a larger family. This helps explain why their share of government spending has grown so rapidly, and it explains a good part of the overall rise in government spending on the welfare state.

A somewhat similar change helps explain the growth in welfare for people other than the aged. We've seen that the welfare rolls ex-

The largest part of social spending goes for the needs of a growing population of older people.

panded rapidly during the late 1960s and early 1970s. What caused this rise? Many things, including improved benefits, easier eligibility, and more aggressive assertion of legal rights to assistance by the poor. But underlying all of these was another broad demographic change — the increase in families headed by women. In 1960 about one in every ten American families was headed by a woman; by 1981, the ratio was better than one in seven.

For reasons we'll examine further in Chapter 6 (including gender discrimination in the labor market and the lack of adequate child care), this trend has resulted in a growing number of families who are dependent on public aid. (It is sometimes argued that the welfare system itself is responsible for the rising proportion of families headed by women. We will look at this issue, too, in Chapter 6, but we'll anticipate the conclusion here: Most research suggests that if welfare *does* have a negative effect on the likelihood of starting families or keeping them together, it is not a large one.)

Both trends — the rise in the proportion of older people and of families headed by women — mean that the number of people on welfare who are of working age, able-bodied, and without very young children is quite small (Table 4-6.) Almost two-thirds of AFDC recipients are children, and among them, over nine in ten are ten years old or younger. In only one in seventeen AFDC families is there a couple in which the husband is able to work. (Note that Table 4-6 also undermines another common stereotype about welfare in America: Most welfare families are *not* large — almost three-fourths have one or two children.)

Does all of this mean that there are no welfare cheaters — able-bodied, working-age people collecting welfare when they could be working? Of course not. But it does show that *most* of the benefits and services of the welfare system go to people who genuinely need some form of public support.

And the problem of welfare cheating is counter-balanced by the fact that many poor people who *are* eligible for public benefits don't get them. Only half of the poor children in the United States participate in the AFDC program; only about three-fifths get any in-kind benefits, with two-fifths receiving food stamps and one-seventh receiving public housing benefits (Select Committee on Children, Youth and Families, 1985, p. 111; *Statistical Abstract of the United States*, 1986, p. 358).

The fact that the welfare system is mainly a response to the needs of the old, the ill and disabled, and women facing obstacles to steady

Table 4-6
Who gets welfare? Characteristics of families and children on AFDC, 1975 and 1982

Families	1975	1982	Children	1975	1982
Number of families receiving benefits (in thousands)	3,420	3,390	Number of children receiving benefits (in thousands)	8,121	6,624
Percent distribution			Father is		
Families with			Deceased	3.7	.9
1 child	38	43	Incapacitated	7.7	3.5
2 children	26	31	Unemployed	3.7	6.0
3 children	16	15	Absent from Home:		
4 or more children	20	10	Divorced	19.4	20.6
Number of years receiving benefits:			Separated	28.6	19.0
			Not married to mother	31.0	46.5
Less than 1 year	28	32	Other	4.3	2.2
1–3 years	27	30	Mother is absent, not father	1.6	1.3
4–5 years	19	15	Age		
6–10 years	19	16	Less than 6 years	34.6	41.1
more than 10 years	6	8	6–11 years	33.7	32.4
			12–17 years	28.5	25.1
			18–20 years	2.4	1.5

Source: Adapted from *Statistical Abstract of the United States*, 1986, p. 382.

(or well-paid) work should make us look hard at some popular beliefs about how welfare hurts the economy — and how reducing welfare will help it. It isn't clear how cutting back on benefits to the disabled or to unskilled single mothers with preschool children could boost the incentive to work — and hence boost the economy — in any meaningful way. This is *not*, by any means, to say that the present welfare system is necessarily the best or the most efficient way to meet the needs of these groups. It does mean that those needs must be taken into account if we want to think about realistic alternatives to the current system.

At the same time, the portrait of the welfare population helps us understand one of the reasons why the growth of the welfare state hasn't much changed the pattern of income inequality. Most welfare spending doesn't shift money so much from affluent to poor as from people of working age to the old and the very young, and from the healthy to the ill and disabled. To an important extent, then, the system transfers money "sideways" rather than up and down the income ladder (Gough, 1979).

A Permanent "Underclass"?	A final issue about the distribution of welfare deserves mention. It is commonly assumed that the welfare population consists of a vast "underclass" (Auletta, 1981; Lemann, 1985) of people who are more or less permanently dependent on the welfare system. This perception, in turn, is partly responsible for the widespread belief that welfare itself fosters dependency in those who receive it (Kristol, 1979; Mead, 1986). Many people believe that welfare demoralizes the poor, that it turns its recipients into incompetent wards of the government. But the University of Michigan's Panel Study of Income Dynamics (Duncan, 1984) found that the vast majority of welfare recipients do *not* fit the stereotype of the underclass. Over a 10-year period, almost a fourth of the U.S. population received some kind of welfare benefits. But fewer than one in one hundred lived in families who were dependent on welfare for more than half of their income throughout those 10 years. Contrary to another common assumption, most people who received welfare *also* worked; and relatively few were dependent on welfare for years at a time. For most of those who received it, welfare operated as a kind of insurance to tide people over temporary hard times.

The Michigan study did find a group of recipients who appeared to fit the image of a permanent underclass, but it was only a fraction of the total welfare population. About 8 percent of welfare recipients depended on welfare benefits to provide more than half of their income for at least 8 of the 10 years studied. For this smaller group, the more normal process of eventually moving out of dependency seems to have been blocked.

But there's an important complication. Though they were only a small percentage of *all* people who ever had to go on welfare, this persistently dependent group made up a substantial proportion of the poverty population at any one point in time — and they account for an oversized part of our total welfare spending. In other words, being on welfare is, for most people, a short stopover on the road out of poverty; for a small percentage, however, it's more like a permanent home. They are trapped in long "spells" of poverty from which it is difficult to escape (Bane and Ellwood, 1986). Given that most people who go on welfare do *not* get trapped this way, it seems unlikely — as we've said — that welfare itself is a major cause of that dependency. But something is. And as we'll see in the next chapter, the forces that lead to long-term dependence on welfare don't strike all Americans equally. Black children, in particular, are not only more likely to be poor in the first place but are *much* more likely to be caught in a "spell" of poverty that may last throughout their childhood — or their lives.

We will come back to the issues of poverty and dependency — and how they are related to changing patterns of work in America — in later chapters. But first let's consider a final reason why government policy has had less impact on the distribution of American income and wealth than many people believe. We have just seen one of the reasons: The scope and generosity of government benefits to the poor is often exaggerated. We now need to consider another reason: The government does not simply transfer money *downward* from the affluent to the poor. It also, in a bewildering variety of ways, transfers money *upward*, to the middle class and the wealthy.

The "Upside-Down" Welfare System

The government is often seen as a huge, bureaucratic Robin Hood, taking from the rich and giving to the poor. But the reality is far more complicated. The poor are by no means the only group that receives welfare — if by welfare we mean money and other forms of support that are not earned in the free market and that are paid for by public funds. We've already encountered some of these benefits — government subsidies to business, for example. But there are many others. In modern American society, the government is less a Robin Hood than a giant machine that sifts and sorts the country's wealth in several directions at once. Virtually every decision made at any level of government, about how it will get money as well as how it will spend it, has consequences — sometimes very large ones — for the pattern of economic inequality in America. Taken together, these decisions add up to a largely hidden welfare system, alongside and often counterbalancing the more visible one.

How much is transferred to the affluent, and to large corporations, through the hidden welfare system is unknown. (For some attempts at arriving at a figure, see Eisner, 1984, and Page, 1983.) We know much more about the scope of welfare for the poor, since every penny is doled out under the watchful eye of public officials. But no one looks as hard at the many forms of welfare for the affluent. It's safe to say, though, that the amount is enormous — and growing. Let's look at three ways in which public resources are shifted upward by the government toward the more affluent: through loopholes in the tax system, through special subsidies and loans, and through the broader pattern of government spending in support of some activities rather than others.

The Hidden Welfare System I: Tax Expenditures

Most people think of the tax system as a *collector* of money. But the tax system also *spends* money in a number of ways. Most importantly, it can allow an individual, or a corporation, to pay lower taxes or no taxes at all. In the United States, the government does this for many different groups, for many different reasons.

Popularly, these mechanisms are called tax loopholes. Officially, they are called *tax expenditures* because, by offering these tax breaks, the government is doing indirectly what it does when it spends money directly. In both cases, the money cannot be used for other purposes. And, in both cases, someone wins and someone else loses. Most often, as one study put it, tax expenditures "result in an upside-down welfare program — the richer the taxpayer, the greater the benefit he, she, or it receives" (Common Cause, 1978, p. iii).

Tax expenditures have been a fast-growing form of hidden welfare. In 1975, they amounted to about $93 billion; by 1985, about $355 billion (*Statistical Abstract of the United States*, 1987, p. 297). And as a proportion of gross national product, they have grown much more rapidly than ordinary government spending.

Some of this hidden spending benefits low-income people; public assistance benefits, for example, are generally not taxed, and they cost the government about half a billion dollars in lost revenues in 1985. But a big part of the government's tax expenditures benefits middle-income people, notably through the tax deduction for mortgage interest for homeowners, which cost the government $25 billion in 1985, or about double what it paid out in housing assistance for low-income people. And, historically, many of the biggest tax expenditures have favored the affluent and/or private businesses. Matched against government spending on the poor, these benefits can be impressive indeed (Table 4-7).

Some examples: In 1985 the federal government gave $1.9 billion to the oil industry to pay for exploration and depletion of oil and gas reserves — $400 million more than it spent for the nutritional program for low-income women, infants, and children (WIC). The exclusion of interest on certain state and local bonds cost the government about $9.7 billion, more than half a billion more than it spent on AFDC; about 90 percent of such bonds, according to the Joint Economic Committee of Congress, are owned by the "super-rich" and the "very rich."

Tax expenditures help explain why corporate taxes have fallen consistently in recent years, as we saw in Chapter 3. And they are the source of the spectacular tax inequities often reported in the media. In 1982, according to the Internal Revenue Service, tax loopholes enabled more than 299 couples and individuals with incomes over $200,000 to pay *no* federal taxes (*San Francisco Chronicle*, January 10, 1985).

Even more importantly, tax expenditures help explain a sometimes puzzling fact — that the American tax system, on balance, has had little overall impact on the distribution of income. Though the *absolute* amounts of money the government takes from rich individuals (or corporations) are larger than those taken from the less affluent, the best evidence suggests that the *proportions* taken from different income groups are roughly *equal*. In the language of economics, the tax system is thus a roughly *proportional* one when all of its various parts

Table 4-7
Federal government benefits

Open . . .	and Hidden
Community health centers $375 million	Mineral depletion allowance $330 million
Job corps $615 million	Capital gains treatment of agricultural income $605 million
Head Start $1.1 billion	Exclusion of interest on industrial development bonds $2.6 billion
WIC Nutrition Program $1.5 billion	Oil and gas depletion and exploration allowances $1.9 billion
AFDC $9 billion	Exclusion of interest on state and local bonds $9.7 billion

Note: Figures are for 1985 and have been rounded.
Source: Statistical Abstract of the United States, 1987, pp. 297, 343.

are put together, including state and local sales and property taxes as well as income taxes. (Taxes that take a greater share as they move up the income scale are called *progressive* taxes, while those that take a greater share at lower income levels, such as sales taxes, are called *regressive*.)

But the tax system has probably become tilted toward the "regressive" end of the scale in recent years, especially because of a rise in Social Security taxes and a decline in income taxes on corporations and the affluent (Pechman, 1985). Poor people's taxes — as a proportion of their income — rose fivefold between 1981 and 1985 alone, while those of middle- and upper-income Americans generally fell (*New York Times*, December 12, 1985). Changes in the federal tax laws in 1986 had a complicated effect on the tax system — in some ways making it more progressive, in some ways more regressive. Taxes on low-income people were reduced, and some of the important tax expenditures mainly benefiting the affluent — such as the investment tax credit and special treatment of some capital gains — were reduced or eliminated. But, at the same time, the maximum income tax rate on affluent families was cut almost in half — from 50 to 28 percent, a substantial "expenditure" indeed.

The Hidden Welfare System II: Subsidies and Credit

Besides tax expenditures, the government offers many special subsidies and loans that, by serving some social groups at the expense of others, also affect the distribution of income and wealth. They take many forms, from outright bailouts of corporations in trouble and loan guarantees enabling businesses to compete more effectively against foreign corporations, to federally backed loans, at favorable rates, for home mortgages or farm expansion.

In 1986 the federal government spent an estimated $200 billion on these credit arrangements. About one-fifth was in the form of direct loans; the rest were loan guarantees (in which the government promises to back up loans issued by other sources). Most of this sum escapes attention in the usual debates about government spending. But, as the Congressional Budget Office bluntly put it, "some people — those who get more credit and income — are made better off; others, who get less, are made worse off" (U.S. Congressional Budget Office, 1980, p. 20).

The best-known examples of this kind of "public welfare" are the huge federal bailouts of major corporations (like the Chrysler Corporation) that, like other welfare recipients, have failed to make it in the "free" market. All told, federally assisted credit to a few key, troubled industries, such as shipbuilding, aircraft, steel, and autos, came to about $4 billion in 1981, or about the same amount as the government paid for all child nutrition programs. But other, less spectacular subsidies have been more important — and costly — over the long run.

The federal government has provided substantial subsidies to agriculture since the 1930s. The most important are price support programs that guarantee farmers a predetermined level of prices for many crops, whatever may happen in the market. Such supports came to about $23 billion in 1986 (U.S. Office of Management and Budget, 1987, pp. 5-54). The government also lends money on favored terms to farmers for new land and other investments, provides emergency loans in case of natural disasters or poor market conditions, and in many other ways provides farmers with protection against the ups and downs of the economy.

Like most items on the hidden welfare budget, these subsidies provide more money for the affluent than anyone else. The biggest beneficiaries are the largest farmers. In 1984, according to the U.S. Council of Economic Advisers, the largest 14 percent of farms receiving payments under the price support program got about 66 percent of the total payments (*Economic Report of the President*, 1986, p. 131).

There are many other kinds of federal subsidies for *business* — most of them little-known. For example, there is the Export-Import Bank, a federal agency that grants credit at reduced rates to American businesses engaged in exporting goods to foreign countries. The goal is to give them an edge against foreign competition. In 1986 the special low interest rates on direct loans amounted to a tax-supported subsidy of about $4 billion. Like most of the hidden welfare system, these loans work in ways that are mysterious to most people. For example, in 1980 American taxpayers (though few of them were aware of it) loaned the national airline of Belgium, Sabena, $31 million (at reduced interest) and promised to guarantee another $62 million so that Sabena would buy two American-made DC-10 jets instead of the European-built Airbus (U.S. Congressional Budget Office, 1980, p. 40). By loaning money to the Belgians, the public helped support the McDonnell-Douglas Corporation and its stockholders — again, a process that shifted money upward toward the higher end of the income scale.

All of these programs, then, transfer money upward, from people of average or lower income to people with more money or to corporations. The money is not earned as the fruits of hard work in the free market: It is a government benefit. This is not to say that there is anything necessarily wrong about the *purposes* of these benefits. Crop subsidies may mean the difference between a farm's economic survival and its collapse. A timely loan to a floundering corporation may save thousands of jobs and bring a whole community back from the brink of economic disaster. There's plenty of room for argument over the merits of any of these measures. What's important, for our purposes, is to understand that government benefits aren't only for the poor.

The Hidden Welfare System III: The Direction of Government Spending

Before leaving this subject, let's make a final, more general, point about the hidden welfare system. Government spending on goods and services now amounts to about a quarter of our gross national product. Given the sheer size of the government's economic role, every major spending decision it makes affects the living standards of many people and alters the distribution of income and wealth.

The government's decision to shift money into defense production, for example, offers a long-term subsidy to the corporations which win most large defense contracts. This means more money and a higher living standard for high-level technical and managerial workers in defense industries and for the stockholders in those corporations. But it also means *less* money, fewer jobs, and a declining standard of living for (among others) teachers, construction workers, and the unskilled unemployed in the inner cities. The decision to build superhighways that serve suburban commuters, instead of mass transportation for central cities, transfers public funds from inner-city residents to suburban ones. In both cases, inequality increases. The effect of these decisions is hard to measure, and it doesn't show up in official statistics on the distribution of income and wealth. But it is crucially important in understanding how different groups fare in the welfare state.

Inequality and the Future

Looking at all the ways the government is involved in the distribution of income and wealth, then, helps explain why America has become a less equal society in the last quarter of the twentieth century, despite earlier expectations of shared affluence. We'll see in later chapters that these fundamental economic inequalities influence almost everything else in American life: the chances of getting adequate health care (and of falling ill in the first place); the chances of losing a job (and of getting a good one to begin with); the risks of being the victim of a crime (and of committing one). Thus, what happens to the trends in inequality in the future will profoundly influence the quality of life in the United States. What does that future look like? No one has a crystal ball, but three recent trends are especially troubling: changes in work, in family structure, and in government policies toward the disadvantaged.

We've seen that one of the main sources of poverty and inequality in America has been the rising number of people who can't make enough money from working to live decently without public help. And the outlook for the near future isn't encouraging. Unemployment, as we saw in Chapter 3, has crept ever-higher, even during times of economic growth. International competition and automation are leading many American corporations to trim their work forces — and/or to lower their wages. And a shrinking union movement has found it difficult to resist those trends. Meanwhile, though we've created millions of new jobs and will doubtless create millions more, too many of them have been low-paying ones that can't raise workers out of poverty and are often unsteady sources of income.

Changes in Work Opportunities

As we'll see in Chapter 8, there is considerable debate over the long-term impact of these changes in the job structure. Some people fear that the middle class may be shrinking, replaced by an "hourglass" economy with some very affluent people at the top and a growing proportion of poor and "near-poor" at the bottom (see Currie, Dunn, and Fogarty, 1987; Ehrenreich, 1986; Harrington and Levinson, 1986). Others think that these fears are exaggerated (Rosenthal, 1985). But one thing is certain: Many people have been pushed out of the kinds of jobs that used to offer a ticket into a steady middle-level income — and haven't been able to find new jobs that can match the ones they lost. This has been most obvious in some of the blue-collar industries especially hard-hit by international competition, like steel. But increasingly it's also a problem in white-collar jobs — in banking, in communications, even in some parts of the computer industry.

No one knows how far this trend may go, or what exactly will happen to those who have been displaced by it. What's not really in debate is that the future of work in America is more uncertain than ever before — and so are the prospects for good jobs and incomes for many people, especially the young. So far, this trend has aggravated inequality in America. Barring changes in the shape of work that we can't yet foresee, it will do so even more in the future.

We've seen that the family plays an important role in shaping the patterns of poverty and inequality. It is not the only thing that determines an individual's economic chances, and indeed the role of family

Changes in Family Structure

breakup in causing the rise in poverty has been somewhat exaggerated lately. (We'll look more carefully at the relationship between family disruption and poverty a little later.) But the family's influence *is* important, and the fact that family breakup is still increasing doesn't bode well for our capacity to reverse the rise in poverty in the near future. This is especially true in the context of a troubled outlook for jobs and earnings and the recent growth of a less-generous public policy toward disadvantaged families.

Changes in Government Policy

Finally, what we've called the shrinking of the welfare state has disturbing implications for the future. Perhaps without intention, the United States has been involved in a massive experiment in recent years (Ellwood and Summers, 1986): We've cut back government benefits to the poor on the theory that the benefits weren't helping — and might be hurting — their beneficiaries and that by cutting public spending we would also free up the private economy, which would, in turn, pump out more jobs and higher incomes for the poor.

The final results aren't in, but so far the verdict on this experiment isn't positive. The reduced role for government in income support, job training, and other benefits has gone hand-in-hand with sharply rising poverty, family disruption, and other social disorders — along with a widening gap between the poor and the comfortable.

How much farther will that gap widen? Are we on the road to becoming a society sharply and irrevocably split between the haves and the have-nots — a society ever more deeply torn by social tension and conflict? We'll return to these questions in later chapters, but to begin to answer them we'll need to consider two other aspects of inequality in America that we've held, somewhat artificially, out of the discussion so far: the effects of race and gender. These are the topics of Chapters 5 and 6.

Summary

This chapter has examined recent trends in economic inequality in the United States. Though it's often argued that American society has become quite egalitarian — even excessively so — in the distribution of income and wealth, the evidence suggests otherwise.

The distribution of income is highly skewed toward the most affluent fifth of the population. Though this pattern improved slightly up until the early 1970s, it has worsened somewhat since then. Personal wealth is distributed even more unequally and is often handed down from generation to generation.

Poverty in America declined during the 1960s, remained roughly stable throughout most of the 1970s, and has risen sharply in the 1980s. The slowdown in the War on Poverty has had especially harsh consequences for children and for those living in the inner cities.

The spread of inequality in the United States is considerably wider than in most other advanced industrial countries — including many whose economies have performed better than ours in recent years.

The American welfare system is neither as large, as expensive, or as wasteful as many critics argue. Our welfare benefits are meager compared with those of many other advanced industrial societies; most states pay benefits that are well below the poverty level; and most welfare recipients are needy women and children who lack strong opportunities for jobs and earnings under current economic conditions.

At the other end of the scale, the government provides many benefits — often hidden — to corporations and affluent individuals, which distribute income upward and thus help maintain the pattern of inequality.

For Further Reading

Blaustein, Arthur I., ed. *The American Promise: Equal Justice and Economic Opportunity*, New Brunswick, N.J.: Transaction Books, 1982.

Danziger, Sheldon and Daniel Weinberg, eds. *Fighting Poverty*. Cambridge: Harvard University Press, 1986.

Duncan, Greg. *Years of Poverty, Years of Plenty*. Ann Arbor: University of Michigan, 1984.

Green, Philip. *The Pursuit of Inequality*. New York: Pantheon, 1980.

Harrington, Michael. *The New American Poverty*. New York: Simon and Schuster, 1984.

Katz, Michael B. *In The Shadow of the Poorhouse: A Social History of Welfare in America*. New York: Basic Books, 1986.

5

Social Inequality II: Race

The ideal of racial equality, like that of economic equality, has had an ambiguous history in America. Officially, Americans believe that people of all races are created equal and that all should have an equal chance at society's benefits. But American history is also the history of the conquest, enslavement, and exclusion of racial minorities. The vision of racial equality and the harsh reality of unequal treatment have coexisted uneasily from the beginning.

That uneasy balance was upset in the 1950s and 1960s as first blacks and then other minorities challenged the social, legal, and economic bases of racial inequality. These challenges created a legislative and judicial revolution that established equal treatment as the law of the land — in the school desegregation decision of 1955, the Civil Rights Act 10 years later, and the rise of affirmative action programs by the 1970s.

And these weren't just paper victories. They quickly began to produce results in the even tougher realm of social and economic practices. Minorities began, in significant numbers, to move into schools, jobs, and income brackets from which they had traditionally been excluded.

For a while it looked as if we might have broken the cycle of racial discrimination and disadvantage for good. In the early 1980s, one national magazine wrote that economic "discrimination seems no longer of major significance," since "blacks as a community have now

136

entered the mainstream of American economic life" (Guzzardi 1981, p. 100). Some even argued that the movement for racial equality had "gone too far"; whites were becoming resentful of the preferential treatment given to minorities.

But by the 1980s it was apparent that something had gone wrong. The social and economic gains blacks and other minorities had achieved were real enough — but in many cases they had been halted or even reversed. And worse, while many had "made it" in American society, many others seemed trapped in an underclass wracked by unemployment, family disruption, drug abuse, and crime. Today few people would deny the existence of this tragic contradiction. The issues are how to explain it — and what to do about it.

Some argue that a faltering economy and a society still tainted by pervasive racial discrimination are largely to blame (Swinton, 1987); others put more of the burden on broad transformations in the economy that have had an especially adverse impact on minorities (Wilson, 1978; Wilson and Neckerman, 1986). Some pin the blame on cultural obstacles that keep some groups from taking advantage of the opportunities available to them (Glazer, 1981; Kaus, 1986); and still others blame government policies — especially the expansion of the welfare state and the rise of affirmative action — for encouraging dependency and blocking minorities from pulling themselves up by their own bootstraps (Sowell, 1981; Williams, 1982; Loury, 1984).

We can't resolve all of these complex issues in this chapter; but we can sort out some of the facts that lie behind them. We'll look at the evidence on minority progress in recent years, focusing on basic trends in income, employment, wealth, and poverty, and we'll consider a variety of explanations for the continuing differences that exist in these areas for whites and minorities. Again, we'll save most of the discussion of other aspects of racial inequality (such as differences in the quality of health care or in victimization by crime) for later chapters.

Gains and Losses: Income and Poverty

We've seen that income distribution in the United States has remained highly unequal, more so than in most other advanced industrial societies, and that the inequality has increased in recent years. The egalitarian "revolution" that has so disturbed some observers has yet to take place. But what about the relative position of minorities within that income spread? How have different groups fared under the impact of changes in the economy and in public policy?

A simple comparison of different minority groups and whites shows that measured in terms of median family incomes, most minority groups (with the partial exception of some Asian-American groups, as we'll see later in the chapter) are far behind whites. The general pattern shown in Table 5-1 is one we'll see repeated in many other areas of social and economic life: Whites are still well ahead, with blacks and Puerto Ricans toward the bottom and Mexican-Americans somewhere in between.

As usual, these figures must be qualified in several ways. For one thing, official statistics on income ignore a large part of the income that comes from owning property, especially capital gains. Minorities much less often own income-producing property (it's estimated that only about 1 percent of all capital gains income goes to blacks, for example, though they are almost 12 percent of the population), so that conventional income statistics underestimate the inequality between minority and white incomes. Further, the usual statistics on income are not adjusted to reflect differences in family size. Because minority families tend to be larger than white families, the same level of family income equals a lower per capita income and, presumably, a lower level of family well-being (Bianchi, 1981, p. 115). But the limitations of the official figures work the other way, too. Minorities receive a higher proportion of in-kind welfare benefits, such as food stamps and subsidized housing, which are also not counted as income. To that extent, the figures understate minority groups' income.

Table 5-1
Race and income: Median family income, by race and Spanish origin, 1984

Race or Spanish origin	Median family income
White	$27,686
Black	$15,432
Hispanic	$18,833
Mexican-American	$19,184
Puerto Rican	$12,371
Central and South American	$19,785

Note: In most Census statistics, Hispanics are both counted separately *and* included on some figures for whites and blacks. Figures on white income and poverty, therefore, include a substantial number of Hispanics; figures on black income and poverty include a smaller number. Of the approximately 17 million persons of Hispanic origin in the United States in 1985, about 10 million were Mexican-American, 2.5 million Puerto Rican, 1.7 million Central and South American, and 1.7 million Cuban.

Source: Statistical Abstract of the United States, 1986, p. 450; and U.S. Bureau of the Census, "Persons of Spanish Origin in the United States: March 1985," Washington, D.C., 1985, p. 2.

Challenges to racial inequality: Troops enforce the integration of Little Rock, Arkansas, High School, 1957.

More importantly, such raw figures don't convey either the complexity or the direction of the trends in minority living standards. Let's consider first the troubling pattern of black versus white incomes. Here, as with other economic measures, *the economic gap between black and white Americans is widening.* In 1965, when Congress passed the Civil Rights Act, the median income of black families was about 55 percent of white income, a proportion that had hardly changed since 1950. By the early 1970s, stimulated by antidiscrimination efforts and a growing economy, that ratio reached a peak of about 61 percent. At its highest level, in other words, black family income has never been more than a fraction above three-fifths that of white family income.

As the national economy slid downward after the mid-1970s, blacks fell farther behind. By the mid-1980s, black median family income had dropped back to about 57 percent of white income — depressingly close to its position at the end of World War II and, for that matter, not far from its estimated level at the *turn of the century* (Reich, 1981, pp. 18–19).

A similar trend has affected Americans of Hispanic origin — only more so. Between 1972 (the first year for which comparable statistics are available) and 1985, their average family income dropped from 71 percent of the income level of non-Hispanic whites to about 65 percent — bringing them considerably closer to the income level of black families. Overall, as we saw in Chapter 3, the average income fell for families of *all* races after the early 1970s, a casualty of an uneven economy, rising unemployment, and falling wages. But it has fallen *faster* for minorities.

Looking at income from another angle, we see that blacks, who made up about 11 percent of American households in 1983, brought home only about 7 percent of the country's total income; Hispanics, who accounted for almost 6 percent of households, brought home less than 4 percent. Had blacks taken home a share of income equal to their proportion of the population, they would have had an extra $86 billion in 1983, or a sizable $9,300 for every black household in America. Hispanics would have enjoyed an extra $36 billion, or about $7,600 for every Hispanic household.

The Disaster of Minority Poverty

An even more disturbing picture emerges for trends in minority poverty. As of the mid-1980s the poverty rate among Mexican-American families was two and a half times the white rate; for blacks, it was three times the white rate; and for Puerto Ricans, four times (Figure 5-1). What's worse, minority poverty has been increasing — dramatically so for Hispanic Americans. From 1979 to 1985 alone more than 700,000 blacks and over 2 *million* Hispanics were added to the poverty rolls, and as Figure 5-2 (page 150) also shows, a disturbing proportion of them were children. The risks of poverty for a Hispanic child have come close to those of a black child; around two in five children in both black and Hispanic families are poor. Black poverty has reached levels we haven't seen since the mid-1960s, at the beginning of the War on Poverty and the antidiscrimination programs sparked by the Civil Rights movement.

Moreover, these broad figures obscure several other troubling aspects of the trends in minority poverty:

- The minority poor are *poorer* than the white poor. In 1984, a stunning 15 percent of American blacks — versus just 4 percent of whites — existed on incomes that were less than half the poverty level (U.S. Bureau of the Census, 1985b, p. 23).

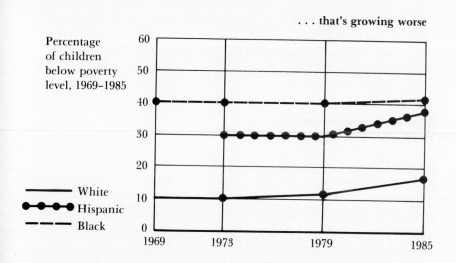

A disaster . . .

Percentage of families below poverty level, 1984

- Puerto Rican: 41.9
- Black: 30.9
- Mexican-American: 24.1
- White: 9.1

Figure 5-1
Minority poverty

Source: Data from U.S. Bureau of the Census, *Current Population Reports,* Series P-60, No. 154, pp. 22–23.

. . . that's growing worse

Percentage of children below poverty level, 1969–1985

- White
- Hispanic
- Black

1969   1973   1979   1985

- Generally speaking, staying in school reduces the risks of poverty for people of all races. But a black American with some *college* education has about the same chance of being poor as a white with a *grade-school* education. Hispanics who have graduated from high

---

Gains and Losses: Income and Poverty   **141**

school have only slightly lower poverty rates than non-Hispanic whites who never finished the eighth grade.

- Similarly, how much you work makes a big difference in the likelihood that you'll be poor; and working full time vastly decreases the chances of poverty for all groups. But a white family with *no one* working is considerably *less* likely to be poor than a black or Hispanic family with one family member at work (U.S. Bureau of the Census, 1985b, p. 28).

- Families with more children generally have higher risks of poverty than those with fewer children. But a black family with only one child has the same chance of being poor as a white family with *four*.

- Even more disturbingly, minority poverty isn't much affected by economic growth. Other things equal, poverty declines when the economy recovers from a recession. But there were about a million and a half more poor blacks and over 2 million more poor Hispanics in the "recovery" year of 1985 than in the recession year of 1975.

- Finally, minorities are overrepresented among the *persistently* poor — those who remain poor year after year. The likelihood of moving *out* of poverty is much greater for whites than blacks. More than three-fifths of the households characterized as "persistently poor" in the University of Michigan's Panel Study of Income Dynamics — those who remained poor in 8 of the 10 years studied — were black (Duncan and Coe, 1981, p. 98). A black child born into a poor family, according to the study, will endure a "spell" of poverty lasting an average of 10 years (Bane and Ellwood, 1986).

Progress and Paradox

By the 1980s, then, the economic condition of many blacks, Puerto Ricans, and Mexican-Americans appeared to be deteriorating. Gains achieved in the 1960s had slowed in the 1970s, and the 1980s witnessed sharp setbacks for minorities. What makes this trend especially disquieting is that it has occurred in spite of a number of social changes that should have *improved* the position of minorities.

One such favorable change is the increasing similarity in years of schooling between whites and minorities, especially blacks. By the beginning of the 1970s, the median years of school completed by blacks were almost equal to those of whites; and among people under age 35, schooling levels had become completely equal (*Statistical Abstract of the United States*, 1983, p. 145). Levels of schooling for Hispanics had not improved as much, but they had also increased dramatically. In 1970 less than a fourth of Mexican-Americans and Puerto Ricans in the United States had finished high school; by 1985 almost half of the Hispanics in the United States were high-school graduates (U.S. Bureau of the Census, 1986c, p. 1). Although they were still distinctly behind both whites and blacks in median years of schooling, they had experienced a sharp improvement that many expected would bring their incomes more into line with those of non-Hispanic whites and reduce their chances of poverty.

Furthermore, the resistance of white Americans to minority progress, at least on the level of attitudes and beliefs, seemed, according to virtually every survey taken by opinion pollsters and social scientists, to have subsided. Whites were more likely to express a willingness to live next to blacks, to work alongside them, to send their children to school with them, and to support their claims for a better chance at the good life. And they were less likely to hold some of the most glaring prejudices against minorities (Governor's Task Force on Civil Rights, 1982, pp. 124–125). To be sure, prejudice, both overt and subtle, did remain, as numerous studies discovered (Crosby et al., 1980; *Public Opinion,* 1981). And whites were much more willing to support racial equality in the *abstract* than in the concrete, as seen by their resistance to the practical implementation of programs like mandatory school busing and affirmative action (Schuman, Steeh, and Bobo, 1985). But, on the whole, racial attitudes improved just when, paradoxically, racial economic inequality began to increase.

A similar paradox appears when we look at residential segregation in the cities. A 1983 study by the sociologist Karl Taeuber shows that most major American cities with large black populations (with some notable exceptions) became somewhat less segregated during the 1970s, continuing a slow shift that began during the 1960s (Taeuber, 1983, p. 5). In several cities, including Gary and Oakland in the North and West, and Dallas, Jacksonville, and Houston in the South and Southwest, the 1970s brought relatively rapid declines in residential segregation. Again, though the successes were far from uniform, they were an improvement, probably resulting both from more effective laws mandating fair housing practices and from the decline in overt racial prejudice.

A final aspect of the paradox is that the minority *economic* losses took place simultaneously with rises in black and Hispanic political representation. Between 1972 and 1982, for example, while urban black poverty rates were increasing, the number of black mayors in America rose from 86 to 223 and the number of black state legislators rose from 169 to 347, according to data from Howard University's Joint Center for Political Studies (*Newsweek,* April 11, 1983, p. 24).

And the stagnation in Hispanic economic gains appeared just as Hispanics, especially in parts of the Southwest, were beginning to flex their political muscle.

How do we explain the stagnation in minority economic progress, especially in the face of these favorable trends?

Class versus Race?

One line of thought holds that the negative picture of racial progress that emerges from these broad figures on income and poverty is misleading. Those who hold this view point to different data, especially those that distinguish racial gains and losses by age and family structure, to argue that the economic situation of blacks is much *better* than it seems at first glance. (At least by implication, this would be true of some other minority groups as well, though the argument has been usually about black progress.) In this view, it's not that *all* blacks are suffering from the effects of continuing discrimination and economic stagnation. Rather, the slowing — or reversal — of black gains in recent years reflects an increasing split between two parts of the black population.

Inner-city minority poverty has worsened in the past decade . . .

Bruce Davidson/Magnum Photos, Inc.

On one side (according to this argument) is a growing, affluent middle class, mainly composed of younger, better-educated families who have been able to take advantage of the improved racial climate and declining discrimination and prejudice in the schools and the job market. Such families, it's argued, now do as well as comparable white families. And because they are the first generation of nonwhites to show the full effects of changing attitudes and forceful antidiscrimination policies, their situation is a more accurate indication of the future of racial equality.

On the other side, however, is a growing underclass of families disproportionately headed by women and often trapped in the inner cities in a self-defeating cycle of welfare dependency, crime, drug addiction, and other social pathologies.

The implications of this view are far-reaching. To some observers, it implies that racial discrimination itself is no longer the real problem. Blacks (or Puerto Ricans or Mexican-Americans) with the right characteristics (good education and a sound family) can now expect to do as well, or nearly as well, as whites in the competition for jobs and income. And they can expect to pass these advantages on to their

while rural poverty improved — until the 1980s.

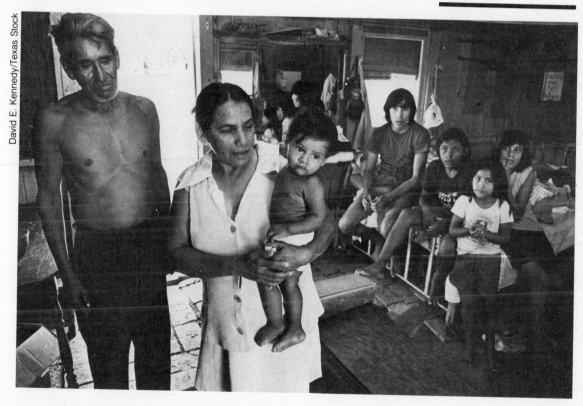

David E. Kennedy/Texas Stock

children, in the traditional pattern of upward mobility followed by many other American ethnic groups (Kilson, 1981; Loury, 1984).

Those who hold this view don't argue that blacks and other minorities no longer face serious problems. But they argue that these problems are now due mainly to cultural deficiencies and the effects of *past*, rather than present, racial discrimination.

For some (though by no means all) of these theorists, this growing separation between a healthy, thriving middle class and a "pathological" lower class also implies that many of the policies developed to combat racial inequality in recent years need to be reconsidered. They argue that affirmative action and other antidiscrimination programs designed to overcome barriers caused by racial discrimination are less and less important today — and may even be counterproductive. Government transfer programs, especially AFDC, are often held largely responsible for the growth and persistence of the minority lower class.

How accurate are these views? The best evidence suggests that they contain some important insights, but also considerable exaggeration. A minority "middle class" *has* emerged — but it isn't as affluent, as secure, or as free from the impact of discrimination as some theorists have argued. And it has suffered serious setbacks in the less favorable economic and political climate of more recent years. At the other end of the spectrum, the relationships among poverty, family disorganization, welfare, and economic discrimination are far more complex than this argument suggests.

A Growing Middle Class?

It's true that the minority middle class has grown. According to one recent study, the proportion of black families who could be considered either "middle class" or "affluent" rose from less than half in 1950 to more than two-thirds by 1980 (Billingsley, 1987, p. 108). But several things make this growth less encouraging than it first seems.

First, minority families achieved middle-class status in recent years primarily by putting more people to work. It's only in black families headed by a married couple — *and* with both spouses working in the paid labor force — that income levels have come even to approach (at 82 percent) those of middle-class white families. In married-couple black families in which the wife didn't work outside the home, family income was only about 60 percent that of whites. (The figures are similar, only a little less extreme at both ends, for Hispanic families.) The overall rising incomes in these dual-earner minority families mask the fact that minority men still make far less money than white men and that black couples make an income approaching that of whites only because the wives work more regularly and more often than wives in white families (Shaw, 1981).

Even these more affluent and hard-working minority families, moreover, represent what one writer calls a "precarious middle class" — one in which the possibility of downward mobility is always present (Billingsley, 1987, p. 109). The University of Michigan's study of 5,000 American families found that blacks are far more likely than whites to fall out of the upper levels of the income scale, if they've arrived there at all. Only two out of every one hundred black men, for example, earned enough money to keep them in the top fifth of the income distribution for 4 years in a row — versus eleven out of one hundred whites (Duncan, 1984, p. 133). The "snapshot" picture of an apparently stable middle class, in short, is misleading; the number of minorities who manage to remain in that position for any length of time is drastically smaller than the number of whites.

Finally, statistics on income alone understate the differences in economic conditions between minority and white families in America. As we saw in Chapter 4, the distribution of *wealth* is in many ways a more telling measure of economic power and well-being. And here the racial and ethnic gaps are vastly wider. We've just seen that white family income is about one and one-half times that of Hispanic families, on average, and closer to twice that of blacks. But white households have *eleven* times the net worth of black households and almost eight times that of Hispanics. (*Net worth,* again, means total assets minus debts.) And while less than one in ten white households have zero — or negative — wealth, a third of black and a fourth of Hispanic households do. Some minority families, then, have "made it" if we measure "making it" by the size of their paychecks. But far fewer have accumulated the kind of assets that can confer economic power or cushion the impact of economic troubles, such as loss of a job.

Minority Poverty and Family Structure

Substantial economic gains, then, have taken place for a growing part of the minority population. But (1) these gains were largely confined to a relatively small proportion of families that are both intact and in which both husband and wife worked outside the home, (2) they were achieved in part only through extra work on the part of minority families, (3) the affluence of these families is often precarious, and (4) they have rarely accumulated much wealth. And the other side of the picture of minority progress is far gloomier. At that end of the scale, it is widely agreed that things have gone from bad to worse. Why?

The growth of minority poverty in recent years, even in times of economic growth and lower unemployment, is often linked to the breakup of the conventional husband and wife family and the resulting rise in the proportion of minority families headed by women. Some observers have even argued that minority poverty and the social problems that flow from it are the result of family instability *rather than of discrimination* (Gilder, 1981, Chapter 6). According to this argument, since intact minority families have done so well in recent years, the source of poverty and other social problems among minorities must be the growth of female-headed families. Thus, one writer argues that female-headed families "regardless of race, display a seemingly endemic incapacity to foster social mobility comparable to husband-wife and male-headed families" (Kilson, 1981, p. 61). Such families tend to "pass on interpersonal pathologies," which "result in low proclivity for coping and achievement."

Again, there is a kernel of truth here. The growth of families maintained by women *is* strongly related to the trends in minority poverty and income inequality. Such families are much more likely to be poor and to need public assistance. And among some minority groups, especially blacks and Puerto Ricans, the growth of female-headed families has been especially rapid. By the middle of the 1980s more than two out of five black and Puerto Rican families were maintained by a woman, as compared to less than one in eight white families, and two-thirds of black children in these families and almost three-fourths of Hispanic children were poor (U.S. Bureau of the Census, 1986c, p. 152).

But this isn't the whole story, as a 1982 Census Bureau study made clear. The Census researchers estimated what the poverty rate *would* have been in 1980 *if* there had been no increase in the proportion of families headed by women. They found that the family changes *were* important but not the only factor. In 1980 the black family poverty rate was about 29 percent — only a little lower than in 1970. Adjusted for changes in family composition, the 1980 rate would have been about 20 percent. In other words, without the growth in the proportion of families headed by women, black poverty would have dropped by a third. A substantial difference — but even so, one in five black families would still have been poor.

This suggests that the impact of the rising number of minorities families headed by women needs to be put in careful perspective. The breakup of the conventional family doesn't necessarily lead to poverty; nor is maintaining an intact family a guarantee against poverty, especially for minorities.

While over half of all familes headed by Hispanic or black women are poor, for example, only a little over a fourth of families headed by a non-Hispanic white woman are. On the other hand, about a *fifth* of *intact* Hispanic families are poor — a rate not all that much higher than that of non-Hispanic white families headed by a single woman. And a substantial proportion of minority families headed by *men* are found not just in the ranks of the poor but of the persistently poor. In the University of Michigan study, about 20 percent of families that were poor at least eight out of ten years were headed by working-age black men (*Employment and Training Reporter*, 1982, p. 98).

Clearly, then, something besides family disruption alone is responsible for the higher rates of poverty among minority families. What is it? To understand the continuing racial inequality in economic well-being and the risks of poverty, we need to look beyond the (admittedly important) role of family disruption — to the world of work.

Minorities and Jobs

Work, or the lack of work, decisively shapes the way all of us live. So it isn't surprising that the distinctive pattern of significant gains for some groups coupled with stagnation and even decline for others is intimately connected to the kinds of jobs members of those groups have held — if any — and the kind of money they've earned at work.

As with income and poverty, trends in minority employment are a mixture of good news and bad news. Minorities have made real gains in breaking into jobs that were once almost exclusively the preserve of whites. They still have a long way to go, and the celebrations of the arrival of genuine equality are premature. But today, the chances of blacks or Hispanics getting high-level jobs with good pay are considerably better than they have been in the past, and the chances of their being confined in the lowest-paid, poorest-status jobs, though still harshly disproportionate, are less overwhelming.

But there is an underside to this progress. While the proportion of minority lawyers, bank managers, and engineers has risen, so has the proportion who are unemployed or who have dropped out of the labor force altogether. And even among those who work regularly, substantial inequalities in wages and earnings remain — inequalities that are not wholly explained by differences in the skills, education, age, or other qualifications that different groups bring to the labor market.

Let's look first at the most troubling part of the problem: minority joblessness.

Minority Joblessness: Bad and Getting Worse

Joblessness has become a major crisis for minorities in America. Minority unemployment rates are far higher than those of whites. And for some groups — including black youth and minority men in the economically stricken areas of the old industrial "heartland" — joblessness has reached levels that can only be described as disastrous.

Figure 5-2 shows that unemployment is much higher for blacks and Hispanics (especially Puerto Ricans) than for whites. But — as bad as these statistics are — they understate the growing severity of the problem.

To begin with, they don't count everyone who is actually out of work. As we'll see in more detail in Chapter 8, the official unemployment rate includes only the jobless who are actively looking for work. But the number of jobless people who have stopped looking for a job is probably almost as large as the number who are "officially" unemployed. According to studies by the National Urban League, inclusion of all those "hidden unemployed" would give us a true unemployment rate for blacks that's almost double the official figure — about 28 percent in 1984, versus the official 15 percent (Tidwell, 1987, p. 223).

And joblessness is even worse for the young. Teenagers of all races have higher unemployment rates than adults. But the difficulties of youth in finding and keeping jobs are greatly aggravated by color. The official unemployment rate for white teenagers, though more than twice the rate for white adults, is about the same as the rate for blacks of *all* ages. Meanwhile, even the official rates for minority teenagers, let alone the "hidden" rates, have reached catastrophic proportions: A quarter of Hispanic youth and better than two in five black youth are unemployed.

Figure 5-2
The minority job crisis: Unemployment rates by race and Spanish origin, 1984

Source: Economic Report of the President, 1986, p. 296; U.S. Bureau of the Census, "Persons of Spanish Origin in the United States, March 1985," Washington, D.C., 1985, p. 4.

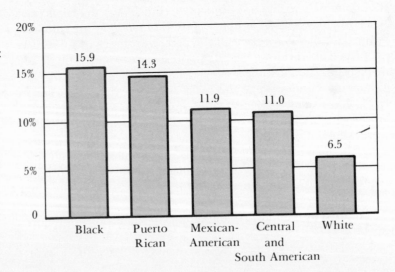

The numbers are even worse in many inner cities. A recent study of young black men in Boston, Chicago, and Philadelphia found less than half of those between the ages of 16 and 24 working (Freeman and Holzer, 1986, p. 8). In Detroit, Buffalo, and Pittsburgh, less than two out of five blacks of working age have a job (Swinton, 1987, p. 62).

As we'll see, this has enormous consequences for every aspect of minority life. It is a main source of the stunningly high minority poverty rates we've described. It increases the probability of family disruption, teenage pregnancy, and domestic violence. It increases the risks of street crime, drug abuse, infant mortality, and preventable disease. And — like the poverty to which it contributes — minority joblessness is growing. From the middle of the 1970s to the start of the 1980s, the unemployment rate for black men averaged about 11 percent; from the beginning of the 1980s until 1986, about 15 percent. Like minority poverty, too, it has proven to be disturbingly impervious to economic growth. A young black man in the United States was more likely to be out of work during the economic "recovery" of the mid-1980s than in the depth of the recession of the mid-1970s.

This doesn't mean that economic growth has *no* effect on minority unemployment. It does mean that the broad economic changes we described in Chapter 3 — the decline of some manufacturing industries, the loss of jobs even in thriving industries to automation and to low-wage countries, the failure of the emerging "service" economy to provide enough new jobs — have struck even harder at minorities than at whites.

The grave problems of joblessness for some minority groups, particularly urban blacks and Puerto Ricans, lend some credence to the view that their economic problems are concentrated among a workless urban underclass and that problems have receded for those with a foothold in the labor market. As the economist Richard Freeman put it in a review of black economic progress since the mid-1960s:

Minority Earnings: Differences and Explanations

> The big problem in the labor market [for minorities] is not wage or occupational discrimination within businesses, but lack of employment altogether. . . . For those "in the system," particularly those with more education and better background, the improvement in the job market after 1964 has greatly reduced economic differences between blacks and whites. For those who have not yet entered the mainstream of the labor market, for whatever reasons, sizeable problems remain. (Freeman, 1978a, p. 68)

What this says about the plight of those outside the system is on target. But the assumption that discrimination in wages and jobs for

Peeter Vilms/Jeroboam, Inc.

In the 1970s, some minorities began to reach the higher rungs of the job ladder . . .

while others didn't get on the ladder at all.

United Press International

the employed is no longer a problem is premature. In fact, substantial inequalities in earnings remain between minorities and whites even among full-time workers. And though it is difficult to pin down, with the methods of social science, how *much* of those inequalities are the result of discrimination, research shows that significant inequality remains even when a variety of factors are taken into account.

Table 5-2 shows the very large racial differences in earnings among people working full time: And it also shows that Hispanics are much more severely disadvantaged in the job market than their unemployment rate alone would suggest. They work more often than blacks but earn even less.

How do we explain these low wages? Differences in regional distribution, age structure, and levels of education, skills, and training explain part of the disparity (Sowell, 1981). But, even in combination, they do not explain *all* of it. Part of the explanation, for example, is that blacks and Hispanics are concentrated in the South and Southwest, respectively, where wages for *all* workers are lower. But minority workers make less money than whites in *every* region (Bianchi, 1981, p. 99; National Commission for Employment Policy, 1982; Reimers, 1982).

Another part of the explanation is the differing age structure of the various racial and ethnic groups. A group with a higher proportion of young people of working age will have lower average earnings (as well as higher rates of unemployment). Younger workers have had less time to gain the skills, education, and experience that lead to higher earnings, and they are more likely to work intermittently, moving in and out of jobs. Since most minority populations, particularly Hispanics, are younger on average than the white population, age may help account for what appear to be racially determined inequalities.

And indeed, age distribution *does* explain *some* of the differences in earnings (and in unemployment) among the different groups. But studies show that the effect of age is small (U.S. Commission on Civil Rights, 1982b, pp. 50–53; National Commission for Employment

Category	Median wage	As percentage of white median wage
White	$370	100
Black	$291	79
Hispanic	$277	75

Source: Data from *Employment and Earnings,* January 1987, p. 214.

Table 5-2
The racial earnings gap: Median weekly earnings of full-time wage and salary workers, 1986

Policy, 1982, p. 51). And when we look at racial and ethnic economic inequalities by age, we can also see another troubling pattern. Inequality in earnings *increases* sharply with age. Youth of *all* groups start out in the labor market by working intermittently, in poorly paying jobs. But white men move *out* of those jobs much more often and much more quickly, acquiring work experience, skills, and job advancement in a much steadier fashion — while minority men all too often remain trapped in them (U.S. Commission on Civil Rights, 1982b; Shapiro, 1984).

Still another part of the explanation for racial inequalities in earnings involves education and skill levels. Workers with limited education and few marketable skills, unsurprisingly, make less money. And though differences in education level are narrowing, they still exist, particularly between Hispanics and whites. How much does this affect their different fortunes in the labor market?

Some, but not enough to account for all of the inequality in earnings. Studies show that limited schooling has important consequences for Hispanics' jobs and earnings, which are compounded by the language difficulties still faced by many Hispanics. Up to 45 percent of Hispanic adults, according to one estimate, have difficulties with English; almost half of Mexican-Americans and two out of five Puerto Ricans aged 25 to 34 have not graduated from high school (*Statistical Abstract of the United States*, 1986, p. 135). But though these differences are real and important, they don't explain all of the inequality these groups suffer in the labor market. At *every* level of education, there are still large differences in earnings (*and* in unemployment) between whites and minority groups.

Black men with four years of college earn less than white men with four years of *high school*, and Hispanic men with four years of college earn only slightly more. More elaborate research consistently finds that what researchers call the *returns to education* (the payoff in jobs and earnings for each further stage of school completed) are greater for whites than for minorities.

Even studies that have put all of these factors together — region, age, education, and others — still find that a substantial amount of inequality is left unexplained (Bianchi, 1981; Darity, 1982; Reimers, 1982; U.S. Commission on Civil Rights, 1982b). Not all of that unexplained inequality can *necessarily* be attributed to current discrimination, but the presumption that discrimination in jobs and earnings is still with us is strong.

Moreover, the argument that economic inequality is now due mainly to "background" characteristics, *rather* than current discrimination, sidesteps the fact that many of those characteristics are themselves the product of discrimination *outside* the labor market. Thus, despite the growing equality in levels of schooling completed among

Minority youth often
remain trapped in
low-wage jobs.

blacks and whites, few would argue that the *quality* of the schools they
attend is the same — or that the differences in school quality are
unrelated to racial discrimination. Poor health also influences the
chances of success in the job market, and the risks of poor health, as
we'll see in detail in Chapter 9, are increased for minorities — in part
because of discrimination in living conditions and the quality of
health care.

Part of the reason for the differences in economic condition between
minorities and whites, then, is that whites are more likely to have jobs;
another is that they are paid more when they have them. Related to
both is the fact that whites still have far *better* jobs. And though this
gap has narrowed considerably as a result of antidiscrimination pro-

**The Job Ladder:
How Much
Progress?**

grams and some favorable economic changes, it is still very wide. And it may become wider in the future.

Consider first the types of jobs minorities have. As can be seen in Table 5-3, blacks and Hispanics are greatly underrepresented in higher-level jobs — as executives, professionals, and, for blacks, skilled craft workers. On the other hand, minorities are *overrepre-sented* in lower-level jobs — as service workers, laborers, and farm-workers, for example. Together, blacks and Hispanics accounted for a little more than 16 percent of working Americans. But they were less than 10 percent of professionals, executives, and managers — and 25 percent of laborers and over 35 percent of private household workers.

These disparities matter — in part because, as the table also shows, they translate into wide differences in economic status. In 1985, executives earned, on average, about $31,000 a year; laborers, a little over $7,000; farmworkers, under *$4,000* (both of the latter provided less than the poverty level for a family of three).

What about trends over time? Here the picture looks somewhat more encouraging. As Table 5-4 shows, blacks made up a substantially higher proportion of lawyers, bankers, doctors, and engineers in the United States in the 1980s than at the start of the 1970s; and fewer were laborers, farmworkers, and household servants. But though these gains are real and important, they must be qualified in several ways.

Table 5-3
The job gap

Occupation	Median earnings (1985)	Percent of total workers (1986) who are: Black	Hispanic
All occupations	$17,779	9.9	6.6
Executives, managers, and administrators	$30,792	5.2	3.7
Professionals	$29,698	6.7	3.3
Technicians	$23,367	8.2	4.0
Sales workers	$20,058	5.7	4.9
Service workers	$ 8,123	16.6	9.0
Private household workers	NA	23.9	12.9
Precision production and craft workers	$18,956	7.5	7.7
Machine operators and assemblers	$17,000	14.7	12.1
Laborers, handlers, and helpers	$ 7,330	16.6	10.5
Farmworkers	$ 3,968	6.5	10.5

Source: Employment and Earnings, January 1987, pp. 179–183.

Occupation	Black men		Black women	
	1972	1980	1972	1980
Total	8.6	8.4	11.0	10.6
Accountants	2.1	3.6	5.2	7.4
Computer specialists	3.5	4.1	6.5	9.3
Engineers	1.4	2.2	*	*
Physicians and dentists	2.1	2.1	*	*
Lawyers and judges	1.3	3.1	*	5.0
College teachers	3.6	3.3	*	7.1
Bank officials and financial managers	*	2.6	5.4	5.3
Postal clerks	16.0	14.8	*	4.6
Carpenters	5.1	4.4	26.7	32.7
Electricians	2.8	4.1	*	*
Clothing ironers and pressers	28.9	*	*	*
Laundry and drycleaning operators	24.0	21.9	38.4	40.4
Busdrivers	21.7	24.0	28.7	23.3
Taxicab drivers and chauffeurs	22.5	24.0	7.0	13.1
Laborers	19.2	15.5	*	*
Construction laborers	24.7	15.4	12.0	12.2
Garbage collectors	33.3	32.8	*	*
Farm laborers	19.3	14.3	*	*
Cleaning service workers	25.4	22.8	23.5	15.7
Health service workers	24.5	32.1	35.3	30.2
Private household workers	*	*	23.7	21.0
Maids and servants	*	*	39.8	31.9
			71.1	52.5

Table 5-4
Climbing the job ladder: Blacks as a percent of all employed men and women in selected occupations, 1972 and 1980

* Data not shown where numerator is less than 4,000 or denominator is less than 35,000.

Source: Adapted from Diane N. Westcott, "Blacks in the 1970s: Did They Scale the Job Ladder?" *Monthly Labor Review,* June 1982, p. 32. Reprinted with permission.

To begin with, the improvement in minority jobs in the 1970s and 1980s came at a much slower pace than it did in the 1960s. The number of blacks in professional jobs, for example, grew only about half as fast in the 1970s as in the previous decade of economic expansion and the first flush of the civil rights effort (Westcott, 1982, p. 29). And an important part of the progress in jobs represents a shift in the American economy, as a whole, away from farm work and domestic service — a shift that helped blacks, in particular, move up the job ladder. Just before World War II, two out of five black men worked on farms, and six out of every ten black women who worked were domestic servants (Allen and Farley, 1986, p. 286). The decline of agriculture and domestic service coincided with the opening of new opportunities in better-paying jobs, especially in manufacturing for men and in clerical work for women. But that specific shift won't happen again.

Still more important, even considerable gains have left us with huge disparities in job chances between minorities and whites. Thus, although the percentage of black lawyers and engineers has more than doubled since the early 1970s, only about one in forty lawyers or engineers is black. And that's in a society in which about one in ten workers is black. In addition, the flip side of having the opportunity to work in a good job is not having to work in a bad one; and whites, who make up about 90 percent of the employed work force, make up only a little over half of the cleaners and servants.

Overall, then, the picture shows both encouraging change and troubling continuity — a continuity that is apparent not only in the still-small numbers of blacks in many of the highest-level jobs but also in their longstanding concentration in some of the poorest-paying and lowest-status jobs in America. In 1972 the job category with the highest percentage of black men was garbage collectors; it still was in 1980. The job category with the highest percentage of black women — in both years — was maids and servants.

Racial Inequality and the Future

Recent trends in racial inequality, then, present a mixed picture. On the positive side, important gains have been made, especially in occupational status, helping to bridge the economic gap between minorities and whites. But those gains, though impressive, have been limited in crucial ways. *Most* of the progress against inequality took place in the late 1960s and early 1970s; it has slowed or even reversed since then. And even during the period of greatest progress, the gains were unevenly distributed among the minority population. The growth of an upwardly mobile, relatively affluent middle class, though often exaggerated, was a significant development. But it was accompanied by the stubborn persistence of wide — even growing — disparities in rates of poverty and unemployment, especially in the inner cities. While the chances of upward social mobility improved for some, the chances of being trapped in an urban underclass increased for others.

What is the outlook for the future? On balance, it's troubling. To a large extent, the progress against racial inequality was the result of several *specific* favorable trends, some of which are not likely to be repeated, at least to the same extent, in the future. And new developments, both in the economy and in public policy, threaten to undermine the progress that has been made. We've looked at some of these developments already in discussing the outlook for poverty and income inequality in Chapter 4. Now let's look closer at what they could mean for minorities.

We've already noted one bad omen. Some of the most dramatic recent gains for minorities resulted from broad social and economic changes that are unlikely to reappear, at least not with the same magnitude or intensity. Improvements in minority poverty rates and in income inequality were partly a by-product of the social and economic transformation that brought the South closer into line with the rest of the country. Likewise, some of the most significant improvements in

Economic Threats to Racial Equality

Asian-Americans: Trials of a "Successful" Minority

The experience of Asian-Americans is often taken as proof that anyone who really works at it can succeed in America in spite of discrimination. The same kinds of discrimination and exclusion that are often held responsible for some groups' poverty, dependency, and social pathology, in this view, have actually strengthened the resolve of others to get ahead. One noted sociologist, for example, drew these lessons from the status of Asian-Americans:

> The gross discrimination, the collective frustrations, to which Chinese and Japanese have been subjected ordinarily result in a pattern of poor education, low income, high crime rate, and unstable family life. . . . Efforts to assist members of such "problem minorities" in achieving parity with the general population have seldom been altogether successful. However, these two minorities . . . themselves broke through the barriers of prejudice and, by such key indices as education and income, surpassed

the average levels of native-born whites. This anomalous record, like the earlier one of Jews, challenges the premises from which the etiologies of poverty, crime, illegitimacy and other social ills are typically deduced. (Peterson, 1978, pp. 65–66)

In other words, from this perspective, discrimination creates real problems only for groups who are already, in some sense, "problem" minorities. This separation of different groups into problem minorities versus successful ones, however, has two unfortunate consequences. One, often noted by Asian-American writers, is that the image of success tends to mask the real problems the "successful" group faces. Asian-American communities have often wound up on the short end of government funds for social programs because of this bias; for that matter, they are often ignored even in the collection of government statistics (U.S. Commission on Civil Rights, 1980a).

The second consequence of the success stereotype is that it implies that other groups' relative lack of success is their own fault. In this view, if blacks or Puerto Ricans haven't "made it" in American society to the same extent as Japanese- or Chinese-Americans, the problem must lie primarily in their attitudes or culture and not in continued discrimination by the larger society — or in economic disadvantage. After all, Asian-Americans have suffered their own harsh history of exclusion and persecution; as recently as the 1940s, Japanese-Americans were interned in camps and lost much of their property.

Some version of this reasoning has been used to argue against special consideration for other minorities. Blacks, Puerto Ricans, Mexican-Americans, and others are urged to pull themselves up by their own bootstraps, with the same perseverance that has presumably brought status and success to Asian-Americans (Sowell, 1979; Glazer, 1981).

What should we make of this argument? A careful analysis of the complex historical differences among the various Asian-American groups, and between those groups and other minorities, would take much more space than we have here. (For some useful leads, see Steinberg, 1980; Bonacich and Modell, 1981; Lieberson, 1981.) For now,

let's look harder at the stereotype of Asian-American success itself, on which the broader arguments about ethnic culture and progress are based.

Have Asian-Americans really succeeded in America? Naturally, the answer depends on what we choose to define as "success." Without undervaluing the very real achievements of these groups, a closer look shows that their progress — while substantial (see Figure 5-3) — is also limited in revealing ways.

It's important, first of all, to distinguish the experience of different Asian-American groups. Japanese-Americans uniformly show the highest income and the lowest rates of poverty, while among Chinese-Americans and Filipino-Americans, median income is considerably lower and rates of poverty are relatively high. Like blacks and Hispanics, the Chinese- and Filipino-American communities show a sharp division between those with better jobs and higher income and those suffering high rates of poverty and rising unemployment, especially for youth.

Success, then, hasn't been uniform among Asian-American groups. Data from the 1980 census indicate the dimensions of poverty among Asian/Pacific Islanders, a diverse category that mixes the experiences of quite different groups — but the data are illustrative. In California, the state with by far

Figure 5-3
Median family income by race and Hispanic origin, 1979

Source: U.S. Bureau of the Census, *1980 Census of Population and Housing, Supplementary Report, Provisional Estimates of Social, Economic, and Housing Characteristics,* Washington, D.C., March 1982.

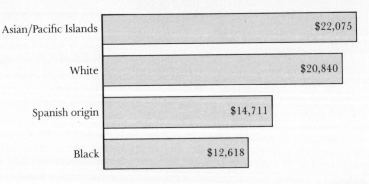

Asian/Pacific Islands	$22,075
White	$20,840
Spanish origin	$14,711
Black	$12,618

Note: Asian/Pacific Islands combines Japanese-, Chinese-, and Filipino-American groups, as well as other Pacific- and Asian-American groups. This masks important differences among the specific groups in family income; not all have higher income than whites.

the largest Asian/Pacific Island population, their rate of poverty was about 13 percent in 1979 — well below the Hispanic and black rates, but well above the white rate. In New York, a state with a high proportion of Chinese-Americans within the Asian population, the rate was about 15 percent, one and a half times the white rate. And in Texas, at 23 percent, Asian/Pacific Island poverty was double the white rate and approached that of Hispanics and blacks.

But there were more subtle problems with the "success" stereotype. Most income comparisons fail to adjust for the fact that Asian-Americans are, on the average, more highly educated than whites, and bring, in other ways as well, *higher* qualifications to the labor market. Studies adjusting for these differences show that in terms of income and occupational status, Asian-Americans fare less well than whites *with comparable educations*. A study of minority gains in academic employment, for example, found that when the quality of their training and professional accomplishments were considered, Asian-American faculty members were consistently underpaid relative to both whites *and blacks*. "The presumption," the economist Richard Freeman noted, "is of some market discrimination" (1978b, p. 197).

Asian-Americans — like other minorities — also have to put more family members to work to make the same income as whites. When income is adjusted for the fact that Asian-Americans average 1.7 workers per household, versus 1.3 for whites, their income is only about four-fifths of white income (Takaki, 1985). In a 1978 study, the U.S. Commission on Civil Rights calculated the earnings of different minority groups as a percentage of white earnings, both before and after differences in age, state of residence, education, and weeks and hours of work were taken into account. When all these factors were considered, some groups' earnings relative to whites' improved over the picture given by the conventional statistics. But the opposite held for both

Chinese- and Japanese-Americans. Both have high median earnings, measured conventionally — higher than whites in the case of Japanese-Americans. And both improved through the early 1970s relative to the white average. But both groups tend to be older, to live in high-income areas, to be better educated, and to work longer and more regularly than whites. When these facts are considered, the adjusted earnings of both groups *dropped* relative to those of whites — and both turned out to have *lost* ground during the 1970s. In fact, measured this way, *the relative earnings of Chinese-Americans were the lowest of any minority group in America* (U.S. Commission on Civil Rights, 1978, p. 54).

Occupationally, Asian-Americans have done well — but again, not uniformly. Asian-Americans are highly concentrated in professional and technical fields. More than 30 percent of Asian-Americans, according to data from the Equal Employment Opportunity Commission, are in those two categories — double the proportion of whites and more than four times that of blacks and Hispanics. But they are also underrepresented in managerial and administrative positions. Though the proportion of Asian-Americans in those positions is nearly twice the comparable proportion of blacks, it is only about half that of whites. One interpretation of this distinctive pattern is that though Asian-Americans have high levels of education and achievement, they have only rarely been able to translate those qualities into economic power or official influence. Such a view is borne out by the position of Asian-Americans in business. According to a report from the U.S. Office of Minority Business Enterprise, Asian-Americans "are *not* in the mainstream of American business" and "are not competing well in securing a proportionate share of the market" (U.S. Commission on Civil Rights, 1980a, p. 10). Asian-Americans make up less than one-half of 1 percent of the officers and directors of the largest 1,000 American companies (Ramirez, 1986, p. 152).

occupational status came about mainly through one-time shifts in the structure of jobs: from domestic service to clerical work, from farm labor to manufacturing industries. It's conceivable that similar changes may come again — but it isn't clear what they would be or when they might come.

And one of the most troubling portents for the future is that some of the jobs and industries in which minorities have made the most gains are precisely those that are being most undermined by the massive, rapid changes now under way in the American economy. Since the start of World War II, for example, well-paying blue-collar jobs in manufacturing have been a main avenue of job security and mobility for blacks and Mexican-Americans. But these jobs are threatened as many basic industries have either undergone decline or are "restructuring" to meet growing international competition. In the late 1970s, for example, black workers held about 9 percent of all jobs. But they held more than 15 percent of the jobs in auto and steel, two of the industries most hurt by foreign competition and now rapidly shifting to greater automation and a smaller work force (B. Anderson, 1982, p. 8). More generally, blacks made up about 18 percent of

The State of Native America

American Indians — native Americans — are often neglected in discussions of the social problems of minorities in America. Part of the reason for this neglect may be that their numbers are relatively small (about 1.4 million, including Eskimos and Aleutian natives, according to the 1980 census); many are also isolated in rural areas and on reservations where their problems are less publicly visible. And urban native Americans, though a substantial population in several cities, are nevertheless a group that is dwarfed in size and political influence by others. During the 1970s, too, the energy boom in the American west brought some wealth to some of the native American tribes, which sometimes led to exaggerated portraits of newly affluent reservations growing rich from their mineral rights. But data from the 1980 census show that native Americans are one of the most severely disadvantaged groups in America.

Nearly half of all native Americans live in the five states with the largest native American populations: California, Oklahoma, Arizona, New Mexico, and North Carolina. As a *proportion* of the population, they are most highly concentrated in New Mexico — about 8 percent of the state's residents.

New Mexico can serve as a microcosm of the condition of native Americans in the United States as a whole. In 1979 the median family income among New Mexico's native Americans was $10,826; among blacks, $12,063; and among whites, $18,429. Thirty-eight percent of native American families in the state were below the poverty line, compared to 10 percent of white and 26 percent of black families. And among those below the poverty line, native Americans were typically poorer than either blacks or whites.

Similar disparities show up in employment and education. The native American unem-

unskilled and semiskilled manufacturing workers at the beginning of the 1980s, but the role of less-skilled blue-collar labor seems likely to decline *permanently* in the American economy. Similarly, Hispanics, who made up less than 6 percent of workers in American industry, were about 11 percent of manufacturing laborers (*Employment and Training Report of the President,* 1983, p. 340).

The accelerating flight of jobs and industries from central cities also has an unequal impact on minorities. The industries most likely to shut down or relocate tend to be those with a higher proportion of minority workers; and those that start up anew in the suburbs and outlying areas tend to hire fewer minority workers. Thus, between 1970 and 1976, the city of Chicago lost 92,000 jobs, about 7 percent of the city's total. But of those jobs, 50,000 were in predominantly black communities. Meanwhile, the counties surrounding the city, where the number of jobs *grew* by 72 percent, had very small minority populations (U.S. Commission on Civil Rights, Illinois Advisory Committee, 1981, pp. 20–42).

So the problem is not just that recession and economic decline hurt minorities disproportionately. More ominously, the new patterns of

ployment rate in 1980 was about 15 percent in New Mexico, compared to 13 percent for blacks and 6 percent for whites. Thirty-two percent of young native Americans aged 16 to 19 were neither working nor attending school. Native Americans, indeed, were the only racial/ethnic group in the state whose *median* level of education was below high-school graduation.

For native Americans living on reservations, these problems are even worse than they are for the population as a whole. Many large reservations are among the most depressed pockets of poverty, joblessness, educational deprivation, and famly breakup in the United States. On the largest reservation in the country, the Navajo reservation extending through parts of New Mexico, Arizona, and Utah, the poverty rate in 1980 was *50* percent. Only a third of residents older than 25 had completed high school; three out of ten youths aged 16 to 19 were high-school dropouts. On the Pine Ridge reservation in South Dakota, 49 percent of the

population was below the poverty line, the unemployment rate was more than 21 percent, and less than 50 percent of all children under 18 lived with both parents.

At least on the surface, as measured by census indicators, living standards are somewhat better for urban native Americans — but they remain severely disadvantaged. In Los Angeles (which, with about 19,000 native Americans, is the largest single urban concentration) native American family income, at $16,556, was well above that of blacks ($12,778) in 1980 but far below that of whites ($23,300).

Sources: Data from U.S. Bureau of the Census, *Current Population Reports,* Series P-20, No. 374, "Population Profile of the United States, 1981," Washington, D.C., 1982, p. 22; U.S. Bureau of the Census, *1980 Census of Population, General Social and Economic Characteristics,* volumes for New Mexico (pp. 40–266) and South Dakota (pp. 268–269); U.S. Bureau of the Census, *1980 Census of Population and Housing, Advance Estimates of Social, Economic, and Housing Characteristics,* volumes for California (p. 131), New York (p. 112), and Minnesota (p. 67), Washington, D.C.: Government Printing Office, 1983.

economic *recovery* may not, by themselves, help minorities' economic situation very much. At worst, the changes now under way in the national economy threaten to block some of the most important past avenues to economic security and upward mobility without offering substantial new alternatives. Economic growth itself, in other words, once a key means of reducing racial inequality, now may even widen it — in the absence of programs specifically designed to ensure that its benefits are made equally accessible to all groups.

Minorities, Public Policy, and the Welfare State

These economic trends are not inevitable: they are shaped by deliberate public policies. Policies that encourage industries to pack up and move from one state to another, or out of the country, in search of lower labor costs, lighter taxes, and fewer regulations aggravate racial inequality through their disproportionate impact on minority workers. Likewise, policies to tighten the supply of money or credit in order to slow down the economy widen the racial economic gap by increasing unemployment unequally among white and minority workers.

Even more clearly, public policies designed to curb the growth of government — and of the welfare state in particular — have disturbing implications for minorities. We saw in Chapter 4 that much of the progress against economic inequality in the United States since World War II has been connected with the growth of government. This is particularly true for progress against minority poverty and racial inequality, for several reasons.

The growth of government employment has been a main source of minority gains in jobs and income in recent years; growth in the private economy, on the other hand, has brought disappointingly small benefits for minorities. Only 5 percent of all new jobs in private industry went to blacks, for example, during the 1970s. But minority representation in government employment grew substantially. A 1982 study estimated that fully 55 percent of the growth in employment for black workers between 1960 and 1976 was in the public sector, as compared to 26 percent of the growth in *white* employment. And much of the growth in professional and managerial jobs for blacks in this period was in education and social welfare occupations (B. Anderson, 1982, p. 7; Brown and Erie, 1982). Moreover, these public-sector jobs have proven more stable than jobs in the private economy; blacks in public jobs have been less likely to suffer downward mobility (Hout, 1984). So the recent drive to cut back government spending and employment, in the name of freeing the energies of the private sector, threatens to block what has been a main ladder of upward mobility, especially for the minority middle class.

An even more troubling development is the sharp reduction in the social programs that have provided jobs and transfer payments for the minority poor. We've seen that minority unemployment has remained at crisis levels, and that even in periods of economic recovery, a significant part of the black community remains in a state of "permanent recession." Without public employment and training programs, minority joblessness would have been even worse. It's been estimated, for instance, that the much-criticized Comprehensive Employment and Training Act (CETA) employed in the late 1970s almost one in every four black teenagers who were employed at all. The argument that similar jobs will now be provided by a revitalized private economy requires us to assume that the private economy will prove capable of providing steady employment for groups it has never steadily employed in the past — and that is a very large assumption indeed. We have, in fact, been cutting spending on jobs and training while "unleashing" the private economy for many years. But the job crisis among minorities has gotten worse, not better.

The reduction of government spending on *income transfers* also affects the future of racial inequality. The minority poor are even more dependent on the welfare state for basic survival than are the white poor, especially because of the high proportion of minority women heading families with dependent children. Under present conditions — with inadequate provisions for child care and job training — these families won't be helped greatly by the growth of the private economy alone.

The past few years have also seen an attack on the antidiscrimination and affirmative action programs that have been responsible for many of the economic gains minorities have achieved since the 1960s. Some argue that these programs, once necessary, have now done their job and can safely be de-emphasized, if not abandoned altogether. Others argue that they actually accomplished little that would not have been achieved anyway — and that they may even have hurt minorities' chances for equality by making them dependent on the help of the state rather than on their own efforts (Williams, 1982). But research consistently shows that without affirmative action programs minority gains in jobs and income would have been much less significant (Freeman, 1978a; B. Anderson, 1982; Leonard, 1984). Minority employment in good jobs, for example, grew much faster in companies that had government contracts — and thus were more directly subject to federal affirmative action guidelines (Rich, 1985).

The combination of cutbacks in government programs and the restructuring of the economy, then, has been especially hard on minorities in America. It has perpetuated — even exacerbated — the plight of the minority underclass and has undermined the security of the more successful. In the process, it has made us a less equal society. Whether this trend will continue depends both on the technological and economic changes that we can expect in the future and on the social policies we develop in response to them. We'll look at both in the second part of this book. First, however, we need to look at trends in another kind of inequality — that between men and women, the subject of Chapter 6.

Summary

This chapter has examined trends in economic inequality between minorities and whites. After narrowing slightly during the 1960s and early 1970s, the racial economic gap has once again been widening. Minorities remain overrepresented among the poor, and minority poverty has increased sharply.

Some writers have attributed these trends mainly to the high rates of family breakup among some minority groups. But though this is surely part of the explanation, it isn't all of it. Whatever their family structure, minorities tend to have lower incomes and greater risks of poverty than whites.

Another part of the explanation for the racial gaps in income and poverty is the difficulties minorities face in the job market. Minority joblessness is disproportionately high, and among some groups — especially black youth — it has reached disaster levels.

The problem of lack of jobs is compounded by low earnings for minority workers who are employed. Some of the disparity between minority and white earnings can be explained by educational differences, geographical concentration, and the younger age of the minority labor force. But these factors leave much of the earnings difference unexplained.

Still another part of the problem is the continued concentration of minorities in poor jobs. Though minorities have achieved important gains in breaking into more rewarding jobs, they remain greatly overrepresented in low-paying, dead-end occupations and underrepresented in higher-level jobs with better pay and greater opportunities for mobility.

The decline of blue-collar industries and the reductions in government spending and social programs threaten to reverse some of the gains minorities have made toward greater equality.

For Further Reading

Blauner, Robert. *Speaking of Race.* Berkeley: University of California Press, 1987.

Dunbar, Leslie, ed. *Minority Report.* New York: Pantheon, 1984.

Lieberson, Stanley. *A Piece of the Pie.* Berkeley, Calif.: University of California Press, 1981.

Reich, Michael. *Racial Inequality.* New York: Cambridge University Press, 1981.

Sowell, Thomas. *The Economics and Politics of Race.* New York: Morrow, 1983.

Steinberg, Stephen. *The Ethnic Myth: Race, Ethnicity, and Class in America.* Boston: Atheneum, 1980.

Wilson, William J. *The Declining Significance of Race.* Chicago: University of Chicago Press, 1978.

6

Social Inequality III: Gender

Like the drive for racial equality, the movement for women's equality came alive, and won many of its most significant gains, in the 1960s. A strong women's movement had been active in the nineteenth and early twentieth centuries but had declined during the Great Depression and during and after World War II. By the 1950s the position of women in American society was rarely raised as a public issue or considered a major subject for social science research. It had become what the feminist author Betty Friedan (1963) called a "problem that had no name."

Yet little more than a decade later, a revitalized women's movement began to transform public and private life in every corner of American society. This transformation was aided by some of the same laws and policies that helped pave the way for progress for minorities — the Civil Rights Act, laws requiring equal pay for equal work, and affirmative action programs. And, like the reaction to minority progress, there was soon a chorus of disapproval. Critics argued that the egalitarian impulse had gone too far for women as well as for other groups that had traditionally suffered discrimination. The efforts to fight present discrimination, however justified in the beginning, had, in this view, overstepped proper bounds.

Some argued that the attempts to ensure equality between the sexes in workplaces and schools were costly, unrealistic, and threatened to interfere with "rational business practice" and even with "the fundamental institutions of society" (Hoffman and Reed, 1981, p. 23). Others felt the drive for equality was upsetting a "natural" balance between men and women, with what could only be dire results for social and personal stability and family integrity (Gilder, 1981).

Affirmative action programs have been the most frequent target of these criticisms. They have been accused of fostering "discrimination in reverse" by penalizing qualified men — barring them from jobs, educations, and training in favor of less qualified women. One American senator publicly described affirmative action as "an assault upon America, conceived in lies and fostered with an irresponsibility so extreme as to verge upon the malign" (Senator Orrin Hatch, Republican from Utah, cited in *Working Women*, 1981, p. 2).

The criticism of antidiscrimination laws and policies usually rests on the belief either that women have already made enough (or too much) progress toward social and economic equality or that they would achieve more *without* the aid of government intervention. Even some feminist writers (though from a much more supportive viewpoint) began to argue in the 1980s that many of the most important battles to ensure women's equality in job opportunities and income had been largely won. At least by implication, women could now, in this view, safely concentrate their energies more on improving personal and family life (Friedan, 1981). And some younger women have been able to take the accomplishments of the women's movement for granted: As one 30-year-old lawyer put it, "I feel a certain sense of personal accomplishment and satisfaction with my own position and with my own ways of dealing with feminist issues, which don't seem to be as much of a problem as they used to be" (quoted in *New York Times*, December 1, 1986).

But just how much progress has *really* been made? In this chapter, we will look carefully at women's gains in jobs, income, and social services. We will consider the dimensions and sources of continuing economic inequality between men and women and of what some writers have called the "feminization" of poverty (Pearce, 1982). Finally, we will assess the prospects for women's equality in the future, in the light of recent economic developments and trends in public policy. Later chapters will take up, in greater detail, the position of women in the family, in health and medical care, and other areas.

Let's begin by considering one of the most important social changes of recent years — the rapid increase in the proportion of women in the American work force.

The "Revolution" in the Labor Force

At the turn of the century, less than one in five American women worked for pay outside their homes. By the 1980s, over half did. This dramatic change has appropriately been called a revolution (Smith, 1979), and it has had enormous effects on virtually every aspect of American life — from childrearing to the workplace, from patterns of unemployment to the relations between the sexes. Let's take a closer look at the nature and magnitude of this change.

Over the past decade, almost seven out of every ten new entrants to the American work force have been women. Between 1975 and 1985 alone, more than 13 million women entered the work force. By 1986, 55 percent of all women over the age of 16 were working outside the home (Table 6-1).

Figure 6-1 shows that the rapid increase of women in paid labor has been accompanied by a less dramatic, but steady, decline in the labor-force participation of men. As a result, the chances of a man or woman being in the work force have become increasingly similar. In 1950 a man was about two and a half times as likely to be in the paid

Table 6-1
Labor-force participation rates of men and women, by race, 1960–1986

| | Percentages | | |
	1960	1970	1986
Total			
Women	38	43	55
Men	83	80	76
By race			
White women	37	43	55
Black women	48	50	57
Ages 20–24			
Women	46	58	72
Men	88	83	86

Note: Figures for blacks include blacks and other races. Rates are rounded to nearest whole number.
Source: Adapted from *Employment and Earnings* (Washington, D.C.: Government Printing Office, January, 1987).

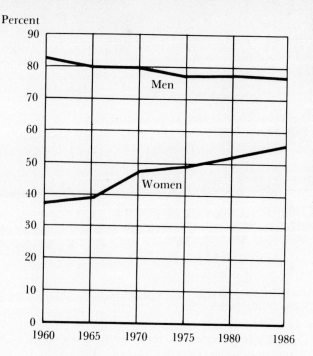

Figure 6-1
Trends in labor-force participation, by sex, 1960–1986.

Source: Data from *Statistical Abstract of the United States, 1982–1983* (Washington, D.C.: Government Printing Office, 1983), p. 377, and *Employment and Earnings* (Washington, D.C.: Government Printing Office, January 1987).

work force as a woman; by 1986 this had dropped to less than one and a half times.

But even these figures somewhat understate the changes in women's role in the labor force. Like most such statistics, they are a kind of snapshot that freezes the action at one point in time. But while about half of all women today are in the work force at any given point, more than *90 percent* of women alive today have been or will be working outside the home at *some* point in their lives. And while women's labor force participation as a whole is about 72 percent that of men's, it is over 80 percent of the comparable male rate for women aged 20 to 24.

To complete the picture of the "revolution" in women's work, we need to add two qualifications to the description of a recent rapid shift of women into paid labor. Though the average numbers of women in the work force historically were relatively low until recently, this has not been true for all groups of women. Black women have traditionally had a much higher rate of labor-force participation (the rate for white women has only recently largely caught up). Similarly, immigrant women have often been an important part of the paid labor force in many American industries. And, in general, work in the

The continuing struggle for women's equality: then . . .

paid labor force has long been a common experience for lower-income women (Kessler-Harris, 1982).

Moreover, this is not the first time in American history that women have moved rapidly into the paid labor force. During World War II, millions of women entered what had formerly been considered men's jobs. When the war began, less than 30 percent of women older than 16 were in the paid labor force; at its end in 1945, more than 38 percent were, a rate that was not reached again until the early 1960s. In a story often told, many women who had worked throughout the war years in traditionally male jobs were ousted from them at the war's end to make room for men returning from military service. By 1947, only two years after the war, women's labor-force participation rate had fallen back to just over 30 percent (F. D. Blau, 1978; K. Anderson, 1981).

Still, even in wartime, the proportion of women in the work force never came close to its current level. And even more significant than these sheer numbers is the change in the marital status of women who work outside the home. Traditionally, the highest labor-force participation of women was among those who were never married or who had lost husbands through death, separation, or divorce — and who were often childless. Women most often were expected to leave their jobs once they married (Hareven, 1984). In 1890, the first year for which we have reasonably reliable data, all but a million of the 3.7 million women in the American labor force were single. Less than 5 percent of all married women worked outside the home. As recently as 1940,

EQUALITY OF RIGHTS UNDER THE LAW SHALL NOT BE DENIED OR ABRIDGED BY THE UNITED STATES OR BY ANY STATE ON ACCOUNT OF SEX

and now.

nearly half of the female labor force was single; but only a quarter was by the beginning of the 1980s (R. E. Smith, 1979, pp. 3, 18).

The increasing tendency for women with *younger children* to work outside the home is another major, dramatic change. Where once it was considered inappropriate for a woman to work while her children were young, today the difference in labor-force participation between women with and without young children is fast narrowing. Since the 1950s, the labor-force participation of married women with no children under the age of 18 has risen by a little more than half, and that of women with children under 6 has *quadrupled*. Indeed, by 1985, half of all married women with infants less than a year old were in the paid labor force — twice as many as in 1970 (Hayghe, 1986, p. 45).

Increasingly, then, women from all types of family situations — single, married, divorced, with or without children — have come to occupy similar roles in the paid work force and to share similar needs with regard to jobs, earnings, and supportive services.

The Earnings Gap: How Much Progress?

Some have argued that women's growing role in the work force has put them well on the road toward economic equality with men, even if they haven't yet arrived at that goal. But this hopeful expectation is belied by the stubborn fact that women are still *far* from equal to men in the economic rewards that work ought to bring. The paradox of increasing labor-force participation coupled with persistent inequality in wages and earnings is one of the most enduring aspects of American women's experience in recent years.

Let's look at the pattern of men's and women's relative earnings. The ratio of women's earnings to men's has fluctuated around 60 percent throughout the past two decades — that is, for every dollar men earn, women earn roughly 60 cents. (Historical studies suggest that this pattern extends back throughout the twentieth century.) These figures, moreover, refer to *full-time* work; they ignore the additional inequality resulting from women's more often having to work part time when they want to work full time. In 1985, about two-thirds of all part-time workers were women (Nardone, 1986, p. 16).

From what we have seen about the persistence of racial inequality, it should not surprise us that minority women fare less well than white women, as Table 6-2 shows. For every dollar earned by a white man in 1986, Hispanic women earned 56 cents, black women 61 cents, and white women 68 cents.

Note, however, that these racial and ethnic differences among women are *far* smaller than the gap between women of any race and white men. Indeed black women's income has increased faster than that of white women, narrowing the gap between them significantly. That faster increase, coupled with smaller recent rises in white women's earnings, has brought women's income a little closer to men's in the past few years. But they are still *far* from equality. And even these *relative* improvements must be qualified by the fact that, in part, they reflect the decline of men's earnings in the 1980s rather

Table 6-2
The earnings gap: Average weekly earnings, 1986, and earnings as a percentage of white men

	Median weekly earnings	Earnings as percent of white men's
White men	$433	100
Black men	318	73
Hispanic men	299	69
White women	294	68
Black women	263	61
Hispanic women	241	56

Source: Adapted from *Employment and Earnings* (Washington, D.C.: Government Printing Office, January 1987), p. 214.

Table 6-3
Same work, different pay: The earnings gap within occupations

Occupation	Median weekly earnings, 1985		
	Men	Women	Women's earnings as percentage of mens'
Financial managers	$677	$400	59
Engineers	673	544	81
Computer scientists	625	523	84
Physicians	656	507	77
Nurses	492	431	88
College teachers	638	487	76
High school teachers	485	408	84
Lawyers	776	558	72
Real estate agents	507	323	64
Secretaries	369	279	76
Police	432	352	81
Bartenders	227	177	78
Bus drivers	403	262	65

Source: Data from Earl F. Mellor, "Weekly Earnings in 1985," *Monthly Labor Review,* September 1986, pp. 30–32.

than the rise of women's; in other words, it wasn't so much that women were doing better in the 1980s as that men were doing worse.

These differences in *average* earnings between men and women translate into even sharper, more specific differences in their chances of bringing home relatively high or relatively low earnings. Women are greatly overrepresented among low-wage workers. In 1985 more than half of working women, but less than a third of working men, brought home less than $10,000 a year. At the other end of the scale, almost a million and a half men made over $75,000 a year — but only about 80,000 women did, or about 1 out of every 680 working women (calculated from *Employment and Earnings,* 1987, p. 17).

Moreover, the earnings gap is felt in all kinds of jobs. As we'll see, a good part of the explanation for the unequal economic position of women is that they typically work in different kinds of jobs than men do; however, they also earn less than men within the *same* kinds of jobs, even when they work full time, as Table 6-3 shows.

Life-Cycle Differences

But there is an even more significant gender difference that is not revealed by the statistics on average earnings. As we've seen, at any given point, women's rewards for full-time work are considerably less than men's — and dramatically so in many kinds of jobs. But beyond

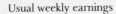

Figure 6-2

Earnings profile of full-time wage and salary workers, by sex and age, 1981

Source: Earl F. Mellor and George D. Stanas, "Usual Weekly Earnings: Another Look at Intergroup Differences and Basic Trends," *Monthly Labor Review,* April 1982, p. 17. Reprinted with permission.

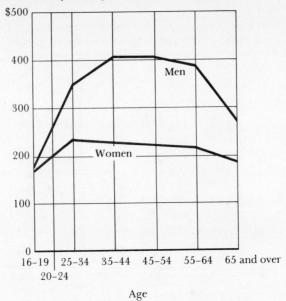

this, there is also a sharp difference in the pattern of earnings *over time*, in what economists call *life-cycle earnings*. Figure 6-2 illustrates this graphically. Men's earnings tend to rise steadily once they leave school, and to continue rising until at least their middle 40s. After that, their earnings tend to fall, especially, of course, after retirement age. Men, in other words, can usually look forward to a steadily rising income as they move more deeply into careers. Women's earnings, on the other hand, typically rise very little from the start and peak much sooner, at about age 30. This flatter "earnings curve" means that women and men start out much closer to each other — at all levels of education and across all kinds of occupations — than they end up.

It is sometimes argued that these different life-cycle patterns result from women dropping out of the labor force to have children. Because their work experience is interrupted, in this view, they usually have to start all over again in entry-level jobs and thus never get the chance to develop a "normal" career pattern. It is true, of course, that women often interrupt their work lives to have children. But it also turns out that women who have *never* married and who do *not* have children tend to have earnings over their life cycle quite similar to those of married women with children — despite the fact that their job commitments resemble those of men. In other words, even though single women's typical work patterns are like men's, their earnings are like other *women's* (Barrett, 1979a, p. 38).

Many other common explanations for the persistence of the earnings gap (like those purporting to explain *racial* inequalities) are based on the idea that women earn less than men because, in one way or another, they bring less to the job than men do in terms of skills, education, or experience — what some economists call *human capital*. How much do these characteristics matter? Research suggests that they *do* make a difference, but not nearly enough to explain all of the gender inequality in earnings (Bergmann, 1986).

Education, for example, is one path to higher earnings, and, other things being equal, more education *does* improve women's earnings — as it does men's. But, as is so often the case, other things are not equal, for the *effects* of education are very different for women than for men. This is strikingly clear from Table 6-4: Full-time working women who have graduated from high school *earn less than men with a grade-school education or less*, and women with four years of college earn far less than men who have only graduated from high school.

Another way of illustrating this is by estimating how much money additional years of education are worth to men and women. One study, aptly titled "Does College Pay?," found that a college education does pay, for both sexes. But within every level of education, the women in this study, members of the high-school class of 1972, earned less than their male classmates during the 1970s. Women who went to work straight out of high school had starting wages that were about 95 cents an hour less than men who did the same; those with an undergraduate degree earned 72 cents an hour less than comparably educated men; and women who earned advanced degrees started work at 38 cents less an hour (National Center for Education Statistics, 1982).

Studies have generally found that *some* of these differences in the

Years of schooling completed	Median weekly earnings	
	Men	Women
8 years of school or less	$259	$169
Less than 4 years of high school	290	180
4 years of high school	363	222
4 years of college	459	299
5 years of college or more	507	362

Table 6-4
Schooling and earnings, full-time workers, 1981

Source: Adapted from Earl F. Mellor and George D. Stanas, "Usual Weekly Earnings: Another Look at Intergroup Differences and Basic Trends," *Monthly Labor Review*, April 1982, p. 16. Reprinted with permission.

payoff to education can be explained by differences in *other* characteristics that women and men bring to their jobs, such as training, work experience, and age. For example, because a larger proportion of women workers are either young women new to the job market or older women returning after long absence, they are more often found in entry-level jobs, which, of course, have lower pay. Men also more often work overtime, spend more hours at work, work more continuously through the year and through the life cycle, and invest more in skill training (Duncan, 1984, Chapter 6).

Having said this, however, it is still true that virtually all studies find that a substantial part of the earnings gap remains unexplained even when all such factors are taken into acount. How wide is this unexplained part?

Different studies have arrived at different estimates, depending, in large part, on the kinds of jobs and workers being investigated. A review by the National Research Council, for example, concludes that all these characteristics combined "usually account for less than a quarter and never more than half" of the earnings differences between men and women (National Research Council, 1981, p. 42).

Moreover, there is an important caution to be kept in mind in weighing the evidence in such studies. By their very nature, they tend to *understate* the role of discrimination in the male-female earnings gap. This is because so many of the factors that are being "controlled" or "held constant" in these studies are themselves often shaped by past or present patterns of discrimination. Thus, many studies have found that the most damaging job-related characteristic women bring to the workplace is a lack of experience: Women have less experience in the work force in general, less in their present job, and less relevant on-the-job training. But, obviously, the fact that women have less job experience is likely to reflect both discrimination in hiring and training policies and the constraints of household work and child care (Bergman, 1986, p. 80). The same point applies to many other current "explanations" of women's position in the labor force, as we will see in the next section.

Women in the Labor Force: Some Myths and Realities

As women have moved into the work force in greater and greater numbers — but without gaining economic equality with men — a number of myths have emerged that serve to "explain" the continuing gap between men's and women's economic status and sometimes to justify the social policies in education and job training, child care, taxes, and other areas that help perpetuate it.

Most of these myths revolve around one of two basic assertions: first, that women are only temporary or marginal participants in the work force, with less commitment to work than men; second, that they don't really need to work and that any paid labor they do is, in some sense, "extra" work. Both ideas are deeply rooted in our culture and social institutions — both are increasingly distant from the reality of most women's lives.

Are women less committed to paid work than men? It's certainly true **Less Committed** that, on average, women still work less — *outside the home* — than **Workers?** men and are likely to have a shorter work life in the paid labor force. (We will look more closely at the patterns of work *in* the home in Chapter 7.) But that difference is fast diminishing. In fact, one of the main reasons why women's overall labor-force participation rate has risen is that more women are not only entering the labor force, but, once in the labor force, are staying longer. At the same time, the average length of time *men* spend in the labor force has declined slightly. A woman born in 1970 can expect to work about 25 years in the paid labor force, on average, as compared to about 15 years for women born in 1950. Men's expected years of labor-force participation, on the other hand, were about 40 for those born in 1970 and 41 for those born 20 years earlier (U.S. Department of Labor, Women's Bureau, 1980, p. 11).

Pregnancy and childrearing once meant long-term interruptions in most women's work experience. This helped define women of child-bearing age as unpromising candidates for jobs requiring extensive training or long-term commitment. But recent studies show that, increasingly, most working women stay on the job until only a few months before the birth of their first child, and they often move back into the work force very shortly afterward. In general, as one study concluded, "the lifetime work orientation of women is gradually approaching the more continuous pattern followed by men" (Mott and Shapiro, 1978, p. 49).

Besides their reputation for a less enduring commitment to the labor force, women are often typed as unreliable workers who quit jobs easily and often. Again, the conventional statistics appear to grant a superficial support to this view. On average, women have higher turnover rates than men do. But a harder look shows that this statistic mainly reflects women's greater concentration in low-level jobs — ones with low pay, little intrinsic interest, and few chances for advancement — which have traditionally high rates of turnover for *both* sexes. When job status is taken into account, men and women

The Bettmann Archive, Inc.

Women have always worked; pictured here, an early twentieth-century "sweat shop."

show similar levels of attachment to jobs. This is indicated, from another angle, by the fact that though women tend to quit jobs somewhat more frequently than men do, they generally get another one very quickly — showing, as some studies put it, that women often develop a stronger attachment to *work* generally than to the specific (often unsatisfying) *jobs* they hold at any given point (Barrett, 1979a, p. 45).

Another study, by the sociologist Paul Osterman (1982), sheds an interesting light on this issue. Osterman found that the enforcement of federal affirmative action guidelines reduced the amount of job quitting among women workers. Industries more closely watched by federal antidiscrimination agencies, and more dependent on federal contracts, had lower turnover among women. The study concluded that antidiscrimination enforcement probably created better job opportunities for women and, therefore, more incentive to stay on the job. This was confirmed by a recent study showing that women who have landed "nontraditional" blue-collar jobs once dominated by men actually quit their jobs slightly *less* often than men do (Waite, 1985).

These issues are further complicated by the fact that many of the statistical differencs that lend superficial credence to traditional arguments about the "irresponsibility" of women workers are, themselves, partly reflections of pervasive gender differences in expectations about work and family life.

Work, Family, and Gender Expectations

In American society, men's work, unlike women's, is rarely viewed through the lens of home and family responsibilities. In this sense, men's relationship to the labor force is a simpler one: Their job opportunities and career tracks are rarely much influenced by such things as the number of children they have or the competing responsibilities of housework. But women's *are* — and this distinction affects every aspect of their working life.

We will examine how these different norms affect the division of labor within the American *family* in Chapter 7. For now, we want to focus on how they affect women's role in the paid labor force and, through that role, their income and earnings. For, though traditional attitudes about the sexual division of labor are changing (Cherlin and Walters, 1981), they are not changing fast enough to remove the obstacles most women face in moving into the paid labor force.

The result is that many women are placed in a kind of double bind. A growing number both want and need to work outside the home, but they are granted inadequate support to do so comfortably, either at home or by the larger society. The assumption that women will remain responsible for running the household, for example, means they must often drop out of the labor force periodically or work part time. The reasons men and women give for working part time are revealing. When men work part time, their most important reasons for doing so are that they can't find full-time work and that they are in school. For women, the most important reason for working part time is that they are taking care of the home. Similarly, about 1.3 million women who aren't working but want a job give home responsibilities as their primary reason for not looking for one. Virtually *no* men give the same answer. For men, being in school is, again, the most important reason for not working; illness or disability is second (*Employment and Earnings*, 1987, p. 197).

All of these expressions of the traditional sexual division of labor in the home are compounded by others in the larger society, especially by the lack of effective social services to lighten home responsibilities for working women. The most important example is child care. Studies show that the lack of adequate child care is a powerful constraint on women's ability to take outside work and is an even stronger obstacle to their being able to follow the kinds of career paths typically followed by men. Close to one in five women with children who are not in the labor force, according to one survey, said they would look for work if satisfactory child care were available at reasonable cost. One in four women working part time said they would work more hours if such care were available (Presser and Baldwin, 1980).

Without either equality at home or adequate child care and other supports outside it, a vicious cycle is created. Many women are effectively locked into low-status, poorly paying jobs — often part-time or intermittent ones that allow frequent movement in and out of the labor force. In turn, women's confinement in these jobs reinforces the view of women's work as "secondary," which helps justify the expectations that women will continue to do most of the housework, stay home with the children when necessary, and relocate or leave school or training in order that a husband's career can be furthered.

This vicious cycle helps explain why women sometimes fail to take opportunities for higher-level jobs or training when they have the chance. Some writers (especially those critical of affirmative action programs for women) make much of this phenomenon in order to argue that the reason women aren't well represented in higher-level jobs is not that they face real discrimination in the labor market, but that they don't really *want* the better jobs. One analysis, for example, revealed that a main reason why women in a large Fortune 500 corporation were underrepresented in higher-paying jobs was that many were insufficiently motivated to compete for promotions. Those women who *did* have the level of aspiraton and motivation that most men had did considerably better in moving up in the company. On this basis, the study concluded that sex discrimination had nothing to do with the unequal position of women in the company (Hoffman and Reed, 1981).

The problem with this line of reasoning is that it doesn't take into account the connection between what happens to women's expectations *outside* the workplace and what happens *inside* it. A variety of studies have shown that women's expectations about their future work are often highly traditional. Teenaged women still most often aspire to typically "female" jobs, such as beauticians, nurses, or secretaries, and less often to nontraditional jobs. Surveys of high-school seniors show that well before they enter the labor force, young men and women are already "lined up" for very different kinds of work. Though most high-school women expect to be employed by the time they're 30, they mostly choose clerical work, almost never skilled craft jobs (Lueptow, 1981; Herzog, 1982). And young women often underestimate the extent of their future attachment to the work force, expecting to achieve most of their economic status through marriage. As a result, they often don't prepare adequately for what will in reality be many years of labor in the paid work force, too quickly accepting dead-end jobs in place of long-term training and investment in career planning (Mott and Shapiro, 1978, p. 140). But to argue that this means that these women "choose" not to strive for better jobs is simplistic. For many women, opting for traditional jobs is less a matter of real choice than the expression of a deeply ingrained set of expectations, rooted in the realities they face, in and out of the home.

There is an enormous body of social science research on the ways in which these gender-typed expectations about work roles are inculcated in both women and men from childhood onward, but we can only touch on it here. (For comprehensive summaries, see Maccoby and Jacklin, 1974; Laws, 1979; Richardson, 1981.) It's important to emphasize how *early* the process begins. A recent study of children aged two and a half to eight years found that even at the *youngest* ages, children of both sexes already clearly defined certain occupations as "women's" and others as "men's" (Gettys and Cann, 1981).

Absenteeism is another case in point. On average, women are more likely to be absent from a job, on any given day, than men are, a fact that is sometimes taken as yet another indication of women's flighty attitude toward paid work. Part of the problem, obviously, is that this fails to take into account differences in the kinds of jobs men and women hold. But, more importantly, it may simply reflect the degree to which women's paid work is defined as secondary to their other socially defined roles. When problems come up at home, for example, women are most often called on to take care of them, whether or not they work full time at an outside job. Data from the University of Michigan's Survey Research Center show that when both husband and wife work outside the home, if one must stay at home to cope with some household problem, four out of five times the one who stays is the wife (Wirtz, 1979, p. 214).

Such conflicts between home and work remain pervasive at all levels of American society. Even for women in high-level professional occupations, demands of home and family are often given priority over career development. In a recent study of men and women microbiologists, 93 percent of the women said they would accept a job in another part of the country *only* if a good job could also be found there for their husbands. Only 20 percent of *male* microbiologists, on the other hand, would have made a job for their wives a criterion for their own career relocation (Safilios-Rothschild, 1979, p. 424). This attitude helps explain the frequent finding that when working-couple families move, the husband's earnings generally *rise*; while the wife's earnings generally *fall* (Barrett, 1979a, p. 44).

In general, then, the reasons why women drop out of the labor force, or move in and out of it without building up substantial experience on the job, are different from men's. The assumption that women should bear most of the responsibility for running a home means that their work *outside* the home is still taken less seriously — by employers, by social service agencies, by their families, indeed, sometimes by women themselves — which, in turn, justifies denying them access to more stable jobs and longer-range training.

Do Women Need to Work? Another often-heard argument is that most women in the labor force don't really need to work. Again, the underlying premise is that most women are secondary earners who could be living comfortably enough on their husbands' paychecks. When they do work, it's mainly because of boredom or the desire to earn a little "extra" money. This argument serves to minimize the social and personal costs of both the low earnings women workers typically bring home and their high rates of unemployment. It is also often marshalled against vigorous antidiscrimination efforts for women. Since women don't really *need* the jobs, the argument runs, it's unfair for them to "take them away" from men who do — especially when the economy is faltering and jobs are scarce.

How does this argument stand up against the facts? Certainly, most working women see the issue differently. In 1983, 71 percent of working women in a *New York Times* survey said they worked mainly to support their families (U.S. Congress, Joint Economic Committee, 1986, p. 2). Nearly half of all women who work are single, widowed, divorced, or separated; and many others are married to men with wages not far above the poverty level.

Especially in times of periodically high inflation and persistently high unemployment, women's earnings are often essential to basic economic security — in some cases, to economic survival. This is obvious when a woman maintains a family or lives alone. Of every eight women in the labor force, one maintains her own family (*Employment and Earnings*, 1987, p. 166). But it is also true in many married-couple families as well, for a wife's earnings are sometimes all that stands between some of these families and poverty. An Ohio State University study found that the rate of poverty among husband-wife families would have been 50 percent higher if the wives had not worked (Shaw, 1981). And even for families not so close to the poverty line, the wife's earnings often provide the critical edge that allows them to buy a house, send the children to school, or pay off debts. Those earnings also provide a cushion against such catastrophes as a husband's illness, death, or job loss. On average, according to the Ohio State study, white working women contributed about 28 percent of their family's income, black women 37 percent. Such dual-earner families (as we saw in Chapter 3) were the only ones who managed to maintain a rising standard of living during the 1970s and 1980s.

Because of the size of women's contribution to family income, women's *loss* of a job can be a devastating experience even in married-couple, dual-breadwinner families. A recent study of women laid off from production jobs in declining industries in New England, for example, found that the majority lived in two-earner families, and their earnings had amounted to between 35 and 45 percent of their families' total incomes (Rosen, 1982, pp. 96–97).

Occupational Segregation: How Much Change?

If these "explanations" fail to explain the earnings gap between men and women, its stubborn persistence presents something of a paradox. How can it be that women are still so far from economic equality, in the face of laws and programs that, since the 1960s, have mandated "equal pay for equal work"?

The data we've already examined offer a clue to one part of the answer. Much research suggests that some of the earnings gap reflects the persistence of overt or subtle discrimination in pay and promotion practices. But there is another, and deeper, problem. An even larger part of the economic gap between the sexes reflects differences in the *kinds of jobs* men and women hold. It's not just that women are often paid less for doing the *same* work as men (though that remains the reality in all too many workplaces). The more pervasive and more stubborn problem is that — despite some breakthroughs into less traditional occupations and industries — most women still do *different* work than men do (Reskin and Hartmann, 1986).

The vast majority of women in the paid labor force are still channeled into a small number of typically "women's" jobs, most of which are poorly paid, unstable, and offer few chances of advancement. The technical term for this sex-typed channeling is *occupational segregation,* and it has so far proven difficult to combat through antidiscrimination laws.

The problem of job segregation is actually two somewhat different problems rolled into one. On the one hand, occupational segregation reflects the obstacles hindering women from taking jobs traditionally defined as "male" jobs — those with predictably higher status and pay. On the other hand, it reflects the *undervaluing* of the jobs that most women *do* perform. "Women's" jobs often bring less pay and other rewards than many "men's" jobs requiring considerably *less* skill — a disadvantage that has led to demands that jobs be rewarded according to some assessment of *comparable worth*. Let's now look at these problems in more detail.

Women's Jobs

Why hasn't the rush of women into the labor force had much effect on their level of income? A good part of the answer is that women have moved mainly into those jobs and industries that have *always* employed most working women, such as clerical work, retail sales, and the "service" occupations. (We'll describe this pattern of job growth in more detail in Chapter 8.) Women's gains in breaking into higher-paying jobs and industries have been counterbalanced by an even greater crowding of women into lower-level, traditionally "female" jobs.

Despite gains, most women still work in routine jobs.

Alan Carey/The Image Works

Table 6-5

The job gap: Workers by major occupational group, by sex, 1972 and 1985

Occupational group	1972 Thousands of employed wkrs. Men	Women	Percent women	Percent distribution among occupations M	W	1985 Thousands of employed wkrs. Men	Women	Percent women	Percent distribution among occupations M	W
Managerial and professional specialty	10,795	5,314	33	21	17	15,151	11,104	42	25	23
Executive, administrative, managerial	5,846	1,433	20	11	5	7,988	4,353	35	13	9
Professional specialty	4,948	3,881	44	10	12	7,163	6,751	49	12	14
Technical, sales, and administrative support	9,561	14,058	60	19	45	11,715	21,715	65	19	46
Technicians and related support	1,188	740	38	2	2	1,780	1,584	47	3	3
Sales occupations	5,093	3,473	41	10	11	6,554	6,095	48	11	13
Administrative support, including clerical	3,280	9,845	75	6	31	3,381	14,036	81	6	30
Service occupations	4,216	6,614	61	8	21	5,673	8,614	60	9	18
Private household	35	1,405	98	*	4	41	925	96	*	2
Protective service	1,122	78	7	2	*	1,480	233	14	2	0
Service, other	3,059	5,131	63	6	16	4,152	7,456	64	7	16
Precision, production, craft, repair	9,853	493	5	19	2	12,169	1,202	9	20	3
Operators, fabricators, and laborers	13,201	4,183	24	26	13	12,697	4,256	25	21	9
Machine operators, assemblers, inspectors	5,278	3,322	39	10	11	4,697	3,076	40	8	6
Transportation and material moving occupations	3,996	146	4	8	*	4,211	358	8	7	1
Helpers, laborers, others	3,926	715	15	8	2	3,789	822	18	6	2
Farming, forestry, fishing	3,250	593	15	6	2	2,992	579	16	5	1
Total	50,876	31,255	38	100	100	60,397	47,470	44	100	100

* Less than 0.5 percent.

Source: U.S. Bureau of Labor Statistics, *Employment and Earnings* (January 1984 and October 1985). The 1972 figures are annual averages, while the 1985 figures refer to September.

Women have made substantial gains in the labor force in the past two decades, as Table 6-5 shows, especially in managerial and technical jobs. But their job prospects remain vastly different from men's. To begin with, half of all women — but just 15 percent of men — are concentrated in two broad job categories — clerical work and services. Nearly half of men — but just a fourth of women — are executives, professionals, or skilled craft workers.

And looking at the broad categories *obscures* the extent of women's job segregation. If we look at more specific jobs, or at specific employers, the astonishing concentration of women in jobs where *other* women work becomes clearer. More than half of all women work in jobs that are at least 75 percent female; one-fifth of all women, in fact, are found in just ten types of jobs, all of which are at least 95 percent female (Bergmann, 1986, pp. 317–318). One recent study calculated a "segregation score" for several hundred California employers. Three out of five of the employers wound up with a score of 100 percent — that is, there was not one woman working in a job with any men and not one man working in a job with women (Bielby and Barron, 1984, p. 8).

One reason this matters so much is that the jobs where women are heavily concentrated nearly always pay less than those that are overwhelmingly male — which tend to pay well even if they require little education (Table 6-6).

To be sure, there is more movement by women into and out of male-dominated jobs than these snapshot figures suggest (Duncan, 1984, p. 164). And women's representation in better-paying jobs *has* been increasing — sometimes dramatically. But it's important to keep

Table 6-6
The job gap II:
Earnings in men's and women's jobs, 1985

Occupation	Percent women	Average weekly earnings	Occupation	Percent women	Average weekly earnings
Secretaries	99	$279	Firefighters	1.4	$437
Nurses	96	$434	Electricians	1.7	$456
Maids	92	$154	Engineers	4.7	$661
Waiters	85	$170	Police	5.3	$452
Elementary school teachers	82	$412	Stockbrokers	17.1	$593
Sales clerks	60	$210	Lawyers and judges	20.7	$724

Source: Data from Earl F. Méllor, "Weekly Earnings in 1985," *Monthly Labor Review*, September 1986, pp. 29–32.

these very real gains in perspective. In 1970, women were less than 2 percent of the engineers in the United States; by 1986, they were over 6 percent. That's a threefold increase, but it still means that only one in sixteen engineers is female. The numbers of women in skilled construction trades, such as electrical work, carpentry, and plumbing, have grown by more than half since 1970. But women still total only one in *fifty* workers in these traditionally well-paying jobs. And even at this rate of change, the ratio will be only one in forty-two by the year 2000.

Moreover, the movement into male-dominated jobs doesn't always mean quite what it seems at first glance. Often, a rising proportion of women in a particular occupation goes hand-in-hand with *falling* wages. One study, for example, found that each 1 percentage-point increase in the proportion of women in an occupation reduces its annual pay by $42 (Reskin and Hartmann, 1986, p. 10).

And, again, new openings at the top have not been accompanied by any significant lessening of the concentration at the bottom. Although almost half a million women began to work as engineers, lawyers, judges, doctors, architects, college teachers, and managers in banking and finance (traditionally male-dominated jobs) between 1970 and 1986, well over a million joined the ranks of secretaries *alone* during the same years.

Moreover, what is remarkable about the separation between men's and women's work is the extent to which it reappears, over and over again, in a variety of different forms and settings. In every broad occupational category, women are still found clustered in the jobs at the lower-paying end. In sales work, men are manufacturing or wholesale sales "representatives," or they sell stocks, bonds, insurance, or real estate; women are mainly clerks in retail stores. In service jobs, women are waitresses, household workers, or nurses' aides; men are police officers and firefighters. In the professions, men are doctors, lawyers, and engineers; but more than half of the 6.8 million women professional workers are school teachers or nurses. Even in the generally female-oriented realm of clerical work, certain jobs (like mail-carriers) remain largely male preserves, and they are invariably better paid than most clerical work.

Even in relatively sex-integrated jobs, women are often disproportionately found in specific workplaces or functions that are different from men's. Women accountants, for example, are often employed by a relatively few employers in a particular city, who tend to hire mainly women — and to pay them less (Blau, 1977; National Research Council, 1981, pp. 49–50). Women in academic teaching are much less likely to teach in large universities than men and much more likely to teach in two-year colleges (National Center for Education Statistics, 1980, p. 2) — and they are less likely to have tenure wherever they teach.

At the highest job levels — whether in academia, in private corporations, or in government — women remain strikingly segregated, often blocked from advancement by what some have called a "glass ceiling." In American universities, on average, only one senior administrative job is held by a woman. At Harvard in the mid-1980s, only one in twenty tenured faculty members was female. And just one in twenty members of the boards of the country's largest corporations are women (*New York Times*, December 21, 1986; *USA Today*, October 15, 1986).

What keeps the glass ceiling in place? The barriers are often subtle. For example, women are often excluded from the established networks of information, sponsorship, and support that are crucial in both landing a top job and advancing high up in a job hierarchy — the so-called old boy networks. One result is that women, even those with prestigious business-school degrees, tend to leave corporate jobs more often than men, frustrated by the intangible, but effective, barriers to advancement (*Business Week,* 1987). Moreover, success often requires extraordinary sacrifices from women who 'make it' to the upper levels of corporate America. Half of the women in a group of fifty of the highest-ranking female executives profiled by *Business Week* magazine had never married or were divorced; a third of those who were married had no children (*Business Week,* 1987, p. 73).

Authority and Women's Work

Women's work, even at the *highest* levels of conventional status and pay, often becomes defined as an extension of the type of work women have traditionally done at home: teaching, nurturing, feeding, cleaning. Likewise, certain functions tend to be predictably male-dominated, even within groups of professional or managerial workers. This is especially true for the exercise of *authority.* Women in science and engineering, for example, are overrepresented in basic research and are very rarely found in managerial roles with authority to set policy or supervise other professionals (National Academy of Sciences, 1980). Women in education are typically teachers, more rarely administrators with authority over curricula or educational policy (Barrett, 1979a, pp. 4–6).

The power to hire and fire or to determine others' pay or their working conditions is disproportionately lodged in men's hands. A University of Michigan survey found that about one-fourth of working men have some supervisory responsibilities that give them a say over other workers' pay or promotion; only one-tenth of working women do (Hill, 1980). Like other inequalities in jobs and earnings,

Nontraditional work:
Women's gains have
been important, but
limited.

this difference is partly explained by the other differences men and
women bring to the workplace — but only partly. Better education
and training help a worker of either sex land a position of authority
and responsibility — but they are far more likely to do so for men
than for women. Women are more likely to remain in subordinate
positions even *with* high levels of education.

These differences must be kept in mind when assessing women's
progress in breaking the barriers of job segregation. But, as with

Better for Younger Women?

minorities, it can be argued that the magnitude of the progress becomes more visible if we look specifically at the experience of younger women. Presumably, their situation more accurately reflects the beneficial impact of antidiscrimination laws and policies, as well as a more accepting attitude in society as a whole toward nontraditional work.

And, indeed, the statistics do show a trend toward improvement: Younger women are more often found outside of traditional

The "Women's Economy"

Within the American economy as a whole, we can discern the outlines of a distinct "women's economy," an economy with its own special characteristics that profoundly shape the lives of the majority of working women in America. The outline of the women's economy coincides, to some extent, with what we've called the "secondary" sector of the economy (see Chapter 2). But it has some specific, and sometimes unpredictable, boundaries all its own.

One of the most obvious is that a high proportion of women workers in a given industry goes hand-in-hand with relatively low wages — even for work that seems comparable to work in other, higher-paid industries that are quite similar but employ more *men*.

In addition, the "women's" industries are less likely to be unionized. The highest-paid workers are those in the oil and coal industries. The lowest-paid workers are those who work in private households. Nine-tenths of workers in private households are women, but only one-fifth of workers in the petroleum and coal industries are.

But, even more tellingly, the women's economy also appears *within* industries. It can be detected by the presence of sharp, sex-linked pay differences for virtually the same kind of work. Within the food and beverage industry, for example, the workers who earn far away the most money are brewery workers. In 1986 they earned $728 a week,

quite high on the scale of American industrial workers. The lowest-paid food industry workers are found in poultry dressing plants. They earned an average of $234 a week in 1986, a wage that, for year-round, full-time work, amounted to almost exactly a poverty level income for a worker with three dependents. Eighty-five percent of brewery workers are men; 53 percent of poultry dressers are women.

Much of American industry has, historically, been based on the organizing principle of the factory assembly line. But how much a worker *earns* on an assembly line depends greatly on just *what* is being assembled. People who assemble motor vehicles made $627 a week in 1986, while people who assembled electronic components made only about half as much. More than half of electronic component assemblers, but only one in nine auto assemblers, are women.

Sometimes the rationale for these distinctions between the men's and women's economies is extremely difficult to comprehend. For example, more than 90 percent of the workers who make tires or inner tubes out of rubber are men, and they earned about $605 a week, in 1986. Two-thirds of the workers who make *footwear* out of rubber are women, and they earned $237 a week. Or consider the apparel (clothing) industry, which has traditionally been among the poorest-paying industries in America. Apparel workers averaged only about $217 a

"women's" jobs. But a crucial question we are not yet able to answer is whether (or how much) these better *initial* job opportunities will be translated into greater chances for advancement and upward mobility. We have seen that women's earnings, unlike men's, tend to stay at much the same level throughout their life cycle. To a large extent this is because they tend to stay in relatively low-status jobs over the course of their lives, while men more often move upward through the job hierarchy over the years. One study even showed that a substantial

week in 1986, again barely above the federal poverty level for a family of four. By now it shouldn't surprise us that three out of four clothing workers are women. Yet within this generally poor industry there is a category of workers who make automotive and apparel trimmings. In striking contrast to all *other* apparel workers, these workers make over $450 a week — far *above* the average for American manufacturing. And *half* of these workers, also in striking contrast to other apparel categories, are men. At the other end of the scale in the clothing industry are the workers who produce women's blouses. At about $182 a week, these women — for *nine out of ten* are women — cannot support three dependents at the federal poverty level through full-time, year-round work without an extra job or welfare.

It is sometimes argued that these inequalities in pay reflect basic differences in the type of work performed. Among the highest-paid industrial workers in America in 1986 were those in the basic steel industry, who averaged $580 a week. (Steelworkers, of course, have also suffered devastating unemployment in recent years.) Steel is one of the *durable goods* industries, which tend on the whole to have higher-than-average wages. But there are some low-paying durable goods industries. The lowest paying is costume jewelry manufacturing, whose workers averaged only $220 a week in 1986. The fact that less than one in ten steelworkers, as compared to three out of five costume jewelry makers, are women might, in this viewpoint, be explained by the nature of the work. Steel-mill work is

heavy and dirty, while costume jewelry manufacture requires dexterity, patience, and other characteristics long considered typically "feminine." But that explanation just doesn't help us understand why workers in, say, meat packing, who make only a little over half of what steelworkers do — and *also* work at heavy, dirty jobs — are almost four times as likely to be women as workers in steel mills.

The same logical difficulty appears if we look at people who work in stores rather than factories. Like the clothing industry, the retail sales industry is one of the poorest paid in the United States. Unsurprisingly, it is a very large employer of women, employing about 9 million women in 1986 — about half the industry's work force. But within the retail industry there are sharp, revealing differences. All retail sales workers sell something for a living — but *what* they sell depends heavily on their gender, and is, in turn, fateful for their standard of living. Though women are half of all retail sales workers, they are only 19 percent of auto dealers, the highest-paid people in retail industry. The people who sell women's ready-to-wear clothing are nearly all (89 percent) women, and in 1986 they made only $129 a week — oddly enough, $50 a week less than the people selling men's and boy's clothes, more than half of whom are men.

Source: Data from U.S. Bureau of Labor Statistics, *Employment and Earnings,* January 1987.

proportion of women workers experience *downward* mobility in the job hierarchy over their life cycle. Women reentering the labor force in their middle years most often enter in a job with *lower* prestige and pay than the one they first held (Rosenthal, 1978).

It isn't certain, then, that women's gains in landing a good job in the first place will be followed by the chances for advancement and mobility that many men enjoy. And, as we've seen, for many women the chances of *ever* landing a well-paying job remain elusive in the 1980s. This is one reason why poverty in America is increasingly a women's issue.

Women, Work, and Poverty

We saw in Chapter 5 that economic progress for American minorities has followed an uneven path. Some, with better access to good jobs and earnings, have gained a foothold in the middle class; others are trapped in a stubborn cycle of poverty and unemployment. The trends in women's economic progress show a similar division. Some women have moved into nontraditional, better-paying jobs, reaching a more equal footing with men. But at the other end of the spectrum is what the sociologist Diana Pearce (1982) has called the "feminization of poverty." Two out of every three adults living in poverty are women. One in three American families maintained by a woman is poor, as compared to just one in eight families maintained by a single man and only one in fifteen intact husband-wife families. And, as Figure 6-3 illustrates, this gap has generally widened in recent years.

We have already seen that poverty in the United States increased sharply in the 1980s afer declining up to the early 1970s. But a closer examination reveals that most of the gains even in the period of greatest success against poverty took place for poor *men* and their families. Figure 6-3 illustrates this disturbing trend. Between 1959 and 1985, the number of poor Americans living in families headed by a woman grew by almost 6 million, while the number in all other families *fell* by 12 million.

The result has been a striking, fundamental change in the composition of the poverty population. In 1959, more than three time as many poor children lived in male-headed families as in families headed by a woman; since the mid-1970s, the majority of poor children have been in female-headed families.

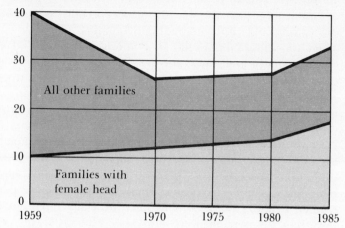

Number of poor
persons (millions)

All other families

Families with
female head

1959   1970   1975   1980   1985

Figure 6-3
Poverty in families with female householder and in all other families, 1959–1985

Source: Data from U.S. Bureau of the Census, *Current Population Reports,* Series P-60, No. 152, 1986, p. 6.

Even more disturbingly, this trend shows up most strongly among the young. While some young women have reaped the advantages of changing attitudes, laws, and social policies, winning better jobs and higher incomes, a rising number have been left behind in a trap of poverty and dependency. About a third of all women heading families are poor — but almost three-fourths of those under 25 are (U.S. Bureau of the Census, 1986b, p. 62).

From what we've seen already about women's jobs and earnings, it shouldn't surprise us that *persistent poverty* (the rare and more stubborn variety that entraps families year after year) is disproportionately a *women's* problem. Among those of the persistently poor who are not aged, two-thirds live in households headed by women, according to the University of Michigan's Panel Study of Income Dynamics (*Employment and Training Reporter,* August 1982, p. 99). Thus, women are not only more often poor, but more importantly, they are far more likely to *stay* poor.

Why? How do we explain this dual character of women's experience today — substantial gains on the one hand, deepening poverty on the other? How can so many women be entering the ranks of the welfare poor while others are moving into executive suites? And why haven't years of antidiscrimination efforts stopped the widening inequality between the sexes in the risks of poverty?

The answers lie in several trends we've already noted: job segregation, the persistence of the women's economy, the sexual division of labor in childrearing and family responsibilities. All of them combine to force many women into poverty, especially, though not exclusively, when they are the heads of families. These gender inequalities generate poverty among women in several, often overlapping ways.

One is high rates of joblessness — especially for minority women, the young, and those maintaining families. Unemployment among women heading families has been at crisis proportions for years. But the problem of joblessness for these women is much greater than the unemployment statistics alone indicate, since official unemployment statistics minimize the extent of joblessness by ignoring people who have dropped out of the work force and those who work only part time when they need full-time jobs. As we've seen, mainly because of their traditional responsibilities for childrearing, women drop out of the labor force more frequently than men do, and they also more often take part-time work in order to balance income needs with the demands of the home. Thus, although only about 12 percent of the women heading poor families were officially unemployed in 1984, less than 28 percent were *employed*. The other 60 percent were counted as "not in the labor force" (U.S. Bureau of the Census, 1986b, p. 21).

Another important reason why so many women are increasingly found in the American underclass is the low wages they make when they do work. This shows that the *sources* of poverty are typically different for men than for women. Men are *most* often poor because they don't have a job; when they *do* have one, they almost always earn enough to bring them over the poverty level. But one of the most telling effects of the segregation of men's and women's work is that a substantial proportion of women who work fairly regularly — even a significant minority of those who work year round and full time — remain poor. In 1984 about 7 percent of women heading families who worked full time, year round were poor as compared to about 3 percent of male family heads (U.S. Bureau of the Census, 1986b, p. 20). Moreover, the number of poor families headed by a male full-time, year-round worker dropped dramatically during the 1960s and has not risen even close to its pre–War on Poverty level. The number of poor *women* family heads who worked year round, full time dropped much more slowly in the 1960s and is now *higher* than it was in 1959.

The problem of low women's earnings helps explain the persistence of poverty among married-couple families as well, for though women's earnings help bring many such families over the poverty line, they are insufficient for others. Overall, as the National Advisory Council on Economic Opportunity has noted (Blaustein, 1982, p. 10), "If wives and female heads of households were paid the same wages that similarly qualified men earn, almost half of the families now living in poverty would not be poor."

Finally, women's high rates of poverty reflect inadequate levels of public and private support. We've seen that the American welfare system has been attacked for excessive generosity — and we've noted some of the misunderstandings that often underlie that view. How well *do* women fare in the welfare system today?

In 1984, the average income from public assistance of all families maintained by women was about $3,400 — about $5,000 below the poverty level for a family of three, the average size of an AFDC family (U.S. Bureau of the Census, 1986b, p. 100).

Not only is the welfare state considerably less generous than is sometimes supposed, but its generosity divides sharply along gender lines — not unlike the economy as a whole. In one "sector," the welfare state offers support through unemployment insurance, trade adjustment assistance, and other programs to those people, mainly (though not entirely) men, who lose high-paying, often unionized jobs in the "primary" economy. This part of the welfare state offers more substantial benefits (though not *as* substantial as some critics have argued) — and generally provides them with less hassle and degradation. But the other "sector" is for those people, disproportionately female, whose work outside the home is confined to the lower reaches of the women's economy and whose main source of support in case of job loss or other catastrophe is AFDC or local public assistance. The benefits of this sector of the welfare state are usually granted grudgingly and are rarely sufficient to lift these women out of what has aptly been called a "workhouse without walls" (Pearce, 1982, p. 31).

Prospects for the Future

On balance, then, women's progress against inequality has been decidedly mixed. Better jobs, with higher pay and better chances for advancement, have opened up for some women. And, to some extent, traditional attitudes in the home and in the larger society are shifting toward greater acknowledgment of the importance of women's work outside the home. But there is a dark side to this progress. Even in those areas where they have achieved the most success in breaking down traditional barriers, women have a very long way to go before they reach anything close to equality with men. The segregation of women's work still pervades the entire economy, even at its highest levels. And despite the velocity of change in some male-dominated fields, women are still underrepresented in most of them — and, even at current rates of change, will remain so far into the future. Moreover, the persistence of the gender-based division of labor in the home, in spite of women's increased work outside it, helps feed a vicious cycle of poor jobs, lowered expectations, and interrupted careers.

But what is even more ominous is that the progress of some women has been offset by a decline for many others. It is not just that progress hasn't been rapid enough. The deeper problem is that many of the forces that have brought greater equality and improved life chances for some women have largely passed others by. The feminization of poverty continues, with its crippling features of low-wage work in segregated jobs, high levels of joblessness, and welfare dependency.

What can we say about the future direction of these trends? For women, as for minorities, the prospects for equality depend crucially on larger trends in the economy, in cultural attitudes, and in public policy. All currently show some troubling signs.

Women's Work and Economic Change

Most projections estimate that a still greater proportion of American women will move into the work force, though there is some evidence that the trend may be slowing. But what is virtually certain is that *most* women entering the paid labor force will continue to move into "women's" jobs. With some exceptions, most of the fastest-growing sectors of the economy will probably continue to be those that have traditionally employed high proportions of women, such as service and clerical work. (We will explore these trends further in Chapter 8.) There will be more jobs for women, but they will still be in some of the poorest parts of the economy. As a result, the earnings gap between women and men is unlikely to be narrowed much in the near future.

Some women will also move into fast-growing, male-dominated jobs outside the largely segregated women's economy. But many of these jobs, especially in engineering, computer science, and other skilled technical fields, are among those where women are now *least* represented and where, even at present rates of change, they will still be underrepresented in the future. Short of an unprecedented shift in the sex composition of these occupations, their growth seems unlikely to have a very strong effect on the distribution of women in the job hierarchy. Overall, it seems likely that the shift to a "service" economy will mainly serve to enlarge the ghetto of "women's jobs" (Women's Economic Agenda Working Group, 1985, p. 14).

Other changes in the American economy seem likely to have a powerful, if not easily predictable, impact on gender inequalities. The long-term process of deindustrialization has so far struck hardest at blue-collar jobs and industries that, on the whole, have traditionally been male-dominated. Many of the "new poor" displaced in this process have been men. Yet the same trend has also hit some women particularly hard, especially those who recently gained a foothold in well-paying blue-collar jobs, only to see them eliminated through economic decline and technological change. Moreover, as we'll see in Chapter 8, those parts of the economy that have been less devastatingly hit by the economic shifts of recent years (particularly clerical and service work) may themselves soon undergo fundamental technological changes as automation moves more and more into the office. And since these are the sectors of the economy that have traditionally employed most women, these changes may have profound repercussions on women's economic position and prospects.

Complicating all this is the rise of a kind of "backlash" against the changes in women's status in recent years. Though it's hard to measure precisely, many saw a change of mood in the United States in the 1980s — a growing, or at least more vocal, resistance to women moving away from traditional roles and into male preserves. One noted writer described it this way:

> I've talked to women who have jobs, good jobs, that they got in the era when the doors were being opened — jobs that women never had before — and these women tell me that if their job were open today, a woman wouldn't get it. You can hear jokes putting women down again, jokes that a few years ago weren't permissible. All it would take would be a serious economic downturn — which can always happen given the shaky nature of today's economy — and there could be a really serious attempt to send women home again. (Friedan, 1986, pp. 153–154)

On the level of public policy, the outlook for women is similarly precarious. Three related trends, in particular, have ominous implications for women: the unsteady commitment to affirmative action, the shrinking of the public sector, and the attack on the welfare state.

Public Policy, Affirmative Action, and the Welfare State

We've seen that women's recent gains in jobs and earnings, though limited, have been real and significant. It's sometimes argued that they would have occurred *without* government antidiscrimination efforts, simply as a by-product of economic growth and changing attitudes. But the evidence suggests that, on the contrary, much of the progress women have made in jobs and earnings has been, in part, the result of vigorous antidiscrimination policies. For example, the greatest improvement in women's job distribution in the banking industry came during the 1970s — a time of slow economic growth but relatively strong federal affirmative action efforts. Between 1950 and 1960, before affirmative action, the percentage of bank managers who were women rose barely at all — less than 5 percent. From 1970 to 1979, after affirmative action plans, the percentage rose by more

Automation in the office may deeply affect women's work in the future.

than 80 percent (*Working Women*, 1981). Similarly, sex discrimination in promotions among public-school teachers, according to one study, was cut in half during the 1970s by federal antidiscrimination enforcement (Eberts and Stone, 1985).

It's often argued that these programs, while well intentioned, are too costly. But some facts about the costs of antidiscrimination programs gathered by Working Women, a national organization of office workers, are enlightening. In 1977, for example, the nation's third largest bank, Citicorp, spent more to sponsor auto racing than it did on affirmative action programs. The chairman of Citibank was paid almost twice as much as the bank spent on affirmative action. And, as of 1980, the budget for the agency that oversees the *entire* federal effort to ensure compliance with antidiscrimination provisions in companies with federal contracts (the Office of Federal Contract Compliance) was only about $50 million (*Working Women*, 1981, pp. 5–10). A study of 48 large corporations by the Business Round Table, a major corporate lobbying organization, found that the costs of affirmative action programs amounted to about 0.01 percent of their revenues, or a little more than $12 per employee per year (*Working Women*, 1981, p. 9).

The attacks on the programs that have helped bring gains for women are compounded by the broader attack on government. Like racial minorities, women have generally fared much better in the public sector than the private, in terms of jobs and pay. Though total employment in the federal government did not grow in the 1970s, the fastest growth of employment *shares* for women took place there. The earnings gap between men and women scientists and other professionals is *far* less wide in the federal government than in private industry. Women are much better represented in management jobs in public administration than in the private sector — and their pay is much more equal in them. Regardless of occupation, in fact, women's earnings, relative to men's, are *consistently better* in public sector jobs, though gaps still exist. (Women high school teachers, for example, earn 84 percent of what males earn; women police officers, 81 percent; see Table 6-3.)

These differences strongly suggest that antidiscrimination policies for women have been much more firmly promoted in the public sector than in private industry (National Academy of Sciences, 1980). This makes the recent shift toward reliance on the private sector to accomplish social goals an ominous one for women.

Cutbacks in public programs — ranging from education and health care to food stamps and AFDC — also have harsh implications for women in America. This is true for both those who have been relatively successful in jobs and income and those who remain dependent on the welfare state. On the one hand, women in higher-level jobs are disproportionately concentrated in some of the parts of the public sector most vulnerable to budget cutting. Most women professionals are teachers, nurses, or social workers — all fields that grew rapidly through the expansion of state and local government spending in the 1960s and 1970s. That growth was responsible for much of the increase in the proportion of women in professional jobs. (We saw in Chapter 2 that though government spending is often identified with a vast, bloated, and distant bureaucracy, *most* of the growth in domestic public spending in recent years was state and local spending for education and health care, and most of the "bureaucrats" thus funded were teachers and nurses.)

At the other end of the spectrum, the prognosis is even worse. Because of their high rates of joblessness and their inadequate earnings when they *do* work, poor women are extraordinarily dependent on the income support provided by the welfare state. As we have seen, the welfare state's support for poor women — especially for young women maintaining families — is rarely, by itself, sufficient to raise them out of poverty. For those it *has* lifted over the official poverty line, the margin of safety usually remains narrow. Less than one child in three in a family maintained by a woman enjoys a family income more than 1.5 times the federal poverty level (U.S. Bureau of the Census, 1986b, p. 23). Severe reductions in benefits and services bear part of the responsibility for the rapidly rising numbers of women and their children living in poverty in the 1980s.

In defense of these policies, it's often argued that reducing the drain of welfare spending will stimulate economic growth, which, in turn, is the most effective way to reduce poverty. The vision is appeal-

---

Women, Work and Pay in Other Countries

Like many other American social problems, the wide economic gap between men and women is often regarded as an inevitable fact of life. For some, it reflects biological necessity (Goldberg, 1974). For others, it's simply another aspect of "the way things are." Both attitudes imply that not much can be done through deliberate social policy to reduce these inequalities.

Few would deny that there are biological differences between men and women and that they influence social and personal relations. But looking at the economic situation of women in other societies shows that the way in which gender affects employment, wages, and living standards is very much affected by *social* policies.

If women were intrinsically less suited for some kinds of work than others, for example, we would expect their occupational distribution to be similar across different countries. But this isn't the case. It's true that women in other advanced industrial societies also remain, *on the whole*, concentrated in lower-paying, traditionally female occupations like clerical work and underrepresented in skilled crafts and many technical and professional jobs (United Nations, 1985). But there are important exceptions, and the range of variation is wide.

Thus, the proportion of women doctors in England, Sweden, France, Denmark, and Austria is about double that in the United States; in Finland and Germany, closer to three times. In Eastern Europe, the proportions of women doctors are typically even greater: More than 40 percent of doctors in Czechoslovakia are women, more than *70 percent* in the Soviet Union. These differences are even more pronounced for engineering, one of the areas in which women are most dramatically underrepresented in the United States. In 1970, 4 percent of engineers and architects in the United States were women (about 6 percent by 1986). In most European countries women were relatively unlikely to be in these fields in 1970, but they were much *more* likely to be in them than women in the United States: There were, proportionately, between two and three times as many women engineers and architects in England, Switzerland, Belgium, and Denmark as in the United States. In most of the countries of Eastern Europe roughly 20 percent (or more) of architects and engineers were women; in the Soviet Union, 45 percent.

And these differences aren't limited to the highest-level jobs. In the Soviet Union, for example, a number of blue-collar occupations that are male bastions in the United States

ing; it professes to offer a way out of the present morass of welfare dependency and its accompanying pathology. But would this kind of growth really address, by itself, the roots of women's poverty? Probably not. Unfortunately, as one critic noted, women are disproportionately "denied access to the additional employment oportunities which faster growth could create" (Sawhill, 1979, p. 545). We have seen why: Many lack either the training, the mobility, or the freedom from home responsibilities to benefit from the higher-level jobs that conventional growth in a high-technology economy might create.

For these women, it seems clear that real change will require much

are dominated by women, including electricians, metal workers, and painters (United Nations, 1980, pp. 40–51).

Women earn less than men, on the average, in every country in the world. But the range of this inequality is wide. There are formidable problems in measuring the earnings gap across different countries, but careful studies show that women's pay ranges from a low of about 65 percent of men's in the United States to more than 80 percent in France, Italy, and Australia and over *90* percent in Sweden. "American women," as a recent study from the Organization for Economic Cooperation and Development shows, "are singularly disadvantaged in their earnings" (*New York Times,* December 21, 1986).

Most of this difference remains even when a number of potentially complicating factors (such as the age of the work force) are taken into account. Moreover, in many European countries, pay differentials by sex have been *decreasing* faster in recent years as a result of the vigorous enforcement of clear-cut national antidiscrimination policies (United Nations, 1980, p. 118).

What accounts for these differences? The specific policies used to reduce women's economic inequality vary widely among European countries (Ratner, 1980). The Swedish approach is one of the most interesting and, so far, most effective. Part of Sweden's success in reducing (though not

eliminating) wage disparities between the sexes is the result of what Swedish planners call a *solidary wage policy* (Cook, 1980). Swedish unions have long adopted the policy of bargaining with employers to reduce the *overall* inequality of wages throughout the economy. "The goal," as one observer described it, "is to abolish low incomes [by] narrowing the gap between high and low earnings. . . . Equality in Sweden means accepting a system under which all workers earn a reasonable but not a widely differentiated standard of living" (Cook, 1980, pp. 64–65). Since the biggest proportion of low-wage workers are women, this policy has the effect of raising women's wages substantially relative to men's.

The solidary wage policy is complemented by measures to lower the barriers *outside* the labor market that hinder women from equal access to good jobs. As we'll see in more detail in Chapter 7, this includes a strong commitment to public provision of child care and to extensive leaves and more flexible and shorter working hours for both sexes. All of these policies are designed to lessen the conflicts between work and family life. They have not yet entirely succeeded; nor have they eliminated deeply entrenched gender differences in the traditional division of labor in the Swedish family (Liljestrom, 1980). But they do represent important — and partly successful — *steps* toward equalizing work and family roles in Sweden.

more direct intervention on many levels — in the workplace, in the division of labor in the home, and in the provision of child care and other social services. To explore these questions, we need to examine a range of further issues — especially the changing nature of work and trends in the structure of the family — in more detail than we've allowed so far. We will turn to these issues in Part II of this book.

Summary

This chapter has looked at trends in inequality between the sexes. Women have entered the labor force in unprecedented numbers; their participation increasingly resembles that of men. But this shift has not brought women to a position of economic equality with men.

The earnings gap between women and men has remained relatively unchanged for decades. Women still earn roughly 60 cents for every dollar men earn. And women's earnings, unlike men's, tend to remain low over the life cycle.

These differences are only partly explained by differences in women's educational levels, work experience, or patterns of movement in and out of the work force. A major source of the inequalities in income and earnings is that traditional sex role expectations and inadequate child care often limit women to intermittent and poorly paid jobs.

Despite genuine gains in their representation in some high-level jobs, occupational segregation remains the norm for women in the American economy. Women still most often work where *other* women work, especially in clerical and service jobs.

Job segregation, along with the low level of public and private supports for single women with children, helps explain the increasing "feminization" of poverty in the United States.

Attacks on public services, affirmative action programs, and public sector employment are likely to widen gender inequalities and stall the progress that has been achieved in recent years.

For Further Reading

Bergmann, Barbara. *The Economic Emergence of Women*. New York: Basic Books, 1986.

Hartmann, Heidi, ed. *Comparable Worth: New Directions for Research.* Washington, D.C.: National Academy of Sciences, 1985.

Kessler-Harris, Alice. *Out to Work: A History of Wage-Earning Women in the United States.* New York: Oxford University Press, 1982.

Pearce, Diana. "Women in Poverty," in Arthur I. Blaustein, ed., *The American Promise: Equal Justice and Economic Oportunity.* New Brunswick, N.J.: Transaction Books, 1982.

Reskin, Barbara, and Heidi Hartmann, eds. *Women's Work, Men's Work: Sex Segregation on the Job.* Washington, D.C.; National Academy of Sciences, 1986.

Part II

Impacts and Institutions

7

The Family

Americans of every generation have worried about the state of the family. In the 1920s, rising divorce rates, changing attitudes toward birth control and premarital sex, and the stirrings of greater independence for women led to fears that the family was in deep trouble. A textbook on social problems written in 1925 devoted its first 11 chapters to the problem of "Family Disorganization and Personal Demoralization" and noted ominously that "probably no social fact is more commented on in popular discussion than the increase in the divorce rate" (Queen and Mann, 1925, pp. 57–58).

During the period immediately following World War II, these fears were moderated by what seemed to be the considerable strength and durability of the family. This was particularly true of what many social scientists of that era regarded as the family's "ideal" form: the intact nuclear family of wedded parents who either had or planned to have children. For most of the late 1940s and the 1950s, divorce rates were relatively stable, and the strong commitment to raising a family was clearly demonstrated in the rising birth rates of the postwar "baby boom."

But the sense of complacency about the family turned out to be short-lived. The stable patterns of family life that seemed, at least on the surface, to characterize the 1950s soon began to crack in highly visible ways. Divorce rates shot upward in the 1960s and 1970s, as did illegitimate births. Conventional marriage and childrearing was rejected, at least temporarily, by a small but conspicuous minority of the young. And a variety of alternative approaches to intimacy and sexuality were increasingly explored. Birth rates fell, in strong contrast to the baby-boom era immediately before.

To some observers, all this seemed to signal the approaching doom of the family. Assertions that the family was "dying" were common among both supporters and detractors of the conventional nuclear family, and the question of whether the family "had a future" was hotly debated (Cooper, 1970; Lasch, 1977).

But this rather apocalyptic view of the family's problems has lost popularity in the past few years, and it's widely acknowledged that the family, as the sociologist Mary Jo Bane put it, is "here to stay" (Bane, 1976). After all, surveys have found that the vast majority of Americans still consider having a good family life their *most* important goal — ranking it even higher than good health, self-respect, and general happiness. Among younger people, the central importance of family life is slightly — but only *slightly* — lower; in a recent Gallup poll, more than three-fourths of those 18 to 29 ranked a good family life at the top of the scale of personal values (Gallup Poll, 1982).

Even so, the family has become a focus of even hotter public debate in the 1980s than it was in the past. But the terms of the debate have shifted. Today, those who describe themselves most vociferously as "pro-family" rarely argue that the family is on the verge of extinction. Instead, they worry that the family's strength is being eroded — by "years of assault on traditional family values" (Bauer, 1987). The erosion of the family's strength is often held responsible for

> not only the juvenile crime rate, but the adult crime rate; the fact that only one-eighth of our youth have got enough sense of responsibility to register for the draft; the fact that we have so much drug addiction; the fact that we have so much loss of drive in terms of the work ethic (Denton, 1982, p. 5)

among other social ills.

The villain in this drama is sometimes portrayed as the "permissiveness" of American society, sometimes as a decline in the values of personal responsibility, self-denial, and respect for the traditional roles of men and women. Especially disturbing to many people are several recent trends that have deeply affected American families: more tolerant attitudes toward divorce, sexuality, and childrearing; the spread of birth control, abortion, and family planning information; the rising participation of women in the labor force; the growth of public welfare and of demands for day care for children of working parents. All of these are often said to be undermining the independence and self-sufficiency that American families are thought to have enjoyed in the past. As one U.S. senator argued:

Many of the family's historical responsibilities have been taken over by the State. . . . The strength of American society has come from families' awareness that they are working together and helping one another. Parents took care of their own children. . . . What might be called the modern welfare state has removed much of that awareness of loving and being loved and working together and has removed much of the sense of responsibility. . . . It is not surprising that as government expenditures on social welfare increase, our concerns over the family and who is taking care of the nation's children have also increased. . . . We must restore the American family to self-sufficiency. (Denton, 1982, p. 5)

Restoring that self-sufficiency, in this view, often means cutting government benefits and services for low-income families, discouraging women's employment outside the home, and limiting family planning and sex education, especially for the young.

But others argue that American families have never been independent in this sense — that they've always been helped by government, through aid to education, tax breaks, and much more. In this view, the problems American families face today cannot be resolved unless society as a whole takes on more responsibility for dealing with their causes (Schroeder, 1987).

We can't address all of these issues in this chapter, but we will look carefully at some of the evidence that should inform contemporary debates about the family. First we'll examine some recent trends in family structure, particularly the rates of separation and divorce and the growth of single-parent families. Next, we'll consider some of the *consequences* of these trends for American families. In the following sections, we'll look at three of the most important problems facing many American families today: the continuing gender inequality in the home, the inadequacy of social services and public supports for families and children, and the persisting tragedy of family violence — a set of problems that are often intimately connected. Finally, we'll conclude with some thoughts on the effects of social policy on family life.

Some Trends in Family Structure

Both critics and defenders of the traditional family often agree that cultural and demographic changes are eroding the historical role of the family as the basic source of care, socialization, and support.

On the surface, there is much evidence supporting that view. The proportion of Americans who, through choice or necessity, no longer

Type of household	1986		1970	
	Number	Percent	Number	Percent
Total	88,458	100.0	63,401	100.0
Family households	63,558	71.9	51,456	81.2
Married-couple family	50,933	57.6	44,728	70.5
Other family, male householder . . .	2,414	2.7	1,228	1.9
Other family, female householder .	10,211	11.5	5,500	8.7
Nonfamily households	24,900	28.1	11,945	18.8
Living alone	21,178	23.9	10,851	17.1

Source: Adapted from U.S. Bureau of the Census, *Current Population Reports,* Series P-20, No. 412, Washington, D.C., 1986, p. 3.

Table 7-1
The changing family: Household composition, 1970 to 1986 (numbers in thousands)

live in an intact nuclear family of husband, wife, and children all under the same roof has increased remarkably in recent years. In 1970 about 71 percent of all households consisted of married couples; by 1986, only 58 percent did (Table 7-1).

Several different trends help account for this change. One is that more people are living outside of families altogether; another is that more people are living in families maintained by a single parent rather than a married couple. About 10 million more people lived alone in 1986 than in 1970. Some of them (about 3 million) were aged. Some were couples living together without being married. Yet contrary to some rather sensational exaggerations of the latter trend, there were only a little over 2 million of these couples in 1986, and they represented only 4 percent of all couples in the United States. Ninety-six percent of couples who live together, in an age supposedly characterized by a rejection of enduring commitment, are formally married.

But young people today are more likely to set up their own households rather than remain with their parents, and growing numbers of people are *delaying* marriage — both of which help account for the rising proportion of people living outside of families (Cherlin, 1981, pp. 72–73). In the mid-1950s the average woman married at about age 20; today it's 23. The average man married before his twenty-third birthday and now marries somewhat before his twenty-sixth. Indeed, women now marry at a later age than at any time since marriage statistics were first recorded in the late nineteenth century (U.S. Bureau of the Census, 1986d, p. 2). This trend toward a longer period of singlehood may or may not mean that a substantial proportion of those now single will never marry. As the sociologist Andrew

Cherlin has pointed out, more than 90 percent of all Americans, from the mid-nineteenth century onward, have *eventually* married, despite variations in the age at which they did so (Cherlin, 1981, p. 10).

What will happen to these couples once they do marry, if they do, is another story. While the vast majority of Americans will get married at some point, their chances of staying in their original marriages have dropped sharply. There are two ways of measuring the trends in the rate of divorce: We can describe the proportion of those who are divorced (as compared to those still married) in any given year, and we can estimate the proportion of married people who will divorce at *some* point in their married lives. Measured either way, the recent changes are dramatic.

In 1960 the *divorce ratio* (that is, the number of divorced people as a proportion of current married people) was 35 per 1,000. By 1985 it had more than *tripled* to 128 per 1,000. The rise was even greater for black marriages. By 1985 the black divorce rate was 251 per 1,000, up from 62 in 1960 — meaning that one in four blacks who had ever married were now divorced (and had not remarried). The picture becomes even more disturbing when we look at divorce among young married people. The rate for people under 30, for example, has more than quadrupled since 1960.

This suggests that the long-term chances of a married couple divorcing are increasing; and, in fact, this trend is a long and remarkably steady one, reaching back at least to the late nineteenth century, (Figure 7-1). And it is a *dramatic* one — a marriage begun in the

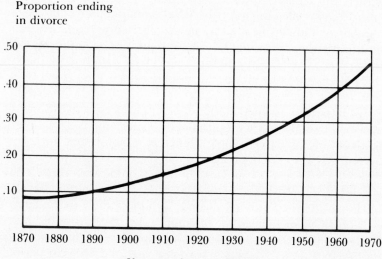

Proportion ending
in divorce

Year marriage was begun

Figure 7-1
Proportion of marriages that will end in divorce, 1870–1970

Source: Adapted from Andrew J. Cherlin, *Marriage, Divorce, Remarriage* (Cambridge: Harvard University Press, 1981). Copyright © 1981 by the President and Fellows of Harvard College. Reprinted with permission.

1970s has about five times the chance of ending in divorce as one begun in 1890. The trend has begun to level off a bit in the 1980s. But even if it doesn't rise any further, more than half of today's marriages will end in divorce.

The Growth of Single-Parent Families

The rising divorce rate is a main reason, though not the only one, for a key social trend we've already encountered: the fast-growing proportion of families headed by a single parent. Today almost one out of four American children live with only one parent (nine out of ten of them with their mothers), as compared to fewer than one in ten in 1960. And not only has the number of single-parent families risen, but their make-up has changed as well. Women maintaining families today are typically younger, and they are more likely to be divorced, separated, or to have never married, and to have young, dependent children. There have always been "broken" families in America. But in the past, death, rather than conflict or incompatability, was the primary disrupter of marriage. As recently as 1970 more than 43 percent of women heading families were widows, about double the proportion who were divorced. By 1985, only 27 percent of women heading families were widows, while 38 percent were divorced (*Statistical Abstract of the United States,* 1987, p. 49).

The rising divorce rate, then, accounts for a sizable part of the increase in single-mother families. But there has been an even faster growth of families with children maintained by women who have *never* married. Like the number of unmarried couples who live together, this trend is often exaggerated: America is not about to be inundated by "illegitimate" babies. Yet the rapid pace of change in the number of families headed by never-married mothers is a real and significant phenomenon. Only about 6 percent of American children live in these families. But their numbers have grown more than *sixfold* since 1970 and have more than doubled since 1980 alone (U.S. Bureau of the Census, 1986d, p. 72).

It's important to keep all these factors in perspective. Some of the growth in single-mother households results simply from a greater tendency on the part of single women to establish their own separate households after the breakup of a marriage or the birth of a child out of wedlock, instead of moving in or remaining with other relatives, which was often the case in the past. And data from the University of Michigan's Panel Study of Income Dynamics show that a large proportion of women heading families move, fairly rapidly, into new relationships. About 16 percent of families in that survey were headed by a woman during at least one year of a five-year period, but

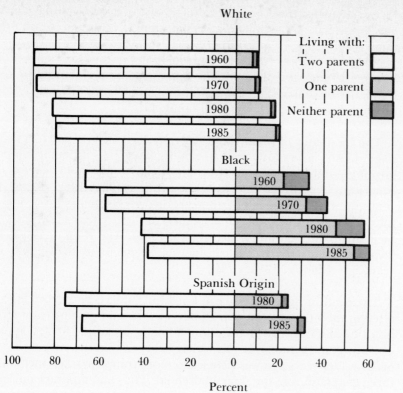

Figure 7-2
Living arrangements of children under 18 years: 1985, 1980, 1970, and 1960

Source: U.S. Bureau of the Census, *Current Population Reports*, Series P-20, No. 412, Washington, D.C., 1986, p. 8.

only 9 percent were headed by a woman for *all* five years (Levitan and Belous, 1981, pp. 113–114).

Despite these qualifications, however, the growth in single-parent families remains one of the major social trends in recent years. And it has even greater significance if we look at its racial dimension. The rise of single-parent families has been *much* more rapid among blacks (as we saw in Chapter 5), and the result has been a widening racial disparity in family structure. By the mid-1980s, four out of five white children — but only *two* out of five black children — were growing up in a home with two parents (see Figure 7-2).

The fact that the intact nuclear family has lost some ground is often taken as a sign of what one critic called a "growing cultural rejection of individual moral responsibility, robbing the family of its natural and transcendent role as the vital center for human life, growth, and development" (MacGraw, 1982, p. 640). Assessing this kind of claim

Is the Family Still a "Vital Center"?

isn't easy; measuring the degree to which American culture has or hasn't rejected "individual moral responsibility" is no simple task. But there is some significant counterevidence suggesting that — for *most* people — the family is a long way from losing its role as a vital center. The increasing rate of family disruption is counterbalanced by the frequency of remarriage, the continuing importance of kinship, and the high level of satisfaction with family life.

The frequency of remarriage. Increasingly, the breakup of a marriage doesn't necessarily lead to a permanent state of being single; growing numbers of divorced people remarry. About 15 percent of Americans over 40 have been married twice (Miller, 1982, p. 29). At 1980s rates, about five out of every six divorced men and three out of four divorced women will remarry, most of them within a few years of their divorces (Duncan and Hoffman, 1985). And the rate at which divorced people remarry is considerably *higher* today than it was 40 years ago (Cherlin, 1981, p. 10).

The continuing importance of kinship. Until recently, sociologists often argued that the nuclear family was the end product of a long historical shift away from the *extended* family (including uncles, aunts, cousins, grandparents). It was widely believed that the typical family of 75 or 100 years ago was richer and more complex, often including three generations in the same household. The contemporary nuclear family was said to have become more and more isolated, lonely, and atomized as these traditional kinship systems eroded.

There is still probably some truth in this view — and many people can point to something similar in their own family histories. But both sides of the portrait have increasingly been challenged by historians and sociologists. Many historians now dispute the idea that the multi-generation extended family was ever as typical a form as we once thought (Hareven, 1984). And recent sociological research has almost uniformly turned up evidence that extended kinship ties are still important in American communities today.

When Theodore Caplow and his co-workers looked at family life in "Middletown" 50 years after Robert and Helen Lynd's classic sociological study of life in a middle-sized midwestern town in the 1920s, they found that extended kinship ties were still surprisingly strong. Far from being "isolated urbanites," Middletown's residents were enmeshed in a varied and complex system of mutual supports and obligations with their relatives. Strong relationships were the norm between adults and their older parents, and there was a substantial amount of regular social activity among relatives. The researchers concluded that kinship was, in the 1970s, still by far the most important "affiliative bond" in Middletown — a conclusion reached by numerous studies of other modern American communities (Caplow et al., 1982).

Similarly, a study of working women by the sociologist Sheila Kamerman found that relatives and family were by *far* their most important source of support and help. Some of the families in the study felt these ties so strongly that they had actually moved in order to be closer to relatives. These women saw their families and relatives as "the focus of daily living" and as a "source of essential help and support, whether concrete and practical or reassuring and nurturing" (Kamerman, 1980, p. 115).

These findings put the contemporary difficulties of the *nuclear* family in a broader perspective. Most of all, they suggest that the (very real) troubles faced by modern couples (Peltz, 1982), and reflected most clearly in the rising divorce rate, don't necessarily mean that family ties *in general* have been as badly eroded as some think.

This is especially important in assessing the ramifications of the high rates of divorce, separation, and single-parent households among blacks. The difficulties faced by black single-parent families are certainly real (as they are for whites), but they don't mean that these families are necessarily unstable and unsupportive. Often, the parent and children in these families can call on a diverse and rich network of relatives for aid (Stack, 1974; McAdoo, 1981).

Satisfaction with family life. Despite the rising rates of divorce and the tendency to delay marriage, sociological research has found a high, and very likely *increasing*, level of satisfaction with the quality of family life in America. Whether it's measured in terms of parents' interactions with their children, the strength and quality of relations with aged relatives, or the quality of couples' sex lives, the evidence *often* suggests that things are getting better, not worse. As we've seen, most opinion surveys find that people of every age still value family life above most other things; they are also, at least on the surface, remarkably happy with it. The recent Middletown study suggests that for blue-collar workers, family life has distinctly improved since the 1920s, when it was often dreary, bleak, and burdened by the twin afflictions of too much work and too little income. By all accounts, it was also characterized by what we would now regard as appallingly restricted communication between husband and wives and a similarly unsatisfying and narrow sexuality (Caplow et al., 1982, pp. 117–135).

There is also evidence that parents now spend more time with their children than they did 50 (or 30) years ago. Again, the change is probably most significant for working-class families, where the crushing burden of work once meant that some parents spent virtually *no*

There is no longer any "typical" American family.

time with their children or that the time they did spend was typically harried and stressed (Caplow et al., 1982, p. 114).

The sources of the improvement in the quality of family life are no mystery. Advances in material well-being — in shorter working days and weeks, higher earnings, and better housing — have clearly helped make a more satisfying family life possible. So, equally clearly, have the spread of both technical knowledge and more flexible beliefs about sexuality, contraception, and family planning. These have not only enriched the relationships between men and women, but have also made possible smaller, better-timed, and therefore less harried and burdened families.

We will return to these issues later in this chapter. But now it will be helpful to examine some of the ways in which, despite its strengths and apparent durability, the family does remain an arena for a number of persistent social problems: the sometimes devastating personal and economic consequences of family disruption, the gender inequalities in the division of family roles, the inadequacy of social services for families and children, and the disturbingly widespread problem of domestic violence.

Michael Hayman/Stock, Boston

Susie Fitzhugh/Stock, Boston

The Consequences of Family Disruption

While the family seems remarkably resilient and often even thriving in the face of important social and demographic changes, this shouldn't blind us to the very real problems many families *do* face. In reaction to the sometimes overwrought fears that high divorce rates, fewer children, and the growth of one-parent families are signaling the "death" of the family, some commentators have too quickly leaped to the opposite view — arguing that the increase in marital disruption and the rapid changes in family composition represent only a healthy ferment, a benign diversity that will leave us all better off in the long run by expanding our "options" to choose from among a wider range of "life-styles."

The reality is more complex than either extreme suggests. Changes in family composition *are* often painful and disruptive, but there is little evidence that — by themselves — they cause the amount of social pathology often attributed to them. At the same time, the problems accompanying these changes, especially for single parents, create profound challenges for American society. With the goal of separating real from imagined problems, let's look at what recent social research tells us about the consequences of family disruption.

The Impact of Divorce

What happens to spouses and children after divorce? Research on the effects of divorce has often led to conflicting findings, but some common themes have begun to emerge.

For husbands and wives, there is — not surprisingly — every indication that divorce is a difficult and, at least initially, disorganizing experience. Studies that have closely followed the lives of divorced men and women have found that, especially in the first year or so, they are likely to have difficulty organizing their home lives, sleep and eat poorly, and function badly at work. Often, at least for a while, the divorced also suffer a restricted social life, as mutual friends and associates drop away or align themselves on different "sides" (Goetting, 1983, pp. 367–372). Typically, they experience a period of anxiety and depression (Cherlin, 1981, pp. 76–77). And a large body of research has consistently linked separation and divorce with higher rates of mental disorder. But it's difficult to be sure whether the change in marital status *causes* mental ill-health, is caused *by* it, or is some combination of the two. Suicide rates, too, are typically higher among the divorced than either the currently married or the never married, and there is evidence that death rates from cancer and other *physical* ills are also disproportionately high for the divorced and separated (Goetting, 1983, p. 371).

Marital disruption is obviously a powerful source of stress, which can underlie or at least aggravate a wide variety of physical and emotional problems, some very serious. But another frequent research finding complicates this picture. Studies have generally found that unhappy, conflict-ridden marriages are even *more* likely than broken ones to cause emotional and social stress (Goetting, 1983, pp. 371–372). In some cases, divorce can be a way of escaping the conditions that breed the physical and psychological problems often associated with divorce itself. And though the picture of divorced people leading chaotic, isolated, and unhappy lives is certainly true for some, perhaps true for *most* in the beginning, it must be qualified by the high proportion of the divorced who remarry, and do so happily.

Divorce, then, may have its "benefits" as well as its "costs" (Cherlin, 1981, pp. 88–92). The authors of the recent Middletown study contend that higher divorce rates may have helped make possible the *improvement* in the quality of marriage that, on balance, seems to have taken place both in Middletown and in the country as a whole. The growing social acceptability of divorce as a solution to a bad marriage may, in this view, mean that truly unhappy marriages are now likely to be terminated rather than continued out of inertia or convention (Caplow et al., 1982, p. 135).

The same seems to hold true for the impact of divorce on *children*. As with adults, the initial period after divorce seems to be the hardest for children. Those of preschool age are especially likely to feel frightened and upset, and often blame themselves for their parents' separation, while older children often become deeply angry at one or both parents (Hetherington et al., 1978; Wallerstein and Kelly, 1980). One study of affluent children of divorced parents in Marin County, California, found that a third of them were still unhappy and dissatisfied five years later (Wallerstein and Kelly, 1980).

A 1976 national survey found that about twice as many children in divorced as compared to intact households were described by their parents as "needing help" or as actually seeing a mental-health professional. But this was only about 14 percent of the children of divorced parents — meaning that about six out of seven of those children were *not* regarded, at any rate by their parents, as needing any special help with emotional problems (Cherlin, 1981, p. 79). And several studies suggest that the initial impact of divorce on children is most often eased over time. This is especially true where the marriage itself was conflict ridden; one study reported that many divorced parents felt their relations with their children generally *improved* after the end of a conflictual marriage (Hetherington et al., 1978).

And, more recently, a study in New York, following children from infancy to early adulthood, found a strong correlation between parental conflict when the child was three years old and a variety of psychological problems in young adulthood. Children who had spent their early lives in families marked by strong disagreement and conflict between the parents over such issues as childrearing and discipline were considerably more likely, as young adults, to have problems with their families, school, or work, and to be troubled by substance abuse and psychological problems (Chess et al., 1983).

Single Parents and Social Pathology

These findings also throw light on some commonly held beliefs about the consequences of single parenthood. Families headed by women are often held responsible for many of the social problems that bedevil American society, from juvenile delinquency through alcoholism and drug abuse, to the decline of the work ethic. Being a member of a single-parent family, according to one sociologist, is like "having a deformed physical body" (Burr, 1982, p. 232).

These beliefs are often based on the idea that children need a male present in the home in order to grow into well-functioning adults. But what is the evidence for this idea?

There is a long tradition in social research attempting to link the prevalence of "broken homes" with problems like mental illness, delinquency, and school failure. But the answers have not been simple. There *is* frequently an association between growing up in a "broken" home and delinquency and other problems. But most studies that have also examined the effect of conflict, inadequate supervision, and violence in the family have concluded that it's *these* factors that are most strongly related to the social problems. On the whole, it is the quality of family life, not the presence of two parents, that's *most* important in influencing childhood and adolescent development (Bahr, 1979; Goetting, 1983). The quality of life, in turn, is strongly affected by the family's overall well-being, especially its income and the availability of social and economic supports that can help the family cope. According to one researcher, the chief problem such families face is "not the lack of a male presence but the lack of a male income" (Cherlin, 1981, p. 80). Let's now look at how deeply these material problems afflict many families headed by women.

Women, Families, and Economic Supports

Recent research indicates that changes in family structure are the single *most* important determinant of changes in an individual's economic position over time (Duncan, 1984). And the breakup of families strikes women very differently than men.

Data from the University of Michigan's Panel Study of Income Dynamics show that men who divorced or separated saw their income drop slightly in absolute terms. But when their income was adjusted to account for the smaller size of their households, they enjoyed a rise in usable income of about 3 percent during the year following the divorce. For divorced or separated women, however, even adjusting for the shrinkage of their families didn't prevent their income from *dropping* by 9 percent. Meanwhile, couples who remained married enjoyed a rise in real income of about 19 percent. (Thornton, 1986). Some studies suggest that divorced women's incomes may fall even more drastically (Weitzman, 1985). Divorce, in short, typically *improves* men's economic condition — and makes women's *worse*.

Much of this difference results from men's more favorable position in the job market. For women who have been out of the paid labor force during their marriage, moving into it for the first time or reentering after long absence is a course loaded with obstacles, likely to end at best in a low-paying job. For many working women, occupational segregation into "women's" jobs means that their own paychecks usually aren't enough to support themselves — much less themselves *and* their children — once their husband's income is gone.

As this suggests, the heart of the economic problems of these families is that, in *most* cases, women remain responsible for childrearing when their marriages break up or when they have children out-side of formal marriage. As the sociologist Diana Pearce put it, "The typical outcome of a marital breakup in a family with children is that the man becomes *single,* while the woman becomes a *single parent"* (Pearce, 1982, p. 12).

This burden is aggravated by several other economic problems single mothers often face. We've already seen one of them: The welfare system offers very low benefits to most women who lack other sources of income. Another problem is that financial support from the fathers of their children is usually meager, at best. In 1983, according to the Census Bureau, of about 8.7 million women living with children of absent fathers, about 3 million (35 percent) received child-support payments and an additional million were entitled to payments but didn't receive them. The amount of child support averaged only about $2,300 a year for those women who *did* receive it (U.S. Bureau of the Census, 1986c, p. 2).

Another difficulty is that women are less likely to move back into relatives' (especially parents') households after a marriage breaks up than they were in the past (Levitan and Belous, 1981, p. 117). Among other things, this forces them into a housing market they are often unable to afford, at least without sacrificing other needs. Women who head families spend a much higher proportion of their income on housing after divorce or separation than before (and higher, too, than divorced men) — and they are still rarely able to afford a home of their own.

Inequality in the Family: Division of Labor in the Home

Many American families remain distinctly unequal institutions that perpetuate the wider social and economic inequality of women in several ways. For some (though by no means all) women, work in the outside labor force has simply been added on to long hours spent working in the home, creating what some writers have called a "dou-ble burden" and others, more sharply, a "treadmill" (Wirtz, 1979, p. 214; Duxbury and Shelendick, 1982). The dual role of traditional housewife and outside breadwinner helps keep some women con-fined to the least desirable and least rewarding kinds of jobs.

Recent research shows strikingly how *little* the "revolution" in women's labor-force participation has affected the conventional role structure of family life. "A family with two wage earners," two rather optimistic observers recently suggested, "may be expected to have a far different pattern of sharing responsibilities than the traditional one-earner household. . . . The slow evolution is toward family work roles based more on equality and less on sexual stereotypes" (Levitan and Belous, 1981, pp. 82, 101). The expectation is reasonable enough, but the "evolution" has been very slow indeed. Two-thirds of women in dual-earner families work 40 or more weeks a year, half work *full time* at least 40 weeks a year (Hayghe, 1981, p. 46). But a great many men (and at least some women) are still reluctant to abandon the traditional stereotypes of the husband as breadwinner and the wife as homemaker (Lein and Blehar, 1979). There is some evidence that this traditionalism is equally persistent among couples who live together outside of formal marriage — a generally younger group often thought to be less bound by conventional gender norms (Caplow et al., 1982, p. 67). Most couples divide the unpaid labor of child care and housework very unequally, and many cannot seriously envision doing things differently.

The Burdens of Housework

How much time and effort does household labor involve today? It's sometimes argued that advances in the technology of housework (such as labor-saving appliances) have dramatically reduced the time needed for home chores. Families, too, are smaller than in the past, which might also be expected to lighten the load of household work. But despite these changes, most research shows that the time spent on housework hasn't diminished nearly as much as expected over the last several decades. One recent study suggests that laundry is the only area of housework in which the amount of labor has clearly been reduced by technological innovation. In other household chores, technological innovation mainly seems to *shift* the hours of work (from food production to child care, for example) or to raise the standards demanded from the work (cleaner homes, more "sparkling" dishes) (Hefferan, 1982, p. 13).

Recent estimates of the hours of work of full-time homemakers range anywhere from about 30 to about 70 hours a week, depending on what is defined as housework and on the age and number of children in the home (Hofferth and Moore, 1979, pp. 111–112). Researchers at the Department of Commerce found that American *adults* average 25 hours of housework a week. They calculated that all that work would have been worth more than $750 billion in 1976 dollars — or an astonishing 44 percent of the country's gross national product at that time. This figure was arrived at by calculating what the same services would cost if they were purchased at prevailing wage rates. Another way of looking at the economic value of housework is to estimate the amount lost in potential earnings as a result of having to do housework rather than working in the paid labor force. According to the Department of Commerce studies, homemakers thus "lose" over half a *trillion* dollars a year (Peskin, 1982, p. 19).

Housework, too, remains disproportionately *women's* work. Men average just 15 hours of household work per week to women's 34. Men and women are also highly "specialized" in the tasks they perform in and around the home: Men do home repairs but still rarely cook, do laundry, or clean up after meals. These figures are, of course, *averages*, and some men do considerably more housework than this. But as many as *a fourth* of American husbands do *no* housework other than some basic child care (Hofferth and Moore, 1979, p. 112). In a survey conducted as part of the recent Middletown study, wives reported doing *all* the housework in almost *half* the households sampled. Less than 10 percent reported that housework was equally shared, and just two out of four hundred couples said that the husband did most or all of the housework while the wife brought in most of the income (Caplow et al., 1982, pp. 109–110).

Housework as Women's Work

How much does this divison of labor change when women enter the paid labor force? Surprisingly little. Most often, the total amount of time devoted to housework shortens somewhat when a married woman enters the paid work force, but women continue to do most of the housework.

In married couples where only the husbands are in the labor force, the husbands typically work long hours outside the home, while the wives average about the same number of hours *inside* it. Since the husbands also usually do *some* housework, they end up (on average) with a slightly longer total "work week" than their wives. But the opposite tends to happen when the wives enter the paid labor force. Even when they work full time, their husbands rarely step in to take on a significantly bigger share of the housework. The wives end up working an average of about 67 hours a week, while the husbands' week averages about 63 hours (Peskin, 1982, p. 10). Thus, the *overall* burden of work within the family shifts to the wives (Bergmann, 1986, Chap. 11).

The time spent in unpaid housework does shrink when wives enter the paid labor force — especially for families able to afford child care, cleaning services, and meals away from home. But, particularly for women with lower incomes, these options can be prohibitively expensive. And some home tasks — time spent with children, for example — cannot reasonably (or happily) be replaced altogether by services bought on the market. According to most studies, working women generally use some of their extra income to buy paid house-

Arthur Grace/Stock, Boston

The traditional division of labor in the family is still with us.

work but *also* lengthen their own working day and week to cope with both paid and unpaid tasks (Vickery, 1979, p. 190). And, obviously, this means less time spent elsewhere. Some studies find that working married women sacrifice an average of about 14 hours of their own time a week, taking it mainly from such activities as sleeping, eating, watching TV, or visiting friends and relatives, and often use their weekends to "catch up" with housework (Hofferth and Moore, 1979, p. 115). This helps explain why 50 percent of women working in clerical, service, retail, and blue-collar jobs reported, in a survey by the National Commission on Working Women in the late 1970s, that they had *no* leisure time (Wirtz, 1979, p. 215).

Changing Attitudes? There is some evidence that the sexual divison of labor in the home is beginning to change. Some recent surveys have found that husbands are somewhat more amenable to sharing household tasks than they were in the past. Working women surveyed in the late 1970s by Sheila Kamerman believed that though the division of household tasks was

still highly unequal in their own lives, it was less so than in the families in which they grew up (Kamerman, 1980, p. 124).

Still, some recent research indicates that the sexual divison of labor in the home is widely accepted even today by both sexes — at least on the surface. Middletown's husbands *and wives* still apparently agree that husbands should be the main providers and experts in home and auto repair, wives the primary housekeepers and specialists in the care and nurturing of children. Only a fifth of the men and women surveyed supported an egalitarian approach to housework (Caplow et al., 1982, pp. 67, 112).

How deeply these attitudes go — and how slowly they seem to be changing — is illustrated by a recent study of the sexual division of household chores (and outside jobs) among *children*. In this study of children aged 2 to 17, the sociologists Lynn White and David Brinkerhoff found that though the kind of work boys and girls perform is roughly similar at very early ages, it begins to diverge as they get older. Boys soon do less and less kitchen and general house-work, girls less and less outdoor work. As they get older, girls also begin putting in more *total* hours on chores than boys. Children's work *outside* the home is even more sex-typed: The primary job for girls is baby-sitting, with restaurant work a distant second, while boys typically work on lawns and sidewalks. The study found that parents with higher levels of education and more flexible attitudes about sex roles were more likely to encourage both sons and daughters to adopt less stereotyped tasks, in the home and outside it. But the researchers concluded that "the major changes in women's adult roles within the last two decades have yet to reach childhood" (White and Brinkerhoff, 1981, pp. 177–181).

Housework and the "Vicious Cycle"

One result of the gender division of labor in the family is the perpetuation of the vicious cycle we observed in Chapter 6: Women's domestic roles and their disadvantaged position in the labor force reinforce each other. Shouldering the major burden of household work doesn't prevent women from entering the labor force, but it *does* hurt their opportunities for stable, successful, and rewarding jobs. It leads to frequent moves in and out of paid jobs. This, in turn, means interrupted training, loss of previously learned skills, and the loss of seniority, career contacts, and networks. The process comes full circle when these problems are taken as "proof" that women are flighty or uncommitted workers whose main interest is in caring for home and family. And the cycle is compounded by the lack of adequate, accessible social services and workplace policies to ease the pressures on working women with children — a problem we'll now consider.

Work, Family, and Social Supports

More than almost any other advanced industrial society, the United States has been slow in developing policies to respond to the changing character of family life — especially the rapid rise in women's participation in the labor force and the growing proportion of families maintained by women.

The relative absence of supports in the community and the workplace that could ease the strains of combined work and parenthood reinforces women's unequal position on the job and at home; and it aggravates the stresses on family life — especially for single-parent families and those with lower incomes. For a society that claims to place a central value on both work and family life, we do remarkably little to help make the two compatible. As Sheila Kamerman puts it, "Being a member of the labor force and a full-time parent means trying to manage against overwhelming odds in an unresponsive society" (Kamerman, 1980, p. 129).

Minding the Children

The biggest single problem faced by the 200 working women with young children in Kamerman's study was the lack of accessible and acceptable child care — a finding that reappears in many other studies as well. In 1980, 7.5 million children under the age of 6 had mothers in the paid labor force; by 1990 there will be an estimated 10.5 million (U.S. Bureau of the Census, 1982b, p. 38). According to data from the University of Michigan's Quality of Employment Survey, about one in four employed women find that their child-care arrangements (or lack of them) often cause them to be late for work or to miss work altogether. Child-care problems make it especially hard for women to undertake training or advanced education, especially since evening child care is hard to find. Married women with very young children often find they can only take jobs during the hours their husbands do *not* work, so that the husband can take care of the children (U.S. Bureau of the Census, 1986a, p. 6).

Lack of child care or worries about its adequacy keep many women out of the labor force altogether or confine them to part-time work. Some studies estimate that as many as one in five unemployed women are jobless simply because they cannot find satisfactory child care (U.S. Commission on Civil Rights, 1981, p. 12). Almost one out of three single mothers with preschool children who are not in the labor force, according to a Census Bureau survey, said they would look for work (and half of those working part time said they would work full time) if good child care were available (Presser and Baldwin, 1980).

Child Care in Other Countries

Inadequate child care, then, helps trap many women in low-paying, dead-end work or joblessness. Given the rhetorical importance we place on work and family in America, the lack of adequate day care seems strange indeed. Yet, despite the rapid growth of dual-earner families with preschool children, the primary caretakers of children in the United States are still the nuclear family and the public school. Table 7-2 shows that compared with some other advanced industrial societies, we lag far behind in both the availability and, even more importantly, the affordability of child care.

In many European countries, most preschool children aged 3 to 6 are eligible for free child-care programs that cover the entire school day. The United States *has* such programs, but they are mainly private

Type of benefit	United States	Sweden	West Germany
Cash			
Income replacement	None	Paternity or maternity leave / Care for a sick child at home	Maternity leave / Care for a sick child at home
Income substitution	Aid to families with dependent children	None	None
Income supplementation	Tax allowance for dependents / Child-care tax credit	Child and housing allowances / Child health services / Tax allowance for dependents	Child housing allowances / Child health services / Child-care tax credit
Employment			
Right to leave work and job security	None	Parental leave up to 9 months / Unpaid leave up to 18 months / 6 hour workday up to child's 8th birthday	Maternity leave up to 7½ months

Source: Adapted from U.S. Bureau of the Census, *Current Population Reports,* Series P-23, No. 117, "Trends in Child Care Arrangements of Working Mothers," Washington, D.C., June 1982, p. 36.

Table 7-2
Family supports in three countries

and are often too expensive for low-income people. They also reach a smaller proportion of children and typically enroll them for fewer hours of the day (Kamerman, 1980, pp. 139–140).

Some countries, such as Sweden and France, also have extensive day-care programs for children under 3 years old — in contrast to the United States, where care for *very* young children is especially hard to find. Swedish parents are also entitled — by law — to take off a few days from work with pay to help their children make the transition into a day-care program (Kamerman, 1980, pp. 141, 161).

Most European countries share the belief that society as a whole bears some responsibility to ease the stresses on working parents and to ensure a nurturing environment for all children. In the United States, on the other hand, substantial public support for day care has only been provided during wars and depressions (McConnell-Condry and Lazar, 1982). Legislation to upgrade federal support for child care was vetoed by the Nixon administration in the early 1970s on the ground that it would commit "the vast moral authority of the government to the side of communal approaches to childrearing over the family-centered approach" (quoted in MacGraw, 1982, p. 66).

Part of the reason for this attitude may be the lingering belief that any form of care other than that provided by the mother may be harmful to the child's personality development. Especially during the 1950s, the notion of "maternal deprivation" as a crucial cause of childhood pathology helped give day care a bad name. But more recent research has failed to turn up evidence that outside care is, *by itself*, bad for children. What's important is the quality and consistency of the care and of the transition between home and outside child care (Kagan, Kearsley and Zelazo, 1978; Rutter, 1980). (In any case, those who most fervently argue that the absence of a mother is bad for children often display a notable inconsistency by arguing — equally fervently — that women with dependent children should have to work outside the home as a condition of public support.)

Whose Responsibility?

Our lack of comprehensive support for child care also reflects the broader themes of private versus social responsibility that, as we've seen, have profoundly shaped American institutions in every realm of life. American policy toward child care rests on the idea that caring for children is strictly up to individual families. It's assumed that parents (and particularly mothers, since child care is also seen as primarily a woman's job) will find their own arrangements for care and will come up with the money to pay for them. One result is that more than 2 million school-age children under 13 are routinely left alone without *any* adult supervision after school hours (U.S. Bureau of the Census, 1986a, p. 3).

The Working Day

But child-care problems are by no means the only obstacle working parents face. Another is the inflexibility of work schedules in the United States. Working parents — especially single parents — are often caught in a double bind: It's financially necessary for them to work and increasingly *expected* that they will do so, yet the traditional organization of work simultaneously makes it hard for them to work without straining family life.

The most pervasive problem is the rigid organization of *time* in the American workplace. Most full-time jobs are tightly structured around a nine-to-five working day; most offer little or no time off to cope with family problems and little time off even for childbirth.

Again, the contrast with other industrial societies is revealing. Many European countries have widely implemented some form of "flextime" arrangement, where working hours are allowed to vary, within limits, usually around a central core of a few hours in the middle of the day. But flexible work time is rare in the United States. According to one estimate, only about 12 percent of full-time American workers are on flexible schedules (Flaim, 1986). One result is that women with family responsibilities are often forced into lower-paid part-time work without fringe benefits or opportunities for advancement.

Several European countries also have legislation requiring paid leave for parents to care for their sick children at home — another rarity in the United States. (In Sweden, *either* parent may take paid leave of up to 60 days to care for a sick child.) In most Northern and Eastern European countries, families are entitled to a lengthy (by American standards) maternity leave at childbirth; the average is 6 months (9 months in Sweden). (By contrast, the women in Sheila Kamerman's study of working mothers took an average of 6 *weeks* off after childbirth.) Both Sweden and Norway provide for *fathers* as well as mothers to take parental leave at childbirth. And Sweden has also recently adopted legislation entitling either parent to a 6-hour workday, with income supplements, until a child's eighth birthday (Kamerman, 1980, pp. 125, 131).

All told, over 100 countries — including every industrial society except the United States — provide for some income support for parents who take work leaves at childbirth and guarantee that their jobs will still be there when they go back. Less than 40 percent of American women have that kind of job guarantee, and for most of them, the leave of absence is unpaid (*New York Times*, July 3, 1986).

The Family as a Crucible of Violence

The American family, then, remains highly unequal in its division of work roles and expectations. An even more dramatic expression of inequality in the family is the problem of domestic violence.

How Violent Are American Families?

That question isn't easy to answer, partly because much (perhaps *most*) violence within families is never reported and partly because the answer depends crucially on how violence is defined. We know that violence between husbands and wives, between parents and children, and between siblings is widespread. Just *how* widespread, however, is difficult to judge.

One of the most extensive recent studies of family violence concluded that "violence between family members is probably as common as love" (Straus, Gelles, and Steinmetz, 1980, p. 13). On the basis of a survey of more than 2,000 families, the researchers estimated that in the course of a year, about one-sixth of married people engage in at least one act of violence against their spouse, ranging from pushing, shoving, or "throwing something" to "beating up spouse" and "using a knife or gun." Over the whole course of their marriages, more than one-fourth of the spouses would be involved in an act of violence. The researchers argued that those figures probably *underestimate* the amount of serious violence between husbands and wives, partly because many failed to report or admit family violence and partly because the study didn't include divorced couples, who might be expected to have experienced even higher levels of violence while married. They estimated that *50 to 60 percent of couples* had engaged in violence at some point over the course of their marriages (Straus, Gelles, and Steinmetz, 1980, p. 13).

The same study found an even higher rate of violence by parents against *children* — with close to two-thirds of the couples sampled acknowledging at least one violent act against a child. And almost four-fifths of the families reported violence between brothers and sisters. The survey also revealed a surprisingly high percentage of violence *against parents* by children; the authors recently estimated that almost 900,000 parents are victimized by "severe" violence at the hands of their children each year (Cornell and Gelles, 1982).

These researchers concluded that "the family is the most physically violent group or institution that a typical citizen is likely to encounter" (Straus, 1980, p. 13). This judgment, however, depends on accepting a very *wide* definition of violence, which included pushes and shoves, "grabbing," and throwing almost *anything* at a family member in anger. But even when these minor forms of violence are excluded, levels of family violence are high. About six out of every hundred people had slapped their spouse or worse, and 14 percent had done the same to a child during the previous year (Straus, 1980, p. 13).

These estimates, however, are still higher than most. A more recent survey by the U.S. National Center on Child Abuse and Neglect estimated that about 650,000 American children under 18 suffer *serious* abuse and/or neglect every year — a little more than one child out of a hundred. These more cautious figures nevertheless reveal a human tragedy of enormous proportions (U.S. Department of Health and Human Services, 1982b). According to the survey:

• More than 200,000 children a year are victims of *serious* physical assault.

- More than 100,000 children a year are victims of such severe neglect that they suffer injury, death, or impairment.
- Nearly 45,000 children a year suffer some form of *sexual* exploitation at the hands of a parent (or a parent's lover).
- About 1,000 children a year *die* as the result of maltreatment; another 137,000 suffer *serious* injury.

And these figures are regarded as conservative by the researchers.

Is family violence *increasing*? It's difficult to tell from the current studies because no really comparable surveys were done in the past. Moreover, it's virtually certain that the *reporting* of both child abuse and spousal violence has improved greatly in the past few years. Therefore, though the bare figures suggest a sharp increase in recent years, the opposite is more likely. Historical evidence suggests that both wife and child abuse may have slightly declined over the past half-century (Straus, 1980, p. 28; Caplow, et al., 1982, p. 336). And a recent follow-up study argues that they have fallen considerably since the 1970s (Straus and Gelles, 1986).

The Social Context   What are the roots of family violence? Despite the difficulties of reporting and definition, some of the social sources of serious family violence seem quite clear from the evidence we have. They include economic inequality and instability, the lack of social supports, and gender inequality.

Economic inequality and instability. Many people believe that violence within families is widespread *throughout* American society, afflicting families of all groups and classes. There is superficial truth to this — both wife-beaters and child-abusers *can* be found among the affluent as well as among the poor, among professionals with satisfying and rewarding jobs as well as among the unemployed and badly employed. But, like many other partial truths, the belief that serious violence is distributed evenly across American families — what the sociologist Leroy Pelton has called the "myth of classlessness" (Pelton, 1981) — is misleading. *Serious* violence within families is disproportionately a problem of the poor and the economically insecure.

During the 1980s, several studies found that maltreatment of children was concentrated not only among low-income families, but among what one study described as the "poorest of the poor." Among families poor enough to be receiving public welfare, those with high levels of child abuse and neglect were typically even *poorer* than the rest of the welfare population (Horowitz and Wolock, 1981, p. 138;

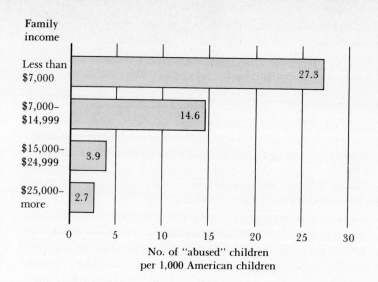

Family income

Figure 7-3
Poverty and child abuse

Source: Adapted from U.S. Department of Health and Human Services, *National Study of the Incidence and Severity of Child Abuse and Neglect* (Washington, D.C.: National Center on Child Abuse and Neglect, 1982), p. 10.

No. of "abused" children
per 1,000 American children

Pelton, 1981, pp. 24–28). Figure 7-3 graphically reaffirms the link between child maltreatment and poverty. The rate of serious reported abuse and/or neglect of children is *10 times* as high among the poorest families as among the most affluent.

These differences *could,* as some have suggested, be due to differences in the *reporting* of child maltreatment. Lower-income people are more likely to come under the scrutiny of public agencies (such as welfare and police) that deal with child abuse, and are probably less able to keep incidents of abuse hidden with the help of discreet private physicians. (As we'll see in Chapter 11, this is a key research issue for other forms of crime as well.) But there is good evidence that these income disparities are *not* simply the result of reporting practices. The *death* of a child through physical abuse, for example, is hard to hide, even among the affluent; statistics on children who die at the hands of their caretakers are therefore fairly reliable. And the picture they give is unambiguous: A study of child deaths in New York City found that 70 percent of the families of murdered children lived in extreme poverty areas (Garbarino, 1981; Pelton, 1981, p. 41).

What is true of child abuse is also true of other forms of family violence. Surveys find several indicators of economic deprivation high on a list of characteristics linked with spouse-beating: low family income; unemployment or manual work for the husband; worries about economic security; and a wife "very dissatisfied with standard of living" (Straus, Gelles, and Steinmetz, 1980, pp. 203–204; Straus and Gelles, 1986).

Lack of social supports. Another factor associated with severe family violence is the absence of *social* supports. Families who are isolated from relatives, friends, and others who can provide support and assistance in times of crisis (or can help lighten the daily load of work, household chores, and child care) are more prone to both spouse abuse and maltreatment of children. Neighborhoods with high proportions of single parents and few strong community ties are predictably neighborhoods where people move frequently and where there are high levels of child abuse and neglect (Garbarino, 1981).

More affluent families can cope better with moving frequently or the lack of close, supportive friends and relatives by being able to buy some of the supports they need, such as day care and help with housework. The combination of severe poverty with social isolation, on the other hand, is a potentially explosive one. It helps produce what the family therapist Donald Bloch calls "a kind of impoverishment of familial social options" in which violence becomes virtually the only response to family problems these families understand. Bloch's summation of the character of many abusive families fits the results of much other research:

> These are under-cared-for families. They are families that are impoverished economically, educationally, in their psychological resources, and in terms of their ability to function in the world. They could be characterized as coerced families. They are families most of whose lives are led in response to reasons they know not why. (Bloch, 1980, p. 35)

Gender inequality. Bloch also describes most violent families as "authoritarian and sexist," with a role structure that is typically "brittle and rigid" (Bloch, 1980, p. 34) — a conclusion shared by many others who have studied such families. Traditional gender inequalities, both in the family and outside it, nourish family violence in several ways.

To begin with, they create expectations about the "proper" roles of men, women, and children that help justify abuse. Wife-beating is, for example, *much more likely* in families where power over major decisions (such as those involving work, expenses, and children) is concentrated in the husband's hands — perhaps as much as *20 times* the rate in families where decision making is democratically shared. This may be especially true where male power, or the belief that the husband *should* be dominant in the home, is not backed by the economic or educational resources to "legitimize" it. In other words, men who *believe* that they should rule the home but who also lack the economic and personal authority to do so are the most likely to use violence against their wives (Straus, Gelles, and Steinmetz, 1980, p. 193).

Police, courts, and other agencies often take a "hands-off" attitude toward domestic violence, which probably helps perpetuate abuse (Berk and Newton, 1985). As we'll see in Chapter 11, there have been some serious efforts to make the police and courts more responsive to domestic violence. But, on the whole, the criminal justice system often retains the traditional attitude that "a man's home is his castle" — that men's use of force in the home, as long as it isn't "excessive," is natural — and emphatically a man's "own business" (Dobash and Dobash, 1981).

Sexual inequality also promotes both spousal and child abuse by limiting the economic and social options available to women. Women who are confined to the home or to low-paying jobs are more vulnerable to being abused — and to abusing their children. They are often faced with a choice between remaining with a violent husband and trying to make their way in an uncertain and unrewarding job market. For women who lack job skills (especially if they also have small children), the alternative to continued abuse is often poverty and welfare dependency. And women who are "stuck" in the home with

American society lags behind many others in the provision of care for children.

Sepp Seitz/Woodfin Camp & Associates

The Family as a Crucible of Violence **237**

preschool children, either because of poor job chances and/or the husband's unwillingness to have them work outside the home, are at high risk for serious child abuse (Gelles and Hargreaves, 1981).

Family violence, then, cannot be understood in isolation from the broader social forces that make *some* kinds of families more likely settings for violence than others. As we've seen, those forces — pov-

---

Does Welfare Break Up Families?

The rising rate of family disruption is one of the most dramatic social trends in contemporary America. As we've seen, it has a profound impact on many other social issues, including poverty, income distribution, and the persistent inequalities of race and gender. But *why* do families break up today at such a high rate — especially among the poor and some minority groups? That question is a large and highly controversial one, and there is no consensus among social scientists on the answers.

Many people believe the welfare system is mainly to blame. In this view, welfare, by providing benefits to women who aren't married, allows them to avoid marrying the fathers of their children and encourages them — or at least allows them — to have children they otherwise couldn't afford (Murray, 1985). The economist Thomas Sowell, for example, echoing many other critics, argued that "the current large and rising number of female-headed families among blacks is a modern phenomenon stemming from the era of the welfare state — when the government began to subsidize desertion and teenage pregnancy" (Sowell, 1979, p. 35). Is this an adequate explanation?

Research shows that the relationship between welfare and family structure is much more complex. The effect of welfare on family breakup — if there is one — is small and unpredictable; and it is overshadowed by the effects of *joblessness* on the chances of maintaining or starting a family.

A first clue is that the proportion of families headed by single women has increased sharply and steadily in recent years — while both the number of people on welfare and the amount of benefits they receive have *fallen*. If the welfare system has been shrinking while the number of broken families has been rising, it's hard to see the connection (Ellwood and Summers, 1986).

Similarly, there seems to be little connection between the proportion of single-parent families in different *states* and the generosity or stinginess of their welfare systems. Since the states vary widely in this respect, with some paying benefits so astonishingly low that they could hardly be regarded as an incentive to have children (see Table 7-3), we must question the belief that overgenerous welfare is the problem. Mississippi, which paid its average welfare mother all of $88 a month in 1980, had almost as high a proportion of single-parent families among blacks as California, which paid the average welfare mother nearly five times as much. Tennessee, which paid $122 a month, had *more*. And more elaborate research, taking into account other aspects of states that might affect family structure, reaffirms that welfare "simply does not appear to be the underlying cause of the dramatic changes in family structure in recent years" (Ellwood and Summers, 1986, p. 8).

But if welfare isn't the underlying cause, what is? Research suggests that the roots of family breakup are complex, involving shifts

erty and economic insecurity, a sex-typed division of labor and segregated job opportunities for women, inadequate social supports for families and children — are much larger than the family itself. This point has broader implications for the way we think about the troubles of the contemporary family and about social policies to address them — issues to which we'll now turn.

in cultural attitudes, in the social and economic roles of women, and in the economic situation of men. And they may also differ to some extent for different races. Among whites especially, the growing participation of women in the labor force has meant greater economic independence for women. Along with the changing attitudes about the acceptability of divorce, that has allowed some women to leave unsatisfactory marriages more easily than in the past. But for blacks, the growing job problems of men — especially young men — are more important in explaining both the breakup of the family and the failure of young fathers and mothers to marry in the first place (Edelman, 1987, chap. 2). The drastically declining proportion of young black men at work — the result of unemployment, dropping out of the labor force, incarceration, and even early death — has meant that "black women, especially young black women, are facing a shrinking pool of marriageable (that is, economically stable) men" (Wilson and Neckerman, 1986, p. 258).

State	Average monthly welfare payment	Percent of all families with children under 18 maintained by female householder	
		White	Black
California	$399	17	40
New York	371	14	48
Illinois	277	12	51
District of Columbia	252	15	51
Missouri	217	11	47
Georgia	133	11	38
Tennessee	122	11	44
Texas	109	12	35
Mississippi	88	10	38
U.S. average payment	280		

Table 7-3
Average welfare payments and percentages of female heads of families, by race, selected states, 1980

Source: Benefit levels from Walter Guzzardi, "Who Will Care for the Poor?" *Fortune,* June 28, 1982, p. 39; family percentages from U.S. Bureau of the Census, *Provisional Estimates of Social, Economic, and Housing Characteristics, States and Selected SMSA's,* Washington, D.C., March 1982, various pages.

Families, Social Policy, and the Future

One of the most important lessons that can be gleaned from this examination of some trends and problems affecting American families is that to speak of the problems of "*the* family" probably obscures more than it reveals. Not all families are alike, and different kinds of families, located at different points in the American social structure, face very different kinds of problems. But there are some recurring themes.

One is the pervasive fact of *gender inequality*. Whether the issue is the division of labor in the home, the pattern of family violence, or the (inadequate) provision of child care, the unequal status of women is revealed at every turn as a major influence on the problems faced by many families — and on the social response to them.

Another theme is the destructive impact of *economic inequality and insecurity*. For some families, poverty and/or unemployment are virtually unchanging facts of life, and they are less constant, but still painful, stresses for many others. Whether the issue is child abuse, the impact of divorce, or the quality of family life for single parents, economic deprivation is a brutally accurate predictor of both the extent and the seriousness of the problem.

Still another running theme is the often harsh impact on family life and a peculiarly American *ideology of social irresponsibility*. That ideology is revealed most clearly in the relative impoverishment of the kinds of social supports (including child-care programs and changes in the workplace) that many otherwise comparable societies have established to help manage the emerging shifts in the labor force participation and family composition.

As we've seen, critics blame the welfare state for undermining the American family. Yet in family-related programs, as in many other respects, the American welfare state is among the *least* developed of any advanced society, and that underdevelopment is itself a source of some of the most stubborn difficulties faced by many American families. Similarly, critics hold the movement for equality for American women partly responsible for the weakening of the family. Yet it is precisely the continuing *inequality* of women that, as we've observed, frequently lies at the root of many family problems, from violence and abuse to unemployment and low income. Others attack the growing openness about sexuality and the increased availability of family planning services as symptoms of an insidious "permissiveness" undercutting family life. Yet the evidence suggests that these trends may be partly responsible for what appears to be an increasing *satisfaction* with family life for a great many Americans.

Reducing economic supports for single parents, eliminating funds for child care, and slicing the budgets of family planning agencies — even the deliberate use of high unemployment to fight inflation — have all been justified on the grounds that the government will thereby "help families" by "boldly promoting a truly productive economy" (MacGraw, 1982, p. 69). From the evidence we've seen, such measures are more likely to reverse the recent, unsteady progress toward improving family life than to help families (Aldous, 1986). But to understand these issues more clearly, we need to examine some trends in other American institutions, such as work and health care, which have profound effects on the character of family life.

Summary

This chapter has examined some problems of the contemporary American family, with special attention given to four issues: growing family instability and its consequences; the gender division of labor within the family; the state of social services for families and children; and violence in the family.

Though some argue that the family is losing its central role in American life, the trends are actually far more complicated. Divorce rates have risen, along with illegitimate births. But remarriage is also common, family and kinship ties are still highly valued, and there is a high level of reported satisfaction with family life.

Still, the consequences of family instability can be severe. Divorce brings social and personal stress for both parents and children. The evidence suggests, however, that many of the problems faced by single-parent families are caused by a low income and inadequate social services.

Despite some evidence of changing attitudes, the division of labor in the home is still dictated by sex-role stereotypes.

The United States has been slow to develop adequate support services for children and families, especially child care and flexible working schedules.

Though its prevalence is difficult to measure precisely, family violence is widespread in America. Both child abuse and spouse abuse are aggravated by poverty, economic insecurity, and the inequalities of income and gender.

For Further Reading

Caplow, Theodore, et al. *Middletown Families: Fifty Years of Change and Continuity.* Minneapolis: University of Minnesota Press, 1982.

Cherlin, Andrew. *Marriage, Divorce, Remarriage.* Cambridge, Mass.: Harvard University Press, 1981.

Edelman, Marian Wright. *Families in Peril.* Cambridge, Mass.: Harvard University Press, 1987.

Finkelhor, David, et al. *The Dark Side of Families.* Beverly Hills, Calif.: Sage Publications, 1983.

Kamerman, Sheila B. *Parenting in an Unresponsive Society.* New York: Free Press, 1980.

8

The Changing Workplace

In the 1980s, Americans found themselves witnessing scenes reminiscent of the Great Depression of the 1930s: long lines outside unemployment offices; once-independent families lined up for free meals and shelter; young people living in their cars or on the street; college graduates scrambling for jobs waiting tables. But these tragedies were only the most recent and most dramatic expressions of a deeper crisis in the institution of work in America.

That institution, like many others in American life, is shot through with contradictions. Despite much talk about the decline of the work ethic, opinion polls consistently find that most Americans regard work as central to their lives and value working hard and doing a job well above most other pleasures and satisfactions (Figure 8-1). The vast majority also believe work is so important that government should ensure that everyone who wants to work has a job. Yet despite this abiding belief in the value of work, Americans have tolerated levels of unemployment that, until very recently, were routinely the highest of any country in the developed world. We spend billions on education to prepare people for a more productive role in society and then allow many of them to languish on public assistance or in jobs that would not challenge a moderately intelligent 10-year-old.

Until recently, the contradictions of work in America were partly hidden by the phenomenon of affluence. Many Americans assumed that good jobs would come naturally, along with so much else, as a by-

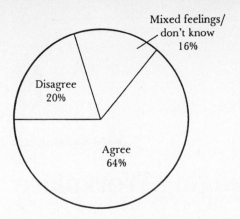

Figure 8-1
Percentage of responses to the question: Do you agree or disagree with the statement that people should place more emphasis on working hard and doing a good job than on what gives them personal satisfaction and pleasure

Mixed feelings/
don't know
16%

Disagree
20%

Agree
64%

Source: From *Public Opinion*, August/September 1981, p. 25. Reprinted with permission of American Enterprise Institute for Public Policy Research.

product of economic expansion. And so they did, for a while. Several severe recessions did throw millions out of work in the 1950s and 1960s, but the economy always bounced back, or so it seemed. The economy of abundance seemed to produce so many jobs that the fear of massive unemployment, so strong in the generation that had endured the Great Depression, largely receded from view. Hard as it may seem to believe today, a college education provided an almost automatic ticket to a good job — good enough, at any rate, to pay for the basic prerequisites of the middle-class life-style. The same was increasingly true for high-school graduates who entered unionized jobs in the big "primary" industries like auto and steel. These were often tough and dangerous jobs, but they also paid the bills.

Two shadows emerged in the late 1950s and 1960s, casting a pall over these expectations. First, it became increasingly clear that not everyone was able to participate fully in the economy and therefore in the general abundance of postwar American life. The excluded were concentrated in the inner cities and were disproportionately young and members of minority groups. By the early 1960s it was widely feared that this "social dynamite" would explode — and it did, to no one's great surprise, in the riots of the mid-1960s.

A second specter was "technological unemployment" — the fear that America's greatest postwar achievement, its growing technical prowess, might have the unintended consequence of creating machines so sophisticated that they would begin to eliminate human labor — and human livelihoods.

More storm clouds appeared in the following years. The recessions of the 1970s and early 1980s threw more people out of work than at any time since the Great Depression. Worse, the economy no longer seemed to recover as well afterward, leaving millions still out of work even in "good" years. The problem of concentrated unemployment in the cities grew worse, not better. The number of urban minority

youth out of work shot up dramatically — despite more than a decade of government job training and education programs for the disadvantaged.

Meanwhile, even college graduates saw their futures shrinking as their degrees became less and less valuable and the competition for good jobs heated up. Industrial workers who had struggled to achieve homes of their own and the good life in stable communities watched those expectations disintegrate as American industry collapsed around them. Not surprisingly, many Americans felt a sense of insecurity, even of betrayal, captured in Billy Joel's popular hit of 1982, "Allentown":

> Well, we're waiting here in Allentown
> For the Pennsylvania we never found
> For the promises our teachers gave
> If we worked hard
> If we behaved
> So our graduations hang on the wall
> But they never really helped us at all
> No they never taught us what was real
> Iron and coal, chromium steel.
> [Copyright © 1981, 1982 by Billy Joel Songs (BMI)]

Massive unemployment is no stranger to American life.

No one disagrees that the job crisis has been one of the most critical social issues of the 1980s, but there is no consensus on what to do about it. Some believe that the best way to create jobs is to "unleash" the private economy. If we just eliminate wrongheaded policies (such as excessive regulations and taxes on businesses, and costly welfare and government job programs), business will invest more, and that investment will generate jobs. But others are less optimistic. They point out that the American economy is already the least regulated, least taxed, and least generous in social spending among industrial societies; moreover, we've already cut social spending, government regulation, and business taxes in recent years — but the job problem has gotten worse. For some, this suggests that we need more government efforts to provide jobs and training, and perhaps an "industrial

---

Counting the Unemployed

The unemployment rate is one of the most common — and controversial — of social statistics. Since it's one of the most important measures of the success or failure of economic policies, its publication in the newspapers each month can cause concern at the highest levels of government. But what does the unemployment rate really measure — and how much does it really tell us about the state of the economy?

A national commission charged with evaluating the government's employment and unemployment statistics once pointed out that a good statistic "measures the right things — and it measures them well" (National Commission on Employment and Unemployment Statistics, 1979, p. 8). It is usually agreed that our present unemployment statistics *do* measure what they measure fairly well. But whether they measure the "right things" is another, more controversial, question.

Most regularly published data on unemployment are collected in a monthly survey of about 60,000 households carried out by the Census Bureau for the U.S. Department of Labor. On the whole, the survey is thought to have a high degree of accuracy, though the sample, while large enough to give reliable estimates of national conditions and of the working population as a whole, may be less reliable for smaller population subgroups and geographical areas. And like other census based data these may undercount some groups (like inner-city blacks) especially hard-hit by unemployment.

But the more serious question concerns the way the surveys *define* employment and unemployment. Deciding when someone is or isn't "working" might seem simple, but is quite complicated in practice.

Unemployment versus Not Working
The official measure of unemployment includes only a fraction of those people who are not working, and this has very important consequences for the way we understand unemployment as a social problem. Some of those left out are excluded for obvious reasons: Both the very young and the very old who do not work are not usually considered as unemployed, nor are those too seriously ill

policy" to help guide investment in ways that create more and better jobs.

In this chapter we'll look at some of the evidence that should inform this debate. We'll look first at unemployment: how it is defined and measured; who it strikes the hardest; and some common, if often misleading, explanations for it. But unemployment is only *one* part the problem of work in America. We are also witnessing fundamental changes in the kinds of jobs that will be available to Americans, the kinds of skills the jobs will require, and the rewards they will offer. In the second part of the chapter, we'll examine some of these changes: the emergence of a "service" economy, the changing relationship between education and jobs, and the impact of automation on the workplace.

or disabled to work. Others, however, are excluded for less obvious reasons.

For example, several million people at any given time who are not working *want* a job, and are capable of working, and yet are not classified as "unemployed" but as "out of the labor force." They are excluded because they had not *actively looked for work in the four weeks* before the Census Bureau interviewed them. In 1986, there were nearly 6 million people "out of the labor force" who said they "wanted a job now" — roughly 4 million women and 2 million men. The most common reasons cited for not having looked for work in the past month (and thereby failing to pass muster as truly "unemployed") were

school attendance and home responsibilities, the latter being the biggest single reason for women. As Table 8-1 illustrates, this should change our view of unemployment, especially for women. Measured by the official rate, women's risk of joblessness was about equal to men's in 1986. But when we add those who would be working or looking for work if they didn't have other responsibilities, the risks suddenly aren't equal anymore.

Within this group defined as out of the labor force is a subgroup of "discouraged workers." They differ from the rest of those "out of the labor force" only because of the *reasons* they haven't looked for work. They are classed as discouraged if they believed

	Total	Men over age 20	Women over age 20	White	Black
Unemployed	7	6.1	6.2	6	14.5
Want a job but aren't looking	4.9	2.3	6.5	4.2	10.8
Total	11.9	8.4	12.7	10.2	25.3

Source: Data from U.S. Department of Labor Statistics, *Employment and Earnings,* January 1987.

Table 8-1
Official and hidden unemployed, 1986 (percent of labor force)

that no work was available, that they lacked the necessary skills or education, or that potential employers would think they were too young, too old, or otherwise unattractive as employees. In 1986 there were over 1 million discouraged workers.

Underemployment and Hardship

Another major issue is that the official unemployment rate only counts people *without* jobs (or some of them). It doesn't tell us much about the *hardships* faced by those without work and it ignores the hardships suffered by many of those who *do* have jobs.

Historically, unemployment and economic hardship were very intimately linked. Most people in the labor force were adult men and single women who were usually the sole support of themselves and their families (the main exception was lower-income families in which wives and children often worked). Most families had one earner; fewer teenagers worked for pay; and there were few income-support programs for those out of work. So losing a job often meant a fall into desperate poverty and nearly always meant severe economic hardship.

Today, those conditions have changed. More families have multiple earners, many teenagers are in the labor force, and government transfer programs, particularly unemployment insurance, help cushion the financial impact of losing a job. As we'll see later, the extent to which these changes have eased the burden of joblessness is often exaggerated, but they *have* made the official unemployment rate, by itself, a less direct or precise measure of economic hardship. The unemployment rate lumps together a single mother with two children and no other source of income, a married blue-collar worker with three children and a mortgage, and a teenager from an affluent suburban family looking for a Saturday job. Given this diversity, the real-life experiences that the unemployment rate so coldly measures can

range from minor inconveniences to a life-shattering disaster.

The other side of the coin is that the mere fact of having a job — being counted as employed in the government's statistics — doesn't tell us whether the job provides an adequate living standard. For one thing, an imposing fraction of people counted as employed are working in part-time work. Moreover, as we've seen, even those counted as being employed full time may not be able to make ends meet through earnings alone. In 1985 about 2 million Americans heading families worked *full time* but remained below the poverty level (*Statistical Abstract of the United States*, 1987, p. 445). For these "underemployed" people, economic hardship is typically greater than that faced by those of the unemployed who, for one or another reason, have access to other sources of income.

Working versus "Employment"

One final issue deserves mention. Historically, the government has defined employment as limited to work done for *pay* (a minor exception is the inclusion of people working in a family business). This means, most importantly, that most housework is excluded from the concept of employment. Under this definition, a "housewife" doesn't "work" — and someone who has done housework for years and then stops is not "unemployed." Somewhat curiously, a woman (or, in the much rarer case, a man) doing child care, cooking, and cleaning in her (his) own home is considered not in the labor force unless she (or he) has an outside job, while the same person doing the *same* work in someone else's house for pay is considered "employed," and is "unemployed" if she (or he) *loses* that job. Thus, this definition of work offers a misleading picture of the extent of women's work and of the severity of their employment problems. It also means that displaced housewives are not eligible for unemployment-related benefits.

The Deepening Shadow of Joblessness

The specter of massive unemployment, as we saw in Chapter 3, is no stranger to American life. Unemployment has been a perennial problem that has receded only to return again in disturbingly recurrent cycles. Even during what we now regard as an era of unparalleled economic growth and promise in the 1940s, 1950s, and 1960s, the jobless rate rose to the neighborhood of 6 percent (and even beyond) in several years.

But the job problem has been worsening over time. In the 1980s, the jobless rate reached levels higher than at any time since the Great Depression; in early 1983 the number of unemployed in the United States was roughly equal to the entire Canadian labor force. Moreover, economic recovery wasn't bringing the jobless rates down as much as in the past. Each successive recession of the 1970s and 1980s began with a higher level of unemployment than the one before; the level of joblessness just *before* the 1981–1982 recession began was much higher than any experienced in postwar America before 1975.

The severity of the job problem is hidden, as we've seen, by the conventions of measurement and definition. An unemployment rate of around 10 percent means that roughly 11 million individuals are officially counted as out of work. But the true number of the jobless also includes the more than 1 million "discouraged" workers and the several million others who are "out of the labor force" but want work. And 11 million individuals out of work means that *25 to 30 million people in their families* are affected by unemployment. Moreover, the official unemployment rate is a kind of "snapshot" measure that freezes the action at one point in time. But 11 million people out of work *at any given point* during the year means that close to 25 million people will suffer unemployment *at some time* during that year (U.S. Bureau of Labor Statistics, 1982b).

And beneath the unemployment statistics, as bad as they are, lie several especially critical problems — including the crisis of youth unemployment, the growing problem of the *under*employed, and the troubles of displaced industrial workers.

Youth: Shrinking Opportunities?

We saw in Chapter 5 that joblessness among minority youth has reached crisis levels. But the lack of good job opportunities confronts youth of all races. The unemployment rate for teenagers in the United States has usually been at least three, and sometimes four,

Since the 1960s, unemployment rates for black and white youth have increasingly diverged.

times the adult rate; and it hasn't dropped below 10 percent since the early 1950s. Youth joblessness is a worldwide problem, but it has traditionally been especially high in the United States. Today American youth unemployment rates are much higher than those in some other industrial countries (Table 8-2). An American under the age of 24 is about three times as likely to be unemployed as a Swede or Japanese the same age; Swedish or Japanese youth, indeed, are considerably less likely than American *adults* to be unemployed.

For youth — as for adults — unemployment is concentrated among some groups more than others. About three-quarters of total youth unemployment, for example, is accounted for by the less than 10 percent of jobless youth who are unemployed for 15 weeks or more. Who are they? As we've seen, many of them are black or Hispanic. And a disproportionate number are high-school dropouts — of all races. Less than half of the youth who dropped out of high school in 1985 are working (Cohany, 1986, p. 30).

But though education helps in getting a job, one of the most troubling features of youth unemployment today is that, increasingly, a high-school (and even college) education isn't a guarantee of a

	Percent of youth labor force unemployed
United States	13.0
Japan	4.8
Norway	6.8
Sweden	5.8
United Kingdom	21.7
West Germany	9.5

Note: "Youth" refers to ages 16–24, except in figures for Japan and West Germany, 15–24.
Source: Data from Organization for Economic Cooperation and Development, *OECD Economic Outlook*, Paris, May, 1986, p. 31.

Table 8-2
Youth unemployment in perspective: Selected countries, 1985

job — any job. One out of four graduates of the high-school class of 1985 who didn't go on to college are unemployed; another 18 percent are out of the labor force. And the proportion of high-school graduates who are unemployed was considerably higher during the economic recovery of the mid-1980s than in the recession of 1975 (Cohany, 1986, p. 30).

What makes all of this especially ominous is that, as we'll see in a moment, the prospects for the growth of good, new jobs in the American economy that could reverse this trend — and offer youth a more certain stake in the future — aren't encouraging.

Some argue that youth joblessness is a less critical problem than it seems at first glance, since young people don't really "need" to work. But though that description surely applies to some, it reveals a misunderstanding of the broader picture. A substantial proportion of unemployed youth come from low-income families, where their work could make a big difference in their well-being and that of their families. And a surprising proportion are also supporting their *own* families (or should be supporting them, if they aren't). One study, for example, found that among unemployed teen-aged women, a third of blacks, a fifth of Hispanics, and a sixth of whites had children of their own (U.S. Commission on Civil Rights, 1980b, pp. 14–15).

We've already seen that one of the main reasons for the rise in poverty in recent years is that, increasingly, many people who work don't work *enough* — or at good enough wages — to make a decent living. Let's look more closely at who they are.

In a recent study, the economists Sheldon Danziger and Peter Gottschalk investigated the extent of low earnings among people they

The Underemployed

described as "expected to work" — heads of families who weren't over 65, disabled, students, or single mothers with very young children. Their most striking finding was that the number of people in this category who didn't earn enough to pull a family of four out of poverty had *risen* sharply since the 1960s — from about 19 percent in 1967 to 26 percent in 1984. Part of the increase was the result of higher unemployment rates, but two out of three people in this group *were* working but either didn't work enough hours or didn't make high enough wages to earn a solid living.

Who are these underemployed workers? Like unemployed youth, they are disproportionately likely to be members of minority groups and to be poorly educated: The *average* earnings of high-school dropouts under 24 who work *full* time, all year round, is below the poverty levels for a family of four. But it's *gender* that most sharply distinguishes the underemployed. Almost half of the women "expected to work" in Danziger and Gottschalk's study earned less than the poverty level for a family of four — more than double the proportion of men (Danziger and Gottschalk, 1986, p. 18). In the University of Michigan study of the economic patterns of American families, about one in five women heading families had earnings so persistently low that they wound up in the bottom tenth of the income scale for ten years in a row (Duncan, 1984, chap. 4). What's worse, the difficulties these women face in making an adequate living seem little affected by economic growth. They remain disadvantaged through both the ups and the downs of the economy (Freeman, 1981, pp. 122–124).

Recognizing the growth and stubbornness of underemployment has important implications for the way we think about strategies to combat the job problem. In particular, it suggests that policies designed to create *any* kind of jobs won't do much to address the problems faced by the most disadvantaged men and women in American society. Behind the (bad enough) problem of a shortage of work is an even deeper problem of a shortage of *good* jobs. We'll return to these issues when we examine trends in the structure of the American labor market itself. In the meantime, we turn to the problem of unemployment among displaced industrial workers.

Displaced Workers: Casualties of Deindustrialization

The decline of many traditional American industries during the 1970s and 1980s has been one of the most profound social developments in our recent history. We saw some of the dimensions of this "deindustrialization" in Chapter 3. Here we'll focus on its most troubling result, the displacement of millions of workers from what had been relatively stable jobs that once enabled them to enjoy many of the rewards of American abundance. As the American economy

A disproportionate number of under-employed workers are women.

continues its shift away from basic manufacturing industries, their numbers are increasing — and their chances of regaining jobs comparable to the ones they lost are shrinking.

More than 5 million workers, according to the Department of Labor, lost their jobs between 1979 and 1984 because the plant in which they worked closed or relocated, or their job was cut back or abolished (Devens, 1986). These "new" unemployed are different, in many ways, from the hard-core unemployed and underemployed groups we've looked at so far. They are likely to be better educated and more highly skilled than the rest of the long-term unemployed;

they are also more likely to be white and to have other sources of income after they lose their jobs — either unemployment insurance (sometimes supplemented by other benefits from employers or unions) or the earnings of other family members (Bendick and Devine, 1981). Because of these resources, it's sometimes assumed that they will have few problems "adjusting" to the economic shifts that have cost them their jobs. But the evidence suggests otherwise.

A substantial fraction of displaced workers spend many months, or even years, out of work or drop out of the labor force completely. Only about two-thirds of displaced workers in the Labor Department's study were back at work by 1985 (Devens, 1986, p. 40). Another study found that among workers laid off as a result of foreign competition, even those who were ultimately able to find new jobs had been unemployed for an *average* of nine months — and were receiving wages in their new jobs that were a third lower than those they earned before (U.S. Congressional Budget Office, 1982b, pp. xii–xiv). In a study of more than 1,000 New York City typesetters displaced by automation in the late 1970s, more than 400 went directly into early retirement when they lost their jobs (U.S. General Accounting Office, 1982a, p. 20). Among workers displaced by a steel-plant shutdown in Youngstown, Ohio, 35 percent retired early, 15 percent were still looking for work months after the shutdown, and 10 percent were forced to move from the area in search of work. And the average unemployment of workers displaced by a chemical company shutdown in Massachusetts was 60 weeks (Bluestone and Harrison, 1982, pp. 49–53).

The problems of long-term joblessness and lower earnings strike some displaced workers — especially blue-collar industrial workers, older workers, and women — even harder than others. Many of these workers withdraw from the labor force after losing their jobs — often exhausting unemployment benefits without finding new jobs. And if they do find new jobs, women and older workers typically suffer even greater declines in earnings than other displaced workers. A study of workers laid off from New England's aircraft industry found that 40 percent of the women, but just 14 percent of the men, had suffered a significant long-term loss of earnings as a result of losing their original jobs (Bluestone and Harrison, 1982, p. 61).

The situation of displaced industrial workers is both bleak and ironic. They are generally people who have worked hard and steadily for years and who have never lacked the capacity or the motivation to hold down a job. But — as we'll see in a moment in examining changes in the structure of jobs in America — none of these qualities can guarantee them a secure future. Many may *never* attain the same kinds of jobs or the same level of earnings they enjoyed in the past.

Understanding Unemployment:
Some False Leads

The high levels of unemployment in recent years — especially the stubborn, hard-core joblessness of urban youth — have spawned an almost bewildering variety of explanations from social scientists, economists, editorial-page writers, and politicians. Though the explanations differ widely in specifics, they share some common themes. Often, for example, they blame unemployment on faults or deficiencies in the unemployed themselves. Some add unwise government policy to the list of culprits. But few pay much attention to the structure of the economy itself. The explanations include these:

The belief that unemployed people "really don't want to work" is deeply embedded in American folk wisdom. The accusation is most often leveled at the young and, at least by implication, at minority youth, since they are among the most visible casualties of unemployment. A more sophisticated, but similar, version is offered by some economists who argue that much unemployment, especially among young people, is "voluntary," a deliberate choice of leisure over work — or at least over the kinds of jobs realistically available. People remain unemployed, in this view, because they have inflated expectations, leading them to reject jobs they could easily get if they weren't so choosy.

Bad Attitudes

All of us know people who don't like to work, and it would be silly to suppose that there are not *some* youth (and adults) who fit this description. But acknowledging that this may apply in *individual* cases is not the same as using it to explain unemployment as a *social* problem affecting millions of people. Here the "explanation" fails.

To begin with, studies of unemployed youth have found that (as one study put it) "virtually no unemployed young jobseeker" actually rejects a job offer; nearly all take the first job they are offered. The image of picky young people disdainfully spurning an array of job offers is false. For the kinds of youth hardest hit by unemployment, there are few offers of *any* kind even in the best of times (Freeman, 1981, p. 23; Wrigley, 1982, p. 146).

In a 1982 study, the economist Michael Borus found that many youths were willing to take any of several jobs listed (including dishwashing and working in a hamburger place), even at $2.50 an hour; the great majority would have accepted *any* job at $5 an hour. More than a million 18 to 19 year olds were willing to accept a job at a checkout counter or a hamburger place at well *below* the minimum wage. Even more revealingly, black youth showed considerably greater willingness to accept even very poor jobs at any wage.

Similarly, a recent study showed that the lowest wage young men said they would accept for a steady job — what economists call their "reservation wage" — averaged about $5 an hour for both black and white youth (slightly lower for blacks than whites) (Holzer, 1986). That may be more than many employers want to pay, but it's also just a shade over the poverty level for a family of three. And for a young man supporting a wife and child, $5 an hour is about as low as a wage can get and still provide even minimal necessities. So while these expectations *may* keep some youth from looking hard for very low paying jobs, they don't keep many from looking for ones that could decently support a family — and they therefore don't affect the larger problem of underemployment.

A review of the impact of job training programs on the work attitudes of disadvantaged youth affirms this conclusion from another angle. Few of these programs actually changed young people's attitudes toward work, though many of them tried to. Even when they *did* have some impact on youths' attitudes, the changes didn't help youths get jobs. Why not? Partly, the study concluded, because the

"These People Just Want to Work"

More than 3,000 people, many of them vaulting counters and climbing over desks, converged on a state employment office yesterday to get applications for 250 jobs at a hotel.

"I almost had a riot down here," said Marvin Noll, supervisor in charge of the employment service.

Police were called, but employment service workers had the situation under control by the time officers arrived.

"These people just want to work," said Police Sergeant John Paul.

Noll said more than 3,000 people picked up applications during the first hour his office was open.

"It was just wall-to-wall people. I've never seen anything like this," Noll said. He said a sizable turnout is expected today.

The applicants hope to be picked for the 250 jobs — 200 of them permanent — at the Radisson Muehlebach Hotel in downtown Kansas City.

Ron Juneman, the hotel's personnel director, said the hotel expects to fill all the jobs in March.

The initial plan, Noll said, was to hand out applications and interview the applicants on the spot. "We had to tell most of them to come back later in the week for interviews," he said.

Unemployment in the Kansas City area was 8.7 percent in December and an estimated 9.4 percent in January.

Source: San Francisco Chronicle, February 15, 1983. Used by permission of Associated Press.

youths' work attitudes weren't particularly negative to begin with. Even if their attitudes changed for the better, the real problem these youths faced was the sheer lack of enough jobs in the labor market and of the concrete skills to compete for the few jobs available. These youth often did display what the researchers called an "intermittent and casual" connection with the labor market. But, the study argued, this was largely because the labor market offered only minimal job opportunities for them to "connect" with (Forcier and Hahn, 1982).

A common variation of the "unemployed don't want to work" argument is that the pages of help-wanted ads in the newspapers "prove" that there are plenty of jobs for anyone who wants one. But that argument (popularized by Ronald Reagan during his first year in office) has been shown to be fallacious. The most revealing refutation appears in an article in *Fortune* exploring the realities behind the help-wanted ads in a small city in New York in 1978. *Fortune*'s investigation showed that there was much less to the pages of want ads than met the eye. Of 228 want ads in the Sunday paper, only 142 were actual job offerings within reasonable commuting distance of the city (many others, for example, were ads for "business opportunities," not jobs). Of those 142, only 42 didn't require special skills, like those of nurses, mechanics, or X-ray technicians. What was the response to those 42 ads that offered work for the typical jobless worker?

According to the article, the employers offering those ads were "fairly swamped by a tidal wave of applicants." A $3-an-hour night-clerk job in a motel drew 70 applicants in 24 hours. The city's jobless, the article concluded, "are not people who are out of work because they are overly fussy about how to make a living; they are people who are eager, even desperate, for jobs that pay $3 an hour." Even if all the full-time jobs listed had in fact gone to unemployed people (and none to people moving from one job to another, as is usually the case), the local unemployment rate would have dropped only insignificantly, from 7.4 to 7.2 percent (Meyer, 1978). A more recent study of Boston-area want ads found that even for the poorest, least-desirable jobs, there were an average of 15 to 20 responses to each ad within 2 days of its appearance (Clark and Summers, 1980, p. 14).

Too Much Welfare

Closely related to the idea that the unemployed don't want to work is the belief that unemployment insurance and other social benefits keep people from working by making *not* working too attractive. The economist Martin Feldstein, later head of the Reagan administration's Council of Economic Advisors, argued in the late 1970s that the "private costs" of being unemployed, for many workers, had become "quite small" because of generous unemployment insurance and other benefits. "The relatively low cost of unemployment," according to Feldstein, "is a substantial cause of our high permanent rate of unemployment" (Feldstein, 1978, pp. 155–158). What is the evidence for this view?

Not much. The idea that unemployment insurance or other transfer payments *keep* unemployment high requires us to believe that actual work opportunities are rejected by the hard-core unemployed in favor of living off "handouts" — and we have no evidence that this happens to any *considerable* extent (though again, of course, it doubtless happens occasionally).

The argument also exaggerates both the extent and the generosity of benefits for the unemployed. Consider unemployment insurance, the usual villain in this piece and the most important source of income support for the unemployed. The argument that it causes unemployment ignores, first of all, the fact that only a fraction, and a dwindling fraction at that, of the unemployed actually receive unemployment benefits. Only about 25 percent of the officially unemployed were getting unemployment insurance during the mid-1980s, as compared to about 60 percent in the recession of 1974–1975. In large part this is because the eligibility requirements for unemployment insurance exclude many of the unemployed, including people attempting to enter the labor force for the first time or to reenter it after a long absence and most of those who *leave* their jobs. Moreover, especially during lean economic times, many who are eligible exhaust their benefits before they find another job. One study found that only 65 percent of those who had exhausted their unemployment benefits had found a job even a year afterward (Freeman, 1981, p. 151).

Since youth are less likely to be eligible for unemployment insurance, we would expect them to have lower unemployment rates if this argument were a strong one; but the opposite, of course, is true. (Some European countries, in fact, do *not* exclude youth first entering the labor market from unemployment benefits and still have *lower* youth unemployment rates than we do [Reubens, 1980, pp. 125–126].)

The degree to which unemployment benefits compensate for lost earnings from work (what economists call the *wage replacement ratio*) is also relatively low in the United States compared with other industrial societies, including many with lower unemployment rates (Haveman, 1978).

Studies attempting to estimate more precisely whether, and how much, unemployment insurance may raise unemployment, suggest that though there may indeed be *some* impact, it's certainly a small one — and it can't explain more than a minor fraction of the unemployment problem. No relationship has been found between the level of unemployment benefits and the rate at which workers *quit* their jobs. Some studies do suggest that unemployment benefits may increase the *duration* of unemployment for those already out of work, but the effect is minimal. Thus, one study estimated that increasing the wage replacement ratio by about 25 percent might increase the length of an average spell of unemployment by about 4 days; another, that extending unemployment benefits by 10 weeks might decrease average employment during a year by 1 week. Obviously, neither would make much of a dent in the long spells of joblessness faced by the hard-core unemployed (Danziger, Haveman, and Plotnick, 1981).

Similar findings apply to other benefits for the unemployed. Some have argued that the generosity of the welfare system has made it easy for people not to work. But as we've seen, the benefits of the welfare system have shrunk considerably in recent years while the problems of unemployment and dropping out of the labor force have inexorably grown. And, again, some countries with far more generous social benefits — Sweden, Norway, Austria — also have far lower jobless rates than the United States.

Experiments with guaranteed income plans in the 1960s and 1970s, moreover, found that even when low-income people were guaranteed an income whether or not they engaged in paid work, the effect on their work habits (what in economists' jargon is called *labor supply*) was small. On average, the income guarantees reduced the work hours of family heads by less than 1 percent; somewhat more — not too surprisingly — for other earners in a family. Even with a minimum income assured, then, the work ethic seems to remain very strong at all levels of American society (Danziger, Haveman, and Plotnick, 1981, p. 1018).

The Minimum Wage

Another argument holds that federally enforced minimum wages cause unemployment by requiring employers to pay more for workers, especially youth, than they're "worth." An employer willing to hire a youth at $2 an hour may not find it worthwhile at $3.35, the minimum wage as of 1987. A 1982 *Fortune* article claimed, "By now, of course, many economists have come to agree that the minimum wage has been a cause of unemployment" (Lubar, 1982, p. 121).

Has it? Actually, the evidence shows that the connection between minimum wage and unemployment is by no means that simple. The minimum wage in the United States has risen less rapidly than those in some European countries with lower unemployment rates (Haveman, 1978). Moreover, the minimum wage in the United States has *not* risen, except on paper, in recent years; relative to the average wage American workers receive, the minimum wage is lower today than in the 1950s and 1960s — when unemployment was also lower. In 1961, for example, the minimum wage was an even 50 percent of the average earnings of workers in American manufacturing industries; 25 years later, it had fallen to 35 percent. And inflation has meant that, in real terms, the value of the minimum wage has declined from the late 1960s. Even more damaging to this argument, though, is the fact that unemployment has *never* been as high in the United States as it was during the Great Depression, which began years before the passage of the first federal minimum wage law in 1938 (Currie and Rosenstiel, 1979).

It's often forgotten, too, that many youth — including about half a million students working in small businesses — are already *exempt* from minimum wage legislation; increases in the minimum wage obviously have little to do with their unemployment problems.

Despite these basic contradictions, this argument has inspired an extraordinary amount of research attempting to calculate just what fraction of the unemployment rate, especially for young people, may possibly be attributable to the inhibiting effects of minimum wages. None of this research, though, has convincingly demonstrated large negative effects of the minimum wage on employment. A recent review of dozens of such studies found that most of them estimate that a 10 percent increase in the real minimum wage (that is, the minimum wage adjusted for inflation) might reduce teenage employment by anywhere from 0 to 3 percent, most likely in the "lower half of that range" (Brown, Gilroy, and Cohen, 1982). (At the level of unemployment faced by black teenagers in 1986, this "explanation" might account for somewhere between one-sixteenth and one-twenty-fifth of the problem.)

Another difficulty with this explanation is its failure to plausibly account for the *racial differences* in youth unemployment. The minimum wage, where it does apply to youth, applies to all races equally; but black teenage unemployment has typically been in the neighborhood of 2.5 times that of white youth in recent years. How could the minimum wage be responsible for this difference?

If a too-high minimum wage was what kept employers from hiring young people, we would expect the employers to jump at the chance to hire youth if someone else were footing the bill. But this isn't the case. Experiments in giving government subsidies to businesses to encourage them to hire low-income youth have generally failed to motivate employers. Recent Labor Department studies in Baltimore and Detroit found that only 5 percent of employers eligible for a *50 percent* wage subsidy (the government, that is, would pay half the youth's wage) hired even *one* new young employee. Only *18 percent* of eligible employers hired a low-income youth even when they were guaranteed a subsidy covering *100 percent* of the youth's wage. Clearly, something besides wage costs keeps employers from hiring young people, if they won't even hire them at *no* cost (*Employment and Training Report of the President*, 1983, p. 115).

If the impact of the minimum wage on teenagers is difficult to pin down, it's even more difficult for adults. Researchers completely disagree on whether there is *any* impact of the minimum wage on adult jobs and, if so, in which direction. That is, while some adult workers with low skills might not be hired because of the minimum wage, others are probably kept *on* the job because the minimum wage helps protect them from teenage competition (Brown, Gilroy, and Cohen, 1982). Thus, the often-heard proposals to lower the minimum wage for teenagers run the risk of substituting cheaper teenage labor for that of poor adults (especially women, who tend disproportionately to fill lower-paid adult jobs).

But there is an even deeper problem with the argument about the negative effects of the minimum wage on jobs. As we've seen, the job problem in America is not simply a matter of a *shortage* of jobs. It is also the inability of many of those who *do* have jobs to earn a standard of living adequate to meet fundamental human needs. As we write this, full-time, year-round work at the federal minimum wage provides an income more than $4,000 *below* the poverty line for a family head with three dependents. In this sense, to argue that the minimum wage causes unemployment misses the point, since work at wages *below* the minimum is, itself, part of the problem — not part of the solution.

A less judgmental, and more plausible, explanation of high unemployment (again, one with special relevance for the young) focuses on the effects of demographic changes in the American labor force — in the kinds of people working and looking for work today. Two of these changes have been particularly important in recent years; the growth in the teenage labor force and in the labor-force participation of women. According to some observers, both have helped boost unemployment rates, even when the economy is generally performing well.

A Crowded Labor Market

Growth in the youth labor force means that the work force now contains a bigger proportion of those people who tend to have higher rates of unemployment, which pushes up the unemployment figures as a whole. Relatedly, it's argued that the great influx of young and female workers means there are now simply too many people competing for jobs. In this view, though the economy has performed well, generating millions of new jobs in recent years, the pace of job creation hasn't kept up with the even more rapid growth in the demand for work. (Interestingly, this argument is based on a premise diametrically opposed to some of those we've just examined. Here, the problem isn't that people *don't* want to work, but that they *do*.)

Certainly, there is important truth in this perspective. To some extent, a rapidly increasing number of people wanting jobs is bound to cause some strains on an economy's capacity to put them to work. How *much* of an explanation it provides, however, is another matter.

Again, one important source of insight is the experience of other countries. Some industrial societies saw a less rapid growth in their youth labor force in recent years than the United States did, but others, such as Japan, saw a faster rate of increase — without the high youth unemployment that accompanied that increase here (Sorrentino, 1981, p. 9). In the United States, the growth in the teenage labor force, while quite rapid for many years, began to taper off in the mid-1970s and has declined since. Youth aged 16 to 19 made up almost 10 percent of the American labor force in 1975, but less than 6 percent in 1986. Yet youth joblessness, again, has generally risen. It's been predicted that the decline in the proportion of young people in the labor force will cause a shortage of young workers in the near future and will dramatically reduce the youth unemployment problem (*Fortune*, 1987). But, so far, the decline hasn't produced that hoped-for effect.

Nor is there much evidence that the influx of women into the labor force has been a major cause of unemployment — that women have "crowded out" other groups from the labor market. For the most part, as we've seen, women have moved into traditionally "female" jobs rather than into those traditionally held by men or younger people. Some research does argue that the rapidly rising numbers of women in the work force may have increased the competition youth face in seeking low-paying jobs (Borjas, 1986). But some other countries with a higher proportion of women in the labor force (Sweden is the best example) have also managed to maintain much lower youth unemployment rates.

Are Undocumented Workers Taking Too Many Jobs?

A recent study estimated that several million illegal aliens were in the United States in the 1980s and that perhaps 200 thousand were entering the country each year, mostly from Mexico and Latin America and increasingly from the Carribean and Southeast Asia (Passel, 1986). Since most of these immigrants, whether or not they remain in the country, come here in search of work and income, it's widely believed that they increase unemployment by crowding American workers out of jobs. What do we really know about the impact of illegal immigration on unemployment?

Surprisingly little. Though on the surface it seems logical that the employment of alien workers should displace native workers from jobs, hard evidence that it actually happens is difficult to come by. There is no consensus among researchers on *whether* illegal aliens

Fewer workers now make their living from the land.

displace American workers at all, much less on how *much*. Estimates run the range from *no* American workers displaced to one displaced for every illegal worker hired. The most plausible estimate is that illegal immigration probably does displace some American workers and thus has some impact on the jobless rate, but most likely a small one (U.S. Select Commission on Immigration and Refugee Policy, 1981).

Why such a small and uncertain effect? One of the most important factors is that most immigrant workers, including many legal as well as illegal aliens, apparently work in different labor markets than do American workers. They are typically found in the poorest-paying

Understanding Unemployment: Some False Leads   **263**

service jobs (like dishwashing), in agriculture, or in those manufacturing jobs with the lowest pay and worst working conditions. For two reasons, this concentration may mean that alien labor has minimal impact on American workers. For one thing, these jobs won't support an American worker — at least one with any dependents — since many pay less than the minimum wage. But they may offer much higher wages than are available in most of the immigrants' countries of origin. Thus, the jobs usually filled by immigrants are rarely sought by American workers. At the same time, employers in these low-wage, often marginal industries may not *want* native workers, preferring, instead, an immigrant work force that is likely to be more docile and less inclined to complain about substandard (even illegal) working conditions and subminimum wages (Cornelius, 1982). It's clear, then, that even if most of the jobs illegal aliens apparently fill were "opened" to native workers, the larger problem of *under*employment in the United States would not be helped.

The shortcomings of these explanations suggest that understanding unemployment demands that we focus our attention on the economy itself — and why it fails to produce enough jobs of sufficient quality to put Americans to work at living wages. In the following section, we turn to some of the key changes that have been taking place in the structure of work in the United States and consider what these changes may mean for American jobs in the future.

A "Service" Society?

It is widely agreed that there has been a profound shift in the way Americans earn their livings in the twentieth century. The shift is frequently described as one from a society primarily engaged in the production of *goods* to one primarily engaged in the provision of *services*. Since World War II, this shift toward a service economy has proceeded with extraordinary speed. Just after the end of the war, the goods-producing industries (agriculture, mining, manufacturing, and construction) produced almost half of our gross national product; service industries (including trade, communications, banking and insurance, entertainment, and social services, among others) accounted for the other half. Thirty years later, the production of goods accounted for just a third of GNP, services two-thirds (Ginzberg and Vojta, 1981).

The same shift can be seen in the proportions of people working in agricultural, blue-collar, and white-collar jobs. As Figure 8-2 shows, the most striking trend throughout this century is the sharp decline in

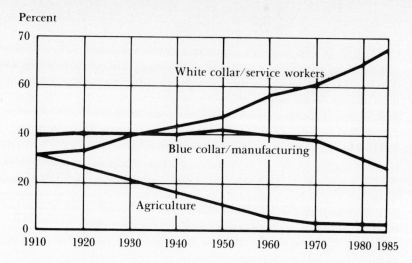

Percent

White collar/service workers

Blue collar/manufacturing

Agriculture

1910 1920 1930 1940 1950 1960 1970 1980 1985

Figure 8-2
The changing struc-
ture of work in
America

Source: To 1980, from *Public Opinion,* August/September 1981, p. 22. Reprinted with permission of American Enterprise for Public Policy Research. 1985 data from *Statistical Abstract of the United States,* 1987, p. 386.

agriculture as a source of jobs and livelihoods. At the turn of the century, agriculture engaged about a third of American workers. By the end of the 1930s, spurred by the economic calamity of the Depression and the growing substitution of machines for human labor on the farm, the proportion had been halved, to about one in six. By 1970 just 3 percent of American workers made their living from the land.

Meanwhile, the kinds of jobs we loosely call white-collar or service work (professionals and managers, technical workers, clerical, sales, and service workers) grew rapidly. In 1910 these occupations accounted for roughly the same proportion of Americans as did agriculture. But by 1970, as farm work dwindled, the proportion of white-collar jobs doubled. Between 1970 and the present, white-collar employment continued to increase, while blue-collar jobs declined.

With the mounting troubles of American manufacturing industries, there has been much talk about the coming end of blue-collar work. This "death" of manufacturing has been exaggerated. Blue-collar jobs still employed almost three out of every ten working Americans in 1985. But the trend in manufacturing remains sharply downward.

The existence of the trend toward a service economy is not in doubt. What it means in terms of the quality and availability of work, however, is another question — and the answers are not yet in. During the 1960s, some social theorists argued that these trends would bring about a "post-industrial" society (in the famous phrase of the sociologist Daniel Bell, 1969) in which, among other benefits, the quality of work performed by most Americans would be "upgraded." Dirty, dangerous, low-skill jobs requiring little more than muscle and endurance would be increasingly replaced by more sophisticated ones calling for brains, not brawn. More recent writers have predicted the coming of a "high-tech" society based on new developments in micro-electronics and robotics, in which increasingly sophisticated machines will do most of society's dull and dirty work. The work humans will do, in this view, will be increasingly challenging and intellectually demanding, requiring, as an article in *Fortune* recently prophesied, "a new order of worker — well-educated, highly skilled, strongly moti-vated, and capable of taking the initiative" (Lubar, 1982, p. 115).

How likely is this hopeful scenario? From the evidence we have, the coming shape of work in America seems much more problematic. While the rapid shift away from traditional blue-collar labor *could* mean an era of more rewarding and fulfilling jobs, it also poses the opposite danger — the threat of eliminating some of the better jobs in the economy without creating enough new ones to take their places. The changes we are now witnessing in the technology and organization of work could bring us a richer, healthier, and more challenging work life. But they could also create even greater and even more stubborn unemployment while eroding the quality of many jobs that now exist.

To assess these different possibilities, we need to look more closely at what the developing service economy and the accompanying tech-nological changes in the workplace have meant, so far, for the kinds of jobs Americans hold. On close inspection, it's clear that, on balance, these changes have *not* brought the general upgrading of work that many observers anticipated.

Though the growth of the service economy has generated millions of new jobs (and at a fairly rapid pace — faster, indeed, than in many other industrial countries), too many of these jobs have been poor ones, with low pay, poor working conditions, and little security or chance for advancement. Between 1963 and 1973, about one new job out of every five paid poverty-level wages or less. Between 1979 and 1985, nearly half did (U.S. Congress, Joint Economic Committee, 1986).

A main reason for this shift is that so many of the new jobs we've created are in traditionally low-paying sectors of the economy. Just two industries alone — retail sales and services — accounted for more than 70 percent of new jobs in private industry from 1973 to 1980. Most of these jobs, indeed, have been in just three specific categories: eating and drinking places, health services, and what the Labor Department calls business services (a broad category that in-cludes everything from photocopying to data processing to janitorial work). The increase in the number of people working in eating and drinking places from 1973 to 1980 was greater than the *total* number working in the auto and steel industries combined at the end of the 1970s (Rothschild, 1981, pp. 12–13).

The problem is that these are often some of the worst jobs in the economy. Not only do eating and drinking places pay the lowest wages of any American industry; but the work is often part time and offers few chances for promotion. And this trend toward the creation of more poor jobs than good ones is expected to continue at least through the near future. According to the Labor Department, by 1990 there will be more than 4 million new jobs in private medical care (mainly in poorly paid occupations, such as hospital aides and nursing-home workers) and another 5 million in retail trade (especially in fast-food restaurants, food stores, and department stores) (Currie, Dunn, and Fogarty, 1987).

Not all jobs in the emerging service economy are poor ones, of course. The service economy includes not only dishwashers and fast-food cashiers, but also doctors, social workers, and systems analysts. Nevertheless, the *typical* workplace of the modern service society is not the computer analyst's or doctor's office but the fast-food franchise, the hospital kitchen, and the "convenience" store. Many of these jobs are in small enterprises that operate with low profit margins in fiercely competitive environments. Only rarely do they offer the protections and amenities that workers traditionally achieved in the more stable, more unionized, and more profitable primary sector of the economy. According to one estimate, between 7 and 8 percent of jobs in very small businesses are lost each year (Greene, 1982, p. 109).

The much-celebrated postindustrial economy, in short, turns out to be heavily (though by no means entirely) made up of jobs that, far from offering unprecedented challenges and rewards, more often provide only low-paid dead-end work that can neither support a family, provide for the future, nor engage the mind. And there is troubling evidence that the growth of automation may aggravate this trend.

The Uncertain Impact of Automation

The rapid spread of sophisticated microelectronic technology, it's widely agreed, will help speed the transformation of American society toward a service-based economy. But how much, and in exactly what ways, this will affect the kind of work we do is an open question. Some argue that this "second industrial revolution" will improve both the quality and the quantity of work. Like the earlier technological transformation of agriculture, it's argued, automation in industry will increasingly enable workers to move from dull and perhaps dangerous jobs into more sophisticated and interesting ones — improving workers' lives and the productivity of the economy at the same time. Those who take this view also usually argue that fear of massive loss of jobs through the new automation is groundless; "there is ample historical evidence," one enthusiast wrote, "that automation in the past has led to greater employment" (Vedder, 1982, p. 25).

Automation and Job Skills

A closer look, however, again suggests that things aren't that simple. It's by no means clear that new technological development, like the growth of the service economy, has improved the quality of work in America — and there is much evidence that the opposite has occurred. The introduction of new technology has often led to what the economic historian Harry Braverman has called the "degradation" of work: eliminating or modifying many jobs with traditionally high skills and replacing them (if at all) with less skilled, more routine and alienating ones (Braverman, 1974; Noble, 1984). Though these new jobs are sometimes called white-collar work, there's little evidence that many of them involve greater skills than the jobs they've replaced in the factory and on the farm. As one critic described the "growing routinization of clerical and sales work": "In modern fast-food outlets, for instance, the cash register keys that clerks punch are marked only by pictures of hamburgers, french fries, milk shakes, and the like. Clerks punch the order in pictures, not prices, and the register does all the numerical computing" (Lucy, 1980, p. 83).

This process has also occurred within many formerly high-skill jobs such as printing, machining, and other crafts. Job satisfaction has generally been high in these jobs, and workers have traditionally enjoyed substantial control over their working conditions. The introduction of electronic technology has often lowered the skills needed in these jobs, simultaneously reducing workers' job satisfaction and control of the work process (Wallace and Kalleberg, 1982; Shaiken, 1985). A description in *Newsweek* of a highly automated jet-engine components plant operated by General Electric illustrates what has often happened to the jobs of skilled machinists:

> Computer-aided design terminals send exacting engineering specifications from distant parts of the country while digital information orders inventories, controls automatic warehouses, keeps records and precisely regulates 137 numerically controlled lathes, milling machines, and drills. . . . It used to take someone three to ten years to become fully qualified as a machinist. GE now can train its Wilmington workers in six months. (*Newsweek*, 1982, p. 81)

As automated production methods reach more and more industries, more and more skilled jobs may undergo the same transformation.

At the same time, it's also true that new high-tech industries have created many jobs that *do* require high-level skills — jobs for computer specialists, technicians, engineers, and others. But fewer than one job in twelve in the American economy falls into this category. And some of these new jobs, like computer programming, are now undergoing some of the same fragmentation into lower- and higher-skilled tasks that has already transformed older skilled occupations (Kraft and Dubnoff, 1986).

Automation has profoundly affected how workers relate to their jobs.

If the new technology's potential impact on the *quality* of work is still uncertain, its impact on the *quantity* of work is even more so. There is no question that, in the short run, some kinds of jobs in certain key

Automation and Unemployment

industries have already been hard hit by automation. The American Society of Manufacturing Engineers estimates that half of all auto assesmbly will be done by automated machines by 1995. Another study estimates that by the 1990s it will be technically possible to replace almost *all* semiskilled manufacturing workers in the auto, electrical equipment, machinery, and metal industries — all bastions of relatively well-paid blue-collar employment — through automation and robotics (Levitan and Johnson, 1982, p. 12). Other studies predict that the impact of automation will be less drastic and point out that, so far, only a few industries have been strongly affected (Fallows, 1984). But no one doubts that many individual workers have already been displaced by automation — and that many more will be in the future.

Beyond the immediate impact on blue-collar jobs looms the threat that automation *could* eliminate millions of jobs in those areas of the economy — especially clerical office work — that have been the main sources of new jobs in recent years, the heart of the emerging service economy itself. According to one estimate, the computer-based technologies that make up what some call the "office of the future" may affect 20 to 30 million white-collar jobs by 1990 (Levitan and Johnson, 1982, p. 12).

But it is much more difficult to predict what effect these trends will have in the longer run. According to rough projections by the Bureau of Labor Statistics, automation may cause job *growth* in almost as many occupations as job *loss*. Table 8-3 lists 33 occupations, employing roughly 8 million people at the end of the 1970s, that will, most likely, be adversely affected by automation. Note that although some of these are low-skill "rote" jobs, others have traditionally offered opportunities for skilled work, both blue and white collar. The table also lists 26 occupations, many computer-related, which should *grow* as a result of automation.

Whether automation will ultimately produce more jobs than it destroys will depend on many factors — including public policy. On the one hand, the modernization of the work process in many industries may make American industry more productive and more competitive in the world market, stimulating enough economic growth at home to boost the number of jobs. But on the other hand, several forces — including some inherent in the new technology itself — make this less likely.

One problem is what is sometimes called the "reproductive potential" of microelectronic technology — the potential for automation *within* the electronics and robotics industries themselves. The possibility of computers increasingly able to program themselves and of "robots building robots" is a qualitatively new development in modern

Adversely affected occupations	Positively affected occupations
Boiler tenders	Accountants
Bookkeepers	Bank clerks
Broadcast technicians	Bank officers and managers
Buyers	Business machine repairers
Cashiers	Ceramic engineers
Central office telephone workers	Chemical engineers
Credit managers	City managers
Drafters	Computer operators
Electroplaters	Computer programmers
Electrotypers and stereotypers	Computer service technicians
File clerks	Economists
Hotel front office clerks	Electrical engineers
Insurance agents and brokers	Engineering and science technicians
Insurance claim representatives	Industrial engineers
Machine setup workers	Instrument makers (mechanical)
Machine tool operators	Librarians
Molders	Maintenance electricians
Motion picture projectionists	Mathematicians
Office machine operators	Medical record administrators
Photoengravers	Metallurgical engineers
Photographic laboratory workers	Physicists
Postal clerks	Political scientists
Printing compositors	Sociologists _social work_
Production painters	State police
Radio and television announcers	Systems analysts
Railroad brake operators	Technical writers
Railroad conductors	
Railroad locomotive engineers	
Railroad telegraphers, telephoners, and tower operators	
Shipping and receiving clerks	
Stock clerks	
Telephone operators	
Tool-and-die makers	

Source: Adapted from U.S. General Accounting Office, *Advances in Automation Prompt Concern over Increased U.S. Unemployment* (Washington, D.C.: Government Printing Office, May 1982), pp. 34–35.

Table 8-3
Occupations expected
to be affected by
automation

industry. It may limit job growth even in the heart of the high-tech industries, even assuming strong growth in the economy as a whole (Levitan and Johnson, 1982, p. 12). Another problem is that the new high-tech industries are just as drawn to the lures of cheaper labor costs in foreign countries as other American industries before them.

It's even less certain that — even granting the most optimistic scenario of economic growth — the emerging high-tech economy will provide livelihoods for the *same* people whose jobs it has eliminated, and will continue to eliminate, in the coming years. The evidence we have so far isn't encouraging. One study of high-tech "reindustrialization" in New England, for example, by the economists Barry Bluestone and Bennett Harrison (1982, p. 97), shows that most of the workers who lost manufacturing jobs in the region's textile industry did *not* move into high-tech jobs, even though a substantial number of such jobs have been created in New England. Instead, most of the displaced industrial workers moved into lower-paying jobs in services or retail trade — or moved out of the labor force altogether. Similarly, studies of typesetters in New York's printing industry who had been displaced by automation found that many remained unemployed for months, retired, or were forced to take poorer jobs much below their former level of skills and pay (U.S. General Accounting Office, 1982a, pp. 23–24).

What these experiences suggest is that nothing *guarantees* that the American work force will automatically adjust to the technological trends now underway in the workplace. How these trends will affect jobs, skills, and the quality of working life will depend on the policies we develop to guide them. What is the outlook for the intelligent development of policies to shape the impact of the new technology? To approach this question, let's consider some recent trends in American policies toward work and unemployment.

The Future: Where Will the Jobs Come From?

The problem of jobs is clearly one of the most urgent issues on the American agenda today. For the past several years, our main response has been to "unleash" the private sector of the economy in the hope that doing so will stimulate business investment, thus creating economic growth and more jobs. Yet, despite incentives to business and the reduction of the government's own role in creating jobs and in training and retraining unemployed workers, the problems of unemployment and underemployment remain with us.

The evidence we've presented in this chapter suggests why the job problem persists — and why the approach we've taken, by itself, is unlikely to "put America back to work" in the future. Some of the reasons:

One problem is that, as we've seen, even substantial prosperity has not, by itself, been an effective remedy for unemployment and under-employment in the past. Even if we regain strong economic growth in the future, there is little reason to believe that the benefits will "trickle down" sufficiently to reverse this pattern. To be sure, economic growth *does* benefit many disadvantaged workers. One study esti-mated that with every drop of 1 percentage point in the national unemployment rate, the unemployment rate for white men heading poverty families falls 1.3 percent, for black men 1.6 percent. But we've seen that hard-core unemployment, as well as the under-employment of the working poor, tend to persist even during the upswings of the economic cycle (Bendick, 1982, p. 252).

The Limits of Conventional "Growth"

This problem is made much more acute by the impact of dein-dustrialization on some of the traditional paths to decent jobs for the less skilled. The automobile, steel, and other basic industries once provided a crucial source of jobs for low-skilled workers; when the economy expanded, these industries pulled in many otherwise hard-to-employ people and put them to work at good wages. The increas-ing automation of these basic industries threatens to close off these traditional avenues for jobs and income even if these industries enjoy a strong recovery. As the Nobel Prize winning economist Wassily Leontieff pointed out, even large investments in industry are unlikely to generate the numbers of jobs they once did. A new copper smelter costing $450 million employs just 50 workers per shift (Leontieff, 1982a, pp. 190–191).

Even an extraordinary spurt of economic growth under these circumstances will not, by itself, create new, good jobs and the neces-sary retraining for workers displaced from blue-collar industrial jobs; nor is it likely to offer much hope for an unemployed teenager in the inner city or a subemployed woman heading a family with preschool children.

The impact of automation on industry's capacity to create jobs is just one part of an even larger problem — the decreasing connection between investment and job creation in the American economy. As we've seen, many large corporations have used the capital they al-ready possess *not* to build job-producing plants or to refurbish old ones, but often to buy other, frequently unrelated businesses — a process that rarely creates jobs and sometimes destroys them. When corporations *have* invested in labor-intensive production, it has often been in foreign countries where labor costs are much cheaper.

In addition, it's equally unclear that small businesses will be able to supply what the large corporations haven't. Although there is some evidence that small businesses may be better at generating jobs than larger ones (Birch, 1982), the jobs they do create are most often both poorly paid and insecure. So the stubborn problems of underemployment and the trend toward a proliferation of inadequate jobs in the lower reaches of the service economy are unlikely to be much affected even by a rapid growth in the small-business sector of the economy.

The Reduction of Employment and Training Programs

Employment and training programs brought benefits for the economy as a whole as well as for participants.

Given these dilemmas, it seems logical for the government to take on a larger role through expanded job-creation and training programs. Some studies estimate that, per dollar spent, a public jobs program specifically targeted to the long-term unemployed would create *twice* as many jobs as would "trickle down" from a general cut in taxes designed to stimulate business (Bendick, 1982, p. 258). But our recent social policy has mainly gone in the opposite direction. The government's role in employment and training was dramatically reduced in the 1980s. It was argued that private employers would do better at hiring the kinds of people who were served by public employment

Tim Jewett/EKM-Nepenthe

and training programs than government could and that the programs were little more than costly and ineffective make-work. But the evidence doesn't bear out either argument.

Education and Jobs: The Declining Returns of Schooling

The idea that a good education will lead to a good job is solidly engrained in our national culture. And it's true that there is a clear relationship between levels of schooling and the risks of unemployment. Increases in formal schooling are almost invariably accompanied by lower unemployment rates.

A recent analysis by the General Accounting Office argues that inadequate education is the *most* significant contributor to hardcore youth unemployment and underemployment. Of roughly 1 million youth aged 16 to 19 who required serious help in the labor market, at least 44 percent had severe educational deficiencies — and a substantial proportion were illiterate (U.S. General Accounting Office, 1982d).

These facts lend support to the view that the job problem results mainly from a mismatch between poorly educated jobseekers and increasingly sophisticated jobs, and that the best way to attack the job problem is through better education and training.

But — though the links between schooling and jobs are real ones — there is another side to the story, one that suggests grave limits to a strategy of attacking unemployment and underemployment *mainly* through education and training. It's increasingly apparent that education is no guarantee of a good job — or even of a job at all — and that Americans, especially young Americans, may be increasingly *over*educated in relation to the jobs they will hold.

One disturbing sign is that the educational level of the American labor force has *risen* steadily throughout the past decade, simultaneously with the rise of unemployment. This trend is expected to continue, with the 1990s seeing sharp declines in the proportion of the work force who have less than a high-school education and a continuing rise in the proportion having four or more years of college.

Increasingly, even a college education is no certain protection against unemployment, as most college students are well aware. This is most apparent for black students; a close look at Table 8-4 shows that in 1982 blacks with some college education had an unemployment rate roughly equal to whites with an *elementary-school* education or less. But college is no longer a guarantee of a decent job for graduates of any race. During the 1950s and 1960s, college attendance expanded dramatically and, in general, so did the demand for college-educated labor. But in the 1970s, "the labor market for the educated underwent a major, unprecedented downturn" (Freeman, 1976a, p. 2), especially for *new* college graduates. This decline is reflected, in part, in growing numbers of graduates forced to take jobs outside the professional and managerial areas their training led them to expect. In 1966, 81 percent of women college graduates were working in professional and technical jobs; in 1978 just 65 percent were. Meanwhile the proportion of women college graduates working in *clerical* jobs rose from about 10 to 15 percent (Rumberger, 1981, p. 14). By the 1970s new college graduates also began to face *higher-*than-average unemployment rates, reversing a long tradition.

	Race		
	Whites	Blacks	Hispanics
Unemployment rate (total)	6.8	13.9	10.8
Elementary: 8 years or less	12.8	15.0	15.0
High school: 1–3 years	11.7	14.0	16.0
4 years only	7.6	16.4	8.0
College: 1–3 years	5.4	12.6	6.9
4 years or more	2.8	7.1	4.8

Source: U.S. Bureau of Labor Statistics, *Education Level of the Labor Force Continues to Rise* (Washington, D.C.: Government Printing Office, 1982), table 2.

Table 8-4
Schooling and unemployment rate, by race and Hispanic origin, 1982 (in thousands)

What happened to the once-glowing job prospects for college graduates? Part of the explanation lies in the generally poor performance of the economy during the 1970s and 1980s. But another part reflects a growing disparity between the increasing numbers of college-trained workers and a labor market no longer providing the same mix of jobs as in the past. During the 1950s and 1960s, the demand for college graduates was fueled by the expansion of jobs in government, education, and certain industries (such as aerospace and computers) that called for large numbers of highly trained professionals, and by the growth of spending on research and development. During the 1970s, however, the rapid growth rates in what the economist Richard Freeman called the "college-intensive" parts of the economy slowed markedly relative to the growth in those sectors traditionally employing fewer graduates. Sharp cuts in the growth of federal employment and in education are especially crucial in causing this shift (Freeman, 1976a, pp. 17–18).

The declining value of the college degree, however, is only the most dramatic expression of a more widespread problem of "overeducation" — or, more accurately, of underutilization of educational skills — throughout the economy. By 1977 more than a third of working adults described themselves as having skills that they were unable to use in their jobs (Rumberger, 1981, p. 17). The relatively unchanging skill requirements of most American jobs coupled with rising educational levels means that overeducation has strongly increased during the past two decades. Though the problem has been worst for the highly educated, "even workers with a high school education hold jobs incommensurate with their level of training" (Rumberger, 1981, p. 17).

Indeed, even the least-skilled workers may be overtrained for many jobs, especially the kinds of jobs usually available to youth. One study of what young workers actually *did* at work found that many "were almost never required to read, write, or use arithmetic skills on the job":

> Most spent their time cleaning or carrying objects; interaction with others was limited. . . . It has been suggested that for many young jobseekers, filling out a job application may actually require more literary skills than doing the job. (Wrigley, 1982, p. 247)

As we noted earlier in the chapter, efforts to lure private business to hire the disadvantaged — through subsidies, tax credits, and other incentives — haven't been successful. Often, employers have used the subsidies to pay workers they had hired already or would have hired even without the subsidy, thus defeating the aim of creating new jobs. Such programs can only be effective, it's widely agreed, if employers are genuinely willing to add new and sometimes difficult workers to their present work force; but most seem to regard the costs of hiring, training, and keeping these workers as too high (Ripley and Franklin, 1981).

But aren't government job programs useless "make-work"? No one argues that all of these programs have been efficient, well-run, or carefully designed. But there is a large body of evidence that some were quite successful — especially for the *most* seriously disadvantaged, for women, and for those with very poor job histories (U.S. General Accounting Office, 1982b). And they've helped the economy as a whole as well as the individuals participating in them. The Job Corps (an intensive skill training program for severely disadvantaged youth), for example, brought benefits that exceeded its costs by 45 percent (Bendick, 1982, pp. 260–261).

In the short run, programs like these are expensive. In the long run, they promise substantial savings in reduced welfare costs, higher productivity, and lower social pathology. In that sense, job programs can be an investment in our human resources. But whether the long-term vision will prevail is an open question. The same tension between short- and long-term goals runs through many other areas of American life, including health and medical care, energy use, and environmental quality — areas we will explore in the following chapters.

Summary

This chapter has examined work as a social problem. Both the problem of unemployment and the longer-run question of the future of work in America have become more urgent with the recurrent economic troubles of recent years.

In many ways, unemployment is getting worse. Jobless rates in the early 1980s reached levels not seen since the Great Depression; and, ominously, unemployment rates haven't fallen as low during periods of economic recovery as they did in the past. Jobless rates for the young have reached disaster levels, and millions of workers have been displaced from declining or "restructuring" industries. Too many of those who are *employed* are working at jobs that can't support an adequate standard of living.

Many common explanations for the severity of unemployment — that the unemployed don't want to work, that the minimum wage or welfare benefits keep them out of jobs, and that teenagers, women, or illegal aliens take away many jobs — are not well supported by the evidence.

Despite glowing predictions, the transition from the production of goods to the production of services in the "postindustrial" economy has not necessarily upgraded the quality of work in America.

The advance of automation in the workplace has eliminated millions of jobs. Whether continued advances in workplace technology will create or destroy jobs, on balance, is uncertain.

Simply stimulating the growth of the private economy will not solve these problems. Private investment no longer leads necessarily to good jobs, partly because of automation and partly because the jobs it does create are often either in foreign countries or, if in the United States, poorly-paid and unstable ones.

For Further Reading

Braverman, Harry. *Labor and Monopoly Capital: The Degradation of Work in the Twentieth Century.* New York: Monthly Review Press, 1974.

Levitan, Sar A., and Clifford M. Johnson. *Second Thoughts on Work.* Kalamazoo, Mich.: W. E. Upjohn Institute, 1982.

Maurer, Harry. *Not Working.* New York: Penguin, 1980.

Noble, David. *Forces of Production: A Social History of Industrial Automation.* New York: Knopf, 1984.

Scientific American. Special Issue on "Mechanization of Work." September 1982.

Shaiken, Harley. *Work Transformed.* Boston: Houghton Mifflin, 1985.

9

Health: Gains and Losses

Few things tell more about a society than the level of preventable suffering and disease it is willing to tolerate. During the 1960s we discovered that in this regard, as in so many others, American society contained some disturbing paradoxes. As citizens of the most affluent society in the world, Americans had access to some of the best health care money could buy. And as a result of rising living standards and the onrush of formidable new medical technologies, we seemed to be on the verge of conquering forever many of the most feared diseases of the past. But there was an underside to this progress. It was perhaps most vividly demonstrated when a group of physicians toured some impoverished areas of the rural South in 1967 and found children who showed startling levels of malnutrition, preventable disease — and even the effects of starvation. The doctors concluded that the children were "living under such primitive conditions that we found it hard to believe we were examining American children of the twentieth century" (quoted in Amidei, 1981, p. 458). Others found similar conditions in the inner-city ghettos of the North.

The discovery of the tragic paradox of starvation in the midst of affluence and of traditional, avoidable diseases side by side with the most advanced medical technology helped spur a commitment to government action to reduce some of the harshest inequalities in health care. And that commitment brought substantial results. The benefits of modern medicine and nutrition were brought within the reach of those too often excluded in the past — the poor, minorities, and many of the aged. The gap between their health status and that of the affluent began to narrow — so much so that by the end of the 1970s, a prominent health scholar wrote: "With respect to the most precious good of all, life itself, the United States is approaching an egalitarian distribution" (Fuchs, 1979, p. 6).

But there were other disturbing discoveries as well. By the late 1960s, it was becoming frighteningly clear that many health problems were linked to technological changes that affected the environment, the workplace, and the consumer products that represented the fruits of the affluent society. Whether it was the discovery of miners crippled by black lung disease, or the threat of cancer from food dyes and preservatives, or of leukemia and neurological damage from poisonous industrial wastes, we were fast learning that the economic growth we had taken for granted had its fearful costs as well as its obvious benefits. Most Americans, to be sure, were getting a bigger share of the economic pie. But the pie, as some put it, was increasingly toxic.

Once again, the response was a new commitment on the part of government — in this case, a commitment to exert some control over the dangers lurking in the air, the water, the shop floor, and the supermarket shelves. And like the commitment to narrowing inequalities in health care, it bore fruit in more stringent control of the hazards of work and consumption.

But by the end of the 1970s, many argued that we had gone overboard in our concern for occupational and consumer health. Government regulations were seen as stifling productivity and economic growth. In an ironic twist, it was even argued that regulation of industrial and environmental health hazards would make people sicker in the long run by undermining economic growth and thus slowing the rise in living standards, which was ultimately the most important source of improvements in health (Wildavsky, 1980). As one critic put it: "With today's consumer advocates heading the way, we are heading toward not only zero risk, but zero food, zero jobs, zero energy, and zero growth. It may be that the prophets of doom, not the profits of industry, are the real hazards to our health" (Whelan, 1981, p. 5).

If the government's regulation of workplace and environmental health hazards was often seen as utopian and counterproductive, its spending on health care for the disadvantaged was often regarded as a source of inflation and a burden on an already strained economy. As a result, we began to move toward reducing the government's role in health care. We cut spending on care for the poor and aged and relaxed occupational health and safety and consumer-product standards, in the name of restoring both economic efficiency and personal freedom. We attacked government spending for family planning services, in the name of restoring traditional morality.

The very idea that health ought to be a matter for *social* concern at all — so basic to the health-care policies of the recent past — is now being challenged in fundamental ways. In its place is a tendency to regard health as being mainly an *individual* matter. We are urged to eat better, to jog farther, to abandon our attachment to coffee and cigarettes, to freely express our feelings, and to avoid stress. All of these are surely important aims, and the evidence increasingly shows their strong influence on the chances of good health. But if the mood of the 1960s was to confront the social and economic aspects of health and illness, the mood of the 1980s is often to look inward and to seek both the sources of illness and the prospects for health in our personal life-styles.

This chapter will address these complex issues. We'll begin by examining how far we've come — and how far we still need to go — in achieving a more healthy society. We will look at changes in life expectancy, infant mortality, and the incidence of serious disease. And we will compare our progress with the progress achieved in other industrialized societies. We will then look more closely at the health of several specific groups: the poor, minorities, women, and industrial workers. Along the way, we'll touch on the arguments for and against a national system of health care. In the final part of the chapter, we'll consider some recent trends in our health-care policy in the light of these developments.

The Picture of Health

It is widely agreed that (with some exceptions) the overall health of Americans has improved substantially in the recent past. But the precise extent of that improvement turns out, like so many other social questions, to be surprisingly hard to measure.

Some of what we know about the health status of the population as a whole is derived from interview studies, mainly from a periodic National Health Survey carried out by the National Center for Health Statistics of the U.S. Department of Health and Human Services. Like any data based on interview surveys, these are subject to a variety of biases and misperceptions; but they do provide a useful, broad picture of the way most people view their own health. And, on the whole, that view is remarkably positive. Today, only about 12 percent say that their health is only fair or poor, and about 40 percent describe it

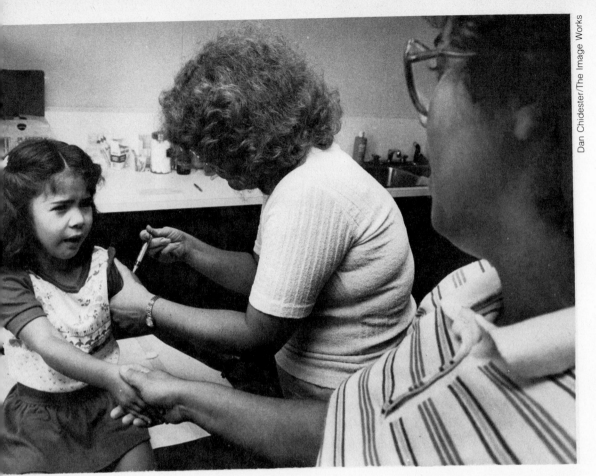

Advances in health
care have made most
Americans healthier
than ever.

as excellent. These proportions have improved slightly since the
mid-1970s. Only about 7 percent of the population describe themselves as limited in some major activity because of health problems,
and that percentage has changed little in recent years.

Another way of measuring health is to look at the incidence of
specific diseases. Here some of the most important data are gathered
from doctors' and hospitals' reports by the Center for Disease Control
of the U.S. Public Health Service. As with all data, however, these are
subject to problems of interpretation. Increases in the reported rates
of a given illness, for example, may mean that more people are
actually getting the disease, or that doctors have come up with a better
way of diagnosing it, or that more people who get the disease are
willing or able to seek treatment for it. For that matter, they may
mean that, because of medical advances, people who get the disease
live longer than they did before.

Disease	Number of cases per 100,000 population			
	1950	1960	1970	1984
Acquired immune deficiency syndrome (AIDS)	—	—	—	1.88
Diphtheria	3.83	0.51	0.21	0.00
Measles (Rubeola)	211.01	245.42	23.23	1.10
Pertussis (whooping cough)	79.82	8.23	2.08	0.96
Poliomyelitis	22.02	3.17	0.04	0.00
Tuberculosis	80.50	30.83	18.22	9.42

Table 9-1
Trends in the incidence of selected diseases

Note: AIDS data are preliminary. Tuberculosis reporting criteria were changed in 1975, so 1984 figure is not exactly comparable to those of earlier years.

Source: Data from U.S. National Center for Health Statistics, *Health United States, 1986.* Washington, D.C.: U.S. Department of Health and Human Services, 1987, p. 120.

Yet, despite these limitations, the general picture is, again, encouraging, with some exceptions. As Table 9-1 indicates, there has been a spectacular decline in some infectious diseases that were still common even fairly recently. Some, like poliomyelitis and whooping cough, have been virtually eliminated. Others, including measles and tuberculosis, have been dramatically reduced. But the darker side of the picture is that an entirely new one has appeared: acquired immune deficiency syndrome (AIDS).

Mortality rates (overall rates of death and death rates from specific causes) are probably the most reliable indicators of broad patterns of health and illness. Even these are not infallible; diagnoses of causes of death can be highly subjective and variable. These problems are aggravated, too, when we compare mortality rates across different countries. But these rates do provide a reasonably reliable portrait of trends in health in this country — and how we stack up relative to others.

Table 9-2 shows recent changes in mortality rates for the most common causes of death. These rates are *age-adjusted* to take into account changes in the age composition of the population. Other things equal, an older population will have higher death rates; and since our population is aging, a simple comparison between years would understate the decline in mortality.

Fewer Americans are now dying from most major causes of death than they were 30 years ago. The declines are especially apparent for some of the most deadly diseases of the past. Heart disease mortality has fallen by a third, and deaths from cerebrovascular disease (mainly

Table 9-2
Trends in mortality
rates (deaths per
100,000)

Causes	1950	1983
All causes	841.5	547.7
Diseases of heart	307.6	183.3
Cerebrovascular diseases	88.8	33.9
Malignant neoplasms	125.4	133.1
Respiratory system	12.8	38.5
Breast	22.2	23.4
Pneumonia and influenza	26.2	12.2
Chronic liver disease and cirrhosis	8.5	9.8
Diabetes	14.3	9.9
Accidents	57.5	35.6
Motor vehicle accidents	23.3	19.2
Suicide	11.0	11.6
Homicide and legal intervention	5.4	8.2

Note: Rates are age-adjusted to reflect changes in the age structure of the population.
Source: Adapted from U.S. Department of Health and Human Services, *Health United States, 1985* (Washington, D.C.: Government Printing Office, 1985), p. 46.

stroke) by nearly half. Tuberculosis was the eighth largest killer of Americans as late as 1950, but had declined to virtual insignificance by the 1970s. Some parts of the picture are less encouraging, though. Cancer — especially lung cancer — has risen, and so have cirrhosis of the liver (a disease usually associated with alcoholism), homicide (as we will observe in more detail in Chapter 11), and suicide. Moreover, the table doesn't include a new killer — AIDS — which had claimed at least 22,000 lives by 1987 and was expected to claim more American lives by 1991 than were lost during the Korean and Vietnam wars combined (Boston *Globe,* May 30, 1987).

The patterns of disease mortality are even more striking if we consider specific age groups rather than the population as a whole. Proportionately, for example, heart disease kills only about half as many men aged 35 to 45 as it did in 1950. Lung cancer, however, kills almost twice as many — suggesting that *part* of the changed American health picture has been a shift in the *kinds* of diseases most likely to take American lives.

Another dramatic decline has been in infant mortality, as Figure 9-1 shows. Today, considerably less than half as many infants are expected to die as 30 years ago. Especially striking was the sharp decline in the late 1960s and early 1970s — when the infant mortality rate dropped by a third. And more than 30,000 babies survived in 1983 who would have died if the 1970 rate had prevailed (U.S. Department of Health and Human Services, 1986, p. 85).

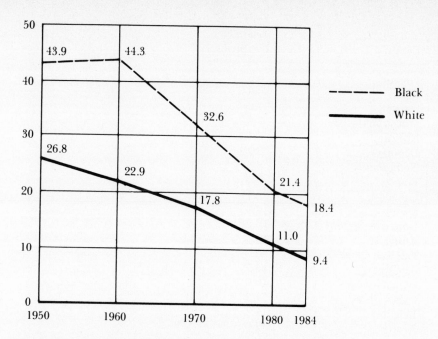

Figure 9-1

Trends in infant mortality: Deaths under 1 year per 1,000 live births

Source: Data from U.S. National Center for Health Statistics, *Health United States, 1986,* Washington, D.C., 1987, p. 85.

Older children, too, are far less likely to die than they were even in the quite recent past. Death rates for children under 15 dropped at a rate of 3 percent a year during the 1970s. If we go only a little farther back in American history, this change is enormous. Of every 100,000 children aged 1 to 4, 564 died in 1930; 139 in 1950; and just 52 in 1984 (U.S. Department of Health and Human Services, 1986, p. 96).

These are genuinely important strides forward. But a different side of the picture appears when we compare some key indicators of health in America with those in other industrial countries. As Table 9-3 shows, our infant mortality rate is worse than that in many industrial societies. Japan's and Sweden's infant death rates are only a little more than half of ours. The Swiss, Danish, Norwegian, and Dutch rates are also far below ours. If we had the same infant mortality rate as Sweden, almost 20,000 fewer babies would die in America every year.

As we'll see, infant death rates in this country are crucially affected by race. But it is important to realize that America's problem of infant mortality goes beyond race as well — even the rate of infant death among whites in the United States is higher than the rates in much of Western Europe and Japan. What's worse, the decline in infant mortality in the United States has been slowing in recent years — and even rising for infants over a month old. In some states and cities, and

The Limits of Progress

Table 9-3
Infant mortality rates:
Selected countries,
1983

Country	Infant deaths per 1,000 live births
Finland	6.5
Japan	6.6
Sweden	7.0
Switzerland	7.6
Norway	8.1
Denmark	8.2
Netherlands	8.4
France	9.0
Canada	9.1
Spain	9.6
United Kingdom	10.2
Australia	10.3
East Germany	10.7
Singapore	10.7
West Germany	10.9
United States	*11.2*
Belgium	11.3
Austria	12.0
Italy	12.4
New Zealand	12.5

Source: U.S. National Center for Health Statistics, *Health United States 1986*, Washington, D.C., 1987, p. 94.

in many poor rural communities, overall infant mortality rates have been rising as well, reversing one of the most important gains in the quality of American life in this century (see *New York Times*, October 24, 1985).

Our high rates of infant mortality are a major reason why Americans' life expectancy, especially for men, is somewhat lower than that of people in many other industrial societies. Thus, the fact that an American male born in the 1980s could expect to live almost 4 years less than a Japanese and 3 years less than a Swede largely reflects the much higher chance that the American might die during his first year. But the differences in the risks of death also persist through childhood and adolescence into young adulthood. An American boy 1 to 4 years old has almost three times the chance of dying as a Swedish boy the same age; an American male aged 15 to 24 has twice the chance of death faced by his Swedish counterpart (World Health Organization, 1986, pp. 257, 618).

Comparing death rates for *specific* causes among different countries is somewhat risky, too, since there are often slight differences among countries in defining and reporting disease. But some broad patterns are unmistakable. On balance, our standing relative to other industrialized societies is mixed, at best. Our death rates from cancer and stroke are in the average range — even better, perhaps, for stroke. But our death rates from heart disease, accidents, and homicide are exceptionally high. Again, too, these *overall* rates mask the tragic fact that Americans are much more likely to be felled by serious disease (particularly heart disease) at *younger* ages. American men in their late 30s and early 40s, for example, are almost three times as likely to die of cardiovascular disease as Swedish men the same age (Sidel and Sidel, 1977, p. 19).

All things considered, then, we have experienced substantial progress — but there are still formidable problems. And the diseases and disabilities that are increasing tend to be ones that have been linked to the stresses of modern social life (like cirrhosis and accidents) or (like cancer) to environmental changes that have accompanied our technological and economic development. These problems take on clearer shape when we begin to look at how health and health care in America vary among different groups.

As we'll see, these differences are pervasive and fundamental. And they show that the problems of health and disease are *social* as well as medical problems. Our chances of suffering disease, accident, or early death, despite improvements in recent years, still depend very much on whether we are born into affluent families or poor ones, whether we are minority or white, male or female, blue-collar industrial workers or professionals. And though some of these differences result from factors over which society has little or no control, others reflect choices about the way we organize our social life: the inequalities of income, race, and gender we tolerate (or encourage); the attitude we take toward the regulation of workplace hazards; and the social priority we place, or fail to place, on the prevention of disease.

Health Care and the Poor: How Much Progress?

Beginning in the 1960s, we began to take strong steps to improve the health of America's poor. We launched the Medicaid program — a comprehensive health-care system for low-income people; developed better nutrition programs for mothers and children; built community health-care centers to provide preventive care to people who often hadn't had access to regular care; and much more. It's generally agreed that these programs have done much to narrow the gap in health between the poor and the more affluent. But there is some debate about just how much that gap has been reduced — and what accounts for the remaining differences in health between the poor and the better-off.

At the end of the 1970s, a noted medical economist declared that "other things being equal, there is no longer any systematic effect of income on health" (Fuchs, 1979, p. 5). Yet two years later, another group of researchers stated flatly that "despite some improvements in health status, the poor are significantly sicker than the nonpoor" (David, Gold, and Makuc, 1981, p. 60).

Which assessment is correct? Evaluating just how equal the health of Americans has become is complicated by the lack of reliable measures (mortality rates, for example, are not usually broken down by income level) and also by some stubborn problems of interpretation. It's difficult, for example, to separate the effects of low income on health from the often simultaneous effects of low education or poor health habits. And since health status doubtless affects an individual's (or family's) level of income, just as income affects the chances of health or illness, it is often difficult to pinpoint the direction in which the relationship runs. But several points do seem clear. Poor people, for example, report that their health is only fair or poor, or that they are limited in activity by some chronic illness or disability, about *three times* as often as people with incomes more than double the official poverty level (U.S. Department of Health and Human Services, 1986, p. 70). These differences *could* reflect the impact of illness on the ability to earn a good living, rather than the other way around. But the same relationship between income and health holds, though somewhat less strongly, for children — for whom the effects of poor health on income are, obviously, less significant. Though even most poor children are rated by the parents as in good to excellent health, they are twice as likely as the national average to be judged as having some health problems (Kovar, 1982, p. 9).

A recent study of childhood deaths by the sociologist Robert Mare (1982) provides further evidence of the independent effect of low income on poor health. Mare found that the differences in the risks of death for children according to their families' income level are at least as great as those for adults, mainly because of a much higher risk of death by accidents faced by lower-income children.

Better health care for low-income people has substantially reduced the risk of those illnesses and disabilities most susceptible to improvement through medical attention: infant and maternal mortality, influenza, and pneumonia, some kinds of cancer (such as breast and cervical cancer) that are often curable with early detection, diabetes, and cerebrovascular disease. But many of these diseases still remain disproportionately afflictions of the poor. One recent study concluded that poor men are 40 percent more likely to die of heart disease than affluent men (*San Francisco Chronicle*, February 21, 1985); overall, according to another investigation, a white man is 12 percent more likely to die at age 50 if he is in the lowest part of the income scale (Duleep, 1986). A Boston study found that if mortality rates for children and youth from the poorest neighborhoods in that city had been the same as those for children and youth from the richest neighborhoods, more than a third of childhood deaths among the poor wouldn't have happened (*New York Times*, August 8, 1985). Cancer, too, is more likely to strike the poor. A recent study of cancer in New York City found that "mortality rates from all cancers increased progressively with decreasing income" (Shai, 1986, p. 547).

How do we explain these continuing inequalities? One line of thought puts the emphasis on differences in *education* (and, by implication, on differences in health habits and life-style). Several studies have shown that the level of education achieved by an individual (or, in the case of children, by their parents) has a strong relationship to health status — stronger than income itself. The relationship holds even when income is "controlled"; that is, even relatively well-off children, for example, may have health problems (such as dental problems, obesity, or anemia) if their mothers have had few years of schooling (M. Grossman, 1982, p. 192).

Some writers take this to mean that it is not income inequality itself that is responsible for the remaining differences in health between affluent and poor, but bad health habits among poor people. At the extreme, this implies that the ill-health of the poor is now, in some sense, "their" problem — that we've done all we can as a society to equalize access to health care, but some people are simply unable to take advantage of that care or to practice elementary methods of prevention (Fuchs, 1979).

No one would deny that people differ in how well they attend to their own and their children's health needs and in their understanding of the importance of good nutrition and exercise. But the argument that the health problems of the poor are mainly a result of their own personal failings stretches the evidence considerably. The best evidence suggests that *both* income and education have independent impacts on health. Robert Mare's study of childhood deaths, for example, found that both the family's income *and* the mother's years of schooling shaped a child's risks of death (Mare, 1982, pp. 541–543); and the same independent effect of low income has been found in the case of high rates of infant mortality among the poor (Gortmaker, 1979).

Unequal Access to Care

The most important problem with the argument that people of all income levels now enjoy *equal access* to health care is that the central premise is, unfortunately, premature. Despite important changes, "equity — equal access acccording to need — has not been achieved" (Kovar, 1982, p. 13). Some of the problems:

- Low-income people are much less likely to have any medical insurance. The problem is especially severe for the so-called near-poor — those not poor enough to be eligible for government programs like Medicaid but too poor to be able to afford private insurance.

- Low-income people are less likely to have a regular source of health care or a regular personal physician and are much more likely to get their care from hospital emergency rooms or outpatient clinics.

- Low-income women are far less likely to see a doctor in the early stage of pregnancy and are less likely to receive other kinds of preventive care. Though periodic exams can greatly reduce the

Not everyone is well protected by the American health-care system.

Michael D. Sullivan/Texas Stock

risks of breast and cervical cancer, for example, poor women have far fewer of them.

- Low-income children are considerably less likely to have had a skin test for tuberculosis or to have received complete vaccinations against common diseases like measles and polio.

Part of the reason for these continuing disparities lies in the limits of government health programs for the poor. Though Medicaid and other public programs have reduced health-care inequalities considerably, they still failed to reach many of the medically needy even at their peak in the 1970s. Medicaid actually covers only about 40 percent of America's poor — down from 65 percent in the mid-1970s — partly because eligibility is limited mainly to the disabled, the aged, or people in single-parent families and partly because different states are allowed to set their own (sometimes very low) income eligibility standards. In Alabama, for example, a family of three had to earn less than $118 a month in 1985 — about 16 percent of the poverty level —to be eligible for Medicaid; in Mississippi, $120 (Rosenbaum and Johnson, 1986, p. 445).

Many of the poor, moreover, live in areas so lacking in accessible health-care facilities that they have great difficulty getting adequate care even if they *are* covered by government programs. This can be seen in the evidence that less than half of the women and children eligible for the federally funded Women, Infants, and Children (WIC) Program, which provides nutritional supplements for low-income mothers and young children, received benefits from it in the late 1970s — and the proportion was much lower in many states (Kovar and Meny, 1981, p. 37). Health care for the poor has improved greatly, but it has never come close to reaching all of the poor.

Minorities and Health: The Persistence of Inequality

Health in the United States is also still sharply stratified by race. There have been significant improvements in recent years, especially because of the spread of health services to poor minority communities, but wide racial differences in health and in access to health care are still very much with us, and in some cases have become even wider.

These differences are seen throughout the life cycle. As Figure 9-1 (p. 285) shows, though rates of infant mortality have fallen for both whites and blacks since 1950, the racial *gap* has remained the same.

About ten out of every hundred thousand white infants died before their first birthday in the mid-1980s — a figure considerably higher than that in many other industrial societies. But twice as many black infants died. In the District of Columbia, Illinois, and Michigan, black infants were less likely to reach their first birthday than babies born in the Third World countries of Jamaica, Trinidad, Cuba, and Costa Rica. The black infant death rate was about equal to the white rate of 15 years before; and if blacks had been blessed with the white infant death rate, almost 6,000 of the roughly 12,000 black babies who died in 1982 would have lived.

The roots of the racial disparity in infant mortality are planted well before birth. Black infants, for example, are twice as likely to be of low weight at birth as white babies, and low birth weight, in turn, is one of the most reliable predictors of early infant death (Hogue et al., 1987).

Nevertheless, the black infant death rate has dropped substantially (especially from the mid-1960s to the mid-1970s) with the spread of health care and nutrition programs into rural poverty areas and inner-city ghettos. That decline also accounts for much of the narrowing of the racial gap in life expectancy. Since 1960, the average life expectancy for blacks has increased by about 6.5 years; for whites, about 4.7 years (U.S. Department of Health and Human Services, 1986, p. 84). But despite the positive trend, a white male, at birth, can still expect to live some 6 years longer than a black; a white female, about 5 years.

At later ages, these differences almost disappear. By the end of the 1970s, life expectancy at age 65 was about the same for both races (for both sexes). But at the *middle* of life, as at the beginning, the risks of death from many causes are strikingly greater for black Americans. For example:

- *Heart disease:* Black men in their late 30s and early 40s have more than double, and black women more than three times, the white rate of death from heart disease. And though heart disease generally kills men at a far higher rate than it kills women, the death rate for black *women* under 35 is higher than that for white *men*.

- *Cancer:* The age-adjusted death rate for cancer is over a third higher for black men than for white men. In general, the chances of dying from cancer increase with age. But the cancer death rates of middle-aged black men resemble those of white men who are about *5 years older*.

- *Stroke:* Black men die from strokes at a rate almost twice that of whites. And though, like heart disease, stroke is typically more common for men than for women, it is much more likely to strike a black *woman* than a white *man* (U.S. Department of Health and Human Services, 1986, pp. 104–105).

Similar, though often less dramatic, differences show up as routinely poorer health and higher levels of disability among blacks. Blacks are twice as likely as whites to report their health as "poor" or just "fair." Washington, D.C., with a population about 70 percent black, has the highest rate of tuberculosis — about four times the national average (Rice and Payne, 1981, p. 129).

How do we explain these differences? The reasons are complex, but it seems clear that part of the disparity reflects some general features of the social, economic, and cultural context of black life in America today, while part reflects the effects of racially unequal health care.

Part of the problem, for example, is inadequate nutrition. There has been much improvement in the nutritional status of minorities since the reports of starvation among southern children in the 1960s, but much remains to be done. As the Children's Defense Fund has pointed out, for most important nutrients, undernutrition is *twice* as common among black as among white children (Children's Defense Fund, 1981, p. 164).

The quality of health care remains unequal for minorities and the poor.

It is increasingly understood, too, that minority health (like that of the poor of all races) is adversely affected by the physical and psychological impact of stress. This is vividly illustrated in the racial disparities in the risks of certain diseases generally understood to be stress related. Hypertension (high blood pressure), for example, is much more common among blacks, which helps explain the higher black rates of death from stroke and heart disease.

A National Health System?

It is often argued that some form of national health insurance for everyone would help alleviate the inequalities in American health care. The appeal of such a system is not hard to understand. Not only do many people receive less-than-equal care, but others are not covered, or only partly covered, by public or private health insurance. An estimated 37 million Americans had no health insurance in 1986; millions more had some coverage, but not enough to pay for high medical bills resulting from long hospital stays or complicated surgery. An even larger number of Americans lacked coverage for long-term care in nursing homes or extended-care facilities.

The uninsured and inadequately insured are disproportionately drawn from the poor and the near-poor (those not poor enough to be eligible for Medicaid or other public programs and neither affluent enough to afford private insurance nor employed in a job that provides health benefits).

Though we usually take this medical insecurity as something we have to live with, the United States is actually the *only* Western industrial society that lacks some form of comprehensive, universal national health program. What makes this situation especially surprising is that most of the American public — about 75 percent, according to recent opinion polls — supports the idea of national health insurance, and that majority sentiment has been with us since the Great Depression.

Why haven't we heeded that sentiment and followed the road every other industrial society has taken? The reasons include successful resistance by the organized medical profession and private insurance companies and the widespread belief that a comprehensive medical program for all represents "socialized" medicine that would necessarily be cumbersome, inefficient, and perhaps most important, costly.

What can we learn about the validity of these fears from the experience of other countries? The exact form that national health programs have taken in different countries varies widely, from elaborate insurance systems (as in Sweden) to public control of most aspects of health care (as in Great Britain). But for an approach that may be most applicable to the United States we might look closer to home: to Canada, which has had a comprehensive national health insurance system since 1947.

Under Canada's tax-supported system, every Canadian is covered for the costs of all medically necessary expenses. Measured against the goal of achieving security against devastating health expenses, the system has been an unqualified success. As a recent study of the Canadian system sponsored by the U.S. Public Health Services put it:

> For all Canadians, the fear of not being able to meet the cost of the hospital or doctor's bills is a thing of the past — and no Canadian citizen has to go begging to the welfare department to pay a hospital or doctor's bill. Canadians have obtained equal access to medical care and medical care with dignity. (Hatcher, 1981, p. 1)

The effects of social and economic disadvantages like poor nutrition and high stress are aggravated by inequities in access to health care. These inequities, too, begin early in life. Thus, though it is now well understood that early screening to detect high-risk pregnancies can significantly reduce infant mortality, and that early prenatal care strongly reduces the chances of both infant and maternal death, black women are far less likely to receive adequate prenatal attention. And

---

Has the provision of quality health care to all caused Canadian health costs to skyrocket? That was the main objection raised in Canada when the system was introduced in the 1940s, and that fear remains a major obstacle in the minds of many people in the United States. If everyone is entitled to "free" care, it was argued, doctors' offices and hospitals would be swamped with patients demanding excessive care and creating a massive increase in costs. But these fears didn't materialize. Health care in Canada now takes a considerably *smaller* fraction of GNP than it does in the United States. In 1960 that fraction was between 5 and 5.5 percent in both countries. By 1978 it had risen to more than 9 percent in the United States but to only a little more than 7 percent in Canada. Our costs of *hospital* care *doubled* in that period as a percent of GNP, while Canada's increased by about a third.

What about efficiency? The Canadian health-care dollar is put to more efficient use, by most measures, than its counterpart in the United States. One way of seeing this is to compare administrative costs. How much is spent simply to manage the health-care bureaucracy rather than deliver services to patients? Administrative costs in Canadian health care are, proportionately, about a fourth of those in the United States; 95 cents of the Canadian health-care dollar goes directly to doctors and hospitals for services. In private health insurance programs in the United States, administrative expenses account for about *20 percent* of the total costs. Our administrative costs rose about 2.5 times between 1960 and 1978 as a proportion of GNP; Canada's were the *same* proportion in both years.

How is this possible? One key to the relative success of the Canadian system is its simplicity, made possible by the standardization of health benefits in a single comprehensive plan, administered uniformly within each province. A crucial part of the plan is that decisions about most issues affecting costs and the quality of services are the responsibility of health-planning authorities and are not left simply to the "market." Standard fee schedules for doctors, for example, are negotiated periodically, and doctors are required to stick to them. Doctors who encourage the overuse of services can be disciplined by health authorities. The introduction of costly new facilities or equipment is carefully regulated according to need — it is not simply left to the decisions of hospital administrators.

The simplicity of having only a single package of benefits helps reduce costs considerably. We often think of government planning as being inevitably cumbersome and bureaucratic. But the opposite seems to be true of health care. In the United States, the effort to devise many different and competing structures of benefits for different kinds of people (in the hope that no one will get more than they "ought to") generates complex exclusions and rules about eligibility, which in turn require an enormous — and expensive — bureaucracy just to enforce them. Paradoxically, our concerted attempt to ensure that no one gets "something for nothing" costs us dearly — and keeps us from reaping the potential benefits of a more efficient health-care system.

Sources: Hatcher, 1981; Schroeder, 1981; Colburn, 1986.

---

they are more likely to receive it, if at all, later in their pregnancy (Kovar and Meny, 1981, pp. 14–15, 32).

Assuming that black children survive the risks of birth and the first year of life, they are less likely than white children (and even less likely than black children at the start of the 1980s) to be completely immunized against common preventable diseases such as polio or diphtheria. They are also less likely to have a regular doctor.

Many black Americans of all ages, and an even higher proportion of Hispanics, have difficulty getting health care at all, despite their usually higher rates of serious illness. About 30 percent of Hispanics, 22 percent of blacks, and 14 percent of whites aren't covered by any health insurance, public or private (*Statistical Abstract of the United States*, 1986, p. 101); and both blacks and Hispanics are more likely to be "dumped" in poorer-quality public hospitals or — increasingly — to have trouble finding care *anywhere*.

Women's Health: Gender and Medical Care

Women are the principal consumers of health care in the United States. However, the problems they face in health care are often obscured by the fact that, according to most (though, as we'll see, not all) measures, women tend to be healthier than men. In some important ways, too, that comparative advantage is increasing.

The most striking gender differences in health status are in life expectancy and the risks of mortality from most major killer diseases and major nondisease killers (such as accidents, suicide, and homicide). Adjusted for age, men die from *every* one of the ten major causes of death at a higher rate than women (though black women die of diabetes at a higher rate than black men) (U.S. Department of Health and Human Services, 1986, pp. 46–47).

These differences begin very early, in higher mortality rates for male infants and much higher male mortality rates among adolescents (especially from accidents and suicide, the leading adolescent killers), and continue into adulthood. Men under 45 have about three times the risk of death from heart disease, the number one cause of death in the United States, as women the same age.

Much of the overall decline in mortality rates in recent years, in fact, is accounted for by the especially rapid declines for women. One result is the well-known difference in life expectancy between women and men. Women's life expectancy at birth in the United States now exceeds men's by about 6 years. Interestingly, American women's longevity comes much closer than American men's to equaling that in other, generally healthier industrial countries.

But focusing solely on mortality exaggerates the healthiness of women compared to men in the United States. There are some disturbing exceptions to the rule that women's chances of death have declined faster than men's. The most striking is the rapid rise in women's deaths from lung cancer (generally attributed largely to the rise in smoking). And it's *only* women, of course, who face death in pregnancy and birth. Though maternal mortality rates have declined greatly in the United States in the past several decades, they remain considerably higher, especially among black women, than in many comparable societies (Moore, 1980, p. 10).

Moreover, though women's health appears better than men's when measured by the risks of mortality from serious diseases, other measures draw a different picture. Although women are less likely to be killed at relatively young ages by catastrophic diseases, accidents, or violence, they are *more* likely, especially at older ages, to suffer some chronic, limiting impairment or disability (Lebowitz, 1980; Moore, 1980). Partly for that reason, women seek doctors' services more often than men do, and are considerably more apt to use many medications. Two-thirds of all prescriptions for tranquilizing drugs are written for women, and the overpromotion of drugs as a typical response to women's medical needs has become a problem of increasing proportions. In a generally overmedicated society, women are the chief targets of legal drug advertising and marketing and are also three-fifths of the people admitted to hospital emergency rooms for drug-related problems (Moore, 1980, p. 37). But this overmedication of women is a response, however inappropriate, to a set of real problems, emotional as well as physical. Women, particularly low-income and minority women, report higher levels of tension and anxiety than men, as well as a lower general sense of psychological well-being and more severe feelings of stress (Moore, 1980, p. 12).

What accounts for these differences? There is considerable debate about the issue, and the answers are not yet all in. One common argument is that they reflect the influence of changes in traditional sex roles. Men tend to be locked into a way of life, particularly at work, which emphasizes competition and striving and generates health-destroying stresses from which, it's sometimes argued, women have been traditionally sheltered. As women move into formerly male-dominated jobs and generally adopt more traditionally "male" social roles, it's argued, their health patterns will come to resemble men's. This argument is sometimes used as ammunition against removing occupational and cultural barriers to women's equality at home and in the workplace. But is it true?

Abortion, Family Planning, and Mortality

The liberalization in the early 1970s of laws and regulations governing such emotionally charged issues as abortion, contraception, and family planning was a significant development in health policy in America. Supreme Court rulings made abortion a matter of choice to be settled between a woman and her doctor. Federal health policy extended legal abortions and improved family services to the poor through Medicaid and other public programs. Teenagers were informed about family planning techniques and contraception, with or without their parents' knowledge. These developments gave women (especially poorer and younger women) much greater control in decisions affecting reproduction.

More recently, these policies — and the deeper philosophy behind them — have been increasingly and sometimes violently attacked. Some court decisions have restricted the scope of legal abortion generally and particularly the use of federal funds to provide abortions for lower-income women. Family planning services have been cut back severely, and family planning clinics have been attacked by opponents of abortion.

Often lost in the debates over these policies are the facts about what women's increased reproductive rights have accomplished, strictly in *health* terms. Whatever one's personal views on contraception or abortion, these outcomes must be an important part of any intelligent discussion of public policy toward them. And the evidence is mounting that the widening of reproductive choice for women was a major factor in reducing deaths related to childbirth and pregnancy — both maternal mortality and, even more strikingly, infant mortality.

The reduction of the number of high-risk pregnancies has been one of the most important health advances in America in recent decades. We've seen one of its effects in the dramatic decline in infant deaths; another has been the reduction of *maternal* mortality to a fraction of its level of even 30 years ago. Dying in childbirth was once an ever-present risk for American women. Even as late as the end of World War II, more than 200 women died in childbirth for every 100,000 live births. Better birth techniques and prenatal care brought that rate down to about 50 per 100,000 by the late 1950s — and, by the mid-1980s, to less than 8 per 100,000 births — a striking and welcome decline in one of the most significant risks of death for younger women (Figure 9-2). This decline reflected several developments: an increase in good prenatal care, especially for low-income women; the spread of knowledge about contraception and family planning, allowing women better control over the timing and planning of pregnancy; and the increased availability of legal abortion. During the 1970s, the number of women receiving publicly funded family planning services increased almost ten times (from 400,000 in 1970 to about 4 million in 1978).

The liberalization of abortion laws also resulted, even more directly, in reducing deaths related to abortion itself. The difficulty of obtaining abortions legally before the 1970s reduced the overall number of abortions, but it also meant that a far greater proportion of those that *were* performed were done illegally, often under dangerous and unsanitary conditions. (Prior to the Supreme Court decision in the early 1970s, there were an estimated 1 million illegal abortions a year.) Liberalization reduced abortion-related deaths dramatically, cutting them by two-thirds between 1972 and 1975 alone, according to U.S. Public Health Service data.

The most precise accounting of the health

impact of liberalized abortion, however, comes from studies of its impact on infant mortality. We've seen that infant mortality declined greatly for both blacks and whites in the 1960s and, even more rapidly, in the early 1970s. A study by the economist Michael Grossman has shown that the increase in the rate of legal abortions was the "single most important factor" in that decline — more important than improved income and levels of schooling, or better health care generally.

According to Grossman, this has crucial implications for the way we think about abortion and public policy. A policy banning legal abortions that reduced them to the pre-1970s level would cause a rise of 1.8 deaths for every 1,000 white births, and 2.8 for every 1,000 nonwhite births. At 1978 birth rates, that translates into the death of more than 1,800 nonwhite and more than 4,800 white infants a year.

Source: Moore, 1980; U.S. National Center for Health Statistics, 1987; Corman and Grossman, 1985; Grossman, 1982; Tietze, 1982.

Maternal deaths
per 100,000
live births

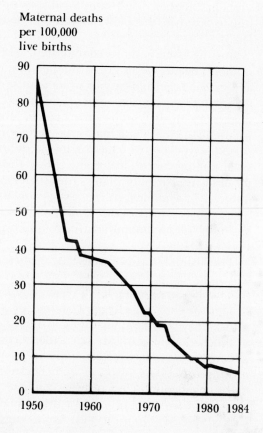

Figure 9-2
The decline in maternal mortality, 1950–1984

Source: Data from U.S. National Center for Health Statistics. *Health United States 1986,* Washington, D.C., U.S. Department of Health and Human Services, 1987.

The evidence suggests that it isn't. Generally, women's rising participation in the paid labor force *hasn't* reduced the male/female disparities in mortality from those illnesses (like heart disease) typically linked to the stresses of competition and achievement. On the contrary, the male disadvantage has usually *grown* (Moore, 1980, p. 10). A recent study of women listed in *Who's Who* shows that women who have achieved considerable social and economic status haven't lost their life-expectancy advantage over men. And a major long-term study of the risks of heart disease has demonstrated that, on the whole, women who work in the paid labor force have no greater risk than those who do not (Moore, 1980, p. 35).

In general, as recent research shows, women who work outside the home are typically *healthier* than those who work only within the home. One study found that housewives reported almost *twice* as many days of restricted activity due to illness as either employed men or employed women. Women who worked outside the home went to the doctor less often and reported their health as excellent much more often than women who worked only in the home. And housewives had higher death rates at all ages up until age 60 than women who worked in the paid labor force (Nathanson and Passannante, 1983).

But the issue is more complicated. The impact of paid work on women's health varies greatly, depending on the nature of the work and on the other obligations women must shoulder at the same time. "Women's" work is sometimes thought to be inherently less stressful, dangerous, or demanding than "men's." But women workers actually predominate in several highly dangerous industries. Fifty-six percent of textile workers, who face high risks of brown lung disease (byssinosis) and lung cancer, are women. Two-thirds of the workers in laundry and dry-cleaning plants, who suffer high rates of some cancers induced by chemical solvents, are women. Similar risks abound in many other industries that mainly employ women, such as electronics assembly, plastics manufacturing, and hospital work (Stellman, 1979; Lebowitz, 1980).

The health hazards for working women, moreover, aren't confined to blue-collar industrial or service work. Evidence is accumulating that health-threatening levels of stress are associated with many kinds of clerical work, the biggest source of jobs for American women (Linsenmayer, 1985). According to one study, three features common to much clerical work are particularly correlated with heart disease among women: lack of job mobility, suppressed hostility, and an unsupportive boss. Among women clerical workers with children, these negative job chracteristics combine with the "double duty" of household work to produce a much higher susceptibilty to stress-related disease (Moore, 1980). As this suggests, what counts in determining women's health (as it does, of course, for men as well) is not simply the fact of working itself, but the quality and quantity of the work and the way it fits with the rest of one's life. In a nutshell, though there is no evidence that achieving rewarding jobs will hurt women's health, there is every evidence that overwork in poor jobs coupled with an unequal division of housework *will*. All of this helps to explain the frequent finding that single mothers with children tend to have poorer health than men (Clark et al., 1987; Gove, 1984).

Health and the Changing Workplace

It is now widely understood that medical care is only one of many influences on health, and that what we broadly term "environmental" factors are also crucially important. Indeed, some writers have argued that medical care has had no significant positive impact on health in the modern age and that our highly technological medical system causes more harm to health than it does good (Illich, 1978). It's clear, however, that some medical advances have made an important difference — including improvements in immunization against major diseases and improved screening and detection techniques for many others, which make possible early and effective treatment (Fuchs, 1979).

Still, few now doubt that the environment has a profound effect on health and illness. One recent study estimated that between 15 and 25 percent of all deaths in the United States each year (between 270,000 and 480,000 people as of 1979) are "related to technology" — including a considerably higher proportion of two major causes of death: accidents and cancer (Derr et al., 1981, p. 8).

The implications of this, however, are hotly debated, especially as they affect the way we think about society's responsibility to regulate health dangers in the environment and the workplace (Efron, 1984). We will look more closely at the relation between health and the broader environment in Chapter 10; now, we'll focus on the heated issue of the problems of health and safety in the workplace.

We know that many workers are injured or made ill on the job — but how many? The answer isn't easy to find. For one thing, the time lag between exposure to a disease-causing condition at work and the appearance of the disease itself is often very long for many occupational illnesses, notably cancer and some other long-term chronic

Occupational Illness and Injury: Dimensions

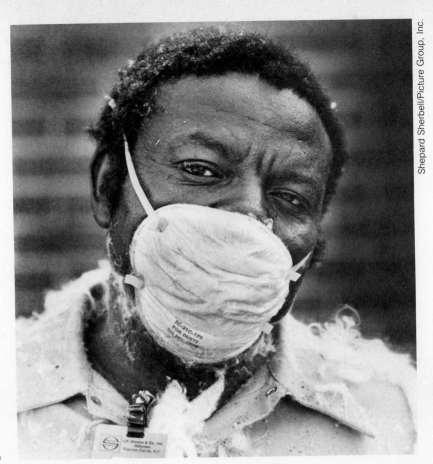

Shepard Sherbell/Picture Group, Inc.

An estimated 1 in 4 Americans are exposed to a major health hazard at work.

diseases — as long as 20 years and more for many work-related cancers. It's difficult, too, to separate out of the effects of occupational exposures from other factors (such as smoking or poor diet) that may have helped bring on or aggravated a disease. And some of the potentially most useful sources of information, like employers' health records, are likely to be biased for financial and public relations reasons (U.S. Department of Labor, 1980, p. 1). But we have a ballpark idea of the magnitude of work-related health problems, and they are staggering:

- An estimated one in four American workers (more than 25 million people) are potentially exposed to a major health hazard at work; about 5.5 million were injured or made ill during 1984 (U.S. Bureau of Labor Statistics, 1986, p. 2).
- An estimated 75,000 deaths a year are "job-induced" (Derr et al., 1981, p. 9), and close to 4,000 workers a year are killed on the job.

We allow levels of exposure to toxic chemicals in the workplace that would be illegal if inflicted on the public.

• Estimates of the percentage of cancers that are occupationally related vary widely, from less than 5 percent up to 20 percent and more. But even if the *lowest* estimates are correct, occupational exposure accounts for close to 20,000 cancer deaths a year (D. L. Davis, 1981, p. 36). About 9,000 workers a year die from asbestos exposure alone (LaFraniere, 1984).

All of these estimates, moreover, almost certainly understate the magnitude of the problem of industrial health. We may only now be beginning to see the long-term health impact of some of the new technologies that expanded so rapidly after World War II, especially the enormous proliferation of industrial chemicals. The federal government now lists about 26,000 chemicals on its roster of known toxic subtances, 2,000 of which are suspected of causing cancer. About 1,000 *new* chemicals are put on the market every year. We know a great deal about the effects of *some* toxic chemicals but almost nothing about the vast majority of new substances that are constantly being introduced into the workplace. And because of the long lead time for the apperance of cancer and other industrially related diseases, the rates we see now may be only the tip of the iceberg. Some evidence for this frightening prospect is provided by estimates that the specific forms of cancer most often associated with industrial exposure rose at about 4 percent a year during the 1970s, while other kinds rose at about 1 percent (D. L. Davis, 1981, p. 36).

Health and Safety Regulation: Limits

Given the enormity of these threats, it isn't surprising that the debate over the proper role of the government in regulating occupational health and safety has intensified. On one side are those who believe that the risks of occupational disease are so great that they call for a larger commitment of social resources to control them — and that we may be heading for catastrophe if that commitment isn't forthcoming (Epstein, 1980). On the other side are those who believe that government regulation of the workplace has already gone too far, putting such an intolerable burden on businesses that it threatens to strangle the economy (Whelan, 1981). Economic growth and workers' health have been increasingly pitted against each other as mutually exclusive goals. Is that perception accurate? Does an effective attack on occupational illness and accidents necessarily hinder economic efficiency?

An adequate answer must begin by noting the *limits* of existing health and safety regulation in the United States. Since the early 1970s, much of the regulatory task has been shouldered by the federal Occupational Health and Safety Administration (OSHA) and its state-level counterparts. OSHA is sometimes described as an all-powerful bureaucracy capable of harassing and intimidating employers. But the reality is considerably less imposing. Of the roughly 25 million American workers routinely exposed to hazardous substances, only about half a million are in workplaces inspected by OSHA each year (U.S. Department of Labor, 1980, p. 114). In the late 1980s, there were only enough OSHA inspectors to visit every American work site about once every 50 years (Celis, 1987). The agency's 1984 budget of about $360 million equalled roughly one-eighth of what the Department of Defense spent on ammunition.

Once standards for workplace health *are* established, moreover, the government's ability to inflict serious penalties on employers who violate them is minimal. In the chemical industry, according to a study by the Council on Economic Priorities (1981), the average fine per violation in 1979 was less than $75. (The giant DuPont chemical company, which the study labeled the "worst violator" in the entire industry, endured an average fine per violation of about $415 in 1979. In 1981 DuPont — the twelfth largest American industrial corporation — had about $24 billion in assets and earned about $1.4 billion in profits [*Fortune,* May 2, 1983, p. 260].)

Health standards for American workers, too, are usually far less stringent than for the public as a whole. We permit levels of chemical exposure in the workplace that would be grossly illegal if they were inflicted on the general population. OSHA and the Environmental Protection Agency (EPA), which regulates air and water quality for the general public, are often charged with setting standards governing the same substances — but the EPA standards are generally far more stringent. The EPA's standards limit the allowable level of carbon monoxide in the air to about 9 parts per million over an 8-hour period; OSHA's workplace standard is 50 parts per million. The OSHA standard for exposure to sulfur dioxide (a major culprit is respiratory disease) is about *12* times the level the EPA allows for the public, and the disparity for many highly toxic chemicals (including such cancer-causing agents as lead and beryllium) is much greater still (Derr et al., 1981, pp. 13–14).

As in many other health measures, the United States lags behind many other industrial societies in the stringency of its regulation of occupational safety and health, as Table 9-4 shows. American standards for exposure to a number of toxic chemicals are considerably more permissive than in many Western European countries and in the Soviet Union. These differences show up in other ways as well. Finland, for instance, had about 500 specialists in occupational health research serving a work force of about 2 million in the early 1980s, while the United States had about 700 for a work force of more than 100 million (A. Anderson, 1982).

Country	Nickel	Benzene	Cadmium Oxides	Carbon Monoxide	Lead	Mercury
Sweden	0.01	30	0.02	40	0.1	0.05
USSR	0.5	5	0.1	20	0.01	0.01
United States	1	30	0.1	55	0.2	0.05

Table 9-4
Occupational exposure standards for various chemicals, three countries (in milligrams per cubic meter)

Source: Adapted from Patrick Derr et al., "Worker/Public Protection: The Double Standard," *Environment,* September 1981, p. 15. Reprinted with permission.

Health and Safety Regulation: Costs and Benefits

Beyond these sheer quantitative differences are broader differences in underlying philosophies. In many other industrial countries, standards for exposure to hazardous conditions are based almost wholly on *medical* considerations. Conditions that are believed to be harmful for workers are treated as a first priority, and industries must often, if necessary, redesign their work processes or technology to eliminate them. In the United States, medical considerations must *compete* with other concerns — in particular, with the "economic feasibility" of a proposed health standard or the *prior* existence of "available control technology" (Derr et al., 1981, p. 31). More than many other countries, in short, we balance the value of workers' lives and well-being against the presumed economic costs of reducing workplace hazards.

What, exactly, *are* those costs? Most studies find them to be less formidable than is often supposed, particularly when balanced against their benefits. One example comes from the Council on Economic Priorities' study of the chemical industry. With one of the worst violation records of any American industry (second only to mining), the chemical industry was a main target of OSHA regulation during the 1970s. What were the results? Recorded rates of work-related illness and injury dropped by about 23 percent after the adoption of OSHA standards — translating into the prevention of as many as 90,000 illnesses and injuries. The cost to the industry was estimated at about $140 per worker per year, or only 1.8 percent of total capital invested. Moreover, the chemical industry's output per hour rose faster *after* the introduction of OSHA standards (Council on Economic Priorities, 1981, pp. 1–4).

In comparison to the United States, the Swedish government regulates many workplace chemicals more stringently, and also spends *more* annually on workplace health and safety training, though its work force is only about one-twentieth the size of ours. One estimate is that Sweden's rate of industrial accidents is about half ours (Early and Witt, 1982). But the tougher regulations haven't visibly hurt the Swedish economy, which outperformed ours on virtually every measure of efficiency in the 1970s.

Despite the lack of evidence that health and safety regulation has damaged the economy, that belief has already led to basic changes in workplace health policy in the United States. Increasingly, measures to lower workers' risks of illness or injury are required to be justified in narrow cost-benefit terms — balanced on a scale against employers' beliefs about the hardships of complying with them. That shift is only one part of a broader thrust in American health-care policy. Where it will take us is not entirely clear, but it does involve far-reaching changes — changes we'll now consider.

Health and Social Policy:
The Prospects

We've seen that, in many respects, Americans' health has improved significantly in recent years. Can we except those improvements to continue? Some suggest trends in health policy give us cause for worry.

There is, first of all, the unmeasurable but troubling threat of further increases in occupationally and environmentally related illnesses. The rise in incidence of cancers that are closely linked to industrial chemicals is especially disturbing — particularly because, as we've already noted, we may not have yet seen the full impact of the chemicals already massively introduced into the workplace, the air, and the water.

Unfortunately, that threat has recently been made worse by cutbacks in our already thin effort to control workplace hazards. And this is only one part of a broader change in the way we've approached health issues in recent years. In general, we've been de-emphasizing society's responsibility for the health of its members in favor of a reliance on the free market to distribute health care — on the premise that health care is, or should be, just another commodity to be bought and sold. At the same time, we've tended increasingly to view health in more individual terms. We often hear that most of our remaining health problems can mainly be corrected through individual effort. There is a new tendency to regard many health problems as the result of voluntary actions (or inactions) — and to argue that similar voluntary changes in life-style hold the key to better health.

That view certainly contains *some* truth, and in the case of some major health issues, such as diet and smoking, it is critically important. But an overemphasis on the "voluntary" and personal sources of health and illness can be misleading. Even in the case of smoking, to take an obvious example, habits that seem on the surface to be personal turn out to be influenced by larger social and economic factors. How voluntary or "private" an act is smoking, for example, in a society in which tens of millions of dollars a year are spent to advertise cigarettes — and in which the full power of government is used to divert tax monies to subsidize the tobacco industry?

If smoking is a less "personal" act than it might first appear, the same is even more true of the kinds of jobs we hold, the air we breathe, and the water we drink. Yet some writers have gone so far as to argue that, for example, the decision to accept a hazardous job is also a "voluntary" act (Wildavsky, 1980), with which government has no right to interfere. But — especially in an economy in which unemployment among blue-collar workers has been endemic for several years — do we really believe that taking a dangerous job is simply a matter of individual choice?

This tug-of-war between public and private responsibility also affects the provision of health care to the poor, the aged, and the disabled. Few disagree that better care for the disadvantaged has been a crucial factor in improving their health status (and thus in improving the American health picture as a whole). Some studies of the impact of specific programs illustrate this even further. Primary and prenatal care furnished to mothers and infants through publicly funded community health centers, according to one study, may have reduced infant mortality in their client populations by up to 50 percent. Preventive care for childen in those centers may have reduced the rate of some preventable diseases (like rheumatic fever) by as much as 60 percent (Davis, Gold, and Makuc, 1981, p. 177). A study in Louisiana found that the WIC program of supplemental nutrition for infants and children brought what the researchers called "significant enhancement" of "most intellectual and behavioral measures" (including IQ, attention span, and school grade-point average) for enrolled children (Hicks et al., 1982). And a New York study showed that a systematic screening program for breast cancer eliminated the long-standing differences in survival rates from the disease between black and white women, while simultaneously increasing the overall rate of survival for women of *both* races (Shapiro et al., 1982).

Yet all of these programs, as well as many others providing preventive care for lower-income people, have come under attack (Aldous, 1986; Edelman, 1987). Cutbacks in support for public programs in maternal and child health, family planning, community health centers — even in the Childhood Immunization program — have been justified in the name of reducing the costs of government. But that argument fails to consider the cost advantages of *preventive* care — the type of care that has been most fostered by the programs for the poor. Studies indicate, for example, that community primary-care centers reduced the rate of hospitalization among their clients by as much as 25 percent by offering a wide range of screening, prenatal care, and other preventive services (Davis, Gold, and Makuc, 1981, p. 177). Since hospitalization is the most expensive way to deal with illness, and preventive care the cheapest, we may expect an actual *rise* in the costs of health care (in addition to a decline in health status) as a result of the cutbacks in preventive care services. Similarly, a Harvard University study, finding that the incidence of low birth weight was three times as great for infants of mothers who did *not* receive benefits from the WIC program, estimated that every dollar spent on delivering nutritious foods to these mothers would save *three* dollars in later health-care costs for their children (Amidei, 1981, p. 459).

This issue goes beyond the specific question of the impact of reductions in care for the disadvantaged. Most of health-care programs introduced in recent years can be seen as experiments in improving our capacity to *prevent* disease by confronting its social, economic, and environmental sources. To the extent that we sidestep that confrontation in the future, we will shift the direction of American health-care policy back to an earlier, more passive role — attempting, *after* the fact, to undo the health damage wrought by unchecked social, technological and economic forces. Something very similar is also at issue in our environmental policy, and we'll turn to that problem in Chapter 11.

Summary

This chapter has considered recent trends in health and health care in the United States. Most of these trends are positive, but there are troubling exceptions.

According to most measures, Americans' health has improved in recent decades. Death rates from most diseases have fallen, sometimes dramatically, and infant mortality has declined considerably.

But the United States lags well behind many other advanced industrial societies in many measures of health, including life expectancy, infant mortality, and childhood death rates. And contrary to the general trend, some health problems — especially AIDS and some forms of cancer — are increasing.

Progress in achieving a healthier society has also been markedly uneven. Many groups (especially minorities and people with low incomes) still suffer unequal access to health care and far higher risks of health problems. And workers in some industries suffer much higher risks of certain health problems than the general public.

The introduction of thousands of new, potentially harmful chemicals into America's workplaces has made occupational health an issue of growing concern. But we now devote few resources to the task of protecting workers' health, especially as compared to other industrial countries.

Changing health policies that reduce public responsibility for health care (especially cutbacks in preventive health services) have slowed or even reversed some of the recent gains in Americans' health.

For Further Reading

Fein, Rashi. *Medical Care, Medical Costs.* Cambridge, Mass.: Harvard University Press, 1985.

Sidel, Victor W., and Ruth Sidel. *A Healthy State,* 2d ed. New York: Pantheon, 1983.

Starr, Paul. *The Social Transformation of American Medicine.* New York: Basic Books, 1982.

Titmuss, Richard. *The Gift of Blood.* New York: Random House, 1973.

10

Energy and the Environment

Americans have historically taken abundant natural resources for granted. The prosperity of the 1950s and 1960s was fueled by what we now recognize as a shockingly wasteful use of energy and a carefree disregard for the impact of growth on the natural environment. Energy use *doubled* between 1950 and 1972, increasing as much in that brief period as it had in the entire 175 previous years of American history (Union of Concerned Scientists, 1981, p. 3). In the 1950s, few Americans worried about world oil supplies as they sped down highways in ever bigger, more powerful cars; few reflected on the potential environmental dangers created by the production of the attractive consumer goods that contributed to our affluent life-style.

One of the most important social and cultural changes of our time has been the end of that state of environmental unconsciousness. Growing concern over the environment prompted an extraordinary spurt of protective legislation, including the Clean Air Act in 1970, the Clean Water Act in 1972, the Safe Drinking Water Act in 1974, and the Toxic Substances Control Act in 1976.

And what came to be called the "energy crisis" has caused even greater repercussions in American life. The country that came of age with the private automobile found itself in the 1970s seemingly running out of gas. Suddenly our capacity to maintain a high standard of living, to sustain a growing and vibrant economy, and to preserve national security were all thrown into doubt with the awareness of our dependence on imported oil.

Two very different responses have emerged to the twin crises of energy and the environment. On one side are those who believe that the lesson of these crises is that we must learn to become a more *conserving* society, reducing dependence on scarce, nonrenewable fuels and exerting greater control over the environmental consequences of growth. On the other side are those who call for a decreased role for government in regulating the quality of the environment and in shaping energy policy. In their view, the government has itself been a large part of the problem and its control should be reduced in favor of "unleashing" the forces of the private market. Behind this attitude is the assumption that environmental regulation has hobbled the economy, slowing economic growth and putting an intolerable and self-defeating burden on business. One critic goes even further, attacking the concern over the environment as an "elitist" view that opposes progress, industry, and prosperity — a doctrine "fearful of the future, despairing of human effort, worried about change, and wed to the status quo" (Tucker, 1982, as quoted in Stegner, 1982, p. 35).

Few issues more sharply illustrate the contrasts between competing social philosophies in America today — and few involve such high stakes. The choices we make about how to manage the problems of energy and the environment will shape not only our social and economic life but also the condition of the natural ecology, on which both ultimately depend, for decades to come. The debate involves questions of enormous significance: the risks of nuclear catastrophe, of potentially irreversible contamination of water supplies, even of basic atmospheric and climatic changes affecting all life on earth.

In this chapter, we can't, of course, do justice to all aspects of these complex and highly technical issues. Instead, we will focus on the social and political questions they raise and on some of the evidence available to help sort them out — for the problems of energy use and environmental policy are *social* issues, not just scientific or economic ones. Whether the issue is balancing the costs and benefits of environmental regulation or the choice between alternative and conventional energy sources, the questions raised involve our deepest social priorities: our assessments of the relative importance of economic growth versus the quality of urban and rural life, the benefits of producing goods in the present versus reducing the risks of illness and environmental degradation for future generations.

We'll first focus on energy use and policy, examining some of the potentials and limits of conventional energy sources (oil, gas, and coal), nuclear power, and alternative energy sources (conservation

WARNING!!

• SURFACE WATER UNSAFE TO DRINK
• USE WATER FROM APPROVED SOURCES
• AVOID UNNECESSARY CONTACT WITH THE SURFACE WATER

The environmental debate involves questions of enormous significance.

and solar power). We'll then consider some of the social aspects of the problems of the environment, paying particular attention to recent debates about the costs, benefits, and consequences of environmental regulation.

Energy:
The Hidden Revolution

With 5 percent of the world's population, the United States consumes over 25 percent of its energy (Table 10-1). As we entered the 1980s, American energy consumption had reached the equivalent of about 14 tons of coal or 2,600 barrels of oil a year for every man, woman, and child in the country (Union of Concerned Scientists, 1981, p. 4). The total bill for energy in the United States amounts to over $400 billion a year (*Statistical Abstract of the United States*, 1986, p. 659).

Unlike some other industrial countries, the United States is also a major *producer* of energy — the largest energy producer in the world, in fact. But we are nevertheless heavily dependent on outside sources for energy, especially oil. Because of that dependence, the sudden shortages of imported oil in the 1970s quickly rocked the country out of its complacency about energy use. In its place came the sense that assuring an adequate supply of energy was one of the most pressing of social and economic problems.

For several reasons — especially, as we'll see shortly, our increas-

Table 10-1
World energy consumption, by region and energy source, 1960–1983

Region and energy source	Consumption (mil. metric tons)*		Percent distribution	
	1960	1983	1960	1983
World total	3,924	8,523	100.0	100.0
North America†	1,599	2,597	40.7	30.5
United States	1,454	2,175	37.1	25.5
South America	79	247	2.0	2.9
Europe	1,039	2,040	26.5	23.9
Asia	514	1,704	13.1	20.0
Japan	96	404	2.4	4.7
USSR	595	1,612	15.2	18.9
Oceania	41	108	1.0	1.3
Energy source:				
Solid fuels	1,940	2,753	49.4	32.3
Liquid fuels	1,306	3,537	33.3	41.5
Natural gas	593	1,876	15.1	22.0
Electricity	84	358	2.1	4.2

* In tons of coal equivalent. Metric ton = 1.1023 short tons.
† Includes Central America.
Source: Statistical Abstract of the United States, 1986, (Washington, D.C.: Government Printing Office, 1986), p. 563.

ing efficiency in energy use — the United States has recently enjoyed a respite from the most heavy dependence on imported oil; we have even experienced an oversupply, or "glut," of energy. But it is generally understood that this is a temporary condition. Over the long term, ensuring adequate energy supplies will remain a key issue for the United States and for the rest of the world (Brown, 1986).

This much is generally agreed on. But *how* we should respond to the threatened security of energy is not. Since the oil shortages of the 1970s, one response has been a flurry of proposals designed to help the country "produce its way out of the energy crisis." The proposals include removing all controls on the prices of oil and gas, in the hope that this will encourage oil companies to undertake more domestic exploration and production, and continuing the massive subsidies for nuclear power development begun in the 1950s. Several interlocking assumptions underlie these proposals:

1. It is assumed that the main energy problem the United States faces is *not enough* energy — that in order to sustain our standard of living, let alone promote economic growth, we will need ever-expanding energy supplies.

2. It is assumed that *conventional* sources of energy, including some combination of oil, natural gas, coal, and nuclear power, can provide for those expanding needs, if given enough economic encouragement.

3. It is assumed that "alternative" energy sources, including "renewable" energy technologies and energy conservation, can make only a minimal contribution to the country's energy needs in the foreseeable future.

How do these assumptions stand up against the evidence? Though the issues are certainly complex, recent research casts doubt on all three. There is a remarkable degree of convergence, in fact, around these very different points:

1. A greatly expanded overall supply of energy may *not* be necessary for continued economic growth and material well-being; indeed, we are already using less energy per unit of economic output than we did during the 1970s — and we could learn to use even less.

2. The long-term potential for oil and other nonrenewable fuels (and for nuclear power) is probably less than often supposed.

3. On the other hand, the potential of alternative energy sources — including wind and water power, biomass, and solar technology — is probably much greater than often supposed.

Let's consider each of these points.

The Limits of Fossil Fuels The sharp increases in oil prices imposed in the 1970s by the oil-producing countries sent shock waves throughout the world, throwing the economies of both the industrial and developing countries out of gear. But there is wide agreement that these shocks were only the leading edge of a much deeper problem: Most of the energy sources we have historically relied on to do the work of society are finite — they are nonrenewable. This is especially true for two of our most heavily used fuels, oil and natural gas. Both will probably be largely depleted — or so difficult to extract and produce that they will become prohibitively expensive — within an uncomfortably short time. Increasingly, debates over appropriate energy strategies begin from the understanding that we cannot, even if we wished to, continue for too much longer our current level of dependence on these fuels (Flavin, 1986a).

Nonrenewable energy sources (the basic "fossil" fuels such as coal, oil, and natural gas, as well as nuclear fuels) now account for roughly 95 percent of America's energy use. By far the largest single source is oil; over two-fifths of our energy is derived from it, about two-thirds from oil and natural gas combined. This marks a dramatic historical change: In 1920 only about one-sixth of energy in the United States came from oil and gas (Union of Concerned Scientists, 1981, p. 2).

How much oil do we have left? That question is not easy to answer and has been the subject of intense debate. But recent estimates suggest that world oil reserves are in the range of 50 to 88 years' worth, at current use levels (Flavin, 1986a, p. 89).

Much of that oil, of course, lies *outside* the United States. And how much of it we will be able to count on for domestic use is impossible to predict. This is partly because of political uncertainties, dramatized by the behavior of the major oil-exporting countries in the past decade. But it also reflects the growing competition for world oil resources, both from other industrialized countries and from developing countries with rapidly increasing energy needs.

Even if the United States were guaranteed a substantial share of world oil reserves — which it is not — the long-term problem of finite oil supplies would not be changed, only postponed. At some point in the not very distant future, we will have to shift to other sources of energy.

Much the same problem applies to natural gas, though unlike oil, a large proportion of natural gas is domestically produced. About a quarter of the United States' energy now comes from natural gas, which is used especially to power industry and to heat and cook in homes and businesses. Natural gas has the additional advantage of being a relatively "clean" fuel and therefore relatively benign in environmental terms, compared to other nonrenewable fuels. But it, too, is finite. One study estimates that we have another 35 to 60 years

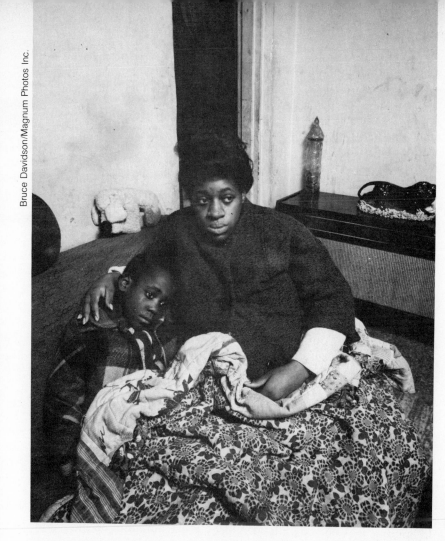

Rising energy prices
are not an abstraction
for the poor.

of domestic natural gas supplies left, at current rates of consumption (Union of Concerned Scientists, 1981, chap. 2).

Some argue that these shortages are mainly artificial, resulting less from scarcity than from unwise social policy. Specifically, they hold the relatively low prices for oil and gas on the American market partly responsible for the supply problem that, they say, is more apparent than real. They argue that government regulation that has historically held oil and gas prices below their potential market values has discouraged efforts by oil companies to locate and develp more domestic supplies. As these supplies become more difficult to discover and extract, the economic incentive to do so begins to disappear. The result, in this view, is that we really don't *know* how much oil and gas may be beneath the surface — and we will only find out when we allow prices to rise high enough to make more intensive exploration worthwhile (Simon and Kahn, 1984).

While it's certainly true that in the short run the supply of oil — like most other things — is heavily influenced by how much it costs, the bottom line is that oil is an intrinsically limited commodity; it is finite and nonrenewable. There is only a certain amount of it in the world, and that amount is shrinking all the time. Looking harder for it can make a difference, but it cannot alter that basic fact (Georgiu, 1987). Indeed, oil companies have increased their exploration for new oil substantially, in recent years — but the rate at which they've discovered it has inexorably declined (Flavin, 1986a, pp. 89–90).

Coal Before the ascendance of the automobile, coal was the most important energy source in the United States; it is still a major source, supplying about a quarter of our total energy (*Statistical Abstract of the United States,* 1986, p. 556). Unlike oil and gas, our coal supplies are a long way from running out. The United States has been called the "Persian Gulf of coal" (Stobaugh and Yergin, 1982, p. 80); we have almost a third of the world's known reserves, enough to last at least 400 years at current rates of consumption.

The problem with coal is not its availability, but the severe environmental problems that accompany its use. These hazards appear at all stages in the process of coal use, from mining it to burning it. Underground coal mining has traditionally been one of the most dangerous occupations; above ground, strip mining (increasingly common, especially in the West) produces fewer occupational hazards but even greater environmental ones.

But the hazards of *burning* coal are even more troubling than those of mining it. Coal burning produces great amounts of hazardous pollutants, especially sulfur dioxide, ash, and carbon dioxide. Historically, these have been responsible for a major part of the air pollution problem in most industrial countries; more recently, they have presented the specter of even more severe problems. Sulfur dioxide emissions from coal-fired power plants are one of the chief sources of the acid rain (see pages 331 to 332) that has increasingly threatened waters and forests, especially in the northeast. The large amounts of carbon dioxide released in coal burning may create what scientists call a *greenhouse effect* — in which a "blanket" of carbon dioxide above the earth's surface absorbs heat radiated by the earth and raises its average temperature, with potentially catastrophic effects on climate, crops, and even the level of the oceans.

Some of these hazards may be mitigated by more advanced technologies that allow coal to be burned in cleaner ways. But though coal will undoubtedly be an important source of fuel for decades to come, enough hazards remain to create wide agreement that coal can only be one part of a long-term energy mix. The hazards of heavy dependence on coal, in fact, are one of the main arguments to justify an even more controversial energy source — nuclear power.

Nuclear Power: High Promises, Grave Dangers

Not long ago, nuclear power seemed to promise an end to worries about America's future energy supplies. In the early stages of the country's budding nuclear program, it was sometimes argued that electricity produced by nuclear power plants would be "too cheap to meter" (Council on Economic Priorities, 1979, p. 2). We accordingly plunged into a huge investment in nuclear energy, fueled by massive government subsidies.

Since World War II, the overwhelming bulk of federal funds for energy research and development have gone to nuclear energy (Union of Concerned Scientists, 1981, p. xvi). And the government has also subsidized nuclear power indirectly through legislation (the Price-Anderson Act) limiting the insurance liability that nuclear power companies face in case of even a massive reactor accident. One study estimated that by the beginning of the 1980s, the public had subsidized nuclear energy to the tune of $37 billion (Friends of the Earth et al., 1982, p. 29). But despite an amount of government support that dwarfs anything allotted to any other energy form in recent American history, it had become increasingly apparent by the late 1970s that, as a Harvard Business School study put it, "the nuclear promise has turned into nuclear disappointment" (Stobaugh and Yergin, 1982, p. 108). Other critics, going even farther, have called the decline of nuclear power "the greatest collapse of any enterprise in industrial history" (Lovins and Lovins, 1980, p. 54). Is this an accurate prognosis?

Certainly the momentum that characterized the nuclear industry in the 1960s and 1970s has subsided. No new nuclear plants have been ordered in the United States since 1978; as of 1984, over 100 previously ordered plants had been canceled (Table 10-2).

Why this sudden reversal in the fortunes and potential of the nuclear power industry? There have been several reasons, including high costs, declining demand, and safety questions.

Cost. Nuclear power advocates seriously underestimated the costs of nuclear power plant construction. Cost overruns have generally

Table 10-2
Nuclear power fizzles:
Nuclear plant orders
and cancellations,
1974–1984

	Orders	Cancellations
1974	26	8
1975	4	11
1976	3	2
1977	4	9
1978	2	13
1979	0	8
1980	0	16
1981	0	6
1982	0	18
1983	0	6
1984	0	8
Totals	39	105

Source: Data from Christopher Flavin, "Reforming the Electric Power Industry," in Lester R. Brown, et al., *State of the World, 1986.* New York: Norton, 1986, p. 100.

been double or triple the initial estimates. Indeed, the industry has faced what the *New York Times* called a "tidal wave of financial catastrophe" (January 20, 1985). Nuclear power may cost, per unit of electrical output, *three times* as much as the average cost for electric power (Flavin, 1986b, p. 101). As a result, nuclear electricity will be less and less able to compete with coal-fired electricity in the marketplace. Many proposed nuclear plants have run so far over projected costs that they may simply never be completed. In Washington State, for example, $4 billion was invested in the early 1970s to build five new nuclear plants. By 1981 the cost had mushroomed to $24 billion; by 1983 construction on two of the plants had been abandoned. Only one of the original five was considered likely to ever produce electricity, and the project's more than $8 billion in debt would probably never be repaid (*Business Week,* 1983).

Declining demand. The nuclear planners also badly misjudged the demand for nuclear power. Current nuclear technology is feasible only for *electric* power generating, but the demand for electric power has not matched early expectations. Increasing energy efficiency and slower population growth, among other causes, have reduced the rate of increase in demand for electricity. Indeed, electricity use has grown at less than half the rate predicted in the early 1970s. By the late 1970s, the United States had an *excess* capacity to produce electric power — an excess more than twice as large as the entire share of electricity generated by nuclear plants (Lovins and Lovins, 1980, p. 61).

Safety. The problem of safety has been perhaps the greatest obstacle to the continued viability of nuclear power and the one most keenly felt by the public. Fears over nuclear safety center on two serious issues: the possibility of major nuclear reactor accidents and the more insidious problem of the disposal of radioactive wastes.

Two years before the terrifying accident at Three Mile Island, one highly placed nuclear advocate wrote:

> The safety of this present generation of nuclear reactors is not a major policy issue. These reactors have operated on ships and on land for over two decades and have never led to a reactor-related fatality. . . . Disposal of low-level wastes . . . is being handled safely, and . . . disposal technologies appear to be nearly at hand." (Laird, 1977, pp. 9–10)

The Three Mile Island accident, which caused over a billion dollars of direct damages and several more billions in indirect economic losses (*New York Times,* November 1, 1982) plus immeasurable psychological damage to residents, made this argument seem less than compelling. So did government studies in the early 1980s demonstrating that the likelihood — and the costs — of catastrophic nuclear accidents were much greater than had been confidently supposed. And the Soviet Union's reactor disaster at Chernobyl in 1986 — which contaminated food supplies in several countries, caused billions of dollars of damage, and may result in several thousand deaths in the coming years from radiation exposure — brought these abstract possibilities home to many Americans (Lee, 1986). Even before Chernobyl about two-thirds of Americans opposed the construction of new nuclear power plants; after that disaster, three-fourths did (Flavin, 1987).

Meanwhile, effective waste-disposal technologies have *not* yet materialized as hoped. It's estimated that the amount of nuclear waste now stored in the United States — about 12,000 tons in the mid-1980s — will quadruple by the beginning of the next century; and these wastes are typically so toxic that they must be isolated for at least 10,000 years (Pollock, 1986, p. 123). By the 1980s some communities were voting to prohibit the disposal of radioactive wastes within their borders. Nuclear waste had become an admittedly intractable problem that nobody wanted in their backyard. In 1980, the residents of Washington State successfully passed an initiative forbidding the shipment of nuclear wastes into the state (*Business Week,* 1983). In late

1982, Congress approved a bill mandating the government to begin building nuclear waste-disposal repositories (probably in deep underground storage areas) by 1989. Most of the proposed sites for these facilities, however, turn out to have built-in uncertainties (like the possibility of contaminating groundwater or of earthquakes), in addition to the probable political resistance of those who will have to live and work near the sites (Carter, 1983).

Estimating the Risks of Nuclear Disaster

For many years, proponents of nuclear energy insisted that reactor safety was not a major problem. The chance of a serious nuclear power plant accident releasing substantial amounts of radioactive material were, they argued, almost infinitesimal. These views were supported by a 1975 study commissioned by the U.S. Nuclear Regulatory Commission (the Rasmussen Report) that estimated the chances of a "worst-case" reactor accident at less than one in a million. The report also calculated that the worst accident would possibly cause about 3,300 "early" deaths (that is, not counting those resulting from the long-term effects of radiation) and that the maximum economic costs would be $14 billion in damages.

But in 1982, a massive, detailed study carried out by the U.S. Department of Energy's Sandia National Laboratories drew much different — and far grimmer — conclusions. On the basis of elaborate computer models of the risks at each of the 80 sites in the United States where nuclear power plants were in operation or under construction, the Sandia researchers came up with the astounding figure that the worst-case reactor accident could cause more than 100,000 deaths in the first year and more than $300 billion in damages.

These estimates were based on a hypothetical, very severe accident involving extensive damage to the reactor's core, partial melting of its nuclear fuel, the collapse of its safety system, and a breach in its containment structure sufficient to allow a substantial release of radioactivity into the atmosphere close to a densely populated area.

Though such an accident would be considerably worse than the most serious one in the United States so far (the 1979 incident at the Three Mile Island reactor in Pennsylvania), the chances of its occurrence, in Sandia's calculations, are much greater than earlier projections had envisioned. The probability of this worst-case accident, according to Sandia, was 1 chance in every 100,000 reactor hours — a seemingly small figure, but one that translates into about *1 chance in 50 of such an accident happening in the United States before the year 2000.*

The toll in death, injury, and property damage from this kind of accident would vary greatly, depending particularly on the population density near the plant, the quality of emergency responses (especially the speed of evacuating the local population), and the specific weather conditons at the time of the accident. The worst site, according to the Sandia study (ranked in terms of potential deaths) would be the Salem nuclear plant in Salem, New Jersey, where a worst-case accident could kill 100,000 and injure another 75,000 in the first year and cause an additional 40,000 deaths from radiation-induced cancer over the following 30 years. An accident at the Waterford plant in St. Charles, Louisiana, could kill 96,000 during the first year and injure 279,000. On the other hand, an accident at the LaCrosse reactor near La-Crosse, Wisconsin, would, according to the Sandia study, kill just 70 people in the first year and 200 over the following generation.

Source: U.S. Department of Energy data as cited in *San Francisco Chronicle,* November 1 and 2, 1982.

Because of these problems, nuclear power is unlikely to supply anywhere near the share of America's energy that its proponents projected in the 1960s and 1970s. As the Harvard Business School's study noted in 1979, even if every nuclear plant then ordered or under construction was added to our current array of nuclear facilities, we would have less than half the nuclear capacity by the 1990s that was predicted in the 1970s (Stobaugh and Yergin, 1982, p. 111). And since that time, the process of "denuclearization" has proceeded even faster.

Over and above the growing public rejection, sheer economics has most deeply undercut the promise of nuclear energy. It has apparently ceased to be competitive with conventional fuels as a means of generating electrical power. "The free market," one study commented, "is killing nuclear power" (Friends of the Earth et al., 1982, p. 29). Without continuing federal subsidies to prop it up, according

The dangers of nuclear power have spurred exploration of alternative energy sources.

John Schultz/PAR-NYC

to some observers, the nuclear industry might well have collapsed already. This judgment is apparently shared even by some in the nuclear industry itself: The chairman of General Electric, a major nuclear plant contractor, declared in 1982, "If we were starting again, we would not enter this business" (quoted in *Environment,* April 1982, p. 21).

Alternative Energy Strategies: Conservation and Solar Energy

If conventional fuels are inherently limited and nuclear energy is burdened with grave and possibly insurmountable problems, what will we do for energy in the future? Strategies to increase conventional and nuclear energy production, even in the face of environmental and social dangers, are often justified on the ground that there is simply no feasible alternative. But there is considerable evidence that the picture may not be that bleak — and the choices not that limited. Reducing our commitment to fossil fuels and nuclear energy need not mean a declining economy, a lower standard of living, or a new "dark age." Two alternatives seem especially promising, according to current research: energy conservation and renewable energy technologies, such as solar power.

Conservation: The Hidden "Energy Source"

Americans have traditionally defined the energy problem as one of a scarcity of energy *supplies.* But that is only one side of the problem; the other is the inefficient use of the supplies we *have.*

Historically, the United States has been one of the least efficient of industrial societies in its use of energy. And it's still true that we use more than twice as much energy per person as many European countries and Japan (*Statistical Abstract of the United States,* 1987, p. 550). This difference shows up in the way we use energy in every realm of life — in transportation, industry, and housing. One study summed up Sweden's ability to use 40 percent less energy than the United States by noting that Sweden has "fewer large cars, flimsy products, leaky houses, and empty buses" (Schipper and Lichtenberg, 1978, p. 26). The biggest difference, historically, has been in transportation — the Swedes, for example, use less than a third the energy, per person, in getting around than Americans, mainly because of much greater use of public transportation — and lighter cars. In the 1970s, America's notoriously big cars used 50 percent more energy, on average, than European cars (Darmstadter, 1981, p. 37).

Studies show that some of these national differences can be traced to different attitudes about the importance of conserving energy. We have tended to squander our relatively vast resources, while many European countries have tended to husband their relatively less abundant ones (see Vernon, 1980). And the United States has lagged behind many other countries in government support for energy conservation — as opposed to oil and nuclear power.

But our attitudes toward conservation have been changing — and with impressive results. "The United States," as one scholar puts it, "starting with one of the world's most energy-intensive economies, has achieved one of the most dramatic turn-arounds" (Flavin, 1986a, p. 84). Energy efficiency in the United States improved by 23 percent from 1973 to 1984, which meant that we managed to use about the same amount of energy in both years despite considerable growth in the economy and in our population. If that turnaround had not occurred, we would be using the equivalent of an estimated 10 million extra barrels of oil a *day* and our annual energy costs would be as much as $100 billion greater than they are.

We managed this in part as a result of broad social and economic changes — notably the shift from an energy-gobbling manufacturing economy to a less energy-intensive service economy (Chapter 8). In part, too, the increased efficiency came from technological advances — smaller and more efficiently-designed cars, more energy-efficient homes and appliances — and in part from changes in our personal habits. For example, we are driving slower and using less heat at home. Changes in the fuel efficiency of the traditionally gas-guzzling American automobile have been a key part of this overall improvement. On average, the American car traveled a third farther on a gallon of gas in 1985 than it did 12 years earlier (Brown, 1986, p. 11).

But much more can still be done to increase energy conservation and bring our level of energy use closer to that of more efficient countries. For example, it's estimated that we can nearly double the efficiency of American cars if we make full use of already-known technology (Flavin, 1986a, p. 86). In this and other ways, the dramatic ability of conservation to "supply" our energy needs can surely be drawn on even more in the future.

These changes indicate that what was once considered an unbreakable link between the amount of energy consumed and the level of economic well-being is actually quite flexible. They mark a kind of quiet revolution in energy use — one that, if encouraged, will surely have an increasing impact in the future. And this emerging shift in energy use has taken place *without* causing major public hardship. As the Union of Concerned Scientists puts it, "No radical transformation of society or reversion to the life-styles of our grandparents is required to hold down growth in energy use" (1981, p. 16).

Solar Power: An Emerging Role

Opinion polls show that solar power is the most widely favored of all sources of energy and the one the majority of Americans most wish to see encouraged. But it is also widely believed that solar energy is at best a technology for the distant future, not an important source of energy for the near term or a significant part of the answer to shrinking supplies of conventional energy. This belief has shaped our energy policy: Only a fraction of federal energy subsidies have been devoted to solar research and development. Solar energy in all its forms (including wind power and wood, an indirect solar source) now accounts for only about 5 percent of America's energy. The idea that much of an advanced society's energy needs could be met from the sun still strikes many people as utopian and farfetched.

But there is growing evidence that solar technology may — if it is adequately encouraged — play a far more important role in meeting American energy needs in the *near* future, and play a much greater role within a few more decades. As with energy conservation, there is a striking amount of agreement in much recent research on the magnitude of that potential contribution. The Harvard Business School's study estimated that with proper government incentives, solar energy could supply from 20 to 25 percent of America's energy by the year 2000 (Stobaugh and Yergin, 1982, p. 183). A report by the federally funded Solar Energy Research Institute (SERI) estimated that 20 to 30 percent of American energy demands in the year 2000 could be met by renewable resources, given a substantial commitment to increasing energy efficiency (Friends of the Earth et al., 1982, p. 66). It's important to note, however, that solar energy's potential is, so far, an uneven one. Solar power is capable of doing some things now, others only in the future.

There is no problem of availability in the case of solar energy; the energy contained in the sunlight that falls on the land mass of the United States over a year is more than 500 times the total energy the country consumes (Union of Concerned Scientists, 1981, p. 110). The problem is transforming that energy into useful applications. Currently, we have the technology for *some* of those applications, while others will require more development. What solar energy does best at present levels of technology is provide space and water heating at relatively low levels of temperature, making it especially suitable for residential uses. Most studies now agree that residential solar heating systems are already economically competitive with conventional fuels. Higher-temperature industrial uses of solar energy are less well developed, as is the direct generation of electric power from sunlight.

The technology for solar electric power generation through photovoltaic cells (which transform sunlight into electrical current) is understood in principle. The obstacles to its large-scale development are now mainly economic; the cells are costly to produce. But they are becoming less so all the time, and many studies argue that this cost disadvantage could be eliminated through sufficient government support, especially through large-scale government purchases of solar cells that would enable the use of more efficient mass-production techniques. Indeed, the cost of photovoltaic power, even without massive government incentives, dropped drastically (about tenfold) since the mid-1970s because of technological advances (Hamakawa, 1987).

These developments suggest that even the large-scale generation of solar electric power, which would make solar energy directly competitive not only with conventional fuels but with nuclear power, may be fairly close at hand — as near as 1995, according to some estimates (Hamakawa, 1987). Wind power — generating electricity through giant windmills clustered in "wind farms" — may, according to one estimate, provide by itself about as big a proportion of the world's electricity as nuclear power now does (Flavin, 1986b, p. 113). Unlike conventional and nuclear technologies, moreover, most solar technologies are environmentally benign. They cause little or no pollution and involve relatively insignificant safety hazards — and they are capable of creating large numbers of jobs.

Despite these advantages, though, recent social policy has not been generous to research and development in renewable energy. Funding for solar research activities by the U.S. Department of Energy (never a high priority) dropped from $570 million in 1979 to $22 million in 1983 (*Environment*, November 1982, p. 23). Why — if the scientific knowledge for the most part already exists — have we done so little to promote the development of solar energy? We will leave the answer to the conclusion of this chapter, but it seems clear that, as the Harvard study put it, "it's the political climate, not the weather, that will govern the future of solar energy" (Stobaugh and Yergin, 1982, p. 212).

Jobs and Energy

Debates about energy issues often become centered with economic questions, particularly the impact of different energy policies on jobs. The stakes can be high — and can generate strong emotions. Especially when unemployment is high, communities, workers, and businesspeople may support energy development programs — even those that bring troubling social or environmental consequences — on the assumption that they will, at least, create jobs. The risks involved in building, say, a nuclear power plant near a community may come to be seen as a relatively small price to pay for its potential benefits in new jobs. The concern for the human and environmental consequences of nuclear development thus becomes pitted against the equally pressing concern for jobs and income.

But a growing body of research suggests that a third option exists: the job-creating potential of investment in alternative energy sources. In particular, solar energy and conservation generate considerably more employment than conventional energy technologies — and *far* more than nuclear power.

Studies comparing the job-creating potential of solar with conventional energy indicate that, for example, investment in solar heating can produce three to four times as many jobs as "hard" technologies producing the same amount of energy. One study estimated that California alone could create at least 375,000 new jobs a year during the 1980s through investment in already existing solar technologies (that is, solar space and water heating) alone (Nordlund and Robson, 1980, pp. 67–68). A study by the California Energy Commission found that *most* energy production typically provides fewer jobs, per dollar invested, than the average for the economy as a whole. But within the range of energy options, solar turns out to be a relatively effective job producer, nuclear an especially poor one.

Why so few jobs from conventional energy production? Like some other industries (the chemical industry, for one), most energy-producing industries are extremely *capital-intensive* — they require very large investment in materials and plant but relatively few workers.

Some alternative technologies, however, including most solar and conservation approaches, are *labor-intensive*. They require relatively little capital investment and relatively large amounts of labor, both in manufacturing (of solar panels or energy-conserving devices, for instance) and in installation.

This job-creating potential is especially strong when these "soft" energy technologies are combined with conservation efforts. One study calculated that a "conservation/solar package" could produce about 30 person-years of work for each million dollars invested, compared to less than 10 person-years in a nuclear power program (cited in Nordlund and Robson, 1980, p. 69). The Council on Economic Priorities (1979), similarly, compared the job-producing effects of investing $4 billion in conservation and solar power for Long Island homes with a scenario based on the existing use of conventional fuels (fuel oil, conventional electricity, and natural gas). The council found that the conservation approach would stimulate up to more than four times as much employment as the conventional one. The conservation scenario was also compared to the effects of building a nuclear power plant. The study estimated that the conservation approach would create more than twice as many jobs in the local economy as the nuclear approaches while costing less and saving considerable amounts of electricity.

Different energy strategies also create different *kinds* of jobs. Conventional energy production is top-heavy with highly skilled professional, managerial, technical, and craft jobs — even more so for nuclear power. According to the Council on Economic Priorities, 42 percent of employees in nuclear energy are scientists, engineers, managers, and other professionals; another 34 percent are highly skilled technicians and craft workers. But most forms of solar energy and conservation are not only labor-intensive but also produce many less-skilled, easily learned jobs; in weatherization, insulation, light manufacturing, and construction, among others. Job growth in "soft" energy technologies, can, therefore, reach a much wider range of potential workers, including the blue-collar unemployed and unskilled minorities (Council on Economic Priorities, 1979, p. 5). (Traditional energy industries are heavily white — and male. The extreme case is coal mining, where 94 percent of the work force in the late 1970s were white men. White men were also 74 percent of workers in oil refining and 79 percent in electric power production [Humphrey, 1979, p. 69].)

Both in the sheer number of potential jobs and the possibility of targeting them to those most in need of work, therefore, an energy strategy that gives special weight to conservation and renewable energy sources could be an important part of the solution to America's job problem.

The Environment: Progress and Perils

Until the 1970s, the United States had no national antipollution program, and the environment was deteriorating at a rapid pace. This changed during the 1970s, as the government began to take on the job of regulating some of the unwanted environmental effects of economic growth. And though not all of the most serious environmental problems have been rolled back (some, in fact, have been barely addressed), many show encouraging changes.

The most visible improvement has been in the quality of the air we breathe. Between 1974 and 1981, the average number of days in which air pollution in a sample of 23 cities reached levels the Environmental Protection Agency defines as "unhealthful" dropped by half, from around 90 to about 45, and the improvement was even greater in some cities (Conservation Foundation, 1984, p. 88). But as of 1987, about 100 counties across the country — most of them urban or industrial — still hadn't met federal standards for pollution by airborne particles, which are believed to aggravate a variety of health problems (Smart, 1987). More disturbingly, the rapid pace of progress was slowed (and even reversed) in the 1980s, as Figure 10-1 shows.

Trends in the quality of water have also been generally positive, though the improvements have been less dramatic. Pollution controls slowed the deterioration of America's waters in the 1970s, but severe problems remain. By 1983, 37 states reported that their waters weren't yet "fishable and swimmable"; and in 1984 alone, about 20 million gallons of pollutants were poured into the country's waters as a result of chemical spills and other polluting incidents. Indeed, the average amount of oil and other contaminants dumped in the water through accidents was higher in the first half of the 1980s than in the

Figure 10-1
Stalled progress on air pollution: Particulate emissions, 1976–1985

Source: Data from Environmental Protection Agency

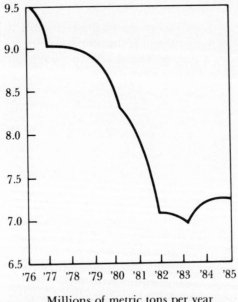

Millions of metric tons per year

last half of the 1970s (*Statistical Abstract of the United States*, 1987, p. 189). And beyond the continuing pollution of surface waters loomed an even graver and more intractable problem, the increasing contamination of groundwater by toxic wastes (see pages 336 to 338).

Moreover, if progress had been made against *some* pollution problems by the 1980s, others were only beginning to be seriously addressed. Three of them, in particular, are among the most urgent environmental problems in America today: acid rain, toxic wastes, and contaminated groundwater. All three promise to be even more stubborn than most of the other problems of air and water pollution that were the main targets of government action during the 1970s.

Acid rain is the name used to describe airborne acid particles — often formed by the burning of coal — that, ultimately, are deposited in distant waters, lands, and forests. Once deposited in lakes or streams, acid rain can kill fish and other aquatic life; in forests, it can destroy vegetation. The economic impact is estimated to be many billions of dollars a year: A recent EPA study calculated that acid rain caused $5 billion damage every year to buildings alone in just 17 states (*New York Times*, July 18, 1985). And much more important is acid rain's impact on the natural environment. The impact has, so far, been greatest in the northeastern and upper midwestern states and in Canada, all of which are downwind from the heaviest concentrations of acid rain sources — the coal-burning industries, especially power plants, in the heavily industrialized midwest. In a 27-state area studied by the U.S. Office of Technology Assessment in 1982 (cited in *Environment*, May 1982, p. 23):

Acid Rain: "Airmailing Pollution"

- Of 17,000 lakes, 3,000 were already damaged by acid rain and 9,000 were endangered.
- Of 117,000 miles of streams and rivers, 25,000 miles were damaged, 49,000 were at risk.

More recent EPA analyses have shown that acid rain is threatening other parts of the country as well, including part of the South, the mountain states, and the West. And some studies suggest that acid rain may have serious health consequences for humans as well (*New York Times*, February 24, 1985).

Though there is now considerable agreement about the major sources of acid rain, there's much less agreement about how to control it, for — like other environmental problems — acid rain raises a number of difficult social and economic issues, as well as technical ones. One issue is the social and economic effects of attempts to reduce the emission of acid rain's components at their source. As we've noted, a major source of the pollutants is coal-burning power plants. A number of technologies are available to reduce emissions from these plants, but many involve high costs. For example, emissions could be reduced by switching the kind of coal used from the high-sulfur-content variety now mainly mined in the East to lower-sulfur coal produced in the West. But this strategy could have a destructive impact on the coal-mining economy (and on coal miners' jobs) in the East, while raising the specter of environmental damage from accelerated strip-mining of coal in the West (Rhodes and Middleton, 1983, p. 32). Other technologies, including techniques to clean or "wash" coal before it's burned and to chemically "scrub" the gases produced afterward, also hold promise, but both are also expensive.

We can't, of course, resolve these technical issues in this book. We raise them to reaffirm a more general point: Problems that seem, on the surface, to be purely technical or scientific ones usually carry broader *social* implications — implications that are sometimes hidden but nevertheless have important human consequences.

Toxic Wastes: Legacy of Neglect

Several highly publicized tragedies — like the toll of illness and social disruption caused by the dumping of toxic chemicals at Love Canal in New York State and the closing of the entire town of Times Beach, Missouri, in 1983 — brought the problem of hazardous wastes strongly into public consciousness. But these catastrophes are only the most visible elements of a *much* larger problem.

In 1983 the U.S. Office of Technology Assessment (OTA) estimated that 250 million metric tons of hazardous wastes were produced annually in the United States, of which just 40 million tons were subject to federal regulation (cited in *Science*, April 1, 1983, p. 34). (The federal government exempts producers of less than a ton of hazardous waste a month from regulation, and a number of specific chemicals, including some of the *most* toxic, fell through loopholes in the regulations.) Other studies estimate that we produce about 2,500 pounds of hazardous wastes each year for every man, woman, and child in the United States (Conservation Foundation, 1984, p. xxiv).

Despite government steps initiated in the early 1980s, the problem continues to grow. Part of the difficulty is the gap between the size of the toxic waste problem and the resources allocated to coping with it. In 1980 Congress authorized a "Superfund" to clean up existing toxic waste dumps (Figure 10-2 maps the location of the worst of these sites). That fund amounted to about $9 billion in 1987, an amount that seems large at first. But the OTA's study estimated that it would

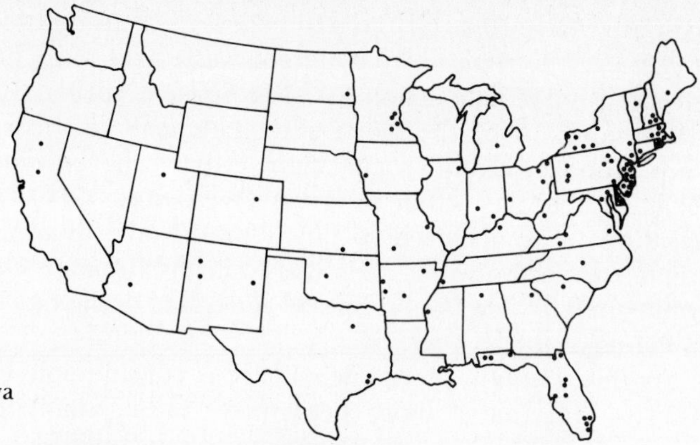

ALABAMA
Triana

ARIZONA
Phoenix

ARKANSAS
Ft. Smith
Jacksonville
Mena
Walnut Ridge

CALIFORNIA
Glen Avon
Keswick
Rancho Cordova

COLORADO
Denver

CONNECTICUT
Naugatuck

DELAWARE
Delaware City
New Castle
Red Lion

FLORIDA
Between Alford
and Cottondale
Clermont
Davie
Ft. Lauderdale
Galloway
Hialeah
Jacksonville
Miami
Pensacola
Tampa
Warrington
Whitehouse
Zellwood

GEORGIA
Athens

ILLINOIS
Waukegan

INDIANA
Bloomington
Seymour

IOWA
Council Bluffs

KANSAS
Arkansas City

KENTUCKY
Brooks

MAINE
Winthrop

MARYLAND
Baltimore

MASSACHUSETTS
Ashland
North Dartmouth
Tyngsborough
Woburn

MICHIGAN
St. Louis

MINNESOTA
Andover
Oakdale
St. Louis Park
St. Paul

MISSISSIPPI
Greenville

MISSOURI
Ellisville
Springfield

NEW HAMPSHIRE
Epping
Kingston
Nashua

NEW JERSEY
Bridgeport
Edison
Elizabeth
Freehold
Hamilton
Marlboro
Monmouth County
Pitman
Pleasantville
Plumsted

NEW MEXICO
Church Rock
Clovis
Milan

NEW YORK
Batavia
Elmira
Niagra Falls
Olean
Oswego
Oyster Bay
Philipstown
Wheatfield

NORTH
CAROLINA
Highway dumping
in fourteen
counties

NORTH DAKOTA
Rural south-
eastern corner

OHIO
Ashtabula
Cleveland
Deerfield
Hamilton

OKLAHOMA
Criner
Ottawa County

PENNSYLVANIA
Bruin
Buffalo
Chester
Girard
McAdoo
Natrona Heights
Old Forge
Pittston

RHODE ISLAND
Burrillville
Coventry
Smithfield

SOUTH CAROLINA
South of Columbia

SOUTH DAKOTA
Deadwood

TENNESSEE
Memphis

TEXAS
Crosby
Grand Prairie
La Marque

UTAH
Salt Lake City

VERMONT
Burlington

VIRGINIA
West of Salem
York County

WASHINGTON
Tacoma

WASHINGTON, D.C.

WEST VIRGINIA
Point Pleasant

Figure 10-2
The worst toxic waste
dumps: hazardous
waste sites with highest
priority for remedial
action under Super-
fund program, 1981

Source: Data compiled by the
Council on Environmental
Quality as it appears in *State
of the Environment: An Assess-
ment at Mid-Decade*
(Washington, D.C.: The
Conservation Foundation,
1984) p. 88.

cost anywhere from $10 to $40 billion to clean up even a substantial *fraction* of the roughly 15,000 toxic waste sites pinpointed in 1983 as needing immediate action (cited in *Science*, April 1, 1983, p. 34). By 1986, only 13 of the worst sites had been cleaned up under the Superfund program — and many critics believed even that number exaggerated the actual progress (Weiskopf, 1986). At the rate of cleanup we've achieved so far, it would take hundreds of years to render even the worst toxic waste sites reasonably safe. And meanwhile, new toxic wastes are being generated at the rate of hundreds of millions of tons a year.

Is this situation inevitable? There is considerable evidence that it isn't — and that a more preventive, rather than merely reactive, approach to the hazardous waste problem could make an important difference. About four-fifths of federally regulated hazardous wastes are now dumped on land. Yet (as a report from the National Academy of Sciences affirmed), "there currently exists some technology or combination of technologies capable of dealing with every hazardous waste in a manner that eliminates the need for perpetual storage" (quoted in *Christian Science Monitor*, April 7, 1983). Many industrial wastes can be safely burned away at extremely high temperatures; others can be detoxified through the use of other chemicals or even bacteria. In West Germany, roughly 85 percent of hazardous industrial wastes are detoxified (Council on Environmental Quality, 1980, pp. 218–219; *Newsweek*, March 7, 1983, p. 24). And some wastes may be reusable by other industries, "on the principle that one company's wastes may be another's raw materials" (Council on Environmental

Figure 10-3
Distribution of hazardous-waste generation, by industrial sector, 1981

Source: Conservation Foundation, *State of the Environment: An Assessment at Middecade* (Washington, D.C.: Conservation Foundation, 1984), p. 72.

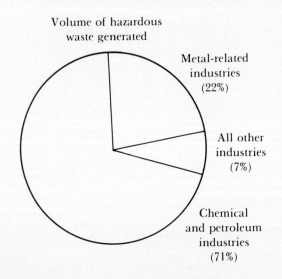

Volume of hazardous waste generated

Metal-related industries (22%)

All other industries (7%)

Chemical and petroleum industries (71%)

HOUSE FOR SALE
TO U. S. GOVT.
YOU TOOK THE
TRASH, BUT
LEFT THE
PEOPLE!

Social consequences of environmental neglect: dioxin contamination, Times Beach, Missouri.

Quality, 1980, p. 218). Also, according to the EPA, about 60 percent of all hazardous wastes in the United States could be safely incinerated; in the Netherlands, half of all hazardous waste is now burned (Conservation Foundation, 1982b, p. 171).

Why don't we make more use of these alternative technologies? One reason, surely, is that they are more expensive — in the short run. Because of that, they have been unattractive to most American industries and have received little encouragement from our government. (Figure 10–3 shows that the generation of hazardous wastes is overwhelmingly concentrated in just a few industries, most notably the chemical industry.) But the short run, as usual, is not the whole story. It's estimated, for example, that proper disposal of the chemical wastes at Love Canal would have cost $2 million or less. But by mid-1980, the costs of dealing with the problem after the fact, including the cleanup and the relocation of residents, already added up to more than $36 million (Council on Environmental Quality, 1980, pp. 220–221).

Troubled Waters: Groundwater Contamination

We've seen that the antipollution efforts of the 1970s at least held the line against further deterioration of the lakes, rivers, and streams of the United States. But by the early 1980s it had become clear that this was only part of the problem with America's water — what was happening *below* the surface was much more disturbing. Indeed, the threat of chemical contamination of groundwater threatens (as one EPA official put it) to become the "environmental horror story of the 1980s" (*Newsweek*, November 1, 1982).

Groundwater is the water trapped underground (in permeable rock strata called *aquifers*) that supplies, through wells, about half of the drinking water in the United States. At one time it was generally believed that groundwater was safe from the kinds of contamination that affected surface waters. The soil usually acts as a giant filter removing most normal contaminants before they reach the water, and the groundwater itself sheds pollutants as it "percolates" through underground rocks.

But the introduction of new kinds of industrial chemicals has created a very different situation. Many of these chemicals are not broken down by the usual processes of cleansing in the soil and rock. And once it has been contaminated by these chemicals, the groundwater may remain contaminated "for hundreds or thousands of years, if not for geologic time" (Burmaster, 1982, p. 9). Groundwater contamination, as the Conservation Foundation noted, "may be essen-

Table 10-3
Toxic chemicals detected in drinking water wells.

Chemical	Evidence for carcinogenicity
Benzene	H
alpha-BHC	CA
gamma-BHC (Lindane)	CA
Carbon tetrachloride	CA
Chloroform	CA
Dibromochloropropane (DBCP)	CA
1,2-Dichloroethane	CA
Dioxane	CA
Ethylene dibromide (EDB)	CA
Tetrachloroethylene	CA
1,1,2-Trichloroethane	CA
Trichloroethylene (TCE)	CA
Vinyl chloride	H, CA

H = Confirmed human carcinogen
CA = Confirmed animal carcinogen

Source: Adapted from David Burmaster, "The New Pollution: Groundwater Contamination," *Environment*, March 1982, p. 33. Reprinted with permission.

Handling toxic waste.

tially irreversible"; unlike some other forms of pollution, it continues *long* after the initial source of the pollution has been stopped (1982b, p. 107). Because of this, groundwater contamination promises to be one of the most dramatic legacies of the heedless attitude toward the introduction of toxic chemicals in the course of America's economic development.

What makes groundwater pollution so threatening is that it strikes at the basic drinking water supplies of many communities. In the late 1970s and early 1980s, contaminated wells were discovered — many by accident — in a number of areas across the country. Some of the chemicals involved are among the most toxic produced by industry, including several known or suspected to cause cancer and/or genetic damage (Table 10-3). Even more disturbing is the fact that so little is known about the precise health effects of these chemicals. About 30 have been conclusively associated with cancer in humans, but only about 11 percent of the chemicals used in industry have even been tested for their ability to cause cancer (Stein, 1984). Less than 2 percent, according to the National Academy of Sciences, have been tested enough to permit a clear assessment of their overall hazards to human health; and we know nothing whatever about the health hazards of an estimated 70 percent of the chemicals in use today (Conservation Foundation, 1984, p. 4). Moreover, some chemicals may have worse health impacts when combined together (as they often are in contaminated groundwater) than they do separately. One study estimated that if a population of a million people were to consume water from one of the most heavily polluted wells so far discovered (near Princeton, New Jersey), there would be an extra 2,500 cancer deaths over the life cycle (Burmaster, 1982, p. 33).

The Costs and Benefits of Environmental Control

So it's clear that while environmental protection measures have accomplished a great deal, much still remains to be done, and some of the remaining jobs are *very* formidable. One response has been to press for stricter, more extensive regulations to more effectively control long-standing air and water pollution problems and to begin to confront the newer, more stubborn ones.

Increasingly, however, another response has become more common — to attack much of the current arsenal of environmental regulations as unwise and unworkable. An overzealous approach to environmental regulation, in this view, however well intentioned, has hobbled the economy and thereby unwittingly made life poorer for everyone: "Through onerous regulations, the total economic pie is reduced to such an extent that all of us — Easterners, Westerners, industrialists, environmentalists — are losers" (Navarro, 1980, p. 44).

The idea that environmental protection has gotten out of hand and has hurt the economy touches a nerve in a time of high unemployment and sluggish growth. Although a majority of the public believes that controlling environmental pollution remains a high priority, these economic concerns have led to demands that we de-emphasize the claims of environmental quality in favor of those of growth. But is this an accurate assessment of the economic effects of environmental regulation?

How Much Does Pollution Control Cost?

Let's consider, first of all, how much environmental protection actually costs. On close examination, it's less than is often supposed.

According to U.S. Department of Commerce estimates, total spending on pollution abatement and control amounted to over $60 billion in 1984. But this figure is misleading because it includes spending on such basic necessities as sewage systems and garbage treatment, not just spending to comply with environmental regulations. Less than $1.3 billion was spent on pollution regulation and monitoring — and, adjusted for inflation, that figure had *fallen* by 17 percent since 1980 (*Statistical Abstract of the United States*, 1987, p. 193). As Figure 10-4 illustrates, federal spending for the environment generally has dropped sharply. American business, meanwhile, devoted only about 2 percent of its total capital spending to pollution control (*Statistical Abstract of the United States*, 1987, p. 194).

The sheer dollar cost of pollution control, however, is of less concern to critics than the wider effects of environmental regulation on economic performance. A number of studies have attempted to estimate the impact of these regulations on inflation, jobs, productivity, and economic growth. Do environmental regulations really hurt the economy, by these measures? The issues are complex, and the problems of measurement difficult, but the overall answer is generally negative. If anything, though it may sometimes involve substantial short-range expenses, environmental protection appears to have a

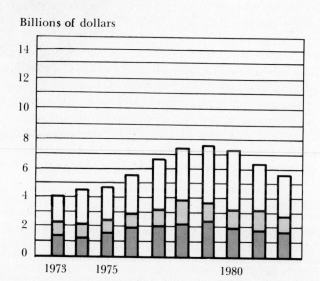

Billions of dollars

Figure 10-4
Federal expenditures for environmental programs in constant 1973 dollars

Source: Conservation Foundation, *State of the Environment: An Assessment at Mid-decade* (Washington, D.C.: Conservation Foundation, 1984), p. 73.

☐ Expenditures for pollution abatement and control (including wastewater-treatment grants to municipalities)

▨ Expenditures on protection and enhancement (includes expenditures for recreation, wildlife, historic preservation, etc.)

■ Expenditures on understanding, predicting, and describing the environment

positive long-run impact on the economy, and could have an even greater one in the future.

Several studies suggest that environmental regulation may have a slight aggravating effect on inflation; but all find the effect to be small, and most find that regulation simultaneously reduces *unemployment*. An EPA study, for example, calculated that environmental regulations may decrease unemployment by 0.2 or 0.3 percent a year (by creating jobs in antipollution-equipment industries and services), while probably causing a 0.1 to 0.2 percent rise in inflation (*Congressional Quarterly*, 1981, p. 128).

Another argument raised by the critics is that pollution regulations require such costly, cumbersome changes in industrial processes or products that they lower industrial productivity. Again, the specter of declining productivity hits home at a time when American industry's productivity gains have slowed, on average, especially in comparison with some other countries. As we saw in Chapter 3, however, productivity is a tricky concept, difficult to measure and even more difficult to interpret. And most studies indicate that to the extent that productivity has declined in the United States, it has been due to a host of factors other than regulatory activity. As one study argued, "the evidence for an adverse impact of environmental regulations on the capital stock and its productivity is very weak" (Haveman and Christianson, 1981, p. 74).

Several studies reviewed by the Council on Environmental Quality found that environmental controls might lower industrial productivity by no more than 0.05 to 0.3 percent — only a very small fraction of America's productivity slowdown. Moreover, the magnitude of this effect had *declined* by the late 1970s, suggesting that part of it reflected one-time expenses of complying with pollution regulations (installing equipment to control emissions from smokestacks, for example) (Council on Environmental Quality, 1980, pp. 388–389).

The Benefits of a Cleaner Environment

The small size of these effects becomes all the more remarkable when it is noted that very few of these studies considered any of the *benefits* of pollution control in their calculations. To be sure, some (though not all) of these benefits are more difficult to measure than their dollar costs. But they are hardly less important: They include better health, reduced mortality, improved environmental quality, and longer-range gains in the productivity of the economy.

Air pollution controls, for example, improve agricultural production, reduce damages to industrial plants and equipment, and lower the costs of cleaning and painting. Water pollution controls increase commercial fishing yields and lower the costs of *treating* water after it has become polluted. It has been estimated that the economic losses water pollution inflicts on recreational activity alone run to several billions of dollars a year (Portney, 1981, p. 50).

Beyond these economic benefits are those associated with human health. Evidence on the adverse effects of pollution on health is growing. Table 10-4 describes the health impacts of some toxic pollutants. Probably the two biggest pollution-related health problems are respiratory diseases and cancer. Industrial pollutants, especially sulfur oxides and particulate matter, have long been linked to respiratory illnesses, particularly in vulnerable groups: children, the elderly, and people already suffering from lung or heart diseases. Children living in highly polluted areas have higher rates of respiratory disease and are more likely to develop chronic respiratory diseases as adults. High levels of air pollutants are also linked with more lost workdays due to illness — another reason to look skeptically at the one-sided way in which the productivity costs of pollution controls are typically calculated (Freeman, 1979; Ostro and Anderson, 1981). The corrosive effect of one kind of industrial pollutant, the acid sulfates, on the respiratory system may account for almost 190,000 deaths a year in the United States, according to a 1981 study (*Congressional Quarterly,* 1981, p. 21). Much of this health impact is hidden because it is usually long-term and subtle, not sudden and dramatic, and because it is often difficult to disentangle from other problems, such as age or excessive smoking, with which it is often combined.

We've already seen that rising rates of some kinds of cancer are the most troubling exception to the overall improvements in Americans' health. We've seen, too, that part of that increase has been linked to environmental factors, especially toxic chemicals in the workplace. Research makes it clear that toxic chemicals *outside* the workplace — in the air and drinking water — are also implicated in rising cancer rates. We've mentioned the potential carcinogenic effects of groundwater contamination. But cancer has been increasingly associated with *air* pollution as well. One study calculated that between 11 and 21 percent of lung cancers in the United States are associated with air pollution and that the threat of pollution-induced cancer is even greater in urban areas (Karch and Schneiderman, 1981). Studies also show much higher rates of cancer among people living downwind from high concentrations of petrochemical plants (*San Francisco Examiner,* July 23, 1985).

Another example of the health impact of air pollution — and the potential benefits from environmental controls — is lead poisoning. Lead is an extremely toxic substance known to cause a number of severe health problems, particularly in children. Long-term exposures to high concentrations of lead can lead to progressive loss of kidney functioning, loss of fertility and risks of fetal damage in pregnant women, and anemia (Hattis, Goble, and Ashford, 1982).

Table 10-4
What toxic chemicals do to you: Health and environmental effects of selected chemicals

| Chemical | Human health effects | | | Environmental effects |
	Potential carcinogen	Potential teratogen	Other effects	
Aldrin/dieldrin	•		Tremors, convulsions, kidney damage	Toxic to aquatic organisms, reproductive failure in birds and fish, bioaccumulates in aquatic organisms
Arsenic	•	•	Vomiting, poisoning, liver and kidney damage	Toxic to legume crops
Benzene	•		Anemia, bone marrow damage	Toxic to some fish and aquatic invertebrates
Cadmium	•	•	Suspected causal factor in many human pathologies: tumors, renal dysfunction, hypertension, arteriosclerosis; Itai-itai disease (weakened bones)	Toxic to fish, bioaccumulates in aquatic organisms
Carbon tetrachloride	•		Kidney and liver damage, heart failure	
Chromium	•		Kidney and gastrointestinal damage, respiratory complications	Toxic to some aquatic invertebrates
Copper			Gastrointestinal irritant, liver damage	Toxic to juvenile fish
Cyanide			Acutely toxic	Kills fish, reduces growth and development of fish

Human health effects

Chemical	Potential carcinogen	Potential teratogen	Other effects	Environmental effects
DDT	•	•	Tremors, convulsions, kidney damage	Reproductive failure of birds and fish, bioaccumulates in aquatic organisms, biomagnifies in food chain
Dioxin	•	•	Acute skin rashes	Bioaccumulates
Lead	•	•	Convulsions, anemia, kidney and brain damage	Toxic to domestic plants and animals, biomagnifies in food chain
Mercury	•	•	Irritability, depression, kidney and liver damage, Minamata disease	Reproductive failure in fish species, inhibits growth and kills fish, methylmercury biomagnifies
Nickel	•		Gastrointestinal and central nervous system effects	Impairs reproduction of aquatic species
PCBs	•	•	Vomiting, abdominal pain, temporary blindness	Liver damage in mammals, kidney damage and eggshell thinning in birds, suspected reproductive failure in fish
Tetrachloroethylene	•		Central nervous system effects	

Notes: In many cases human health effects are based on the results of animal tests. For instance, the identification of a substance as a potential carcinogen indicates that there is at least one animal test that demonstrates carcinogenic effects. However, whether a substance actually produces the effects indicated depends on the duration and intensity of exposure, the form of the exposure (whether it is inhaled, ingested, and so on), the susceptibility of the person exposed, and other factors. If a substance is identified as a *carcinogen*, there is evidence that it has the potential for causing cancer in humans. If it is identified as a *teratogen*, it has the potential for causing birth defects in humans.

Source: Data compiled by the Council on Environmental Quality as it appears in *State of the Environment: An Assessment at Mid-Decade* (Washington, D.C., The Conservation Foundation, 1984), p. 35.

But probably the most telling effect of lead is its tendency to "wreak havoc in the nervous system, to destroy normal behavior and to result in crippling mental damage" (*Environment,* March 1982, p. 22; Bellinger, 1987).

We saw in Chapter 9 that the incidence of many health problems in the United States is profoundly shaped by social factors — including race and income. A 1982 survey from the National Center for Health Statistics found that almost one-fifth of inner-city black children have seriously high levels of lead in their blood, as compared to less than 5 percent of inner-city white children and just 2 percent of white children living outside the inner cities (cited in *Environment,* March 1982, p. 22). How does lead wind up in a child's blood system? Some of it comes from food; some from peeling lead-based paint in older, often dilapidated urban housing; and some from the air, especially from automobile exhausts. Since the mid-1970s, blood-lead levels in children have declined substantially. Why? The regulation of lead in gasoline is the most likely factor: The decline in blood-lead levels parallels the decline in the use of leaded gas.

Overall, according to one study, cleaner air standards could result in a 7 percent reduction of mortality in the United States (*Congressional Quarterly,* 1981, p. 128). Again, these matters of life and death are not easily translated into quantitative cost-benefit terms and are, therefore, typically left out of the conventional calculations of regulation costs. But it is noteworthy that the Organization for Economic Cooperation and Development (OECD) has estimated that the health damage caused by air pollution *alone* may amount to between 3 and 5 percent of the gross national product of industrial countries — which translates (roughly) into a sum of $120 to $200 billion in the United States in 1985 (cited in *Environment,* 1980, p. 22).

Environmental Control, Jobs, and Investment

Most critics of environmental controls would probably acknowledge that cleaner air and water do bring important benefits. But many would nevertheless argue that both the cost and the complexity of complying with pollution regulations have become so great that they discourage investment, hinder the construction of new plants, and generally block economic growth. Horror stories are told of plants closed or unbuilt, and jobs lost, because of "nit-picking" regulations.

But though the cost, in money and time, of meeting environmental standards *can* be significant, the evidence does *not* show substantial adverse effects on investment. And, at the same time, environmental protection turns out to have surprising potential for *encouraging,* rather than hindering, economic growth.

It's often argued, for example, that tough environmental laws discourage businesses from locating in certain states or encourage them to leave the country. But a study by the Conservation Foundation (funded by several business-related organizations) argues that this view is a myth. The study found no evidence that environmental regulations had caused industries to avoid certain states. California, for example, which has very stringent environmental regulations, also had the *largest* gain in manufacturing jobs of any state during the 1970s (Conservation Foundation, 1982a).

Similar findings apply to the specter of plants closing because of the burdens of pollution regulations. Using data provided by private industry (which we wouldn't expect to understate the problem), the EPA calculated that between 1971 and 1981, a maximum of 33,000 American workers may have been displaced by plant closures in which environmental regulations played *any* part at all (Kazis and Grossman, 1982, p. 13). (This was during a period when the average number of unemployed workers never dropped below 4 million.) And many of the plants turned out on closer inspection to have been marginal ones in any case — the inability to meet pollution regulations was often the *least* of their problems. Meanwhile, an EPA-sponsored analysis estimated a net *gain* of over half a million jobs as a result of pollution controls between 1970 and 1987. Some of those jobs are in government pollution-control agencies, but many others are in the private sector. By 1981, according to one estimate, about 600 new companies were in the business of pollution-control equipment manufacturing and installation (Kazis and Grossman, 1982, p. 18).

Of course, the loss of even a *few* jobs as a result of environmental controls is a painful, threatening experience for those affected. But the job losses seem small enough to be offset by serious retraining programs for displaced workers.

More generally, pollution prevention, as an analysis in the *Harvard Business Review* noted, has been responsible for stimulating a substantial amount of new economic development in the United States — and even more in some foreign countries. "Environmental business" had become a $50 billion-a-year industry by the beginning of the 1980s, and was growing at a rate of 20 percent a year — in a time generally characterized by a sluggish economy. "Environmentally induced economic activity" of all kinds, according to this analysis, was now an estimated 2 percent of America's GNP, employing more than 2 million people (Royston, 1980, pp. 12–13).

The importance of environmentally related industry is even greater in some other countries, where it has been deliberately developed as a high priority in order to spur economic growth. Both the Swedes and the Japanese used massive investments in pollution control (stimulated by very strict antipollution legislation) to boost their economies out of the recession of the mid-1970s. According to an

OECD estimate, fully 20 percent of Japan's economic growth in the late 1970s was attributable to new, tough environmental regulations and the resulting antipollution spending. Because of that investment, too, both Japan and Sweden benefited economically by emerging as leading world suppliers of the most advanced pollution-control equipment and technology (Royston, 1980).

Certainly, some forms of pollution control cost money — and controlling some of the more recently discovered problems, like carcinogenic wastes or acid rain, will cost even more. The evidence doesn't suggest that these costs are unimportant — or that *all* environmental regulations are equally sound and wisely conceived. There is certainly room for improvement and careful assessment of the value of particular regulations. What it most clearly suggests is that we need to distinguish between *short-term* and *long-term* costs. Like most other socially useful investments (and like many personal ones) the initial costs to an industry to "clean up its act" may be significant. But the economic benefits *alone* are usually even greater when viewed in a longer time frame. Many European and Japanese companies have saved substantial sums, and increased their profits, by redesigning industrial processes to reduce pollution and to reuse industrial wastes at the same time. And in the United States, some corporations have discovered that, as the economist Ruth Ruttenberg put it, "regulation is the mother of invention" (1981). Corporations that are forced to change their products and industrial processes to meet environmental requirements often design something more productive, more technologically advanced, and frequently more profitable. Unfortunately, though, as in the case of energy use, American industry has more often emphasized the short-term gains at the expense of potential long-term advantages.

The Outlook: Energy and Environmental Policy

That tension between short-term gains and the longer-range health of the economy and society underlies much of the debate over energy and environmental policy in the United States today. And, in the past few years, it appears that, after a decade and more of greater attention to the long-term issues of energy supply and environmental quality, we began to shift back toward the kind of short-range approaches that have been an unfortunate part of the American tradition.

Much of American energy policy in the 1980s has stressed incentives for increased fossil fuel production (and nuclear energy), while downplaying the already minimal support for conservation and renewable energy — the strategies that now appear *most* likely to offer long-lasting, environmentally attractive solutions to the energy crisis (Georgiu, 1987). Tax incentives for energy *production* outweighed those for *conservation* by eight to one in the early 1980s. And this is in spite of the public's often expressed preference for a shift to renewable energy and conservation, and its growing wariness over the costs and perils of nuclear power.

These policies, somewhat curiously, are often justified in the name of allowing the unfettered operation of the free market. But most of these energy policies have little to do with the market — and are most certainly not free. The nuclear power industry has been saved from the market's verdict in recent years by nearly $40 billion worth of government subsidies. America's energy choices, in fact, have *never* been left to the forces of the free market: They have always been shaped by the government's funneling of taxpayers' monies to *some* energy strategies at the expense of others. According to a Department of Energy–sponsored study, from the end of World War I through the 1970s, direct federal subsidies for energy amounted to more than $250 billion: about half for the oil industry, a fourth for electric power, 8 percent for the nuclear industry — and just 0.15 percent for all forms of solar energy (Lovins and Lovins, 1980, p. 112).

Thus, our current dependence on energy sources that are either the least plentiful, the most polluting, or the most dangerous is not simply a result of consumers' free choices, or of fate, or even of technological obstacles to alternative energy strategies. Instead, it is to a substantial degree the result of deliberate government policies. And those policies are now pointing us toward an uncertain and perhaps perilous future in energy.

And the long-term care of the natural environment is also increasingly being counterposed to the short-term imperatives of economic growth. In the name of growth, there has been a shift toward weakening pollution regulations. Funding for federal environmental programs was sharply reduced in the early 1980s, and so were the staffs of pollution control agencies. Most of these changes were heralded as the beginning of a more cost-effective approach to environmental problems. But, as we've seen, assessing "cost" is a much more complicated matter than simply adding up the dollar figures on next year's budget. And the possible longer-term costs are staggering. The Conservation Foundation's summation of these issues is hard to improve on:

> Environmental programs are not an expendable indulgence of an affluent society. The basic purpose of environmental programs is to protect

us from ourselves by assuring that our activities do not destroy the natural functions on which we depend. . . . Delays in pursuing environmental programs may have serious consequences. At stake are human health, the condition of our farms and forests and rivers, and irreplaceable natural areas and animal species. Not only are the stakes high: many decisions are irreversible. (Conservation Foundation, 1982b, p. 8)

Summary

This chapter has examined two closely related social issues: energy use and environmental policy. After decades of heedless attitudes toward these problems, the United States now faces tough choices in both realms.

Among potential energy sources for the future, the traditional fossil fuels (oil, natural gas, and coal) are crucially limited. Oil and natural gas are in relatively short supply. Coal, though more abundant, carries troubling environmental costs.

The potential of nuclear power (once thought to be the answer to America's energy problems) has been derailed by skyrocketing costs and unresolved safety problems.

Alternative energy sources (conservation and solar power) may have a much greater potential role in America's future energy policy than we once thought.

Some aspects of environmental quality have improved significantly in recent years. But other problems — including toxic wastes, acid rain, and groundwater contamination — have barely been touched by public policies.

Though environmental protection is often attacked as too costly, the evidence indicates that pollution regulations have little negative impact on the economy — and can have important economic benefits, in addition to the more obvious benefits in health and environmental quality.

For Further Reading

Conservation Foundation. *State of the Environment: An Assessment at Mid-decade.* Washington, D.C.: Conservation Foundation, 1984.

Schnaiberg, Alan. *The Environment: From Surplus to Scarcity.* New York: Oxford University Press, 1980.

Stobaugh, Robert, and Daniel Yergin. *Energy Future,* rev. ed. New York: Vintage, 1982.

Union of Concerned Scientists. *Energy Strategies: Toward a Solar Future.* Cambridge, Mass.: Ballinger, 1981.

Worldwatch Foundation. *State of the Earth, 1986.* New York: Norton, 1986.

11

Crime and Justice

When Americans are asked what worries them most about their society, crime is always high on the list — usually just below the cost of living and the threat of unemployment. Most of us feel that our streets and communities are more dangerous than they used to be. Opinion polls show that over half of Americans living in cities are afraid to walk in some areas near their homes at night, and about one in six regularly carry some sort of weapon or other device for self-defense (*Washington Post*, March 11, 1985).

The most common response to the fear of crime has been the demand to "get tough" with criminals. Most Americans, according to the polls, believe that the courts are too lenient with criminals. Legislators have responded with stiffer sentences for serious crimes and more funds for new jails and prisons.

Though these sentiments have been with us for some time, the strength of the get-tough position in recent years marks an important shift in public attitudes — and those of some social scientists as well. In the 1950s and 1960s, criminologists often emphasized the social and economic causes of crime. To a great extent, crime was regarded as one of the bitter fruits of disadvantage and discrimination. And it was widely believed that crime could be largely overcome through reform of the larger social conditions that seemed to breed it — poverty, racial discrimination, unemployment — coupled with programs to rehabilitate delinquents and criminals. A former U.S. attorney general put it this way at the close of the 1960s: "Warring on poverty, inadequate housing, and unemployment is warring on

350

crime. A civil rights law is a law against crime. Money for schools is money against crime. . . . Every effort to improve life in America's inner cities is an effort against crime" (President's Commission on Law Enforcement, 1967, p. 6).

But by the 1970s, the view of crime as mainly the product of remediable social conditions was under attack. It was weakened by what some saw as a revealing paradox: The social programs of the 1960s, and the improvements in educational opportunities and income levels, seemed to have had no impact on crime (Wilson, 1975). If anything, crime had increased considerably — leading some critics to argue that efforts at social reform were at best irrelevant and at worst detrimental to public safety. Simultaneously, a series of widely publicized studies of programs for offenders and ex-offenders seemed to show that "nothing worked" (Lipton, Martinson, and Wilks, 1975) — that on the whole, the efforts to rehabilitate criminals were dismal failures.

It's now often argued that we know little about the causes of crime and that even if we did know, we lack the means to intervene effectively to alter them (Wilson, 1975; Wilson and Herrnstein, 1985). For many years, our main reponse to the crime problem has been to put more and more offenders behind bars, for increasingly long terms. But — as we'll see — the results haven't been impressive: America's prisons and jails are overflowing, but the crime rate remains depressingly, frighteningly high — and much higher than in most other industrial societies. What lies behind our unusually high crime rate, and how we can best reduce it?

In this chapter, we will consider these issues through the lens of the most careful research on crime and its control. We will focus on some key questions raised by current debates about crime and justice: Is crime increasing? If so, how much? Who are the typical victims? How much can we rely on courts, prisons, and police to prevent crime? Are we as much in the dark about crime's cause as some writers suggest — and as powerless to develop strategies to combat them? Finally, what is the outlook for the future? Can we expect continuing rises in crime and violence, or is there reason to expect that we may begin to reverse the sense of fear and disintegration in American communities?

Is Crime Increasing?

Despite the complexity of measuring crime, it's clear that some of the most serious, violent crimes have risen since the early 1960s, sometimes sharply (Wolfgang and Weiner, 1985). Table 11-1 shows the

Table 11-1
The persistence of crime

Year		Violent crime	Property crime	Murder and manslaughter	Rape	Robbery	Aggravated assault	Burglary	Larceny–theft	Motor vehicle theft
1960	Number	285,980	1,733,600	9,030	17,030	107,340	152,580	900,400	507,300	325,900
	Rate	159.5	966.7	5.0	9.5	59.9	85.1	502.1	282.9	181.7
1970	Number	732,940	4,848,300	15,860	37,650	348,240	331,190	2,176,600	1,749,800	921,900
	Rate	360.7	2,386.1	7.8	18.5	171.4	163.0	1,071.2	861.2	453.7
1980	Number	1,344,520	12,063,700	23,040	82,990	565,840	672,650	3,795,200	7,136,900	1,131,700
	Rate	596.6	5,353.3	10.2	36.8	251.1	298.5	1,684.1	3,167.0	502.2
1985	Number	1,327,440	11,102,600	18,980	87,340	497,870	723,250	3,073,300	6,926,400	1,102,900
	Rate	556.0	4,650.5	7.9	36.6	208.5	302.9	1,287.3	2,901.2	462.0

Rates are per 100,000 population.
"Violent" crime includes murder, rape, robbery, and aggravated assault. "Property" crime includes burglary, larceny–theft, and motor vehicle theft.
Source: Federal Bureau of Investigation, *Uniform Crime Reports*, annual.

trends in *reported* crime in recent years. For some crimes — perhaps especially rape — the recorded increase may be exaggerated because of changes in people's willingness to report the crime. But the homicide rate, which is much less likely to be biased in this way, also shows a dramatic increase. About twice as high a proportion of Americans died by homicide in the 1980s than at the beginning of the 1960s.

Who Are the Victims?

We have often seen in this book that broad, national figures can be misleading, masking sharp variations in the way social problems affect particular kinds of people in particular kinds of places. Crime is no exception. National crime trends obscure the fact that different groups face dramatically different risks of being victimized by crime. In most respects, these risks reflect the broader inequalities characteristic of modern American society. The victims of serious crime — and especially violent crime — are disproportionately the poor, minorities, and the young.

Crime can strike anyone, but violent crime is mainly an affliction of the poor. With the exception of some property crimes, the chance of being a victim of nearly all serious crimes rises, sometimes dramat-

Uncovering the Crime Rate

At first glance, it might seem simple to determine how much crime we have and whether — and by how much — it has increased. Yet, despite improvements in the techniques of measuring crime, we are still a long way from being able to pinpoint its true dimensions with precision. Because of this, crime statistics are among the most commonly abused of all official data, and their interpretation requires even more caution than most.

The fundamental problem is that there is potential bias both in the way crimes are reported — or not reported — and in the way they are recorded by officials. The first step is the initial reporting of the crime to the police. Most often, this is the responsibility of the victim; but for a variety of reasons, victims may fail to report crimes. Sometimes this is because the crime is a small one; many small thefts are never reported because the victims feel that going to the police is more trouble than it is worth. Sometimes crimes are not reported because victims are afraid, ashamed, or mistrustful of the police and courts. Some victims are afraid of retaliation by their attackers, a problem that is especially severe in such crimes as child abuse and wife-beating. Many rape victims are afraid that the police response will be unsympathetic or degrading.

Some crimes, moreover, are so severe, or

so obvious, that they are nearly always reported. Murder is the best example of the first, auto theft of the second. This makes these crimes easier to compare over different time periods or across different cities, regions, or countries than crimes like theft, which vary enormously in reporting rates.

But the difficulties do not end when crimes are reported to police. Studies show that how the police classify and record the crimes that do come to their attention depends on many factors in addition to the crime itself. For example, a study of robberies in Chicago found that only about a fourth were ultimately recorded by the police as official robberies. Of the rest, some were not reported by the victims, and some that were reported were classified as "unfounded" by the police. Both for the victims and the police, the decision to classify an incident as a robbery or not depended primarily on their assessment of the larger situation in which the robbery took place. Robberies that were successfully resisted, for example, were less often recorded by police; robberies involving guns were more often recorded (Bloch and Block, 1980).

The collection and recording of official crime statistics in this country begins with the many thousands of separate local law enforcement agencies. About 15,000 such agencies provide the information that goes into the FBI's *Uniform Crime Reports,* the annual compilation that is the basic source of official crime statistics in the United States (Federal Bureau of Investigation, 1986, p. 1). In the past, some police agencies tended to record the local crime rate according to their own administrative needs rather than the call of accuracy and impartiality. A stunning example of this took place in New York City in the mid-1960s and is illustrated in Table 11-2. As the table shows, the city's official rates of certain crimes shot up enormously just at the time when the police administration changed hands.

Despite the potential biases, the *Uniform Crime Reports* (UCR) remains the standard source for most of the crime rates and trends that are reported in the media. The UCR describes the number of crimes of various kinds reported to the police, with special attention to eight serious crimes that are often combined to form a *crime index:* murder, forcible rape, robbery, aggravated assault (assault intended to seriously injure, often with a

Table 11-2
Reported crimes before and after a 1965 change in police administration, New York City

Crime	Recorded crimes		Percent change between 1965–1966
	1965	1966	
Murder and manslaughter	631	653	3
Forcible rape	1,154	1,761	53
Robbery	8,904	23,539	164
Aggravated assault	16,325	23,205	42
Auto theft	34,726	44,914	29
Burglary	51,072	120,903	137

Source: Adapted from Alfred Blumstein, Jacqueline Cohen, and Daniel Nagin, eds., *Deterrence and Incapacitation* (Washington, D.C.: National Academy of Sciences, 1978), p. 115. Reprinted with permission of the National Academy Press.

weapon), auto theft, larceny (theft), burglary, and (since 1980) arson. These index crimes are, in turn, broken down into *crimes of violence* (murder, rape, aggravated assault, robbery) and *crimes against property* (burglary, larceny, auto theft). The UCR also records how many of these crimes *known* to the police are "cleared" by an arrest and describes, for some crimes, the characteristics, insofar as they are known, of the people arrested and (for homicide) of the victims.

Like the process of reporting crime in the first place, but even more so, the official figures on *arrests* reflect many things other than the "true" crime rate and must be treated even more cautiously. Police may arrest someone for a wide variety of reasons: a past criminal record, a "suspicious" appearance, or, in some places, unfavorable racial, ethnic, or class stereotypes. And these biases are likely to be more severe for some kinds of crime than others.

Some crimes frequently lead to arrests; others are very rarely cleared in this way. The proportion of index crimes cleared by arrest ranges from almost three-fourths of murders to one-quarter of robberies and about one-seventh of burglaries and auto thefts. As we will see later in this chapter, this low rate of cleared crimes has important implications for how we think about preventing crime.

Because of the limitations of these official data, two other techniques have been used by researchers to get at the "true" rate of crime. One relies on the testimony of crime's victims, the other on its perpetrators.

Victim surveys ask a sample of the population about its experience with crime in the past year. The most comprehensive of these surveys is the annual National Crime Survey of 60,000 households, which is conducted by the Census Bureau for the Justice Department. Because these surveys tap crimes that are not necessarily reported to police, they produce a very different picture than the FBI data. In particular, they show much *more*

crime than official figures reveal. According to the UCR, the 1983 robbery rate in the United States was about 217 per 100,000 population. According to the National Crime Survey, it was about 600 per 100,000.

Since the victim surveys show that a very large proportion of some crimes are not reported to the police, it is often thought that they give a more accurate picture of the trends in crime over time. But victim surveys have limitations of their own. First, they deal only with "street" crime and not with "white-collar" offenses (see pages 379 to 381) — an important, though often neglected, aspect of crime in America. They also underreport crimes within families. Further, the surveys depend on the victims' ability to remember incidents of crime accurately and to have perceived them correctly in the first place. Finally, survey results may exaggerate the real seriousness of crime by including many relatively unserious incidents in the category of serious crimes. Victims may define small thefts as robberies, for example, or consider a minor scuffle as a serious assault.

Another approach to uncovering the crime rate is through "self-report" surveys, in which samples of the general population, or of offenders, are asked about the offenses they have committed. Like the victim surveys, self-report studies generally turn up much more crime than is recorded in official data — and show that the number of people who are willing to admit to having committed *some* sort of crime is very large indeed. But even more than the victim surveys, they are subject to biases reflecting the respondents' ability or willingness to report their own criminal acts accurately. And, again like the victim surveys, they turn up vast numbers of minor crimes that may give a misleading picture of the distribution of *serious* crime (Hindelang, Hirschi, and Weis, 1979).

Sources: Hindelang, Hirschi, and Weis, 1979; Bloch and Block, 1980; Hindelang, 1981; Federal Bureau of Investigation, 1986.

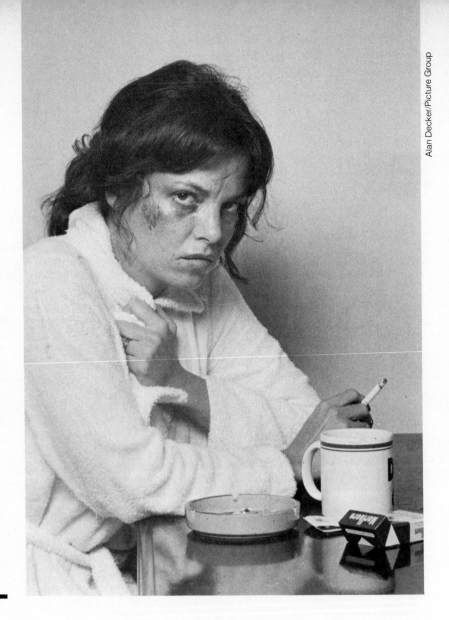

Many crimes against women still go unreported.

ically, as income levels fall. For violent crimes (other than homicide) the rate of victimization for people whose family income is below $3,000 is nearly double the rate for families earning more than $15,000 a year. The poorest stratum in the United States has more than *four* times the risk of rape or robbery with injury than Americans earning more than $15,000 a year (U.S. Bureau of Justice Statistics, 1982).

Crimes against property are a slightly different story. Although poor homes, perhaps surprisingly, are somewhat *more* likely to be burglarized than middle-class homes, the poor are slightly *less* likely to be the victims of simple theft or auto theft. (Some of this, however, may reflect their having fewer cars and reporting smaller thefts less frequently.)

And though crime victimizes people of all races and ethnic groups, it strikes especially hard at *minorities,* particularly blacks. Again, this pattern is clearest for the more serious crimes of violence. Black women have more than twice the chance of being raped as white women; whites have about half the chance of being robbed as Hispanics and less than half that of blacks.

Data on the risks of homicide present a similar picture. Forty-two out of every hundred murder victims in 1985 were black, though blacks were only twelve out of every hundred in the general population (Federal Bureau of Investigation, 1986, p. 19). This translates into a striking racial difference in the *lifetime* risks of death by homicide, illustrated by Table 11-3: at current rates, 1 in every 131 white men, but 1 in 21 black men, will be murdered during their lifetime. Homicide is the *leading* cause of death among black men aged 15 to 35 (U.S. Department of Health and Human Services, 1986, pp. 102–117).

Violent crime is so often associated with cities that the terms *crime* and *urban crime* are sometimes used interchangeably. And the connection is a real one: Cities — especially central cities — are much more dangerous than the suburbs, or especially, small towns and rural areas. The latter have rates of robbery, for example, around one-eighth the rates for cities of more than a million people.

	Probability
U.S. total	1 out of 133
Male	1 out of 84
Female	1 out of 282
White	
Male	1 out of 131
Female	1 out of 369
Black	
Male	1 out of 21
Female	1 out of 104

Source: U.S. Bureau of Justice Statistics, cited in *San Francisco Chronicle,* May 6, 1985.

Table 11-3
Probability of lifetime risk of murder, by race and sex

Frank Siteman/Stock, Boston

Almost half of Americans are afraid to walk at night in their own neighborhoods.

With one very important exception — rape — violent crime strikes men more often than women. Overall, the male victimization rate is more than double women's for violent crimes other than murder; for aggravated assault, the male rate is more than triple women's. (The latter figure should be treated cautiously, though, since assault against women within families is surely underreported.) For homicide, the male victimization rate is even higher: in 1985, 74 out of every 100 murder victims were male. (The factor of race, as in so many aspects of American life, cuts across this distinction, however.

As Table 11-3 shows, black women are somewhat *more* likely than white men to be homicide victims.)

As we'll see in a moment, the young commit much more than their share of violent crime. But it is less often recognized that they are also disproportionately crime's *victims.* For most violent crimes, the worst risks are among youth aged 16 to 24; the risk drops sharply after age 35, and the chances of being a victim of personal violence for people over 65 are less than one-eighth those of young adults.

Of course, none of these differences implies that any group is free from the threat of violence or that some people's fears about crime are more justified than others. What these differences *do* illustrate is the truly disastrous level of violence faced by some kinds of people in some kinds of communties. Not surprisingly, the communities most plagued by crime are those in which a number of risk factors are combined — inner-city residence, minority status, low income. And within these especially violence-ridden communities, some people, notably the young, face particularly high chances of death or injury from personal violence.

Crime, Courts, and Prisons

What can be done about crime? In the beginning of this chapter, we noted that the idea that crime is best attacked through social programs dealing with its causes has lost favor in recent years, while the older notion that the most effective way to reduce crime is to deal more swiftly and harshly with criminals has returned into fashion, fueled by the generally rising crime rates of the late 1970s and the 1980s.

The belief that criminals are treated too leniently is shared by a broad majority of Americans, according to opinion polls. About three-fourths of blacks and more than four-fifths of whites, according to data from the National Opinion Research Center, believe that the courts do not "deal harshly enough with certain criminals" (*Public Opinion,* 1981, p. 40). But "getting tough" with criminals can mean several different things: arresting them more often, convicting them more predictably once arrested, and/or sentencing them to more severe punishment once convicted. Many believe that the reason we have such a serious crime problem is that we have allowed crime's "costs" to fall, relative to its "benefits" (Wilson, 1975; Ehrlich, 1979). In this view, crime is rising because punishment is declining. The remedy follows simply: If we increase our capacity to punish criminals more certainly and/or more severely, we can bring down the crime rate.

The argument has a compelling simplicity that appeals to our fears of being victimized by crime, as well as to our understandable moral feeling that criminals should not go unpunished. But how well does it explain America's crime problem?

On closer examination, things are not nearly so simple. There are two main difficulties with this argument. *First,* it overlooks the crucial fact that the United States *already* has one of the harshest systems of punishment in the developed world and that we have been locking criminals up for many years now at an ever-accelerating rate — without a discernible effect on the crime rate. *Second,* careful studies have repeatedly found that it is much more difficult to increase the real "costs" of crime, in practice, than this argument supposes. Let's look at each point in turn.

Are We "Soft" on Criminals?

Compared to most other advanced industrial societies, the United States has traditionally imprisoned a very high proportion of its population. Table 11-4 shows what criminologists call *incarceration rates* (the number of people in prison as a proportion of the total population) for several European countries and the United States. Our incarceration rate is from almost three to more than eight times higher than that of the other countries (with the exception of Poland). Yet, as the table also indicates, the rate of the most serious of violent crimes, murder, is strikingly *less* in all of the other countries for which data are available.

Obviously, there are many differences in social, economic, and cultural patterns among these countries, making comparisons difficult. But Table 11-4 indicates that the relationship between rates of punishment and rates of violent crime are far more complicated than the "declining costs" argument suggests.

The same point emerges if we compare incarceration rates for different groups in the United States itself. By most measures, black Americans commit a disproportionate amount of street crime. If the *absence* of punishment causes crime, we would expect that blacks are treated more leniently by the criminal justice system. In fact, the opposite is true. The black incarceration rate in state prisons is about seven times that of whites in the United States as a whole. Almost *20 percent* of black men can expect to spend some time in a jail or prison in their lifetime, as compared to less than 3 percent of whites (Blumstein, 1982, p. 1260).

That difference partly reflects the higher crime rate among blacks, but it also seems to result from a tendency for some jurisdictions to deal more severely with blacks than with whites for the same types of

Country	Incarceration rate	Homicide rate
United States	241	8.5
Denmark	67	1.0
France	85	1.3
West Germany	94	1.2
Greece	33	0.9
Italy	57	1.9
Netherlands	27	0.9
Norway	44	1.1
Poland	269	NA
Spain	49	1.0
Sweden	58	1.1
United Kingdom	88	0.7

Table 11-4
Rates of imprisonment and homicide*

Note: NA means not available.
* Incarceration and homicide rates are per 100,000 population. Incarceration rates are mainly for 1980; homicide rates are for 1980 for Spain and for 1983 or 1984 for the rest of the countries.
Source: Incarceration rates from authors' calculations; homicide rates from World Health Organization, *World Health Statistics*, Geneva, 1986.

crimes. The evidence for this kind of racial bias in the courts is mixed (Blumstein, 1982), but several recent studies have concluded that blacks are somewhat more likely to receive a prison sentence than whites once convicted of a serious crime — and that their sentence is likely to be longer (Thornberry, 1979; Thomson and Zingraff, 1981). By the simple logic of the declining costs argument, the disproportionate incarceration of blacks ought to bring their crime rate *down*. Since it has not done so, it seems clear that something other than leniency in the courts must lie behind black Americans' higher crime rate.

The same problem also appears when we examine differences in crime in different *regions* of the country. The South imprisons people at a considerably higher rate than other sections of the United States; with less than a third of the country's population, it holds almost half of all state prison inmates. Moreover, it imprisons people disproportionately relative to its share of serious crime (Mullen et al., 1980). In other words, the "costs" of crime are typically *greater* in the South than elsewhere in the country. But, at the same time, many southern states and cities have among the country's *highest* rates of violent crime.

The country with one of the *highest* rates of imprisonment then, has the worst rate of violent crime recorded; within that country, the group with the *highest* rate of imprisonment accounts for a disproportionate share of violent crime, and the region that uses its prisons

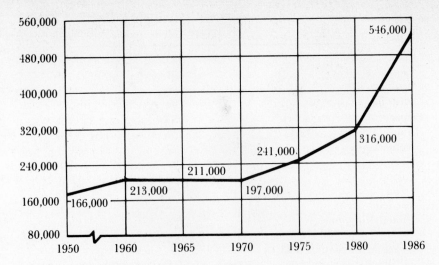

Figure 11-1
Inmates in state and federal prisons, 1950–1986

Source: Data from U.S. Bureau of Justice Statistics, *Prisoners in State and Federal Institutions on December 31* (Washington, D.C.: Government Printing Office, annual).

most heavily has among the highest rates of violence. These facts pose obvious problems for theories that blame the leniency of our criminal justice system for our high crime rate.

So, too, does another piece of evidence — our rates of incarceration have been *rising* sharply for many years. To the extent that there was a period of leniency in the American criminal justice system, it ended in the mid-1970s. Figure 11-1 shows that after a low point in the late 1960s and early 1970s, the American prison population began to increase rapidly, with the incarceration rate more than doubling between 1975 and 1986. The get-tough policies that are *already* in use have resulted in a prison system that is now almost literally bursting at the seams, with grim and sometimes terrifying results.

The problem, then, is not how to understand the growing "leniency" of American justice — but, rather, to understand why the increasing *harshness* of American justice has not reduced crime and, in fact, has been accompanied by generally *rising* crime. To approach that question, we need to look more closely at what recent research tells us about the complex relationship between crime and punishment in America.

Deterrence and Incapacitation

Criminologists have traditionally described two distinct ways in which the criminal justice system may act to prevent crime: *deterrence* and *incapacitation*. Deterrence refers to the inhibiting effect on potential criminals of the risks of being caught and punished. Incapacitation is the crime-reducing effect of taking criminals off the streets and thus preventing the crimes they would otherwise have committed. Thus, imposing a stiff prison sentence on a convicted robber might reduce the crime rate in either or both of two ways: by deterring others who might be tempted to robbery (or deterring the robber from *further* crimes), and/or by taking one active robber off the street. When we talk about reducing crime by building more prisons, giving convicted criminals harsher sentences, or improving the efficiency with which criminals are caught and brought to justice, we are making assumptions about the impact of some combination of these two effects. What do we know about how they actually influence the crime rate?

That question has generated an enormous amount of research, but the results are much less clear-cut than we would guess from politicians' speeches. On the whole, the evidence suggests that our capacity to reduce crime through either deterrence or incapacitation is crucially limited.

Deterrence: Inconclusive evidence. The commonsense idea that punishment deters crime is based on the assumption that people choose their behavior according to some more or less rational weighing of the risks and benefits of different courses of action. According to the argument for deterrence, would-be criminals balance the potential gains of, say, robbery against the risks of being caught and punished. If those risks are high, the potential gains will not seem worth it, and the rate of robbery should go down. If, on the other hand, the chances of capture and punishment are low, robbery may seem a rational option, especially if the benefits of law-abiding behavior are *also* low. The result should be a higher rate of robberies.

Though this argument seems quite simple at first glance, deterrence does not work quite so simply in practice, for at least three reasons:

1. Research suggests that the model of rationally chosen behavior — the notion that would-be criminals think through the relative costs and benefits of their actions in advance — fits poorly with the admittedly limited evidence we have on criminals' motivation. At best, it works better for some kinds of crime than others. Many crimes of violence, those we generally fear the most, are typically less planned and calculated than the model implies. One recent estimate is that between one-half and two-thirds of murders are unpremeditated, spontaneous results of arguments and moments of anger, often between people who know each other, and frequently among family members (Green and Wakefield, 1979). And a substantial proportion of violent crimes — including an estimated 40 to 65 percent of homicides — take place under the influence of alcohol or drugs (U.S. Bureau of Justice Statistics, 1983a, 1983b). This does not mean that such crimes *cannot* be deterred by the threat of punishment, but it does limit the

usefulness of an approach based *mainly* on appealing to criminals' rational avoidance of risks.

2. Another limitation on the deterrent effect of punishment stems from the fact that deterrence is actually a blend of two separate elements: the chances of being caught and punished and the harshness or leniency of the punishment if it is inflicted. Criminologists have traditionally called the first the *certainty* and the second the *severity* of punishment. Most studies show that of the two, it is the *certainty* of punishment that has the more important deterrent effect on crime (Blumstein, Cohen, and Nagin, 1978; Tittle, 1980). Common sense suggests why this should be so: If the chances of punishment are low, the fear of even very harsh penalties is, realistically, likely to be slight. The problem is that the chances of being punished with certainty for a crime are not so much a matter of what happens to criminals once they are in the courts but of whether they are *caught* in the first place (Currie, 1985). As we will see when discussing the effects of incapacitation, those chances are quite small for many crimes, and they depend on factors that lie mainly outside the influence of the courts or prisons.

3. The third important limitation on deterrence concerns the kinds of punishments that may be inflicted on criminals through the criminal justice system. Most studies of deterrence have found that such "formal" sanctions have much less impact on crime than "informal" ones (the approval or disapproval of one's family, friends, and larger community). Sociologists have long argued that these informal, close connections of family and community exert a far more powerful influence on human behavior of all kinds than is usually recognized, and criminal behavior is no exception (Tittle, 1980; Paternoster et al., 1983). Thus, formal punishment may be inherently less effective than other means of social control.

Does all of this mean that tough sentences and the threat of prison have *no* deterrent impact on crime? No; most research suggests that the commonsense notion that punishment can have *some* effect on crime rates is probably correct. But how *much* of an effect — and for what kinds of crimes and on what kinds of criminals — is still a largely unknown quantity. A thorough review of dozens of studies of deterrence by the National Academy of Sciences concluded: "The empirical evidence is still not sufficient for providing a rigorous confirmation of a deterrent effect. Perhaps more important, the evidence is woefully inadequate for providing a good estimate of the magnitude of whatever effect may exist" (Blumstein, Cohen, and Nagin, 1978, p. 135).

Incapacitation: Yes, but. . . . The existence of what criminologists call an *incapacitation effect* is more easily documented. But, once again, the *magnitude* of that effect is difficult to determine. As with deterrence, common sense suggests that, other things being equal, putting known criminals behind bars will reduce crime. But the results of research on how *much* crime would be reduced — and at what cost — turn out to be fairly discouraging. Why?

The amount of crime that can be prevented through incapacitating a given number of criminals depends partly on how much of the total crime in a community those criminals commit. Two extreme examples help illustrate this. Suppose, first, that *all* of the serious crime in a community is committed by a handful of very active criminals. In this case, imprisoning even one of this "hard core" for a long period could have a noticeable impact on the overall crime rate; locking up *all* of these criminals would virtually end crime. But suppose, instead, that crime is more evenly spread among a much larger number of criminals. In this case, locking up any one criminal will have little impact on the crime rate; or, to put it the other way around, making a large impact on crime would require locking up a much larger number of people, with a much greater investment of social resources.

Which example is closest to the truth? The reality clearly lies somewhere in between these extremes. No one knows exactly how much crime is accounted for by particular criminals, since so much crime is hidden and since criminals have an important stake in keeping it that way. Most studies based on official crime records suggest that a disproportionate amount of crime is committed by repeat offenders; one study, by the criminologist Marvin Wolfgang and his co-workers, found that less than one-fourth of all delinquent youth in Philadelphia were responsible for about two-thirds of the city's serious youth crime (Wolfgang, 1981). But most research indicates that the often-heard idea that we could stop crime by getting tougher with a handful of hard-core criminals is greatly exaggerated.

A study of violent criminals in Columbus, Ohio, illustrates this problem. The researchers followed all serious violent offenders who were arrested over a period of a year and calculated how much crime would have been avoided by giving every one of them a minimum five-year prison sentence. Their estimate was that just *4 percent* of serious violent crime in that city would have been prevented by that kind of sentence — one considerably more severe than most offenders actually receive and one that, if adopted, would multiply the prison population many times over (Conrad, Van Dine, and Dinitz, 1979).

Other studies have put the amount of street crime that could be prevented through tougher prison sentences higher; but few argue that even with extremely severe changes in sentencing, the rate of

Longer sentences for offenders have resulted in overcrowded and turbulent prisons.

serious crime could be slashed by much more than 20 percent (Boland, 1978). And most agree that this level of prevention would be possible only through truly dramatic increases in our reliance on prisons. The National Academy of Sciences study concluded that in order to cut serious index crime by 10 percent, California would have to increase its prison population by 157 percent, New York by 263 percent, and Massachusetts by 310 percent (Blumstein, Cohen and Nagin, 1978, p. 176).

Why would tougher sentences have so little payoff? In part, research suggests, because so much crime is *not* committed by repeat offenders — at least, not by repeat offenders who get caught. Among the offenders followed in the Columbus, Ohio study, for instance, only 11 percent had a record of a previous conviction for a violent felony; less than a third had *any* previous felony conviction. (Roughly similar proportions have been found in studies of other urban criminal courts.) Thus, this study tends to affirm the first of our hypothetical examples — serious crime seems to be fairly widely spread among a large population of criminals (Blumstein and Graddy, 1982; Tillman, 1986), many of whom are first offenders and many of whom apparently never reach the courts (Conrad, Van Dine, and Dinitz, 1979).

We noted this problem in looking at the effects of deterrence: For either deterrence or incapacitation to work, criminals must first be caught. We saw in the beginning of the chapter that the "clearance rate" for many kinds of crime is quite low; in the Columbus study, only 40 to 50 percent of the city's serious violent crime was ever cleared by an arrest. No one knows precisely how many of the unsolved crimes were committed by criminals who are ultimately arrested and tried. But we do know that the chances of being arrested for any given crime are small — for most types of crime — while the chances of being dealt with severely once arrested and convicted are much greater than critics often suggest, particularly for repeat offenders.

A Rand Corporation study of imprisoned offenders, for example, asked them to report how often they were arrested in comparison with the number of crimes they had committed. The results are revealing. According to their own testimony, these criminals had about one chance in ten of being arrested for any robbery, slightly less for a burglary, and only one chance in twenty-five for auto theft. Once arrested, on the other hand, these "repeat" offenders were quite likely to be dealt with strictly by the courts. Almost nine out of ten of those arrested for robbery were convicted; of those convicted, almost nine of ten were imprisoned. Other studies have found roughly similar proportions for the treatment of repeat or "habitual" offenders (Petersilia, Greenwood, and Lavin, 1978).

In the past few years, there has been an increasing interest in what some criminologists call *selective incapacitation* (Greenwood and Abrahamse, 1982), the attempt to predict which criminals are most likely to become repeat offenders and to sentence them to appropriately longer confinement. This approach has been criticized on several grounds. For one thing, the state of the art of predicting future criminality is very crude indeed. Any formula for picking out just which criminals will be repeaters in need of special handling will cast its net too wide, snagging many offenders who would *not* have gone on to further crimes. Moreover, there are disturbing legal and ethical issues involved in sentencing people to greatly different punishments when they've committed the same crimes. Finally, and perhaps most importantly, courts *already* use background information and the criminal's past record in deciding how to sentence offenders. It's unlikely that efforts to make this process more exact would have *much* impact on crime, especially given the lack of precision in our capacity to predict future criminal behavior.

Attempts to prevent crime by changing the way we deal with offenders in the courts are probably focusing on the wrong end of the criminal justice system. Some criminals, certainly, do slip through the net of the system, receiving a light sentence, or even no sentence at all, for even very serious crimes. But the evidence suggests that this is not the *main* way in which the criminal justice system "fails." Critics of the "leniency" of American criminal justice often point to figures showing that only a relatively small proportion of crimes ever end in a prison sentence. That is true, as many studies of the criminal courts have shown. But the *primary* reason is the small proportion of crimes that result in arrest — not the failure to punish known, convicted repeaters.

That distinction is important because it helps us understand what "getting tough" in the courts or building more prisons can and cannot do. Ultimately, our ability to increase the costs of crime depends more on increasing the chances of *apprehending* criminals than on dealing more severely with them once they are caught. And that is primarily a function of the police rather than the courts or prisons. We need to ask, then, what we know about the ability of the *police* to prevent crime.

Police and Crime

The evidence suggests that the police, like the courts and prisons, are limited in their capacity to prevent crime. This is not to suggest that the police have *no* impact on crime. Historical studies of the rare occasions when cities have been without police are instructive. In England, a Liverpool police strike in 1919 resulted in mass looting of shops and attacks on the few remaining police officers. In 1944, in occupied Denmark, the Germans arrested the entire Danish police force. Although the Germans greatly increased the *severity* of punishment, the crime rate doubled during the seven-month absence of police. But the *total* absence of police is unusual and transient. Usually when we discuss the effectiveness of the police, we are talking about the ways in which marginal changes in the numbers of police officers influence police effectiveness or about how police effectiveness varies with different strategies of policing.

Consider for a moment how police officers work. They are obviously very dependent on information that they do not themselves generate. And, as we have already seen, victim surveys show that a very large proportion of some crimes do not come to the attention of the police. Obviously, if the police do not know a crime has occurred, they cannot move to apprehend the offender. Also, in one major area of crime, the police rarely, if ever, are offered information about criminal activities. These are sometimes called "crimes without victims," to suggest the consensual nature of the crime, but most accurately, from a law enforcement perspective, these are crimes without citizen complaints. The prevalence of these crimes (such as drug sales and use, prostitution, and illegal gambling) is captured neither by the *Uniform Crime Reports* nor by victim surveys. The narcotics seller and purchaser, the prostitute's "John," and the bookmaker's bettor do not usually feel victimized. Therefore, they don't report such crimes to the police.

How effective are the police in fighting *street* crime? Once again, the answer is: not very. Nor have police strategies for *increasing* effectiveness against street crime been very successful. There's little evidence that simply adding *more* police officers, or spending more money for police hardware, will reduce crime (see Loftin and McDowall, 1982; Greenberg et al., 1983). And varying the conventional police patrol strategies has had only an uncertain impact. As the criminologists George Kelling and Mark Moore argue, research suggests that "there is a limit to the deployment of police resources (squad cars, rapid-response police teams, investigators) beyond which the rate of violent crime is very insensitive" (1983, p. 56).

In the early 1970s, the Police Foundation (a national research organization) carried out a study in Kansas City to test the impact of preventive patrol. The researchers created three types of experimental areas: In one, the police presence was increased by two or three times the customary amount; in another, it was held at the usual level; and, in a third, the police presence was withdrawn except to respond to calls for assistance. The results showed that police patrols had virtually no impact either on the incidence of crime or on citizens' perception of crime (Kelling et al., 1974). Later studies found somewhat different effects of preventive patrols, but they were not as carefully constructed.

Critics of preventive patrols suggest that the tactic contributes to an image of police officers as a remote and alien force — occupying the

© Jerome H. Skolnick

Some communities regard the police as a remote and alien force.

community rather than participating in it. This alienation is both ironic and costly when measured against the fact that police officers actually spend little time on crime-related matters. Considerable research has shown that most police time is spent breaking up fights in bars, clubs, and athletic stadiums; settling family fights; responding to complaints about teenage misconduct; directing the flow of traffic; and maintaining public order in various other ways. Police officers talk the suicidal out of killing themselves; break into houses and apartments for those who have locked themselves out; administer first aid to heart attack victims; get cats down from trees; capture or, if necessary, shoot animals that are threatening people in the community; and rush accident victims to hospitals. These are important services, and some critics argue that the police might be able to increase their ability to provide such "order maintenance" to communities by, for example, getting out of their cars and back into the community on foot (Kelling and Moore, 1983). But while this approach may help bring police officers closer to the communities and help make residents feel more secure, the evidence that it will do much to reduce serious crime is mixed (Police Foundation, 1986; Trojanowicz, 1983). However, there is growing evidence that changes in police practices may have an important impact on at least one kind of crime — domestic violence. Recent studies in Minnesota and California show that arresting men who beat their wives tends to deter them from further attacks (Berk and Newton, 1985).

Understanding Crime: Some Recent Evidence

In emphasizing the limits of the criminal justice system's capacity to reduce crime, we don't mean to imply that we should not continue to search for ways to improve its efficiency and fairness. But the criminal justice system is only one of the institutions that influence the crime rate — and not the most important one. And this, in turn, directs our attention to the larger social context of American crime.

We've noted that the search for the causes of crime lost ground in recent years in favor of an emphasis on increasing punishment. That shift reflected these assumptions:

1. That the most frequently cited explanations of crime — especially the role of poverty and unequal opportunity — were largely irrelevant, since the plight of America's disadvantaged had improved just when crime rates were sharply rising

2. That crime rose not only in the United States but in every other society throughout the world as well — so that attempts to explain crime by reference to the institutions of American society were misguided

3. That programs designed to attack the root causes of crime had turned out to be incapable of either rehabilitating offenders or reducing the crime rate

Are these assumptions supported by the evidence? In this section, we'll look at what recent research tells us about the role of several key factors — inequality, poverty, unemployment, family disorganization — on crime. The literature on these issues is enormous, and we cannot, of course, hope to cover all of it in this chapter. But even a beginning look at the best current research suggests that we know more about the social sources of crime than is often supposed — and that we are not so helpless to deal with it in constructive ways.

Crime, Inequality, and Poverty

The social science of the 1950s and 1960s stressed the close connection between crime and racial and economic inequality. It was widely believed that poverty and discrimination caused crime and that ending those disadvantages would reduce it (Cloward and Ohlin, 1959; President's Commission on Law Enforcement, 1967).

But this view was roundly attacked in the 1970s. Critics argued that since crime and violence increased during a time of rising incomes, improved educational opportunities, and declining rates of poverty, they could not be explained by worsening social conditions.

But more recent research suggests that this conclusion was premature. For one thing, the critics' argument failed to acknowledge the uneven, spotty character of the rise in American living standards in the 1960s (a point we considered in detail in Chapters 4 and 5). Some groups achieved real affluence, while others faced new forms of disadvantage and blocked opportunities. This was especially true of those — particularly minorities — who were uprooted from rural livelihoods and displaced into urban areas where a changing economy left many of them farther and farther behind as other groups advanced. The decline in poverty, too, as we have seen, was considerably less than often supposed and — even more importantly — was concentrated among some groups and regions (the elderly, the South) much more than others. Poverty — accompanied by rising youth unemployment and a growing disparity between minority and white jobless rates — persisted stubbornly in the inner cities. Moreover, national trends in the overall inequality of income and wealth changed little if at all during those years, despite the growth of Great Society programs and the expansion of the welfare state.

So the supposed paradox of rising crime amidst rising prosperity turns out, on closer examination, to be far less paradoxical than it seemed at first glance. And the strong connection between crime and inequality is affirmed by other kinds of research.

Official data on arrests, which are broken down for most crimes according to race, provide one kind of picture — but one that, for reasons we've already noted, needs to be examined cautiously. Arrest data may be biased because police treat different groups differently, and data on convictions and imprisonment may be even more biased (we will return to these issues in a moment). Homicide rates, however, give a more reliable indication of group differences in crime rates (Blumstein, 1982, p. 1274) — and they show startling differences by race. In 1985, for example, blacks were about 12 percent of the American population, but they were about 48 percent of those arrested for homicide. Hispanic Americans were overrepresented too, though less so than blacks. About 16 percent of homicide arrests were of Hispanics, while they amounted to about 6 percent of the total population. Robbery arrests are even more sharply tilted toward minorities: 62 percent of robbery arrests were of blacks; 14 percent were of Hispanics (Federal Bureau of Investigation, 1986, pp. 12, 19).

A similar picture can be drawn from prison statistics. About half of state prison inmates in the United States are black. But that figure only begins to capture the imbalance between the imprisonment rates of white and black Americans. In New York State, for example, young black men aged 16 to 35 are imprisoned at a rate twelve times that of their white counterparts (Murphy, 1986).

Surveys of state prison populations also reveal a striking concentration of people whose "street" incomes before imprisonment were at poverty level or below. As the U.S. Bureau of Justice Statistics summed it up, "Inmates of state prisons are predominantly poor

---

How We Stack Up

It is often said that America is a violent country. How does our level of criminal violence compare with that of other countries?

Those who believe that there is little we can do to reduce crime often argue that crime is increasing everywhere in the world — that rising crime results from inherent forces in modern society over which we have little control (Wilson, 1975). There is *some* truth to that description, but it masks great differences in the picture of violent crime in different societies. First, some countries, unlike the United States, did *not* experience rapid rises in serious violent crime during the 1960s and 1970s. (Japan and Switzerland are two examples in the industrial world, Cuba one in the Third World.) And even among those societies that *have* suffered substantial increases in crime in recent years, some crimes of violence are so rare by American standards that focusing on the increases alone is highly misleading.

Crime rates, as we have noted, are difficult to compare even across different cities in the United States, much less across different countries (many of which use different ways of classifying and reporting crime). But homicide rates are less troublesome in this way, and they provide a fairly reliable indicator of the extent of violence in America vis-à-vis

---

other countries. The United States is not quite the murder capital of the world; but it *is* the murder capital among advanced industrial societies — and by a shocking margin. Table 11-5 shows that men in the United States have from ten to twenty times the chance of being murdered as men in several other industrial societies. And, though death by violence is almost everywhere less likely for women than men, the chances of being murdered are greater for an American women than for *men* in almost every European country. Only Mexico and a number of other Third World countries exceed the American murder rate. If the United States had the same murder rate as the United Kingdom or Japan, we would have less than 1,800 homicides a year instead of the more than 18,000 we now typically have.

A detailed study of crime in Switzerland, where serious crime generally declined in the 1960s and 1970s, found that murder rates in the biggest Swiss cities were considerably lower than those in American cities of less than 10,000 people. Switzerland's largest city, Zurich, is about the same size as Denver, Colorado; but in 1972, Denver had six times as many robberies as Zurich did over the preceding *10 years* (Clinard, 1978).

Table 11-5
Homicide rate, by sex

Country	Homicide deaths, per 100,000 population	
	Men	Women
United States	13.4	3.9
Australia	2.3	1.5
Austria	2.1	1.5
Canada	3.2	1.4
Czechoslovakia	1.3	0.9
Denmark	1.1	1.0
Finland	4.0	1.5
West Germany	1.2	1.1
Greece	1.3	0.6
Israel	2.1	0.8
Italy	3.3	0.6
Japan	1.0	0.7
Mexico	32.7	3.0
Netherlands	1.3	0.6
Norway	1.7	0.5
Paraguay	16.4	1.5
Singapore	3.7	1.7
Sweden	1.4	0.8
United Kingdom	0.8	0.6

Source: Data from World Health Organization, *World Health Statistics*, Geneva, 1986.

	White	Black
Male	94%	92%
Female	6%	8%
Median age	26.7	26.9
Highest school grade attended:		
Less than 12th grade	56%	62%
12th grade or higher	43%	38%
Pre-arrest employment status:		
Employed	56%	50%
Not employed	44%	50%
Median income	$6,312	$4,067

Source: Adapted from *Statistical Abstract of the United States*, 1987, p. 172.

Table 11-6
Who goes to jail? Selected characteristics of jail inmates, 1983

young adult males with less than a high school education" (1982, p. 2). Table 11-6 shows that the same is true of the population of local jails.

Moreover, these broad indicators of the role of race and income are supported by more elaborate studies. A classic analysis that followed the criminal careers of every youth born during 1945 in Philadelphia found that both lower socioeconomic status and being nonwhite — especially the latter — were associated with higher rates of youth crime. Nonwhite boys averaged three times as many offenses as white boys and were much more likely to commit more serious offenses and to be repeat or "chronic" offenders (Wolfgang, Figlio, and Sellin, 1972). A more recent study of Philadelphia youth born in a later year, 1958, similarly found that nonwhite boys were three times as likely as white boys to commit a violent crime (Wolfgang, 1981, p. 141).

These findings (and others based on official criminal statistics) have long been criticized on the ground that they reflect class and racial bias in the criminal justice system more than any real differences in groups' propensity to commit crimes. Critics have noted several potential sources of bias. First, these data deal only with the more serious street crimes — not with other kinds of crime, especially white-collar crime (see pages 379 to 381). If we examine those crimes, ones more accessible to the affluent, a different picture appears. Whites, for example, are almost 70 percent of those arrested for crimes of fraud, 75 percent of those arrested for embezzlement, and about 90 percent of those arrested for drunken driving or violation of liquor laws (Federal Bureau of Investigation, 1982, p. 179). In looking at the way crime is distributed by race and income, then, we need to keep in mind that it is not simply that whites (or the affluent) commit *fewer* crimes, but they commit *different* ones.

Studies of the distribution of crime using self-report methods (asking respondents about their own involvement in crime) also support a somewhat different interpretation than the one provided by official statistics. For the most part, these studies have turned up a great deal of "hidden," unreported crime that, contrary to arrest figures, shows a much more equal distribution of offenses among different races and income groups. Some self-report studies have found *no* significant differences in offense rates by class or race. Such findings have sometimes been taken to imply that the criminal justice system itself, by "labeling" members of some groups as criminals more often than others, is the main source of the differences in official crime rates. Obviously, this has crucial implications for our understanding of the causes of crime. If all groups are equally involved in crime, explanations that stress the role of inequality in causing high rates of crime are false. Is this a reasonable interpretation?

Studies of bias in the courts and by police give a mixed and inconclusive answer to the question of how much the difference in arrests and sentencing are determined by race or income level and how much by the differences in the amount and kind of crime different groups commit. Blacks, for example, are generally more likely to receive tougher sentences than whites for *generally* similar crimes. But when such factors as the seriousness of the crime and the offender's past record are also taken into account, the racial differences are less clear. On balance, the evidence does indicate that there is bias in the treatment of minorities in the criminal justice system. But these biases do not, according to most research, loom large enough to explain the dramatic group differences in official rates of violent crime — especially for crimes like homicide and aggravated assault (Blumstein, 1982, p. 1274).

Most recent research based on victim studies comes to a similar conclusion, suggesting that the official arrest and prison data may be a closer reflection of group differences in serious crime than some critics have thought. One study calculated that offense rates for personal crimes (robbery, rape, assault, and larceny) are about five times higher for black men than white men and that the disparity is even sharper among young men aged 18 to 20 — an especially crime-prone age group (Hindelang, 1981).

Why so wide a divergence from the findings of the self-report studies? In part because those studies rarely survey the most crime-prone groups, particularly poor, urban minority youth, and in part because they turn up a great amount of relatively unserious offenses (like vandalism or petty thefts) that a wide range of people readily admit to having committed. Self-report studies that have focused on more serious crimes have found them much more prevalent among lower-class than among middle-class youth (Elliott and Huizinga, 1983; Currie, 1985, chap. 5).

The effect of class and racial inequality on crime rates can be approached in other ways, as well. For example, recent studies comparing crime rates among American cities have found a strong association between high levels of crime and a high degree of inequality in a city's income distribution. Others have found that *within* cities, the areas with the highest levels of violent crime are likely to be those split by the sharpest income inequalities — where poverty and affluence coexist uneasily side by side. These studies generally find that *poverty*, itself, is less clearly significant as a factor in high crime rates than is *inequality* between the races and between the affluent and poor (Blau and Blau, 1982). The same association appears when crime rates are compared across different countries (Braithwaite and Braithwaite, 1980; Messner, 1982). Measured by their rates of homicide, many poor countries have relatively low rates of violent crime. But harsh inequalities in living standards in both "developing" and developed countries are closely associated with high levels of violence. And a high degree of inequality of income in the United States, relative to most other advanced industrial societies (see pages 000 to 000), goes hand in hand with our devastatingly high homicide rate.

Poverty itself, however — in the stark sense of simply having too little money to survive through legitimate means — *can* be an important factor in crime rates, as the results of recent experimental programs for ex-offenders have demonstrated. Traditionally, ex-inmates coming out of prison have faced not only a difficult job market and the stigma of being an "ex-con" but also an immediate lack of income for basic necessities. The pressure to return to crime for survival needs alone has often been compelling under those conditions. During the 1970s, the U.S. Department of Labor initiated a series of programs designed to give a small stipend (at about the level of unemployment insurance benefits) to ex-offenders while they looked for jobs and tried to reestablish themselves in the community. Careful evaluation of these programs shows that even very *small* amounts of cash, offered for a period of a few months, had a substantial impact on rates of return to street crime (what criminologists call *recidivism* rates). Compared with a control group of ex-offenders receiving no payments, the experimental program groups had rates of rearrest up to 30 percent lower (Rossi, Berk, and Lenihan, 1980).

Unemployment, Subemployment, and Crime

The connection between inequality and crime is closely related to another relationship often affirmed by recent research: the association between unemployment and crime. Even many of those critics who argue that we know little about the causes of crime agree on this one — especially on the effect of the disastrously high jobless rates among urban minority youth.

But the precise relationship between unemployment and crime is more complex than it seems at first glance (Thompson et al., 1981; Currie, 1985). Surveys of convicted offenders give a startling picture of the poor job situation most of them faced while "on the street." American prison inmates are disproportionately drawn from the ranks of the unemployed and intermittently employed. In a recent study of imprisoned felony offenders in California, for example, only about half had been employed and even among those, "most had earnings that were not much above a poverty level." Among these generally poorly employed offenders, those who were described as the "better employed" (meaning that they had worked during at least 75 percent of their "street" time and had earned at least $100 a week) had dramatically lower rates of crime than the rest. Adults in the better-employed group committed less than a *fifth* of the crimes that the less well-employed committed. And the crimes they did commit tended to be not only less frequent but less serious as well (Petersilia, Greenwood, and Lavin, 1978, p. 89).

But this relationship between poor jobs and crime could mean that crime leads to unsteady employment and not, necessarily, the other way around. More elaborate studies, however, throw more light on the independent effect of unemployment on crime. Some have charted the relation between changes in the economy over time and changes in the rate of reported crime or of admission to prisons. In one study, M. Harvey Brenner calculated the effects of economic recession on crime with chilling precision. A 1-percentage-point increase in the national unemployment rate, according to this study, would increase the rate of admissions to state prisons by about 4 percent and, by itself, would account for about 6 percent of robberies, 9 percent of narcotics offenses, and 4 percent of homicides in a given year (Brenner, 1976).

Not all studies have found such a strong and precisely calculable connection between unemployment and crime rates, however (Orsagh and Witte, 1981). There are several reasons why. First, these studies deal with the effects of *changes* in the unemployment rate on patterns of crime. But those economic fluctuations may have less importance in terms of crime rates than the *persistence* of an urban underclass that, tragically, is relatively unaffected by the ups and downs of the economy. Thus, as we have seen, men who have rarely if ever held a decent or stable job now disproportionately fill America's prisons, and their situation changes little as a result of large-scale changes in the economy as a whole. (We will return to the future implications of this in a moment.)

Another reason why changes in unemployment rates sometimes show only a slight connection with crime rates is that unemployment affects different kinds of crime in different, even opposite, ways. A study by the Vera Institute of Justice shows that certain crimes, such

---

White-Collar Crime: Dealing with the Corporate Offender

Most of our discussion in this chapter has been about what is often called *street* crime: crimes against persons and property that strike with stunning immediacy in the streets and homes. But there is another variety of crime, usually less immediately tangible, which since the classic work of the sociologist Edwin Sutherland (1949) has been called "white-collar crime."

White-collar crime is often divided by criminologists into two somewhat distinct varieties. One is *occupational crime:* crimes usually committed by individuals in connection with their occupation (such as embezzlement or employee theft) as well as violations by public officials (such as taking bribes). *Corporate crime,* on the other hand, refers to business violations of laws and regulations that typically involve groups acting together as part of a larger organization (Clinard and Yeager, 1980, pp. 17–18).

We have encountered some aspects of the problem of corporate crime already in this book, such as violations of environmental and workplace health and safety regulations. But corporate crime is a much broader phenomenon, including offenses ranging from price fixing to consumer fraud, from bribery

of public officials to the illegal dumping of hazardous chemicals. Its precise extent is unknown, but it is widely agreed that far from being a rare occurrence in American business, it is both widespread and deeply embedded in American corporate practice.

A study of almost 600 major American corporations, by Marshall Clinard and Peter Yeager, found that in just two years (1975 and 1976), more than 1,500 federal cases were begun against these companies, for an average of 2.7 cases apiece. Overall, *60 percent* of the corporations studied had at least one federal action brought against them (Clinard and Yeager, 1980, p. 113). Some of these corporations were "repeat offenders": 5 percent of the companies accounted for over *half* of all the violations in the two years studied, with an average of an astonishing *24* violations per firm.

The worst violators, in this survey, were the large corporations, and especially those in the oil, pharmaceutical, and motor vehicle industries. The oil industry alone was responsible for more than half of the violations of environmental laws in this survey and accounted for a fifth of *all* the legal actions taken against this sample of firms (Clinard and Yeager, 1980, pp. 116–120).

By many measures, the costs to society of corporate crime may be greater than those of conventional street crime. Violations of federal antitrust laws alone may cost consumers more than $60 billion a year: One admittedly rough estimate put the total annual cost of illegal business activity at more than $200 billion (Green, 1982, p. 229). By contrast, the average street robbery in the United States, in 1981, netted $441; even the average bank robbery brought its perpetrators just $3,564 (Federal Bureau of Investigation, 1982, p. 16). The total "take" from every street robbery in the country in 1981 was a little more than $130 million, while the cost of cleaning up one of the worst known violations of environmental laws in recent years — the illegal dumping of the toxic chemical kepone into the James River in Virginia by the Allied Chemical Company — has been estimated at $8 billion. The hazardous waste cleanup at Love Canal in New York State had already cost more than $35 million by 1981; the total "haul" from every bank robbery in the United States in that year was about $29 million (Federal Bureau of Investigation, 1982, p. 16).

Despite these costs — and the more tragic losses of human lives and health — research consistently finds that corporate crimes rarely incur severe penalties. Sutherland's study in the 1940s found that most white-collar criminals were let off with minor fines at worst, and often received no punishment. Most research since then has turned up a similar, though somewhat less extreme, pattern.

There *have* been some changes in the social response to corporate crime in America, both in public attitudes and in the seriousness with which courts and government agencies approach the problem. Recent surveys show that many kinds of corporate crime are regarded by the public as at least as serious as many "conventional" crimes

(Clinard and Yeager, 1980, p. 5). And one study found a "significant shift" in recent years toward increased prosecution of white-collar cases (Hagan and Nagel, 1982). During the 1970s and 1980s, too, there has been an increase in the attention and resources devoted by the federal government to the problem of corporate crime, a movement described by two recent observers as "a modest redeployment of prosecutorial resources from crime in the streets to crime in the suites" (Braithwaite and Geis, 1982, p. 293).

But though sanctions against corporate crime have been stiffened in the past decade, they remain relatively puny. In the beginning of the 1980s, the maximum penalty for a violation of the antitrust laws was $1 million: violations of consumer product safety laws could add up to $500,000. And these were among the *largest* penalties; others were much smaller. Violations of Food and Drug Administration laws brought a maximum fine of $1,000 for the first offense and $10,000 for each succeeding offense at the end of the 1970s (Clinard and Yeager, 1980, p. 91). (These penalties must be seen in the context of the multibillion-dollar operations of most large corporations.)

In certain cases, criminal penalties may be invoked against corporate officials. In theory, these penalties can put them behind bars. In practice, criminal prosecutions are rare, and actual imprisonment even rarer. Clinard and Yeager's study found just 16 corporate executives who received prison sentences for the more than 1,500 prosecuted violations; 11 of these executives averaged just *9 days* of actual time in jail (1980, p. 291). More recently there have been exceptions to this situation, as some prosecutors and judges have become less tolerant in the face of what some have called the "corporate crime wave" of the 1980s (Williams, 1985). One Tennessee banker convicted of defrauding his customers, for example, received a 20-year prison sentence in 1987 (*Investor's Daily*, May 26,

1987). But such tough penalties remain unusual.

There are several reasons for the leniency in imposing criminal penalties on corporate officials. It is often difficult to penetrate the labyrinth of corporate decision making to pinpoint the individuals responsible for the violation. The complex, technical character of some kinds of corporate violations also makes it difficult to establish criminal intentions. As the criminologists John Braithwaite and Gilbert Geis noted: "Pollution, product safety, and occupational safety and health prosecutions typically turn on scientific evidence that the corporation caused certain consequences. [But] in cases that involve scientific dispute, proof beyond reasonable doubt is rarely, if ever, possible" (1982, p. 299). And, finally, there is a deeply ingrained attitude in America that the kinds of people who offer bribes to officials or conspire to fix prices or evade workplace safety regulations are not "really" criminals — at least, not like the people who commit street robberies or household burglaries. For the former, "respectable" people, being caught and made to suffer public shame is thought, by judges, prosecutors, and fellow corporate executives, to be punishment enough.

This leniency has inspired a number of proposals for more effective sanctions against corporate offenders. They include, among others:

• *Much higher economic penalties:* Corporations convicted of violations might, for example, be required to pay a fine up to double the amount they gained through the violation. This would ensure that the economic sanction isn't dwarfed, as it nearly always is now, by the potential illegal gains a corporation may envision when it, for example, bribes a foreign government official to buy a certain product or fails to correct a dangerous, illegal health and safety problem.

• *Barring convicted executives from performing similar work in the future:* Lawyers, doctors, or other professionals might be barred from practicing their professions if they commit a sufficiently grave violation of law or ethics. On the same principle, corporate executives could be disqualified from holding the same type of job, at least for a specified period of time. At present, corporate officials rarely lose their jobs, even when convicted of very serious offenses. (Some of the financial executives convicted of illegal practices in the Wall Street scandals of the 1980s *were,* however, barred from working in the securities industry.)

• *Holding corporate officials criminally liable for the actions of their subordinates:* Much corporate crime now goes unpunished because managers look the other way while those working under them actually carry out the illegal actions. This pattern could, it's argued, be reversed by making higher-level managers accountable even if they were unaware of the violations going on below them. (This principle would apply only to cases in which a manager's lack of awareness reflected a truly reckless disregard of the duty to oversee the actions of subordinates.)

• *Nationalizing the worst offenders:* As a last, most drastic resort, some critics propose that corporations that are serious, "habitual offenders" might be brought under public ownership and control. Short of that, but on a similar principle, a corporation might be forced to sell the part of its business that had repeatedly violated the law to a different company with a less-criminal track record (Clinard and Yeager, 1980, chap. 13; Braithwaite and Geis, 1982, pp. 307–308; Green, 1982, pp. 231–234).

Sources: Sutherland, 1949; Clinard and Yeager, 1980; Braithwaite and Geis, 1982; Federal Bureau of Investigation, 1982; Green, 1982; Hagan and Nagel, 1982; Williams, 1986.

as employee theft, predictably *decline* when unemployment rises, canceling some of the increases in other kinds of crime (Thompson et al., 1981).

Finally, most research shows that it is not so much the fact of being without *any* job that increases the likelihood of crime, but the lack of reasonably *good* jobs with adequate pay and some chance of security and advancement — what one study called "economic viabilty" (Orsagh and Witte, 1981, p. 1071). Jobs that confine people to the bleak prospects of the "secondary" labor market seem unable to provide a sufficient stake in law-abiding behavior or to promote the values and norms that keep people from crime (Currie, 1985; Sullivan, 1985).

As with the impact of inequality on crime, important evidence on the relation between jobs and crime can be gleaned from the results of social programs — in this case, ones designed to provide jobs for offenders and ex-offenders. A substantial body of reseach now suggests that we can reduce crime through increasing the "benefits" of work at least as well as by increasing the "costs" of crime. The Job Corps program, which provides intensive training and education for disadvantaged youth, has consistently been shown to reduce crime among many of its graduates (Curtis, 1985). And a recent, elaborate experiment in providing supported work for ex-addicts and other high-risk groups also shows important success. This program provides a sheltered work environment for people who have trouble functioning in the regular labor market. Participants start with low responsibilities (and low pay), and with intensive counseling and peer support, they are gradually brought to greater and greater responsibility and higher rewards until they are ready to take on regular work. Extensive tests of this program found that it has worked most effectively for ex-drug addicts — a group that has been especially difficult to reach through other programs — substantially reducing their re-arrests for serious crimes. So far, supported work has proven less successful with some other groups of ex-offenders (Manpower Demonstration Research Corporation, 1980). But it shows real promise and suggests, once again, that we may be less helpless in dealing with the roots of street crime than is often thought.

Family Patterns and Crime

A third set of factors, also widely accepted as being deeply implicated in crime in America, are those involving the family and early childhood development. Social scientists of nearly every persuasion agree that the family, as the primary agency through which children are socialized, is important in forming behavior that is law abiding or criminal, violent or cooperative.

Yet there is considerable disagreement over just *how* the family affects crime. As we saw in Chapter 7, it's often argued that a "breakdown" of the family lies behind the rise in crime. One line of argument blames crimes, as well as a host of other social pathologies, on the growing number of families with only one parent (especially those maintained by women). As the traditional two-parent family has lost center stage, especially in urban minority communities, the family has, in this view, lost the capacity to discipline and socialize its children. How accurate is this view?

A growing body of research does affirm that children in "broken" families face greater risks of delinquency (Rankin, 1983). But most research suggests that the main cause is not having a single parent, or having that single parent be a woman. Instead, research most often pinpoints two other factors as the crucial ones: the tensions and problems that led to the family's breakup in the first place and, even more importantly, the absence of adequate supports for the one-parent family in the larger society — including jobs, income, and child care. Children from two-parent families in which there is much hostility between the parents, capricious discipline, or systematic abuse and neglect fare at least as badly in terms of later delinquency. As Chapter 7 suggested, these facts should direct our attention more to the broader social and economic structures that help shape children's experiences in the family than to the particular *form* the family takes.

We can gain some insight into the relation between crime and family problems by looking at the results of programs designed to reduce delinquency by intervening in family life. For example, there is some evidence that programs offering a wide range of social services to low-income families (including parenting training, health care, nutrition, and educational enrichment) may have a substantial payoff in reduced rates of delinquency (as well as in better school performance and better health) (Currie, 1985, chap. 7). Again, what this suggests is that it is the social context surrounding the family that is most important in affecting the quality of life within it — and in affecting its ability to produce compassionate and nonviolent children. Where basic social services are absent or inadequate, where parental unemployment and poverty-level income is a way of life, that capacity may be seriously crippled.

Crime, Social Policy, and the Future

The sources of our strikingly high crime rates, then, can be found, in part, in some important social and economic differences between the

United States and many other advanced industrial societies. As we've seen in earlier chapters, we perpetuate a much larger "underclass" of the persistently poor; tolerate a much wider spread of inequality and greater economic insecurity; and are much stingier in the supports and services we provide for families and children. It's not just coincidence that the industrial society that has the widest gap between affluent and poor, among the highest infant mortality rates, and the most severe and extensive poverty is also the industrial society with the highest rates of violent crime.

And all of this suggests some troubling prospects for the future. We've seen that inequality in America has been generally worsening and poverty has been generally increasing. We've also seen that the employment picture, especially for the young and for minorities, is disturbing at best. Even if we achieve much better overall economic health than we've witnessed in recent years, it seems clear that the benefits won't "trickle down" to the poor, the badly educated, and the unskilled, without considerable help.

Thus, to effectively forestall crime in the future — as well as a host of related problems, including hard-drug abuse, family stress, and teenage pregnancy — we'll need to pay much more attention to providing skills, quality education, health care, and family support programs for those who are now excluded from a productive and rewarding place in American society. Unfortunately, though, the unfavorable economic and social trends of recent years often have been compounded by reductions in our commitment to provide these and other social services. In particular, we've been cutting back on early education, job training, and job creation programs just when the changes in our economy have made them most needed.

The results — in terms of future levels of delinquency and crime — cannot be precisely calculated. And many of these effects may not make themselves felt for many years. Like our policies toward health care and environmental quality, these economic policies raise longer-term questions about the kinds of legacies we will leave to future generations.

Summary

This chapter has explored the problems of crime and criminal justice in America. The complexity of criminal statistics makes it hard to pinpoint the dimensions of crime with precision, but it seems clear that (1) serious crime has increased since the 1960s and (2) though crime can strike anyone, its victims are disproportionately the young, minorities, and the poor.

Much recent social policy toward crime has emphasized "getting tough" with criminals, and we have been locking up offenders at an unprecedented rate. But this strategy has done little to reduce crime.

The evidence suggests that it is much more difficult to "deter" criminals through tough sentences than is often believed. One reason is that so few crimes ever result in an arrest. And we do not yet know how to increase the ability of the police to apprehend criminals.

Though public concern usually focuses on "street" crimes, white-collar crime also takes an enormous toll and only rarely results in severe treatment by the courts.

It's sometimes argued that we know very little about the causes of street crime. But there is considerable evidence that economic and racial inequality, inadequate employment, and the lack of family supports are all important factors.

For Further Reading

Currie, Elliott. *Confronting Crime.* New York: Pantheon, 1985.

Curtis, Lynn, ed. *American Violence and Public Policy.* New Haven, Conn.: Yale University Press, 1985.

Skolnick, Jerome, and David Bayley. *The New Blue Line.* New York: Basic Books, 1986.

Wideman, John Edgar. *Brothers and Keepers.* New York: Doubleday, 1985.

12

National Security

After the trauma of World War II, Americans deeply hoped for a return to international peace and domestic prosperity. But by the 1950s we were already embroiled in another war, in Korea, and by the close of that decade, the president of the United States warned that what he called the "military-industrial complex" had grown to become a powerful and dangerous fixture of American life.

The military presence in America grew without much scrutiny until the Vietnam War. Before that war, the buildup of American military strength and its deployment around the world was widely accepted as one of the necessary costs of maintaining and extending America's economic growth and that of its allies, and of containing the spread of the power and influence of the Soviet Union.

The Vietnam era brought some important changes of direction. Though this wasn't the first time that many Americans had challenged their government's military priorities, it was the deepest and most serious challenge in decades. As the war in Southeast Asia wore on, taking American lives and resources without much discernible result, more and more Americans began to question the values that lay behind the entire postwar military expansion — especially the fundamental belief that military power should be a primary instrument of our foreign policy.

By the mid-1970s, these sentiments had helped put an end to the Vietnam War. They had also deeply influenced the way many people in the United States viewed the more basic, underlying issues the war had raised: the role of American military power in the international arena, the seriousness of the threats to the United States and its way of life from countries that organized their economies along different lines, and the impact of a vast defense establishment on political, economic, and social life at home.

These new doubts didn't diminish the military's role, at home or overseas, to the degree that many critics have since argued. But the changes they brought in American policy were significant enough to generate a chorus of criticism that the United States was neglecting its military. This neglect, some believed, would have fearful results. America's world influence was being weakened as a result of a posture of "withdrawal, retrenchment, disengagement" (Podhoretz, 1980, p. 2). Meanwhile, according to these critics, the Soviet Union, less "weak-willed" and vacillating, was steadily building up its military strength to the point where it not only exceeded ours in technical terms but gave the rest of the world a signal that it was willing and ready to use force to pursue *its* goals while the United States was not.

This threatened shift in the world's balance of military power, it was often argued, was caused not just by wrong-headed attitudes but by what a later president of the United States called "a dramatic shift in how we spend the taxpayer's dollar." As Ronald Reagan continued, in a 1983 speech:

> Back in 1955, payments to individuals took up only about 20 percent of the federal budget. For nearly three decades, these payments steadily increased, and this year will account for 49 percent of the budget. By contrast, in 1955 defense took up more than half of the federal budget. By 1980, this spending had fallen to a low of 23 percent. . . . The calls for cutting back the defense budget come in nice, simple arithmetic. They're the same kind of talk that led the democracies to neglect their defenses in the 1930s and invited the tragedy of World War Two. We must not let that grim chapter of history repeat itself through apathy or neglect. (Reagan, 1983, p. 13).

By the 1980s many Americans agreed that we needed more defense spending in order to bolster our sagging military capacities. And so what one critic called the "decade of somnolence" (Stein, 1982b) about defense was succeeded by the most rapid and massive military buildup since the early 1950s. But the new thrust toward more money for defense quickly ran into strong opposition. By the mid-1980s other critics were warning about the terrible destructive powers that were being created through the growth of our military weapons and casting doubts about the capacity of those weapons to further the goal of world peace or even to reliably protect the United States in the event of war.

Protest against the Vietnam War helped make America's military priorities a focus of public concern.

The role of the military in American society has, then, once again become one of the most urgent, and fateful, areas of debate about social policy in the United States. In this chapter, we can only consider *some* of the many aspects of this debate. Space doesn't allow us more than a passing glance at most of the broad issues of international policy that have shaped it. Instead, we'll concentrate on the effect of defense spending and military priorities on American social and economic life. Given that we need a system of national defense, we'll address some of the issues about how we should provide it — and what different strategies for national defense really cost.

In the first section, we examine the growth of American military spending in recent years, giving special attention to the problems of measurement and definition that often make the defense budget difficult to unravel. We then consider what research tells us about the impact of defense spending on the economy and some of the reasons for the skyrocketing costs of military weapons. Finally, we'll take a closer look at the weapons themselves — at what defense spending buys — and how they fit (or fail to fit) the realistic needs of America's national defense today.

Understanding the Military Budget

According to recent projections, the United States will spend more than $2.3 *trillion* on the military in the 1980s. In sheer dollar terms, this is the largest military buildup in American history. Figure 12-1 shows that this sharp rise has been a major trend in American social policy in recent years. The rise is frequently justified on the ground that our defense spending dropped to perilously low levels during the 1970s, especially when compared to other kinds of public spending. As the secretary of defense put it in 1983, these enormous expenditures are required to offset a "decade of our neglect" of the military (Weinberger, 1983). In this view, we've tended to ignore the most fundamental needs of defense in favor of government spending for social programs. In the meantime, the military readiness of the United States has crumbled, making the country ever more vulnerable to threats from abroad.

We'll look in a moment at some of the dimensions of those threats, as shown by data on comparative military strength. First, however,

Figure 12-1
Budget authority for national defense (in constant 1987 dollars)

Source: Adapted from U.S. Office of Management and Budget, Historical Tables, Fiscal Year 1988, Table 3-2.

* Preliminary.

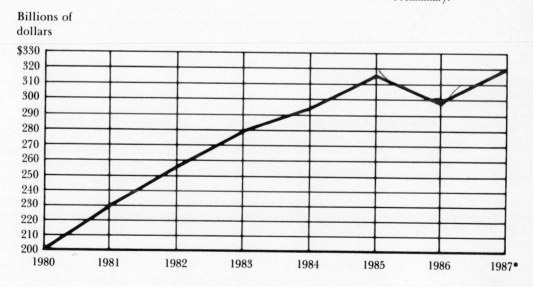

Billions of dollars

let's look more closely at the pattern of military spending in the United States in recent years. Have we shifted the balance too far away from the military, too much toward domestic spending?

Obviously, the answer to that question depends very much on subjective assessments of what we wish to use social resources *for*. But it should also be based on a careful analysis of the realities of the federal budget. Unfortunately, such an analysis is not as easy to make as it might seem. Like most official statistics, the figures on military spending (as well as those on *non*defense spending) are very complicated, and they can be given many different interpretations depending on what kind of argument one wants to make. When read carefully, however, the figures show that military buildup in recent years has been dramatic indeed and that the supposed tilt toward nondefense social spending is a more complicated matter than its critics assume.

Currently, national defense takes over a quarter of all federal spending (or *outlays*) and accounts for about 6 percent of GNP. In the late 1960s, defense accounted for more than 45 percent of federal outlays and 9 percent of GNP. Meanwhile, that part of the federal budget going to what the government calls "payments to individuals" has risen considerably, from about a third of outlays in the late 1960s to about half in the late 1980s (U.S. Office of Management and Budget, 1987, Table 3-2).

Although figures like these are often presented to demonstrate the supposed decline in our military spending in recent years in favor of social programs, they don't tell the whole story. To gain a more accurate perspective, we need to look much more closely at both sides of this comparison. Two issues are especially important. One we've touched on already, in Chapter 4: It involves the nature and definition of the government's spending on domestic social programs. The other involves a more critical look at how we measure military spending.

Types of Government Spending

How much do we spend on social programs? To answer that question, we need to distinguish between two very different ways in which the federal government receives and spends money. *Most* of what the government spends in payments to individuals does not come from the public's general tax money (what in budgetary jargon are called *general funds*) but from another source, called *trust funds*. These are funds based *primarily* on special contributions made by the groups for whose needs the funds will be spent. Beause of this, trust funds are not available for other government purposes and are usually considered relatively "uncontrollable" (not subject to the government's discretion as to how they should be spent). All told, trust funds account for over a third of the budget in the late 1980s; of those funds, the bulk is accounted for by two very large programs: Social Security and Medicare. The most important single part of the nondefense side of federal spending, then, is money for health care and income support for the aged. And as we've seen, the increase in this kind of government spending primarily reflects the overall aging of the population (and partly, too, the increasing costs of health-care services). Neither can fairly be said to reflect a decreasing commitment to defense in the name of *shifting* social resources to the needy.

Another important part of the trust fund component of federal spending is unemployment compensation. Unemployment insurance accounted for about $21 billion of federal outlays in 1986, up from $13 billion in 1975 (*Statistical Abstract of the United States,* 1986, p. 296). This growth does represent an increase in the share of the budget devoted to income security versus defense. But it hardly represents a deliberate policy shift from national defense to pay for expanded social programs. Instead, it is a response to high rates of unemployment in recent years. (Moreover, as we'll see in a moment, those rising unemployment rates are not unrelated to the size of our defense spending itself.)

A more accurate way of depicting the share of the military budget in overall federal spending is to subtract these trust fund outlays from the rest of federal expenditures. This will give us a better picture of the way the government spends the tax dollars over which it has more discretion — expenditures that do not so closely reflect fundamental demographic or economic changes and that are paid for out of general tax funds. Figure 12-2 illustrates this "general funds" measure of the burden of military spending.

The figure also includes two further operations necessary to arrive at a clear picture of the size of the military budget. First, it shows the effect on the military burden of subtracting, along with trust funds, another uncontrollable part of the budget — the interest on the federal debt (what the government owes on its past borrowing of money). In 1986, interest on the debt was about 15 percent of the total federal budget, up from about 7 percent in 1960. It is another reason for the apparent increase in the share of the budget going for nondefense spending. But much of it — *about half* in 1982 — was interest on debts incurred to pay for *past* wars and military purchases (DeGrasse and Murphy, 1981, p. 2). Second, Figure 12-2 also includes in its calculation of the defense burden the addition of an important sum that, in more conventional portraits of federal spending, is placed, curiously, on the nondefense side of the ledger — veterans benefits (which amounted to over $25 billion in 1986).

Seen in this light, the military burden looms much larger, even before the recent buildup, than is usually acknowledged. Instead of a

Figure 12-2
Two measures of the military burden

Source: Based on Robert DeGrasse and Paul Murphy, "Impact of Reagan's Rearmament," *Council on Economic Priorities Newsletter,* May 1981, p. 1. Reprinted with permission. 1986 figures from *Statistical Abstract of the United States,* 1987, pp. 294, 317.

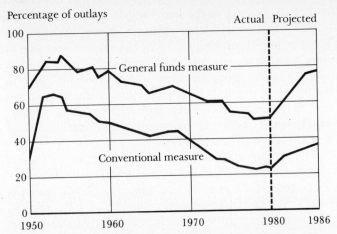

Note: General funds measure: Conventional measure adding veterans benefits to the defense function and subtracting trust funds and interest on the debt from total federal outlays. Conventional measure: Defense function as a percentage of total federal outlays.

fourth of the federal budget, it amounted to three-fifths of the more controllable federal spending in 1986.

What all this means for individual families can be brought home by an example. In 1986, according to one estimate, the average family paid about $5,800 in taxes. Of that sum, $3,103 went to the military, $126 to education, $138 to nutrition programs, and $115 to housing (Jobs with Peace, 1986).

The Military Budget in War and "Peace"

These trends suggest that, measured in dollar terms alone, the military has become an ever-greater presence in American life. This is apparent when we realize that all of the periods in which defense spending as a share of the economy was higher than it is today were periods of *war*. One way of looking at the trends in military spending since the 1940s, therefore, is to note that we have never returned to the low levels of military presence we enjoyed just after World War II. The "peacetime" military system has become institutionalized in America — so much so that by the mid-1980s, the military budget in years of peace had approached the share of the American economy that it held during the height of the Vietnam War in the late 1960s. (Table 12-1).

As we've seen in earlier chapters, our military expenditures are also much larger than those in most other countries — with the principal exception of some of the more troubled countries of the Third World and the Middle East. In the mid-1980s Americans were spending

Year	Outlay
1955	211
1960	192
1965	181
1968	255
1970	226
1975	160
1980	164
1986	232

Source: Data from *Statistical Abstract of the United States*, 1987, p. 317.

Table 12-1
The growth of the 'peace time' military: Outlays for national defense, 1955–1986 (billions of constant 1982 dollars)

around $1,000 per person on the military; the Germans and Swedes were spending about $400 and the Japanese closer to $100. As we'll now see, this has important implications for the relative economic performance of the United States.

The Impact of Military Spending

What is at issue in the debates over military spending is not just the numbers of dollars we spend on defense but the ways in which that spending affects both national security in a volatile world and the fabric of economic and social life at home. We will return to the first issue — how well our current approach to military spending addresses the real problems of national security — later in this chapter. First, let's look at what we know about the effect of defense spending on the domestic economy and society. As we might expect, there is considerable disagreement over this issue.

Some argue that defense production is inherently bad for the economy and that sharp increases in military spending will "wreck" it (Thurow, 1981b). On the other hand, the secretary of defense argued in 1983, in the midst of the largest defense buildup in 30 years, that "fears that the defense budget of this administration will strain the economy are unfounded" (Weinberger, 1983, p. 2). Who is right?

Like so many other questions of social policy, the answer depends very much on judgments about what kind of social priorities we want our economy to serve. With this in mind, let's consider several areas in which the impact of defense spending has been of major concern: jobs, urban and regional decline, and investment and productivity.

Military Spending and Jobs

No one disagrees that military spending creates a great many jobs in the United States. According to estimates from the Center for Defense Information (1986a), more than 3 million industrial jobs in America now depend on the defense budget. Moreover, as we saw in Chapter 2, the Department of Defense is itself one of the largest employers in America; it provided more than a million civilian jobs in the mid-1980s.

But evaluating the impact of military spending on employment involves more specific questions: first, whether defense spending is an *effective* creator of jobs as compared with alternative ways of using government monies; second, whether the *kinds* of jobs it creates are those most needed in American society today — and most helpful in developing a vital economy; and, third, whether the *location* of the jobs created by defense spending represents an efficient or equitable use of the government's resources.

How many jobs from defense spending? Although a substantial number of jobs are created by defense spending, most research has shown that it produces fewer jobs than some other kinds of government and nongovernment spending — especially nondefense government spending.

This is especially true for spending on military hardware and weaponry. Recent estimates by the Council on Economic Priorities, on the basis of data from the Bureau of Labor Statistics have shown that roughly 28,000 jobs are created for every *billion* dollars spent on military procurement. (*Procurement,* in the language of military budgets, means the purchasing of weapons and other supplies — as opposed, for example, to military spending for personnel salaries or maintenance of equipment.) The same amount of spending, however, would create 32,000 jobs if it were spent on public transit and *71,000* if it were spent on education (DeGrasse, 1983a, p. 2). A more recent study estimated that a billion dollars spent for the military generally would create about 85,000 jobs, whereas the same amount in nondefense public spending would create about 92,000 jobs (Blank and Rothschild, 1985).

Why does military spending produce such a relatively small number of jobs? We've encountered part of the reason already, when we discussed the transformation of the American workplace through high-technology, automated forms of production. Most military production is extremely capital-intensive, using very large amounts of money and sophisticated machinery to produce *other* very sophisticated, complex products. (As we'll see later in this chapter, the growing complexity of military weapons systems has disturbing consequences in military terms as well.) This is especially true of some of the most advanced strategic weapons systems, which have been the fastest-growing part of the total military budget in recent years. As shown in Table 12-2, the production of military missiles produces fewer jobs, directly and indirectly, than other industrial production. (Indirect employment refers to jobs created among suppliers, subcontractors, and firms providing services to those working directly in the industry.)

Because the capital-intensive character of military production is increasing, the same amount of money invested in it no longer generates as many jobs for American workers as it once did. (Blank and Rothschild, 1985). As we saw in Chapter 8, this is a growing problem in many American industries; but it is especially apparent in some of the defense-related ones, particularly the aerospace industry — one of those most dependent on military contracts.

Jobs for whom? A second issue has to do with the *kinds* of jobs that military spending creates — and fails to create. Defense spending, like any other kind of spending, creates what economists call a *multiplier effect:* It ripples out through the economy as a whole, providing jobs for many people only remotely connected with the defense industry itself. But it's still true that dollars spent on defense are dollars *not* spent on other things, and like other spending decisions by the government, this has important effects on the distribution of jobs and income throughout the society. And by benefiting some occupations

Alternatives	Numbers of jobs per $1 billion* (direct plus indirect employment)
Guided missile	53,248
Mass transit equipment	77,356
Public utility construction	65,859
Railroad equipment	54,220
Housing	68,657
Solar energy/energy conservation	65,079
Solar energy	57,235

Table 12-2
Jobs and military spending

* 1972 dollars
Source: Adapted from David Gold and Geoff Quinn, "Misguided Expenditure: An Analysis of the Proposed MX System," *Council on Economic Priorities Newsletter,* July 1981, p. 6. Reprinted with permission.

more than others, military spending affects the pattern of social inequality as well as the prospects for employment and unemployment.

An analysis by Employment Research Associates (1982) calculated that the 1981 spending by the Department of Defense resulted in the net *loss* of more than 1.5 million jobs in the rest of the American economy. According to this study, each $1 billion shifted to defense from ordinary purchases by taxpayers caused the loss of about 18,000 jobs. The heaviest losses, the study argued, took place in a few key areas of the nondefense economy, especially retail trade, the textile and clothing industries, automobiles, banking, insurance, real estate, and housing construction.

In dollar terms alone, the military has become an ever-greater presence in American life.

These differences in the sectors of the economy boosted by military versus domestic spending also translate into differences in the types of workers who benefit from each. Relatively few defense-related jobs go to blue-collar production workers; the bulk of jobs created by

Rich Frishman/Picture Group

defense spending go to high-level workers, especially engineers and others with high-technology skills. In the missile industry, two out of five workers are engineers, computer specialists, mathematicians, or scientists, though these workers make up only about 6 percent of the overall American work force (Markusen, 1986, p. 507). Most of the major defense-related industries, generally, employ considerably higher proportions of professional workers and managers than the American manufacturing industry as a whole (DeGrasse, 1983b, p. 2).

Obviously, this is a complicated issue to evaluate in social terms. On the one hand, high-tech defense-related jobs are relatively *good* ones — for those who get them. But relatively few people *do* get them. Defense spending tends to distribute employment benefits toward workers who are relatively affluent, highly educated, and already blessed with relatively low risks of unemployment. To a disturbing extent, these workers are also white and male. (Blank and Rothschild, 1985). Although a few of the industries in which jobs tend to be displaced by military spending (notably construction) are also disproportionately filled by white men, most of the others are large employers of minorities and women — including teaching, health care, nondefense government employment, and semiskilled blue-collar work in civilian manufacturing industries, such as autos and steel. This disparity is even greater if we compare defense procurement spending to other possible uses of public spending, such as job programs targeted toward the unemployed, which (as we saw in Chapter 8) are much more effective in providing jobs for minorities, women, and the disadvantaged. To the extent that military production "crowds out" such more targeted social spending, it tends to deepen, rather than diminish, the inequalities of race and gender.

The Urban and Regional Effect of Military Spending

Defense production is also distributed unevenly across the country. Thus, some areas benefit more than others. To some extent, this is true of any form of government spending. What makes this pattern especially troubling, however, is that shifts of government spending to military uses, on the whole, distribute those resources primarily to areas that are *least* in need of such public support and away from those that have suffered the most from joblessness and economic decline in recent years.

Military contracting is heavily concentrated in what's sometimes called the "defense perimeter" — the states from New England south to Florida, west to Texas, and north through California to Washington state (Markusen, 1986, p. 510). As more and more defense funds are poured into the economy, they obviously increase investment and employment in those areas of high defense-industry concentration.

Most of these regions, however, are precisely those that have been least hurt by the problems of industrial decline we saw in Chapter 3. The resulting imbalance between regional need and government funding was sharply revealed in a University of Michigan study of the impact of recent increases in the military budget in the different states of the union (Anton, Oppenheim, and Morrow, 1982). The researchers began by calculating what they graphically called a "pain index," the combined rates of unemployment and welfare dependency for each state and region of the country. They then calculated the per capita amounts of federal spending each region received. The pain index was worse in the Mid-Atlantic and East-North-Central states of the old industrial heartland than in any other areas of the country. But the federal budget served the former areas *least* — mainly because they received so little from the defense part of the budget. The hard-pressed states of Illinois, Indiana, Michigan, Ohio, and Wisconsin received about a fourth as many defense dollars per capita as the New England and Pacific states.

What is true for the declining industrial areas is generally even more true for many of America's most distressed cities. The shift of employment away from teaching, health care, and housing construction helps ensure that the inner cities remain disadvantaged. Since few of the job opportunities created by defense expansion are accessible to most inner-city residents, particularly the low-skilled and unemployed, the shift of government spending to military procurement cannot deliver in new jobs what it takes from the cities in employment, training, and other supportive programs. Moreover, the evidence suggests that for many older, "needy" cities, high levels of defense spending act as an enormous funnel that channels tax funds in the wrong direction, taking more public monies than it gives back in necessary urban services.

Booming defense, crumbling infrastructure. One long-range result of these priorities has been the steady deterioration of the infrastructure of American cities: highways, bridges, and other public facilities. Most of us can observe this first hand, in potholed streets, unkempt parks, insufficient and dilapidated public transportation. No one knows the precise extent of this problem, but some rough estimates of its dimensions have been provided in a study by Pat Choate and Susan Walter for the Council of State Planning Agencies. "America's public facilities," they wrote, "are wearing out faster than they are being replaced" (1981, p. 1). Among the most pressing problems they reported were the following:

• One out of every five bridges in America needed "major" rehabilitation or reconstruction, at an estimated cost of as much as $33 billion.

- At least several thousand dams in the United States were plagued by "hazardous deficiencies," but not enough public funds were available even to *inspect* most of them, let alone repair them.
- New York City alone would require more than $40 billion of public investment over the 1980s to service, reconstruct, or repair bridges, reservoirs, streets, sewers, subways, public hospitals, firehouses, and other public facilities. The city was expected to be able to invest just $1.4 billion a year to do the job.

Choate and Walter argued that these were only a few examples of a more general "decline in both the quantity and quality of virtually every type of public works facility in the nation" (1981, p. 4). But, meanwhile, the government's investment in public works spending had actually *fallen* considerably. As a proportion of GNP, for example, public works investments dropped from more than 4 percent in 1965 to 2.3 percent by 1977 (Choate and Walter, 1981, p. 7).

Not all of this decline reflects the impact of defense spending, to be sure. Some of it, for example, represents the declining share of spending on educational facilities as the school-age population has become a smaller proportion of the total (Choate and Walter, 1981, p. 7). But it seems clear that the kinds of sums thought to be required to rebuild America's infrastructure will be hard to find in the coming years, given the growing share of our limited public resources now taken by defense.

We will return to the issue of the crumbling infrastructure again in Chapter 13. Now, let's look at some of the ways in which high levels of military spending affect *private* investment — and, therefore, may aggravate the nagging problems of low productivity growth and declining competitiveness in the world economy.

Defense, Investment, and Productivity

As we've seen, many of America's basic industries have fared badly in recent years, especially when compared with those of some foreign countries. We examined some of the possible reasons for this comparative decline in Chapter 3. But there is growing evidence of the importance of another factor, one we haven't discussed yet: the negative impact of high military spending.

Some basic evidence is illustrated in Figure 12-3, based on recent research by the Council on Economic Priorities. The figure shows that countries with a high level of investment — the basic source of economic growth — tend to be those with relatively *low* military spending. Thus, Japan stands out from all the countries in the chart in the amount of its gross domestic product (GDP) devoted to investment — and it also has the *lowest* proportion devoted to military spending. At

Source: Robert DeGrasse,
"Military Buildup Exacts Toll
on Economy," *Council on
Economic Priorities Newsletter,*
May 1983a, p. 3. Reprinted
with permission.

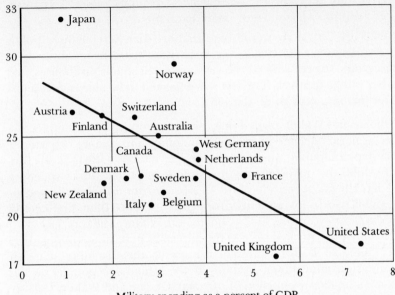

Investment as a percent of GDP

Military spending as a percent of GDP

the other end of the scale, the United States stands out as the country
with the *highest* proportion of its economy devoted to the military, and
it is next to the bottom in its level of productive investment. It is
second only to the United Kingdom, which, not coincidentally, spends
the second highest percentage of its domestic product on defense.

Certainly, disproportionate spending for defense is not the *only*
source of poor investment and declining economic performance in
the United States. (We've looked at some others in earlier chapters,
including the inefficient use of human resources and the substitution
of short-term gains for long-term planning and investment.) But the
destructive role of the extreme diversion of resources to defense is an
important *part* of the explanation. Table 12-3 supports this conten-
tion from a somewhat different angle, by comparing *productivity*
across different countries in relation to levels of military spending.
Once again, as with investment, productivity growth is fastest by far in
Japan, the country with the lowest defense share of domestic product.
It is slowest in the United States, with the United Kingdom also near
the bottom in productivity growth and near the top in spending on
defense.

What causes these effects? In part, extremely high levels of defense
spending apparently drain necessary capital away from civilian industry. This is a complicated issue because, as we saw in Chapter 3, a

Country	1970–1979
United States	
Productivity growth	1.1
Defense share of GDP	6.1
Japan	
Productivity growth	4.5
Defense share of GDP	0.9
West Germany	
Productivity growth	3.4
Defense share of GDP	3.9
United Kingdom	
Productivity growth	2.0
Defense share of GDP	4.9

Table 12-3
Defense spending and productivity growth

Source: Adapted from U.S. Congressional Budget Office, *Defense Spending and the Economy* (Washington, D.C.: Government Printing Office, 1983b), p. 40.

number of industries that have performed poorly in recent years have *not* suffered from a shortage of capital so much as from a misuse of the capital they have. But, nevertheless, across the economy as a whole, it's clear that an extraordinary amount of America's capital is siphoned off to the defense economy, a phenomenon one critic, Seymour Melman, described as "looting the means of production" (Melman, 1982). As Melman noted (1982, p. 4), $46 out of every $100 of new capital formed in the United States in the late 1970s was spent in the military economy, versus $14 in West Germany and less than $4 in Japan.

Military production drains not only capital but also skills and knowledge from the civilian economy. Military-related production employs about a third of all U.S. scientists and engineers and uses almost 70 percent of the federal dollars spent on research and development (Center for Defense Information, 1986a, p. 3). The latter figure compares with about 10–15 percent in Germany and less than 5 percent in Japan (McFadden and Wake, 1983, p. 10).

The result is that most of our scientific and technological resources are channeled into the production of some goods rather than others — increasingly causing a "recomposition" of the entire American economy (Markusen, 1986, p. 502). We're producing more and more of certain kinds of high-technology products — many of them with mainly military uses — while allowing other industries less tied to defense (like steel and consumer goods) to fall into relative decline.

Meanwhile, of course, some other countries are pouring much greater resources into these industries and are increasingly dominating the world market for them.

The Costs and Aims of Defense Spending

All of this suggests that America's commitment to massive expenditures on defense carries some extraordinary social and economic costs — costs of lost civilian production, stifled innovation, inadequate and unevenly distributed job opportunities, and urban and regional decline. But we have not yet paid much attention to the more *immediate* dollars-and-cents costs associated with the military buildup in recent years. The escalating cost of defense — particularly in the production of new, complex weaponry (Table 12-4) — has become the focus of concern and criticism from a surprisingly wide range of critics, from every point on the political spectrum. Whether from left, right, or center, the critics converge in their assessment that defense costs much more than it needs to. Moreover, there is a surprising amount of consensus that the weapons Americans pay for, with a bigger and bigger share of their taxes, are problematic even in military terms. Viewed strictly from the perspective of enhancing the country's military security, what we buy is probably not what we need.

Table 12-4
Costly weapons: Total spending for the ten most expensive weapons systems, fiscal years 1985–1987

Weapon	1985–1987 cost (billions)
B-1 Bomber	$13.8
F-16 Falcon Aircraft	$10.1
Strategic Defense Initiative ("Star Wars")	$ 9.0
F/A-18 Hornet Aircraft	$ 8.4
Trident II Missile	$ 8.1
SSN-688 Nuclear Attack Submarine	$ 7.8
AEGIS Cruiser	$ 7.6
Peacekeeper Missile ("MX")	$ 7.0
F-15 Eagle Aircraft	$ 6.7
M-1 Combat Tank	$ 6.1
Total cost of ten systems, 1985–1987:	$84.6

Source: Data from U.S. Department of Defense, *Program Acquisition Costs by Weapon System,* Feb. 4, 1986, pp. i–ix.

Meanwhile, some things we *might* do to make the country's defense system more efficient and more reliable are usually the *last* items on the military agenda.

Why Defense Costs So Much

No one doubts that military weapons have become staggeringly expensive. As James Fallows has pointed out, the cost of American combat fighter planes rose by a factor of 100, in *constant* dollars, in the 25 years following World War II (1982, p. 37). The vice-president of Martin Marietta Aerospace, a major defense contractor, has said that, at these rates, the *entire* American defense budget would buy a single tactical aircraft by the year 2054 — and the air force, navy, and marines would have to share the plane, a few days a week each (quoted in Fallows, 1982, p. 38). Aircraft carriers cost 20 times what they did in World War II, tanks 15 times. A modern Trident nuclear submarine costs more than 270 times as much, per ton, as a World War II variety of submarine (Kaldor, 1981, p. 25).

Such figures have led even some of the staunchest supporters of increased American military power to accuse the government, as the conservative Heritage Foundation did in 1982, of "throwing money at the Pentagon" (quoted in Anderson, 1983). Why have the costs of defense risen so fast, and why can't they be held down?

The "Military-Industrial Complex" and the Costs of Defense

Some of the reasons defense costs are so high involve the nature of the institutions of defense production in the United States: the large private corporations that account for the lion's share of military production and the military agencies that plan, fund, and ultimately use the weapons. Other reasons for the rising costs of weapons involve the nature of the weapons themselves. Both, as we shall see, are related.

In a famous declaration at the end of the 1950s, former President Dwight Eisenhower warned that what he called the military-industrial complex was achieving a dangerous amount of influence in American life. Today that influence is considerably greater, since the military-industrial complex is considerably bigger — and no less difficult to control. If the American military industry were a separate country, it would have the world's thirteenth largest national economy (Center for Defense Information, 1987a, p. 1).

In addition to the Department of Defense, itself one of the largest economic entities in the world, the military-industrial complex includes many of America's largest private corporations. Six of those corporations (McDonnell-Douglas, General Dynamics, Rockwell International, General Electric, Boeing, and Lockheed) received over 25 percent of all defense contracts in 1985; all are among the country's

40 largest industrial corporations (U.S. Department of Defense, 1986, pp. 1–4).

It isn't just the size of these corporations that gives them great influence over the defense production process, however, but, more importantly, the nature of their connnection with the government. In an economy that is *generally* less and less "competitive" in the classical sense of a large number of firms competing for the customer's dollar, the sector devoted to defense is even *less* competitive. Most defense contracts are not subject to competitive bidding among potential suppliers; they are negotiated with a few corporations that have longstanding ties to the Department of Defense and the various military services.

By itself this lack of competition is extraordinarily costly, as many corporate managers (and Defense Department officials) have frequently pointed out. In 1983, the president's Private Sector Survey on Cost Control, undertaken by a staid assortment of corporate executives, concluded that opening up the military weapons procurement system to more contract competition might save the navy and air force each about $2 billion annually, the army $3 billion (*New York Times*, July 1, 1983). In the early 1980s, the Small Business Administration insisted on opening up the procurement of certain aircraft spare parts to competitive bidding, allowing more smaller companies to have a crack at supplying them. Over an 18-month period, this practice saved the air force almost $7 million (Harvey, 1982). And the inspector general of the Department of Defense later estimated that the military could save an additional billion dollars, on spare parts alone, through this process (Center for Defense Information, 1986b).

Linked with the absence of competition is the tendency for defense corporations and their government customers to develop intimate relations and common perceptions that often allow the defense firms to exert great influence over defense policy and especially over the acquisition of new weapons. According to a study by the Council on Economic Priorities, the ties between the top eight defense contractors and the Pentagon are very close indeed. An astonishing number of high-level executives move back and forth between the defense corporations and the Department of Defense or the National Aeronautics and Space Administration (NASA). The military-industrial complex is in many ways "a closed community in which the private and government interests converge" (1981, p. 4).

In addition, the major defense corporations maintain influential lobbying offices in Washington, D.C. The lobbyists spend large sums of money to develop friendly ties with members of the congress and the executive branch of the government — much of which is ultimately charged to the taxpayers as normal expenses of government contracts. (Some of these expenses stretch the imagination: The

Raytheon Corporation charged taxpayers for lodging, meals, and guide service for goose hunts it organized for its executives and guests; General Dynamics charged to the government the cost of tie-pins it had made in the shape of its F-16 fighter plane, to be distributed as gifts [*Common Cause,* 1983].) The large defense contractors also spend substantial sums, through political action committees and campaign contributions, to support friendly congressional candidates (Center for Defense Information, 1987a).

These intimate relations boost the ability of the defense corporations to shape the aims of national weapons policy. And they help ensure that there are few mechanisms for holding the corporations accountable for the quality or the costs of what they produce. Most defense contracting has traditionally been done on what's called a cost-plus basis: The firm bills the government for what it claims to be its costs to complete a project, plus an adequate margin of profit. The costs are virtually automatically reimbursed by the government, so there is no incentive for the corporation to hold costs down. The mentality encouraged by this process was summed up by Admiral Hyman Rickover (the creator of the navy's nuclear submarine program) as he left the service in 1982: "They don't care how the work goes," the admiral told a congressional committee. "The government pays for it. There's no incentive. There's no real responsibility" (Rickover, 1982, p. 13).

Sometimes this practice leads to outright fraud, as when corporations pad their bills in order to recover the costs of poor contract performance and inept management. One giant defense contractor, for example, was found guilty of falsifying some of its employees' time cards so that their salaries could be charged to a cost-plus contract rather than to another, fixed-cost contract (Center for Defense Information, 1986b). More often, the lack of incentives for cost control and efficiency simply allows the costs of virtually anything the military contractors produce to rise inexorably upward — especially in comparison with the costs of similar products sold on the civilian market. James Fallows (1982, p. 38) and other observers have pointed out that the cost of many *civilian* electronics products, from calculators to large computers, dropped dramatically during the 1970s as simpler, cheaper technology became available and was passed on to consumers in lower prices, but the opposite has happened with military electronics. Over the past decade the electronic systems that represent much of the new technology in advanced aircraft, guided missiles, and other sophisticated weaponry have become vastly more expensive.

This cost escalation affects even the most mundane military equipment, not just the super-sophisticated weapons systems. Among the items recently contracted for by the military, for instance, were airplane ashtrays costing $969 apiece and a $9,606 Allen wrench (Center for Defense Information, 1986b).

The most often-noted result of cost-plus contracts is what are called, in the language of government contracting, *cost overruns:* The costs of particular weapons systems almost invariably escalate far beyond their original estimates. In recent years cost overruns on major military weapons systems in the United States have *averaged* about 100 percent (Kaldor, 1981, p. 71). On some weapons, the cost overruns have been much higher.

Another factor feeding the ever-increasing costs of weaponry is the rivalry among the various armed services — a rivalry built deeply into American military traditions. It causes what a former head of the Joint Chiefs of Staff called "an intramural scramble for resources" (quoted in *Newsweek,* 1982a, p. 32). That scramble for resources — and for prestige — results in massive duplication of weapons systems, as each service comes to believe it needs to outpace the others. Both the navy and the air force, for example, invest in tactical airplanes that are virtually alike, except that they are produced by different corporations. They thus have parts and systems that can't be interchanged and that cost more per unit and require more money and personnel to maintain. In the early 1980s, the overall cost of this duplication was estimated to be as high as $20 billion a year (*Business Week,* 1982c, p. 76).

What the Dollars Buy

At the heart of the cost problem is the nature of much modern military weaponry itself. A growing number of critics have begun to argue that, despite their admittedly awesome destructive power, many modern weapons systems have become so complex that they are not only incredibly expensive, but often of limited use in achieving their stated purpose — the defense of the country in the event of war. They are examples of what the British social theorist Mary Kaldor (1981) has called "baroque" technology: marginal improvements tacked on, at ever-increasing expense, to conventional, and very likely outmoded, designs. Because of the drift toward this kind of expensive but marginally effective technology, as Kaldor (echoing many other critics, in and out of the military itself) noted, there are serious questions about "the ability of modern armed forces to fight wars" (1981, p. 175).

Sometimes the growing complexity of modern military technology results in the production of expensive weapons that simply don't work. Consider the ignominious failure of a weapon termed the "most expensive gun in the world": the DIVAD (a military acronym

for Division Air Defense) antiaircraft gun. The DIVAD was elabo-
rately controlled by sophisticated computers and guided by the most
advanced radar systems available. But during its demonstration in
1982: ". . . the DIVAD trained its sights on a drone Huey helicopter
hovering nearby — and failed to fire. After repairs to a disconnected
cable, the DIVAD fired — this time, directly into the ground 300
yards away" (*Newsweek*, 1982a, p. 31). DIVAD was cancelled in 1985
"after seven years of technical failures, delays, and cost overruns"
(*Science*, 1987, p. 137) — and the expenditure of almost $2 billion.

Other expensive weapons may ultimately perform better. But
many of them turn out to be so cumbersome and complex that they
seem astonishingly ill-suited to any imaginable conditions of actual
combat. Take, for example, the XM-1 tank, developed by the
Chrysler Corporation to replace earlier (and much cheaper) models.
The program to develop the tank was expected to cost Americans
almost $20 billion during the 1980s. (Like most weapons-cost projec-
tions, this sum is almost certain to rise.) In 1983 the XM-1 created a
considerable stir when it became publicly known, as a result of field
tests, that the tank's engine and transmission had to be removed in
order to change the oil (Coates, 1983). The tank is also so voracious in
its consumption of fuel that it must be accompanied into battle by
military gasoline trucks (Children's Defense Fund, 1982, p. 16).

Such complexity often means that the newest weapons are not only
more costly but also require more frequent maintenance, more spare
parts, and more personnel to keep them going. Not surprisingly, the
percentage of time during which many complex weapons — from
combat aircraft to armored vehicles — are out of service has increased substantially over their less expensive predecessors. In the
early 1980s, two-thirds of the military's F-111 D attack aircraft were
out of service; the plane required 98 hours of maintenance work for
every flight (Kaldor, 1981, pp. 175–176).

Such examples can be multiplied many times over. But the main
message of many recent studies of modern weapons systems is clear:
The increasing costs they incur don't bring even remotely comparable
benefits, even in the most quantitative, military terms. And because
the more elaborate, high-technology weapons require such vast sums
to produce, it's impossible to produce very many of them, even in an
age of greatly expanded military budgets. The long-term results are
disturbing, for they mean that we are tending to produce a few highly
destructive, but remarkably unreliable, weapons rather than — *at the
same cost* — producing a larger number of simpler, more reliable
weapons that might serve much better should they ever be needed.

If so many wepaons are poorly designed and developed in relation
to their enormous costs, why do they continue to be ordered — and

We may be building more complex and expensive weapons than we really need.

paid for? The answer, it's increasingly argued, lies in the military-industrial linkage we've already observed, what James Fallows called the "culture of procurement" (1982, p. 38) — a culture in which weapons are built less to suit any conceivable needs of military defense than to sustain the financial and organizational needs of the defense corporations themselves.

Alternatives to Military Spending

We've seen that the defense budget in the United States is swollen by cost overruns and the production of weapons that are sometimes unnecessary and often unreliable. The bright side to this otherwise grim picture is that these inefficiencies create room for considerable savings of money and human resources through changing the way we spend our defense dollars. With careful planning, those savings could be turned to alternative uses — which could help revitalize the American economy and restore domestic social programs.

No one proposes that we scrap the entire defense budget. But research suggests that there are several ways in which it might be reduced without damaging national defense. Critics of our current patterns of defense spending have pointed to three such strategies, in particular: putting a cap on the level of *increases* we permit in the defense budget from year to year, reducing cost overruns, and halting or scaling down the production and testing of nuclear weapons.

The Center for Defense Information, a Washington-based advocacy group, has argued that one way to achieve savings in military spending is to establish a "level" defense budget — that is, a budget that gives the Pentagon the same amounts from year to year, with an added adjustment to account for inflation. If inflation reached 4 percent, for example, the defense budget would be increased by no more than 4 percent. (The budgets requested in the early 1980s were closer to 12 percent above their predecessors.) This strategy could save billions, and it would do so without requiring *cuts* in military spending, only a ceiling on increases.

Putting a ceiling on defense spending, in this argument, would utimately *strengthen* the national defense because it would force greater efficiency on the military and its suppliers — efficiency that is now routinely demanded of all government programs *except* defense. "A level military budget," the center argues, "would encourage military officials to give more attention to *how* money is being spent and for what purposes." It would also "stimulate more careful planning of military programs and improve procurement practices," help to "limit spending on new weapons that may quickly become obsolete or will be too complex to function on the battlefield," and, over the long run, help to "focus attention on better long-range planning and valid military strategies" (Center for Defense Information, 1983, pp. 2–3).

Putting a Cap on Defense Increases

Reducing Cost Overruns

One of the most obvious ways to achieve substantial savings without hurting national defense is to hold down cost overruns in the procurement of weapons. As we've seen, the waste involved here is staggering. As many critics have pointed out, the amount of these overruns is so large that they often dwarf our spending on some supposedly "out of control" domestic programs. Thus, according to the Children's Defense Fund, the cost *increases* in development of the F-15 fighter plane up to fiscal year 1983 could have paid for the entire AFDC program in that year (Children's Defense Fund, 1982, p. 16). Some other examples:

1. The cost overrun on the MX missile during 1982 alone equaled the proposed reductions in federal student loans for the 5 years from 1984 through 1988.

2. If cost increases during 1982 for five major weapons systems (the MX, Trident submarine, Tomahawk missile, C-5 transport aircraft, and SH60B helicopter) had been avoided, the resulting savings could have restored 5 years' worth of reductions in Child Nutrition programs (calculated from U.S. Congressional Budget Office, 1983b, pp. 77–145).

3. The accumulated cost increases by 1982 in any *one* of the three most costly fighter plane programs, if distributed as cash grants, could have brought every poor family in the United States in 1981 above the poverty line (calculated from *Common Cause*, May-June 1983, and U.S. Bureau of the Census, 1983a, p. 150).

Accomplishing such reductions in overruns is no easy task, however, given the deeply entrenched practices of defense contracting in the United States. But there is obvious room for reform. By the mid-1980s, critics representing many different political and social views were calling for legislation to control cost escalation. The suggestions included (Coates, 1983; Center for Defense Information, 1986b):

• Forcing the Pentagon to increase the amount of procurement done under competitive bidding;

• Insisting that the Pentagon require producers of military equipment to provide warranties, like those given with new car sales;

• Creating an independent government testing office to ensure that high-technology weapons actually work *before* they're purchased by the military;

• Requiring that major cost overruns incurred by defense contractors be made public knowledge.

Controlling the growth of nuclear weapons (see pages 413 to 414) could free tens of billions of dollars for other uses. According to a 1983 estimate, a "freeze" on nuclear weapons production in the United States would save at least $84 billion over 5 years, with a potential for much more (McFadden and Wake, 1983, p. 13). The analysis found that the savings from the first year of a nuclear weapons freeze would have been close to $7 billion in fiscal year 1983, a sum that could have restored most of that year's reductions in federal programs for community development, mass transit, child nutrition, student loans, income support, legal services, and subsidized health care (McFadden and Wake, 1983, p. 14).

Halting or Scaling Down Production of Nuclear Weapons

Achieving this amount of savings in defense spending, however, could not be accomplished without significant impact on those workers and communities now heavily dependent on defense contracts (Blank and Rothschild, 1985).

The Importance of Planning

The defense industries, as we've seen, are a major employer of American workers, especially in some parts of the country. The eight companies identified by the Council on Economic Priorities as the top defense contractors during the 1970s employed, among them, nearly 700,000 workers in 1982 (*Fortune*, 1983, p. 228). However, because many defense-related projects are relatively poor generators of jobs, careful, targeted reductions in defense production would boost employment and community well-being over the long run — especially given the insecurity of military-related employment. In the short run, though, reductions could mean serious hardship and economic dislocation.

Because of these problems, proponents of reduced weapons spending have directed their attention to ways of cushioning the impact of reductions through retraining defense workers and developing alternative uses of military production facilities. There is certainly no lack of needed goods that converted defense plants might produce, especially products that require some of the same skills (and even some of the same machinery). In England, one of the most ambitious plans for military conversion, developed by workers at one of Britain's major defense contractors, Lucas Aerospace, identified 120 alternative products their plans might produce (Yudken and Goldenkranz, 1983, p. 5). In Massachusetts, workers at a General Dynamics shipyard, floundering because of reduced military and civilian orders, proposed using the facility to build floating plants to convert ocean thermal energy into electricity (such "plantships" are already being produced in Japan) (Meacham, 1983, p. 3). In southern

Despite growing protest, nuclear-weapons production continues to escalate.

California, workers at a McDonnell-Douglas aerospace plant identified a variety of alternative products that promise to be both marketable and feasible to produce within the plant, given some retooling and retraining — including commuter aircraft, mass transit vehicles, wheelchairs and other medical supplies, and energy-conservation equipment (Yudken and Goldenkranz, 1983, p. 5).

Recently, there have been several attempts to develop legislation to put the conversion of defense production on the political agenda. Though they vary in specifics, they focus on at least these priorities:

1. Providing assistance to workers and communities through retraining programs, income support, and help in developing plans for alternatives production

2. Establishing local committees, representing workers, management, and the community, to develop specific approaches for plant conversion

3. Providing for early notification of workers when the government plans to reduce or eliminate defense-related projects

So far, no such comprehensive conversion legislation has made it through Congress. But with the growing awareness of the excesses and uncertainties of our current pattern of defense spending, the search for alternatives is likely to remain a key public issue.

International Insecurity and the Prospects for Change

For many years there has been a tacit assumption in American social policy that when it comes to national defense, "more is better" — that a more effective defense means more money for armaments and, necessarily, less for other social purposes. We've seen how this attitude has affected the civilian economy and society. But one of the most important shifts in thinking about defense in recent years has been the growing awareness that this assumption has undermined the effectiveness of defense itself.

Thus, the choice often posed to the American public — between pouring ever more money into a "strong" defense and supporting the rest of society's needs — seems more and more to be a false one. "Throwing money" at defense *will* divert resources from other social

The Nuclear Balance

Shortly after World War II, a United States senator advised the president of the United States that public support for spending billions on massive increases in military strength wouldn't be possible without "scaring hell out of the country" (cited in Barnet, 1983, p. 448). In the 1980s, as in the 1950s, what "scares the hell out of the country" is what has come to be called the "Soviet threat." It is widely argued that a rapid military buildup by the Soviet Union has created an unprecedented threat to world peace and security — a threat that can be countered only if the United States rushes to catch up. This belief has fueled the massive increases in defense expenditures in recent years.

Addressing the complex history of Soviet/ American relations is a task far beyond the scope of this book. And comparing the strength and sophistication of American and Soviet military forces is itself a complicated science that has generated an enormous, highly technical literature. We won't, therefore, try to sort out all of these issues here. Instead, we will attempt the much more modest task of examining recent claims about the comparative buildup of nuclear weapons in the two countries — the most critical aspect of the presumed imbalance between Soviet and American military strength. (For some useful starting points on the wider issues of policy and military strategy, see the works by Holloway and by Barnet in the suggested readings at the end of this chapter.)

The dramatic increases in our own development of nuclear weapons have been justified on the ground that the "balance of forces" achieved after World War II has been "upset by the Soviet military buildup, which contrasts sharply with our own military restraint," as a U.S. State Department official put it in 1983 (Dam, 1983, p. 57). Is this an accurate assessment?

The evidence suggests that it isn't. It's certainly true that Soviet nuclear capacity increased significantly, and alarmingly, in recent years; but so did that of the United States. The most dramatic aspect of this buildup, on both sides, is the rising numbers of nuclear warheads (Table 12-5).

On balance, the United States is "ahead" in long-range bombers and in submarine-launched nuclear missiles, two of the "legs" of what in defense jargon has been called the triad of strategic nuclear weapons: those based on land, in aircraft, and at sea. The Soviet Union is "ahead" in the third leg, land-based missiles. One of the most important arguments for the rapid buildup of American nuclear forces in the 1980s has,

therefore, been the need to upgrade the land-based leg of the triad, through heavy investment in missile development.

But the number of nuclear weapons *already* capable of being delivered by the United States is enormous. A single Trident nuclear submarine carries enough nuclear warheads to destroy 192 Soviet cities. The Soviet navy's capacity to destroy American cities is not *quite* so far advanced: It would take three of their most modern submarines to demolish an equivalent number of American cities (Sigal, 1982, p. 57). To date, no effective technology exists on either side to locate and disable these missile-launching submarines. The result is that neither side is capable of stopping a devastating retaliation against even a completely successful attack on land-based nuclear weapons. Since, at any given point, some of these submarines are in port or otherwise out of commission, not all of these sea-based warheads are actually deliverable at any one time. But, by most estimates, this still leaves us with over 3,000 nuclear warheads that are now virtually incapable of being destroyed.

Table 12-5
The nuclear buildup: Total land, sea, and air-based nuclear warheads

Weapon	United States		Soviet Union	
	1972	1985	1972	1985
Land-based (on Intercontinental Ballistic Missiles — ICBMs)	1,254	2,126	1,510	6,420
Sea-based (on submarines — SLBMs)	1,232	5,728	440	2,124
Air-based (on long-range bombers)	NA	2,544	NA	1,000
1985 total		10,398		9,544

Note: NA means not available.
Source: Reprinted with permission from Leon V. Sigal, "Warming to the Freeze," in *Foreign Policy* 48 (fall 1982). Copyright 1982 by the Carnegie Endowment for International Peace.

goals, like providing stable jobs, building affordable housing, or rebuilding America's declining infrastructure. But it will *not* necessarily provide more security — even when security is defined in the narrow sense of military readiness (see Barnet, 1983).

There is a parallel here with the problem of rebuilding American industrial performance, which we discussed in Chapter 3. Simply boosting the amount of money that flows to American business won't rebuild economic vitality if it's used to speculate in real estate or buy other corporations. Similarly, the massive shift of government spending to defense corporations won't ensure national security if the funds

---

Arming the World

So far in this chapter we have been considering the impact of the military on *American* society. But the military role of the United States does not, of course, stop at our own borders. We are also the largest supplier of arms and military assistance to the rest of the world.

The United States supplies the military needs of other countries in three basic ways: sales of military equipment, grants and loans, and training programs for military personnel. American arms corporations can sell directly to foreign governments or foreign firms, particularly such smaller, "nuts and bolts" military products as small arms, ammunition, and spare parts. Most larger sales, especially of costly, sophisticated equipment like aircraft and missiles, are handled through the government's Foreign Military Sales program (FMS). Between 1950 and 1985, military sales totalled more than $108 billion worldwide. Four Middle Eastern countries — Saudi Arabia, Iran, Israel and Egypt — accounted for almost half that total (Table 12-6).

Until the late 1970s, the United States also poured considerable sums into outright military grants to foreign countries, about $55

Country	U.S. military sales deliveries (in billions of dollars)
Saudi Arabia	$30.2
Iran	10.8
Israel	9.1
West Germany	8.0
United Kingdom	4.4
Egypt	3.7
Australia	3.4
Taiwan	3.0
South Korea	2.9
Netherlands	2.9

Source: Data from *Statistical Abstract of the United States*, 1987, p. 324.

Table 12-6
The top ten buyers of American military goods, 1950–1985

billion between 1950 and 1985. But economic realities, among other factors, have caused a shift in policy. Outright military assistance has been increasingly replaced, partly by weapons sales and partly by loans enabling foreign governments to buy American military equipment. Finally, the United States has trained more than half a million foreign military personnel since 1950 under the International Military Education and Training Program (IMET), an enterprise that has cost more than $2 billion.

Who gets this military assistance — and what are the consequences? The American arms industry's foreign customers are an extraordinarily diverse group — and very numerous, indeed. In 1982 the United States sold arms through the FMS program to 96 nations. The two biggest cash customers in the past three decades have been Middle Eastern countries: Saudi Arabia and (until recently) Iran.

What is most troubling is that American arms sales and military assistance have helped support some of the world's most repressive governments — and also probably increased the risks of destructive war, especially in the Third World. According to the Center for Defense Information, the United States has been a key supplier of arms to 28 out of 41 military-dominated governments around the world with records of severe violations of human rights, including torture and arbitrary arrest (Center for Defense Information, 1982, p. 7). During the 1960s and 1970s, the United States trained more than 300,000 military personnel and transferred close to $30 billion in weapons to these countries, which include South Korea, Brazil, and El Salvador. In the late 1970s, some steps were taken by the American government to restrict arms sales to some of the worst human-rights offenders. But these restrictions have loosened in the 1980s.

It has been argued that removing such restrictions and boosting the level of foreign arms sales will both help the American economy and promote world peace and stability.

But the evidence suggests that this argument is wrong on both counts. Massive arms sales aggravate the distortion of the domestic economy already caused by a disproportionate emphasis on military production. And though foreign sales do bring some revenues into the domestic economy, the low-cost loans and remaining military grants offered to those countries to pay for the American arms represent a significant "hidden" expenditure (of the kind we described in Chapter 4) that diminishes the revenues available for other public uses.

And the impacts of arms sales on the foreign client nations themselves are far more troubling. Excessive spending for weapons drains their economies, especially those of some poorer countries of the Third World, making stable, long-term economic development more difficult. In some countries, the weapons and military skills purchased with American help are used in part to repress internal dissent. And the scale and sophistication of the weapons we sell virtually ensures that any military conflict that *does* arise in tense regions of the world will be far more destructive than it would otherwise have been — especially since the United States and its allies sometimes arm *both* sides of potential conflicts (consider Saudi Arabia and Israel, Iran and Iraq, Turkey and Greece).

The usual justification for increasing arms sales and military assistance to foreign countries is that doing so will boost America's influence around the world. But a glance back at the history of two decades and more of military aid should help put this claim in perspective. In the 1970s, the second-largest consumer of American arms was Iran; the second largest consumer of American military assistance was South Vietnam. Obviously, arming these two countries did *not* produce the hoped-for results. It's important to note that the record of the Soviet Union in cementing *its* world influence through arms transfers is almost equally dismal: One of its biggest arms clients after World War II was the People's Republic of China.

are spent to buy elaborate planes that rarely fly or weapons that don't fire.

But the gap between spending and performance in defense, though deeply troubling, has its positive side, too. It opens up the possibility that some of the resources we now devote to a mistermed "defense" effort could be shifted to alternative uses *without* jeopardizing the legitimate demands of a military that works.

Still, the prospects for doing this aren't bright without larger changes in the way the United States approaches its role in the wider world. We've, somewhat artificially, kept that issue out of our discussion in this chapter (it would take at least another book to do justice to the intricacies of foreign policy; some useful leads may be found in the suggested further readings). Still, some general comments are appropriate — and hard to avoid.

As we argued in Chapter 1, the international situation has changed considerably in the past few decades. From the viewpoint of the United States, the world has become in many ways a more volatile, less controllable place. Old balances of economic and military power have shifted, once-dependent parts of the world have begun to flex their political muscles, and the longstanding technological superiority of the United States has been eroded. There are two broad possible responses to these changes. We can adapt to the changed realities,

Given the vastly increased destructive power of nuclear weapons, there may be few — if any — survivors of the next nuclear war.

Martha Tabor/Picture Group

maintain sufficient defensive capacity to cope with the genuine threats an unstable world produces, and also relinquish the idea that we can remold the rest of the world to our liking. Or we can take on the unpromising job of trying to turn back the clock to reassert American power over the destiny of other countries through the threat of military force.

Given what we know about the irrationality and excess of current patterns of defense spending, the first response would very likely allow us to achieve, over time, both a more efficient, truly *defensive* defense *and* a more equitable, more productive use of social resources in civilian society. The second response commits us to building an elaborate, expensive — and terribly perilous — military presence whose purpose is more to project a symbolic image of America's "will" and "strength" than to defend us against realistic threats from other countries.

Ultimately, deciding on a rational approach to defense strategy means that we need to place our concerns about the military in the broader framework of the kind of society we want to build. As Mary Kaldor has argued, "Practical aims, like getting rid of certain weapons or initiating experiments of industrial conversion, need to be located in a wider vision of the future to which we aspire" (1981, p. 23). In Chapter 13, we'll examine some of the different approaches to that future that have emerged on the political stage in recent years.

Summary

This chapter has examined national defense as a social problem, focusing on the social and economic impacts of defense spending and military priorities in the United States.

Military spending has grown rapidly in recent years, and it takes a far larger share of available budget resources than is often assumed.

Compared to most other industrial societies, the United States devotes a much greater portion of its resources to national defense. Research suggests that this has several negative effects:

1. Though military spending does create employment, it creates *fewer* jobs than most other kinds of spending.

2. Rising defense spending has diminished funds available for other purposes, such as rebuilding the country's infrastructure.

3. Military spending hinders economic performance by shifting skills, research, and capital away from nonmilitary industries.

The high cost of defense results, in part, from wasteful and inefficient practices built into the military-industrial complex, such as lack of competition and cost-plus contracting. In addition, the equipment that the defense dollar buys is not only expensive but often also cumbersome and ineffective.

The evidence suggests that it's possible to reduce military spending without damaging national defense. Some approaches include putting a cap on increases in the defense budget, reducing cost overruns, and stopping (or greatly reducing) the production of nuclear weapons.

For Further Reading

Barnet, Richard. *Real Security.* New York: Simon and Schuster, 1981.

DeGrasse, Robert. *Military Expansion, Economic Decline.* New York: Council on Economic Priorities, 1983b.

Fallows, James. *National Defense.* New York: Random House, 1982.

Holloway, David. *The Soviet Union and the Arms Race.* New Haven, Conn.: Yale University Press, 1983.

Kaldor, Mary. *Baroque Arsenal.* New York: Hill and Wang, 1981.

13

Strategies for Social Policy

As we near the twenty-first century, there is an unusual amount of agreement that the social policies of the past 30 to 40 years will no longer suffice to deal with America's problems in the future. The model of social and economic organization based on the economic expansion we enjoyed during the period after World War II was often regarded as an inevitable fact of life. But we can understand now, with the advantage of hindsight, that it was a temporary condition made possible by a fleeting combination of several factors: America's dominance of the international economy; the ready availability of cheap petroleum-based energy; and the still relatively uncluttered natural environment, which, up to a point, absorbed the ecological byproducts of unreflective affluence like a giant sponge.

As we've seen, troubling problems revealed themselves even when that postwar development was at its peak. There was nagging unemployment, high rates of crime and violence, harsh inequalities of race, class, and gender, and the less measurable but equally disturbing coexistence of what the economist John Kenneth Galbraith (1957) described as "private affluence and public squalor." But America's commanding position in the world's economy, coupled with its abundant and seemingly inexhaustible natural resources, acted as a kind of buffer that allowed us to put off reckoning with the larger implications of those problems.

420

Many elements of America's infrastructure are rapidly decaying.

There's now little disagreement that the terms and conditions of American life are changing — and that the only social policies that are likely to be effective will be those that come to terms with those changes: the growing economic role of other countries, the limits of nonrenewable resources, and the limits to the capacity of the human and natural environments to absorb unchecked growth. It's increasingly understood that these changes force choices on us that we have been able to dodge up to now with some success — choices about economic growth versus ecological health, about the distribution of social and economic resources among different groups, and about the balance between private and public needs. And, within the category of public needs, there is the further choice between the social programs of the welfare state and the claims of military spending. In turn, these choices force us to rethink some basic concepts whose meanings may have been taken too much for granted in the past — concepts like growth, security, costs, and welfare. How we define

Strategies for Social Policy **421**

these terms and how those definitions are put into practice are a good part of what social policy is about. And here, of course, the agreement ends.

Strategies for Social Policy

Obviously, it would take another book even to begin to describe the range of ideas for social change stimulated by America's recent problems. But within the bewildering variety of proposals for dealing with particular problems, we can discern some larger themes that lead to fairly distinct *strategies* for approaching social problems. In this chapter, we will sketch the outlines of three such strategies that are now shaping much of the debate over specific social policies. We will outline their most important principles and underlying assumptions — and to suggest what we think, on the basis of the research we've examined so far, may be some of their probable social consequences.

Generalizing about these strategies is inevitably a little risky. In the real world of social action and social policy, such broad themes are only rarely clear-cut or mutually exclusive. The three broad strategies should therefore be considered examples of what one of the founders of modern sociology, Max Weber, called "ideal types": abstractions that help us illuminate the essential features of more complex and subtle realities (Gerth and Mills, 1954). We've already encountered all three strategies at various points in this book. If we now draw out their premises more explicitly, they may provide a framework that can help us understand a variety of more specific policy issues in the 1980s.

The Strategy of Reprivatization

The first strategy calls for what we may term a *reprivatization* of social and economic life. We call it "reprivatization" because it takes the form of demands to reduce the role of government in the economy and in society as a whole in favor of greater reliance on market forces or free enterprise. But, as we've argued before, this is somewhat misleading. More accurately, this strategy has meant making government the powerful, if sometimes hidden, partner of those private

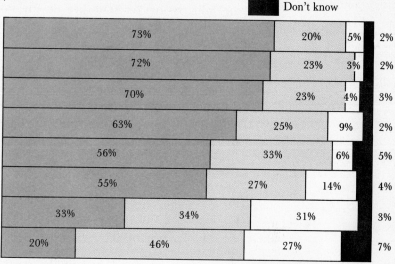

Role government should play in. . .

	Major role	Minor role	No role	Don't know

Seeing to it that all Americans get good health care: 73% | 20% | 5% | 2%

Protecting the environment: 72% | 23% | 3% | 2%

Encouraging economic development: 70% | 23% | 4% | 3%

Seeing to it that there are enough good jobs: 63% | 25% | 9% | 2%

Fostering basic research: 56% | 33% | 6% | 5%

Helping American business compete with foreign business: 55% | 27% | 14% | 4%

Increasing the number of blacks and minorities in good jobs: 33% | 34% | 31% | 3%

Fostering the arts: 20% | 46% | 27% | 7%

Figure 13-1
Public attitudes toward the role of government

Source: Public Opinion, February-March 1982, p. 39. Reprinted with permission of American Enterprise Institute for Public Policy Research.

economic interests considered most able to produce the benefits of economic growth (Lindblom, 1977).

As we've seen in earlier chapters, few segments of the American business community are genuinely opposed to using the resources and power of government or even to large-scale government spending. The important differences in contemporary debates about social policy are mainly over what government is *for*. (For one portrait of how the *public* regards the proper role of government, see Figure 13-1.) Whether the specific issue at hand is energy policy or national security or the supply of medical care, the vision of the strategy of reprivatization is *not* a return to a presumed golden age of small-scale, genuinely competitive capitalism with government a distinctly minor character in the drama of social and economic life. Instead, this strategy is rooted in the belief that the vast resources of the modern state should be channeled toward *some* social ends rather than others. What are those ends?

A "Military-Market State"?

Social critics in the 1960s often warned against the growth of what they called the "welfare-warfare state" — a phrase that described the uneasy combination of the expansion of domestic social programs on the one hand and of massive military spending on the other. Today, the strategy of reprivatization aims at what we could call the "military-market state."

Unlike the architects of the welfare-warfare state, the supporters of the military-market state are deeply hostile to most social welfare spending. Government — despite rhetoric to the contrary — remains of crucial importance to this strategy. But its purpose is seen as mainly strengthening the country's capacity for warfare and reasserting American economic and political influence in the international arena. These goals require a shift of public spending away from many domestic social programs to the military and to those private corporations whose prosperity is now inseparable from government defense spending.

On the domestic front, reprivatization means more than just the frugal trimming of overblown social program budgets or reducing "waste" and "abuse" in these programs. If this was *all* it meant, not many would disagree with it. Most public bureaucracies (like most private ones) can certainly stand some trimming, tightening, and an occasional shaking-up. But this strategy involves something much more fundamental; its long-term goal is to greatly reduce the scope of the institutions developed in the past half-century to cushion the impact of economic forces on individuals and communities.

The social changes in the welfare state that this strategy proposes are profound. The growth of domestic social programs over the past several decades has been based on the principle that modern societies bear some responsibility for the well-being of their members regardless of what happens to them and their families in the economic market. Slowly, often grudgingly, American society has made important strides in that direction, as this book has shown.

The length of those strides shouldn't be overstated, as we've *also* shown. We remain the *least* developed of modern welfare states. We lag behind most other industrial societies in workplace health and safety, in child-care provisions, in cushions against the ravages of unemployment, in accessible and affordable health care. We are more unequal in the spread of personal income than almost every other developed country — mainly, as we saw in Chapter 4, because we allow more severe poverty at the bottom. We have few of the mechanisms for worker participation in decisions affecting their jobs that are now common in many European countries and Japan (see pages 434 to 435). We are already, in short, a far more "privatized" society than most and have been much slower to recognize the obligations and the benefits of a more caring and conserving approach to our human resources.

Yet our recent accomplishments along this line shouldn't be taken lightly. For all its (very real) limits and imperfections, the rudimentary American welfare state has brought many important changes in American life. Traces of those changes have appeared again and again in the statistics we've presented — numbers that, however coldly, represent some of the life and death realities of our society. These include the dramatic decreases in infant mortality and other life-threatening health problems, attributable in part to publicly supported preventive health care; a better life for many of the aged, partly the result of better social benefits and improvements in the quality and delivery of medical care; the achievement of safer, more healthful workplaces through more effective social regulation; and much more.

But not everyone agrees that these benefits have been a good thing. Some believe that they've simply been too expensive — a drain on the economy and an obstacle to growth. Others go further, arguing that it isn't society's responsibility to protect people against the risks of economic life — that we've already gone too far in this direction and that if we go farther we'll make everyone poorer in the long run. Some argue that it's only the fear of failure and deprivation that keeps people working hard; as one writer who supports these sentiments put it, "What the poor need most is the spur of their poverty" (Gilder, 1981, p. 118). In many ways, this view echoes the Social Darwinism of the nineteenth century — the sometimes chilling vision of a social world organized single-mindedly around interpersonal competition in which only the "fittest" will (or should) survive. "How could adaptation take place," wrote one social scientist partial to this view, "if some behaviors and organisms do not die? Is it being suggested that everything live forever? . . . *Neither everything nor everyone can survive*" (Wildavsky, 1980, p. 36).

As we've seen, however, many of those who argue that the poor should be "spurred" by their poverty and insecurity, or that industrial workers ought willingly to accept greater risks to their health in the workplace in the name of economic growth, are *also* among those who clamor the loudest for a variety of cushions and protections — subsidies for investment, cost-plus contracts for defense production, emergency funding to stave off business failure — to shield private corporations from the consequences of their actions. The real issue is not whether protection against economic risks is itself a bad thing — but *whose* risks are to be considered, and who gets to choose.

What are the *consequences* of the strategy of reprivatization for American life — for the strength of the economy, the health of families, individuals, and communities; the quality of the environment? The answers aren't yet all in, but the evidence so far is troubling.

The Consequences of Reprivatization

As we've seen (especially in Chapter 3), even on economic terms alone, a strategy of stimulating the private economy — "throwing money" at those who already have it — does *not* necessarily bring useful growth. Instead, it may lead to the diversion of human resources, capital, and energy into nonproductive uses — into what Robert Reich calls "paper entrepreneurship" (1983) and other critics described as a taste for short-term profit rather than long-term productivity (Faux, 1986, p. 193).

We've seen a great deal of this in recent years — companies buying other companies, often abandoning useful production in favor of takeovers and speculation. All of this activity is counted as part of our GNP, just as more productive economic enterprise is. But not much, if anything, actually gets produced. Our problems of high unemployment, declining competitiveness, and a shaky standard of living aren't helped.

Above all, this approach hasn't been able to address the deeper questions about the *quality* of economic growth. It cannot distinguish between the social and economic virtues of an economy based on fast-food franchises and T-shirt shops and one providing stable, rewarding work and useful services. And its proponents have not, so far, been able to come up with clear answers to questions about how our finite natural resources and environment will be preserved in the face of uncontrolled economic growth.

Even beyond these issues of economics and ecology are other questions about the potential *social* impacts of the strategy of reprivatization. In the introduction to this book, we noted that one of the most important contributions of social science to the analysis of social problems is its emphasis on the *social* dimension — on the complex interconnections of groups, communities, and institutions that make up the fabric of a society. What's striking about what we've called the strategy of reprivatization is its *lack* of this sense of the complexity of the social world — its unfortunate tendency to reduce nearly all social problems to narrowly understood questions of "economics" and, as a result, to ignore or dismiss the social consequences of economic policies.

One very likely consequence of this strategy, for example, is increased social *inequality*. The strategy is *based*, in part, on the argument that inequality is a "good thing," a necessary precondition for economic growth and for ensuring that incentives will work. In turn, economic growth will, the strategy's advocates contend, bring sufficient jobs and income to provide the basis for a healthy social order. "A rising tide," as the economic platitude goes, "lifts all boats." The trouble is that it clearly *doesn't*, under modern social and technological conditions — a fact emphasized by the conservative economist Her-

The benefits of the private economy do not "trickle down" to all Americans.

bert Stein. "It is not sufficient to say that a rising tide lifts all boats," Stein wrote (1982a, p. 50). "It is not true."

Undirected economic growth cannot, by itself, draw all of the poor, the jobless, and the displaced into productive work or ensure them an adequate living standard, for reasons we've touched on in Chapters 4, 5, 6, and 8. Many of the poor are members of groups (welfare mothers, older people, teenagers without salable skills, for example) that have not been effectively pulled into the economy in the past, even in periods of "prosperity." Others (like some displaced industrial workers) are among the "new poor" who, though once sought after for their skills, won't be hired for rewarding work without substantial retraining. And, as we saw in Chapter 8, this problem will be aggravated by the continuing impact of automation in industry and the office. We don't yet know exactly how that impact will make itself felt. But it seems clear that without more attention to job training and retraining, this technological change will sharpen the inequalities between those who, through luck, pluck, or skill, have a foothold in the emerging economy of the coming decades and those who do not.

As in the past, a disproportionate number of the latter are destined to come from the ranks of minorities and women if the strategy of reprivatization prevails. Though it has become fashionable to argue that the worst enemy of minority progress has been "government" and that the best hope for minorities is the removal of such government-created barriers as affirmative action programs (Williams, 1982), the evidence shows that the opposite is the case. We might all *wish* for a society in which access to equal employment, earnings, and educational opportunities comes naturally as a result of the market's even-handed rewarding of individual abilities and motivation. American society, however, is not — and never was — that society of happy abstraction.

A good part of the progress made by minorities in the 1960s and early 1970s (as we saw in Chapter 5) was the result of the expansion of the public sector in general and of antidiscrimination programs in particular. Thus, even for many of the relatively affluent among the minority middle class, a strategy of reprivatization could bring substantial suffering and the prospect of downward mobility. But for many of the minority poor and near-poor, it promises something like disaster. Forced to the margins of economic and social life even when the economy has performed reasonably well, the innner-city minority poor are unlikely to be lifted from that condition simply by more of the same. And if this gloomy prospect holds for the poor generally, it holds doubly for poor women maintaining families, for whom the lack of adequate child care and the still-segregated labor market combine to add extra obstacles to their chances of success.

This tendency to increase social inequality suggests that the strategy of reprivatization has a troubling potential for generating social conflict between those groups with a realistic chance at the "good life" and those without (U.S. Commission on Civil Rights, 1982). A society that offers harsh and bleak futures to a wide stratum of its people — especially its young — while holding out the lure of ever-increasing consumption for others, is not a society that can ensure public order for long. We learned this painfully in the 1960s. The lesson may be equally agonizing in the 1990s and beyond, if this strategy prevails (Currie, 1987).

One response to these issues has been the argument that the plight of many of the poor is the result of a decline in moral values brought on in large part by the welfare state itself (Gilder, 1981; Murray, 1985). "Permissiveness," in this view, has been mainly responsible for the growth of families headed by women and for other social problems among minorities and the poor. From this perspective, what's needed is not more income supports or public services that only encourage the breakup of families, but the enforcement of traditional morality among the poor. Indeed, a characteristic of the reprivatization strategy is that it often seeks to resolve a host of social problems by *increasing* the role of the state in the enforcement of private morality. The fact that this conflicts philosophically with the idea of reducing the role of government hasn't stopped it from being a major theme for partisans of the strategy. They seem more interested in shifting the government's focus from the boardroom to the bedroom than in reducing government's ability to control behavior.

The Strategy of Revitalization

A second broad strategy for dealing with America's social problems in the 1980s is distinguished from the first primarily by its emphasis on the need for a certain amount of government economic planning. We call this the strategy of "revitalization" because its major theme is the need to revitalize the American economy — usually through a partnership between business, government, and labor — in order to increase its productivity and competitiveness. But it also has much broader implications.

Proponents of this approach realize that modern societies are increasingly interdependent systems that require a substantial degree of planning and coordination. Moreover, they recognize that planning done wholly under *private* auspices is unlikely to add up to a coherent effective social policy. They also emphasize the importance of the careful cultivation of human resources for a society's health and are critical of the more simplistic versions of "market ideology" for failing to adequately understand "the importance of human capital for America's future" (Reich, 1983, p. 108).

From this perspective, one of the main reasons America has lost ground in the economic race to countries like West Germany and especially Japan is that the latter have been much better at training and motivating workers as well as making more efficient use of their physical resources. And those countries have also, in this view, been much better at directing economic investment into areas promising long-run productive gains as opposed to the short-run search for profit that has dominated American management.

Because of this, it's argued that what is most needed to recreate American prosperity are new mechanisms of planning and coordination of the economy. In this model, business, government, and labor would enter into a partnership to promote American industry's ability to "win" in international competition. Without some explicit direction and planning, in this view, we will not have a truly productive economy — nor, by implication, a healthy society. Proponents of this strategy understand that sheer growth, as measured by gross national product, is a misleading indicator of economic and social health: It masks too much waste, too much unproductive activity (such as corporations buying other corporations), and too much mere shifting of assets from one firm to another. They are, accordingly, critical of the belief that simply offering ever-greater incentives for private investment will revitalize the American economy. As Robert Reich (1983, p. 107) noted, "It is no secret that the rich are likely to spend large chunks of any new income on Persian carpets, rare paintings, antiques, yachts, luxury cars and vacations" — none of which contribute to sound economic growth.

Instead, this strategy places most of its bets on targeting private investment into more productive uses, particularly through supporting the development of what are sometimes called "sunrise" industries — those that, like microelectronics, genetic engineering, and robotics, appear (at this point) to be the most promising future winners in the international arena. In this view, channeling investment to these industries, changing the tax system to reward productive investment rather than paper profit-making, and investing more heavily in education and training to develop a more sophisticated labor force would lead to a revitalized economy and the return of prosperity — though not, perhaps, the level America enjoyed before the 1970s (Democratic Caucus, 1982; Thurow, 1986).

Given the troubles of the American economy in the 1980s, this vision has a strong appeal — and its critique of the irrationality of American economic policy and its destructive effects on the fabric of society strikes home. It seems likely that *some* kind of approach to public/private planning for economic revitalization will be a major item on the social policy agenda in America for years to come. But this approach also raises a number of troubling social questions.

Revitalization for Whom?

Perhaps the greatest problem with the revitalization strategy is that it generally accepts, without much reflection, the premise that boosting the private economy will bring about a whole range of beneficial *social* consequences. It shares with more traditional ideologies the idea that jobs, income, and an enhanced community life will "trickle down" from the growth of the private economy. It differs, as we've noted, in its belief that some government planning and coordination with business and labor are necessary to achieve that growth, but the assumption that growth will lead naturally to other social benefits remains central. Like the strategy of reprivatization, this approach often seems too enamored of purely economic solutions to social problems and insufficiently concerned with the changing social and technological context of economic life.

One crucial problem can be illustrated by an example. During the early 1980s, some politicians who supported high-tech reindustrialization as a response to America's problems became known as "Atari Democrats" (from the computer corporation best known for its elaborate video games). As one of the most phenomenal examples of the rapid growth of the microelectronics industry in the 1970s, Atari seemed an appropriate symbol for a strategy of social and industrial revitalizaton. But in early 1983, Atari shut down some of its operations in California's Silicon Valley, shipping the production of many components — and thus several hundred California jobs — to the Far East.

The lesson is that there is no good reason to believe that the new industries won't follow the route of older ones in search of lower labor costs and the other advantages of moving abroad. Nor, as we saw in Chapter 8, can we be sure that investment in these industries will generate substantial numbers of good jobs even if they *do* remain within American borders. The technology of many of these industries is impressive, but much of it is designed precisely to *eliminate* jobs, not

High-speed railways, like those in France and Japan, could become an important new industry in the United States.

create them; so even a booming industry is no longer a guarantee of adequate livelihoods for many Americans.

A strategy based so thoroughly on boosting America's ability to compete in the international economy raises other questions as well. Beating other countries at the competitive game often means sacrificing a great deal — particularly since some of our new competitors are low-wage Third World countries with the economic "advantages" of minimal environmental or workplace regulations. Success in such competition often implies a deliberate reduction of the standard of living of *some* groups in order to raise capital for private industry. From this perspective, revitalizing the American economy — especially in the inner cities — may require rolling back many of the hard-won gains of working people, such as minimum wages and workplace regulations (*Business Week*, 1980d). If the past is any guide, the burdens of such a strategy would fall hardest on those groups in American society that are already the poorest and most dependent on public services, such as urban minorities and women.

But it is not clear that, even on its own terms, this strategy can work — if that means sucessfully competing in the world market with countries that provide even *lower* wages, even *fewer* public services, and even *less* stringent social regulations than we could reasonably achieve. And it is even less clear that the kind of society we would create by trying to beat Third World nations at their own game would be one much worth striving for. Advocates of this strategy often tend to agree with those of reprivatization that "if we maximize justice we destroy the conditions of economic growth" (Tsongas, 1981, cited in Harrington, 1982a, p. 413). The lack of evidence for that view hasn't greatly weakened its appeal among political leaders searching for ways of justifying the imposition of a new austerity on some social groups, but not others. An editorial in *Business Week* at the beginning of the 1980s, for example, explicitly declared that the creation of what it called a new "social contract" to boost American industry's productivity "must take precedence over the aspirations of the poor, the minorities, and the environmentalists" (1980d, p. 146). And a noted sociologist similarly argued that reversing America's "industrial obsolescence" in the future would require us to diminish our concern for the "quality of life" — including such social goals as national health insurance, better air and water quality, public support for education, and child care (Etzioni, 1980).

What we've called the strategy of revitalization, in short, often rests on a vision of social life in which many social goals are deliberately sacrificed in the name of improving productivity and international competitiveness. "The world is becoming a race course," one enthusiast wrote, "in which the first producer to gain a dominant share of a new market is able to maintain a lead in future markets, because it enjoys higher profits than its rivals . . ." (Reich, 1983, p. 104). But one problem with regarding the world as an economic race course is that not enough attention is paid to the effects of that "race" on individuals and their communities.

Like reprivatization, this vision often seems a narrowly economic one that views the economy as an abstract system of exchanges, detached from its roots in living human communities. Many advocates argue that declining industries, cities, and even regions should be allowed to "die" so that investment may be channeled to new, more dynamic regions and more promising industries. Presumably, people who are displaced or made jobless will simply move to where new opportunities are. But even if that were true, the result would often be the disruption of established ways of life and the fragmentation of entire communities. The potential human and financial costs — ranging from increased welfare dependency to crime, family violence, and health problems — are rarely accounted for on the balance sheet of revitalization (Bluestone and Harrison, 1982).

Despite its tough-mindedness about some of the recent failings of the American economy, then, this approach is sometimes remarkably myopic about the *social* consequences of economic change and about the limited ability of economic growth to ensure, by itself, other fundamental social values. The view of social life as a race course implies that some will win and some will lose. But this perspective is often uncomfortably silent both about what will happen to the losers — and about what lies at the end of the race.

The Strategy of Social Reconstruction

A third strategy toward America's problems is distinguished by its central emphasis on just those social values and concerns that tend to be ignored or downplayed by the other two strategies. Because of this emphasis, we call it a strategy of *social reconstruction*. It includes, but also moves beyond, the pursuit of economic competitiveness.

Like the others, this strategy recognizes that a productive economy is a necessary foundation for any successful attempt to cope with most social problems (Faux, 1986). And it also recognizes, like the others, that there has been a considerable waste and irrationality in some of the programs of the welfare state. Like the strategy of revitalization, it emphasizes the need for more, rather than less, conscious planning of economic life. As the economist Jeff Faux put it, "National economic policy remains the only significant organized human activity in America where planning ahead is considered irrational" (1982, p. 12). But the strategy also goes further. Less convinced that the social goals of equality, democratic participation, individual well-being, environmental health, and community stability will necessarily be accomplished through economic growth alone, it puts these ends *first*. It thus seeks to tailor economic policies and programs explicitly to social goals, rather than the other way around.

Since these goals may or may not coincide with the search for private profit, such a strategy leads to a much more explicit role for *public* investment and for *public* participation in economic decisions. The means proposed to achieve this extension of democratic norms to

---

Controlling the New Technology: Some Experiments from Europe and Japan

Some of the most profound issues for social policy in the next decade will be those surrounding the development of new technologies in the workplace. Computer-based, microelectronic technology has already had a powerful impact on the nature of work and the problem of unemployment in America, and that impact is certain to be even greater in the future. Yet there has been little effort to develop policies to govern the introduction of these new technologies or to control their social consequences. Like many other social concerns, the impact of revolutionary new technologies has usually not been considered a proper object of deliberate policy in the United States. Our approach has been to leave decisions about technology almost entirely up to the discretion of private employers, while allowing the social costs of those decisions — such as unemployment and its destructive impact on families and individuals — to be borne by society as a whole.

But America may be able to learn a great deal from the experience of other countries. Many of these countries have developed innovative policies that help prevent some of the adverse effects of technological change by giving workers considerably more control over its direction and impact.

Much of the impetus for these policies has come from unions. While the unions accept the need for new technologies, they have also insisted that changes be introduced in ways that enhance rather than diminish workers' skills and working conditions and that maintain jobs and wages. European and Japanese unions have been successful in sparking legislation and agreements with employers that improve workers' access to information about proposed new technical developments and give them a voice in determining how these will be implemented.

In Sweden and Norway, workers have won legislation giving them the right to full information about any new technology planned for their workplace. The Norwegian "data agreement" gives workers access to company data banks and all other information available to a company's board of directors and gives them the right to attend company board meetings. Unions may veto proposed technological changes that could be harmful to workers' safety and health. Workers in several countries (including England, West Germany, Sweden, and Norway) can partici-

the economy vary widely. They include a stronger role for national-level government economic planning. But they may also include other mechanisms for public influence over economic policy, such as worker ownership of some industries and representation of workers or labor representatives on boards of directors, workplace health and safety committees, and other important functions now usually under private control (Harrington, 1986).

We saw in Chapter 2 that the United States is unique among other advanced industrial societies in the relatively small role played by the public sector in the economy — and the extent to which fundamental decisions about investment and economic priorities are concentrated

pate in government- or union-sponsored training programs on new technology, subsidized by special government funds or by employer contributions. (In the United States, any such training must be paid for by workers themselves, through their unions.) Scandinavian, German, and British workers also have access to government funding to develop consulting programs with outside technical experts, such as computer specialists and engineers, of their own choosing.

This access to information on new technologies gives European workers the tools to engage successfully in "technology bargaining" — negotiating with employers over the nature and purposes of new techniques before they are put in place. Thus, German metal workers have won a contract provision guaranteeing that they will not lose income through technological changes in their jobs; Norwegian telephone workers won the right to block new computerized technology that would eliminate jobs or worsen working conditions; a German union of bank workers won a provision forbidding the layoff of workers as a result of technological change. And workers at the Nissan Motor Company in Japan won an agreement that the introduction of new technology wouldn't result in layoffs or wage reductions and that the company would provide retraining and health and safety protection for those employees

who would need them because of the new technology (Klay, 1987, p. 39).

The principle behind these policies is not simply resistance to change for its own sake; the goal is to minimize the social and personal *costs* of such change and to broaden the control over the nature and pace of technological innovation beyond the hands of employers. The contrast between this and the American practice is illustrated in an example of the computerization of machine operators' jobs in Norway and the United States. According to the labor writers Steve Early and Matt Witt, workers in an aircraft parts plant in Norway were given full information in advance about a proposed installation of computer-based machine tools. This enabled them to successfully demand, not that the new tools be rejected, but that the existing machine operators be trained to program and repair them. In a similar situation in a plant in Massachusetts, workers were neither consulted nor given a voice in the introduction of automated machine tools. As a result, the programming and repairing are done by specialized programmers or supervisors, and the machinists have had to settle for lower pay, less challenging work as mere "button pushers," and the prospect of losing their jobs altogether (Early and Witt, 1982).

in private hands. We've encountered this difference, in many ways, throughout this book: in national differences in policies governing health care, employment and training, energy conservation, the regulation of occupational hazards, and much more. Bringing the United States closer to the practice of most other industrial societies is a central thrust of the strategy of social reconstruction. For example, the strategy often calls for a significant expansion of public-sector enterprises, common in many other industrial countries, to ensure investment in areas typically neglected by private industry, such as mass transit and alternative energy development (Carnoy and Shearer, 1980, chap. 2; Faux, 1986, p. 199). It also calls for legislation at both federal and state levels to reduce the arbitrariness of private investment decisions — legislation, for example, for closer regulation of industrial wastes and for advance notification of plant closings (Bluestone and Harrison, 1982, chap. 8).

At least four major themes underlie many of the specific policies offered by proponents of what we've called the strategy of social reconstruction: assuring full employment, reducing the inequalities of race and gender, investing in human resources, and changing the balance of military and domestic spending. Let's consider each in turn.

Assuring Full Employment   The crucial role of unemployment and *inadequate* employment in shaping many of America's problems (from racial inequality to family violence and ill-health) has appeared again and again in the preceding chapters. And, on the surface, there's not much disagreement in America today that dealing with the devastating joblessness that has wracked American society in recent years must be a main priority for social policy.

But this superficial agreement conceals dramatic disagreements about what full employment *means,* not to mention how it should be achieved. Proponents of rebuilding American society through unleashing the "forces of the market" have often opted for deliberately *increasing* unemployment on the ground that, however painful, it will help create the conditions for economic growth. Those who argue for a strategy of revitalization tend to believe that full employment will come as a natural by-product of government-stimulated growth of competitive industries. The limits of the first strategy in producing full employment are obvious. And from all the evidence we've examined, the second strategy's ability to provide adequate work for all is problematic, at best.

Recognizing these limitations, the strategy of social reconstruction emphasizes that full employment will require a commitment to *public* as well as private job creation (Harrington, 1986). Where the private sector fails to produce adequate jobs, public jobs will need to be created if we want to avoid the systematic waste of human resources, the disruption of personal and community life, and the aggravation of social inequality that massive unemployment and underemployment generate.

In the United States, public job creation has often been dismissed as somehow inferior to private employment. As we saw in Chapter 8, government-supported jobs are often regarded as useless make-work. But it isn't clear why, say, a public school teacher's job is less serious than that of, say, someone who sells used cars. It's also sometimes difficult even to *distinguish* public from private employment. What is the difference, for example, between working as a meter-reader for a public utility company or a private one, between working as a nurse in a public health clinic or in a private hospital?

As we've seen, countries like Sweden and Austria, which have very low unemployment rates and have weathered the economic troubles of the last several years very well, have achieved economic success partly through extensive public intervention in the labor market, including public job creation and extensive job training and retraining programs. And opinion surveys have shown that, since the 1930s, the vast majority of Americans have believed that the government should provide jobs for all those who want them.

A basic premise of the strategy of social reconstruction is that high unemployment represents a failure to make the most rational use of our human resources, not a lack of necessary work to be done. (Some concrete suggestions on where such useful work could be found are offered in the proposals from the Joint Economic Committee of Congress, pages 441 to 443.) But many kinds of necessary work do *not* usually get done under private auspices because they are not regarded as sufficiently profitable, at least in the short-range calculations of American private industry. Because of this, the strategy of social reconstruction emphasizes the crucial importance of supplementing the decisions of the private labor market with public investment to create permanent jobs.

A strategy for full employment, from this perspective, is perhaps the most important step toward reducing America's systematic inequalities of class, race, and gender. As the economist Robert Lekachman pointed out, "Full employment is the most efficient agent of equitable income redistribution" that is possible "within the parameters of market capitalism." He noted that, for several reasons, it is a strong catalyst for social equality:

Overcoming Inequality

New strategies for social change will involve increasingly complicated trade-offs.

Full employment sucks into the labor force individuals who now strive desperately to survive on welfare, food stamps, Social Security and unemployment compensation. Full employment improves wages for low-paid workers whose financial situation is only slightly less precarious than that of the unemployed. It is a particular boon to blacks, Hispanics, teenagers, and women, last hired in good times and first fired in recessions. . . . Full employment would substantially narrow the existing indefensibly wide differentials between the earnings of those groups and those of white males. (Lekachman, 1982, p. 201).

But even sustained full employment will not, by itself, guarantee the equal treatment of women and minorities in jobs, education, or other American institutions. For minorities, this became clear in the 1960s: Although we achieved something approaching full employment on the national level, the minority population continued to face high rates of unemployment and income inequality. And, as we've seen in Chapters 6 and 7, the barriers of inadequate child care, sex-segregated labor markets, and traditional sex roles in the family will conspire to perpetuate gender inequality even in full-employment economy.

Nor can we expect the inequalities of gender and race to be wiped out magically by the uncontrolled operation of the market system. After all, these inequalities were even more entrenched in the United States *before* government intervention in the market was so much as a gleam in the bureaucratic eye. Thus, the strategy of social reconstruction recognizes that the position of minorities and women reflects deeply rooted traditions in America that will not simply wither away without deliberate social action. A commitment to reducing these inequalities therefore means that explicit antidiscrimination measures, as well as extensive child care and other public supports that acknowledge the changing roles of American women, must have a central place in the social policy agenda for the future.

Investing in Human Resources

What we've called the strategy of social reconstruction also emphasizes that the welfare state is here to stay. No social order can do without some systematic provision for the ill, the disabled, the very young, and the very old — a principle increasingly acknowledged even by serious conservatives (Will, 1983). And, as we've seen in this book, a number of social changes have made the extension of *public* provision for these needs even more crucial.

One such change is the aging of the population. As we have learned to lengthen the life span, we will also have to learn to accept the responsibility to provide well for an increasing proportion of people who are past the age when they can reasonably be expected to support themselves in the labor force. Similarly, the changing pattern of labor-force participation among American women (especially coupled with the growing number of women heading families) creates greater responsibilities for the provision of child care, income supports, and more flexible approaches to work time.

It has sometimes been argued that these needs should, ideally, be taken care of within the family rather than by government. Or, in the case of women in the labor force and the needs of children in families headed by women, that these needs wouldn't exist if the traditional family had not been eroded by unwise policy and an attitude of permissiveness. As we've seen, this is one reason why the strategy of reprivatization frequently involves efforts to enforce traditional family norms. A strategy of social reconstruction, on the other hand, seeks to support the family not by dictating its "correct" composition

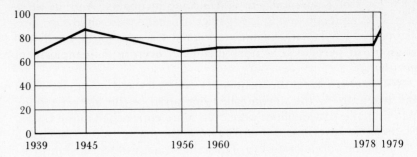

Figure 13-2

Attitudes toward government job creation. Responses to the statement, government should see that everyone who wants to work has a job.

Source: From *Public Opinion*, August–September 1981, p. 34. Reprinted with permission of American Enterprise Institute for Public Policy Research.

or "proper" gender roles but by protecting *all* families from the preventable stresses of economic insecurity, inadequate income, and absent or inaccessible public services (Edelman, 1987).

Again, such a strategy is undeniably costly (though, as we've seen in Chapter 4, not nearly as costly as it's sometimes said to be). But there are several reasons why we need to look more carefully at the way we define "costs." Just as in the business world or in the family budget, some of the "costs" of social programs are more properly seen as *investments*. Preventive health care, early childhood education, and nutrition programs, to name just a few examples, are not simply consumers of scarce funds but investments in the quality of our human resources. And even in the barest dollars-and-cents terms, such investments "pay off" in reduced expenses for later health and mental health care, police and prisons, and — as the experience of many other advanced societies shows — in an economy strengthened by the more productive use of its human capital.

Perhaps even more importantly, many of the "costs" of the welfare state are the result of having to "mop up" the consequences of the frequently preventable irrationality and mismanagement of other social institutions — especially the economy. As the British social theorist Richard Titmuss put it, the modern welfare state is cumbersome and costly in part because it is a response to a larger "*dis*welfare state" that systematically creates "needs" — through joblessness, community disruption, occupational disease — which then require costly, after-the-fact attention (Titmuss, 1968). And this is a major reason for the inefficiency and waste of human resources that often *does* characterize the welfare system in America — as well as its stinginess.

By contrast, the new vision of the welfare state implicit in a strategy of social reconstruction is a more active one — designed, as Norman Furniss and Timothy Tilton propose, to "not merely care for the victims of advanced industrial society" but to provide "preventive efforts to forestall unemployment, disease, waste, and urban squalor"

Reconstructing the Economy — A Congressional View

Many people believe that the American economy hasn't been working well — and that its priorities are out of line with social needs. But some find it difficult to visualize the alternatives — what might be done differently. How can we put people to work at useful jobs? What should we be producing if we want to spend less on defense? How can we discourage unproductive corporate takeovers and promote more productive enterprise? Among the most detailed proposals for restructuring the economy is a set of recommendations offered by the Joint Economic Committee of Congress in 1982. They included the following:

Recommendation No. 6: Practice Credit Conservation

The administration and the Federal Reserve should encourage the banking system to develop an effective means to deter destabilizing bursts of bank-financed lending for unproductive purposes such as large corporate takeovers and speculation in commodities, collectibles, and land. Such measures will have the effect of conserving scarce credit resources in times of need for the use of small business, farmers, housing, automobile financing, and productive capital investments.

The year 1981 was a banner one for predacious corporate takeovers financed by the savings of ordinary American citizens. Spectacular examples included the takeover of Conoco by Du Pont, after a public battle involving Texaco, Mobil, and Seagrams; the takeover of Marathon Oil by U.S. Steel, after a public battle with Mobil; and the attempted takeover of Grumman by LTV. One can only imagine how millions of ordinary Americans who could not get credit in 1981 viewed the spectacle of such massive misuse of their savings by the corporate world and the banking system. . . .

We recommend specifically that a policy in this area take the form of credit conservation. . . . We should effectively discourage bank lending for those few uses which conspicuously absorb large amounts of scarce credit to the detriment of more productive uses. This will not put an end to corporate takeovers. But it will make them more expensive to the acquiring firm, and therefore encourage a reallocation of that firm's efforts to more productive activity, which is the point. . . .

Recommendation No. 19: Promote Catalysts

In chemistry, a catalyst is a chemical which facilitates a reaction, thereby increasing the efficiency with which resources, like heat, can be applied to a process, and sometimes making possible transformations that weren't possible before. Similarly, government policy should seek for areas of enterprise where a little public-private cooperation, a little access to credit, or a little infrastructure development can have far-reaching effects on the efficiency of our resource use, our future pattern of development and growth, and the competitiveness of our final goods industries. The examples are many. [One is] high-speed passenger rail. . . .

The National Transportation Study Commission reported in June 1979 that a "transportation crisis in this country is just around the corner." The commission estimated that, by the year 2000, national domestic person-miles of travel will increase between 81 and 96 percent and national domestic freight ton-miles will increase between 165 and 314 percent. It concluded that the present transportation system will be hard-pressed to handle such dramatic increases.

The U.S. highway system is rapidly deteriorating. The Federal Highway Administration projects that an expenditure of $360 billion over the next 15 years would be required merely to maintain and repair existing far-from-adequate road quality. The nation's many airports and primary air lines are also seriously congested. Many smaller communities are losing service as a result of the increasing costs, especially fuel costs, of providing service.

The nation's railway system is at the present time in no position to pick up the slack. Track and equipment are deteriorating. The increase in the price of petroleum-based fuel has made railroad travel, as air travel, increasingly expensive.

Advanced industrial nations abroad have remained dedicated to the provision of high-quality rail service. Japan inaugurated "bullet train" service almost 25 years ago. Trains between Tokyo and Shin Osaka average 100 miles per hour and attain top speeds of 130 miles per hour. One hundred twenty million passengers a year use these trains. They operate reliably, and the technologies on which they are based are being continually redesigned and improved. They also operate without government subsidies and even make a profit. In September 1981, the Tres Grande Vitesse made its debut as the French entry among bullet trains. It travels between Paris and Lyons, attaining top speeds approaching 160 miles per hour. Throughout Europe and Canada, high-speed trains are either already in operation or currently being developed.

American trains pale in comparison. The average speed of a passenger train in this country has declined from 75 miles per hour in the mid-1950s to a current average of 40 miles per hour. Amtrak today operates only 1,700 passenger cars. Despite smaller populations, the majority of the European nations operate at least five times as many passenger cars. Japan operates 26,000 cars over a rail system that covers only half the mileage of the U.S. system, in a country which is the size of the state of Montana. . . .

The committee . . . has proposed developing [high-speed passenger rail service] in 20 highly populated rail corridors.

The committee believes that such an undertaking would produce not only major direct economic benefits, but indirect ones as well, such as providing an infusion of capital into depressed industries and encouraging technology transfers throughout the economy. Now that much of the nation's highway construction is complete, the highway construction industry's talents and capabilities could be readily channeled to such purposes as grading, building bridges, pouring concrete, and building fences and stations for a new rail transportation system. Moreover, a whole new industry of rail cars, locomotives, and equipment can help reemploy our skilled manufacturing labor force and the excess capacity of our metalworking industries.

In the same way that the development of an automobile industry in the 1920s not only changed the face of America's transportation system, but also created untold new jobs and business, the development of a new high-speed rail passenger service–oriented industry would serve as the catalyst to renewed economic prosperity that the United States is so lacking today. . . .

Recommendation No. 20: Maintain Infrastructure

In large part, our network of highways and bridges, ports and railroads, and adequate water and utility systems are responsible for the nation's productive capacity. In recent years, however, real capital expenditures at all levels of government have declined. . . .

These declines in capital funding have resulted in a deterioration of the basic public facilities upon which our economy relies. Over 8,000 of the 42,500 miles of interstate highways and 13 percent of its bridges have now exceeded their designed service life and must be rebuilt. The costs of rehabilitating and constructing our nonurban highways necessary to maintain existing service levels will exceed $700 billion in the 1980s. The 756 urban areas with populations over 50,000 will have to spend between $75 to $110 billion just to maintain their water systems. And it will cost upward of $33 billion to replace or rehabilitate the nation's deficient bridges. Pat Choate and Susan Walter, authors of *America in Ruins,* conclude that these deteriorated facilities are a major structural barrier to the renewal of our national economy and, combined with an aging industrial plant, have contributed to the decline in American productivity.

The deterioration of the infrastructure adversely affects investment because often firms must bear the additional costs which result from infrastructure problems. According to a recent issue of *Business Week,* U.S. Steel Corporation is losing $1.2 million per year in employee time and wasted fuel rerouting trucks around the Thompson Run Bridge, in Pennsylvania, because it is in such disrepair. Companies in Manhattan, New York, lose $166 million a year for each additional five minutes delay on the public transportation systems. Old or inadequate water and sewer systems also stifle economic development. . . . In older areas of the country, large parts of the water and sewer systems are almost 100 years old. Many of these systems, however, were designed for a maximum of 100 years of serviceable life.

Although discussions of the need to revitalize the nation's decaying infrastructure often revolves around the problems of our urban centers, similar problems which plague rural America should not be minimized. Despite growth and diversification in many rural regions during the past dozen years, nagging deficiencies in rural infrastructure persist. According to a report of the General Accounting Office (GAO) issued in March 1980, as much as one-half of the nation's substandard housing may be found in rural America. . . . Public transportation is used by less than 1 percent of rural people who work away from home; more than 4

million rural people have inadequate sewage disposal systems or none at all; more than 2 million do not have running water in their homes. . . .

Recommendation No. 27: Promote Energy Security

The committee continues to believe that energy conservation and the use of renewable energy alternatives are a necessary component of a comprehensive national program to improve our energy security. Substantial investment has occurred as a consequence of tax incentives for industrial and residential conservation and the installation of solar energy equipment. The continuation of these fiscal incentives is appropriate to ensure that reliance on imported sources continues to decline.

Further gains in our nation's energy security can be realized from continued research into energy conservation and the renewable energy technologies. In fiscal year 1980, federal research, development, and demonstration budget authority for these programs totaled $1.5 billion, and comprised almost 11 percent of the Department of Energy's budget. Private conservation efforts have continued to blossom and renewable energy technologies mature. Yet, administration budget requests for these programs in the current fiscal year were reduced precipitously to less than $400 million, only 3 percent of DOE's budget.

A continued viable federal program of research on energy conservation, renewable energy, and coal technologies is a necessary component of a broad-based national program to improve our energy security. While we support efforts to eliminate waste and fraud and reduce government spending, such motives should not provide an excuse to eliminate support for conservation, renewable energy, and coal research.

Source: U.S. Congress, Joint Economic Committee, *Joint Economic Report* (Washington, D.C.: Government Printing Office, 1982a, pp. 64–155).

(1977, p. 192). As Figure 13-2 suggests, the majority of Americans support that sentiment.

Shifting the Balance of Social Spending

But it's true that there are limits to how much a society can spend. Especially given America's changing role in the world economy, no serious approach to social policy can operate under the assumption that we can endlessly accommodate both "guns and butter" — both soaring military spending and a productive and humane investment in our human resources. The strategy of social reconstruction acknowledges that national security is a legitimate concern for any government. But it also stresses that national security can be achieved both more effectively and less expensively than it is.

As we saw in Chapter 12, the most important issues surrounding military spending concern not just its sheer *size*, but also the *inefficiency* of much defense production. There is plenty of room for serious disagreement over the best size and composition of America's military forces, but there is no real argument for continuing to tolerate the level of waste and inefficiency that has become the hallmark of military spending in this country. As we saw, the cost savings that may be attainable even *without* significantly changing our military priorities are astonishing; the cost *increases* in major weapons systems alone in the course of one year amount to a sum that, if saved, could pay for many of our social welfare programs.

Beyond this, of course, lie deeper questions about the kinds of weapons we really need — and the possibilities for converting some military production facilities to peacetime purposes. A strategy of social reconstruction must carefully reconsider what we choose to mean by "national security" (Barnet, 1981) — and whether a society can be said to be "secure" if it allows its cities, industries, and human resources to deteriorate in the service of increasing its capacity to wage war.

Planning for Social Reconstruction

The strategy of social reconstruction involves substantial economic planning. But so, as we've seen, do the other strategies — though the first often masks this by making planning more a private, corporate function, and less a public one. The idea of economic planning raises many fears — that it could create enormous, powerful bureaucracies, interfere with personal freedom, and concentrate too much power in the hands of a distant and unresponsive State. Most Americans have experienced (or read about) enough bureaucratic abuses, both here and abroad, to have developed an understandable concern about the potential threats from the increased role for government — even a well-intentioned government — that planning seems to involve.

These are legitimate worries. But, as with most important social issues, there are no easy answers. Simply limiting the role of *public* planning will not eliminate these dangers in a society dominated by great concentration of *private* power. Moreover, the demand for a reduced role for government in the American economy has often been accompanied by a simultaneous demand for a greater role for government in regulating private life. And, paradoxically, it also goes hand-in-hand with a willingness to let much of our economic life be planned — usually without much public input — by the military. Again, the realistic issue is not whether there will *be* planning in America — but *who* will do it and what values and social ends it will serve.

Ultimately, the only effective way to diminish the potential for abuse is to develop mechanisms to extend the principles of democracy and accountability to economic life. Sometimes this may mean *decentralizing* the mechanisms of economic planning to bring decision-making power closer to the communities where Americans live and the workplaces where they earn their livings (Faux, 1982). (One example — workers' participation in decisions about the introduction of new technology — has already been discussed.) More generally, it will require what Michael Harrington (1981, p. 326) has called the "democratization of information": ensuring that ordinary people, as workers and citizens, have access to the information that will enable them to participate effectively in the decisions that will govern the fate of their jobs, families, and communities.

Again, the questions raised for American social policy by the tensions of planning versus individual initiative, public decision making versus individual autonomy, are not the kind that permit simple answers. In one form or another, they are sure to be a focus of debate for many years to come. For us, what's important in this book is not to try to produce a blueprint for the future, but to reaffirm the point we began with in Chapter 1: Social science, as we understand it, has an important role to play in helping to provide the tools for participation in what we hope will become an increasingly open and democratic debate over America's future.

We noted in the beginning of this book that one distinctive contribution of social science is that it teaches us about the constraints on human action. Properly understood, it also teaches us about human possibilities. It demonstrates, even in the face of confusion and cynicism, that things need not necessarily be the way they are. It does so by, among other things, demonstrating that things are done differently — and often quite effectively — in societies very much like our own, as we've seen over and over again throughout this book. And it also shows that social action often makes a very real difference. No abstract beneficent force, whether the "invisible hand" of the "market" or the march of historical inevitability, caused the dramatic reduction in infant deaths, the beginnings of regulation of toxic wastes, or the tripling of the number of women lawyers that we achieved in recent years. The limits of social action are real, and they can often seem overwhelming, but the possibilities are real too. And it is arguable that it's when we make the most of these possibilities that we become most fully human. A thought from the late biologist and environmental activist Rene Dubos (1981, p. 9) may be an appropriate way to end a book about social problems: "We cannot escape the past," Dubos wrote, "but neither can we avoid inventing the future."

Summary

This final chapter has considered some directions American social policy might take in the future, based on the analysis of earlier chapters. We've described three broad approaches, or strategies, toward social problems:

1. The strategy of reprivatization emphasizes reducing the role of government (except in defense) and relying on the forces of the market to deal with social problems. Though American society already lags behind other industrial countries in the development of social welfare measures, this approach would reduce those measures still further. Proponents of this view usually accept social inequality and environmental disruption as necessary costs of economic growth. But it's not clear that this strategy could actually deliver the long-term economic growth it promises.

2. The strategy of revitalization would make more explicit use of government planning to direct economic growth and improve America's competitiveness in the world economy. But it leaves many unanswered questions about its ability to generate adequate employment or to address the problems of social inequality.

3. The strategy of social reconstruction also argues for substantial planning — but planning that includes a commitment to full employment, to overcoming the inequalities of gender and race, to investing in human resources, and to balancing military and domestic spending.

For Further Reading

Alperovitz, Gar, and Jeff Faux. *Rebuilding America*. New York: Pantheon, 1985.

Carnoy, Martin, and Derek Shearer. *Economic Democracy: The Challenge of the 1980s*. White Plains, N.Y.: M. E. Sharpe, 1980.

Howe, Irving, ed. *Alternatives*. New York: Pantheon, 1984.

Reich, Robert. *The Next American Frontier*. New York: Random House, 1984.

Thurow, Lester. *The Zero-Sum Solution*. New York: Simon and Schuster, 1986.

Bibliography

Adams, Gordon, and Geoff Quinn. "The Iron Triangle: The Politics of Defense Contracting." *Council on Economic Priorities Newsletter,* June 1981.

Aldous, Joan. "Cuts in Selected Welfare Programs: The Effects on U.S. Families." *Journal of Family Issues,* June 1986.

Allen, Walter, and Reynolds Farley. "The Shifting Social and Economic Tides of Black America, 1950-1980." *Annual Review of Sociology,* 1986.

Alperovitz, Gar, and Jeff Faux. *Rebuilding America.* New York: Pantheon, 1985.

Amidei, Nancy. Testimony, U.S. Congress, House, Committee on Energy and Commerce, Subcommittee on Health and the Environment, October 1981.

Anderson, A. "Neurotoxic Follies." *Psychology Today,* July 1982.

Anderson, Bernard. "Economic Patterns in Black America." In National Urban League, *The State of Black America, 1982.* New York: National Urban League, 1982.

Anderson, Jack. "Big Spenders." *San Francisco Chronicle,* January 10, 1983.

Anderson, K. *Wartime Women: Sex Roles, Family Relations, and the Status of Women during World War II.* Westport, Conn.: Greenwood, 1981.

Anderson, Martin. *Welfare.* Stanford, Calif.: Hoover Institute, 1980.

Anton, Thomas, John Oppenheim, and Lance Morrow. "Where the Shoe Pinches: The 1983 Reagan Budget." *Economic Outlook USA,* Spring 1982.

Ashford, Nicholas. "New Scientific Evidence and Public Health Imperatives." *New England Journal of Medicine,* April 23, 1987.

Auletta, Ken. *The Underclass.* New York: Random House, 1981.

Bahr, Stephen J. "Family Determinants and Effects of Deviance." In Wesley R. Burr, et al., *Contemporary Theories about the Family.* New York: Free Press, 1979.

Bane, Mary Jo. *Here to Stay.* New York: Basic Books, 1976.

———, and David Ellwood. "Slipping Into and Out of Poverty: The Dynamics of Spells." *Journal of Human Resources,* Winter 1986.

Barnet, Richard. *Real Security.* New York: Simon and Schuster, 1981.

———. "Ritual Dance of the Superpowers." *The Nation,* April 9, 1983.

448

Barrett, Nancy. "Women in the Job Market: Occupations, Earnings, and Career Opportunities." In Ralph Smith, ed., *The Subtle Revolution*. Washington, D.C.: The Urban Institute, 1979a.

Bauer, Gary. "Families Fare Best When They Help Themselves," Washington *Post National Weekly*, January 5, 1987.

Behr, Peter. "Has the American Economy Lost Its Competitive Edge?" *Washington Post Weekly*, May 7, 1984.

Bell, Daniel. *The Coming of Post-Industrial Society*. New York: Basic Books, 1969.

Bellinger, David. "Longitudinal Analyses of Prenatal and Postnatal Lead Exposure and Early Cognitive Development." *New England Journal of Medicine*, April 23, 1987.

Bendick, Marc, Jr. "Employment, Training, and Economic Development." In John L. Palmer and Isabel Sawhill, eds., *The Reagan Experiment*. Washington, D.C.: The Urban Institute, 1982.

———, and Judith R. Devine, "Workers Dislocated by Economic Change: Do They Need Federal Employment and Training Assistance?" In National Commission for Employment Policy, *7th Annual Report*. Washington, D.C.: National Commission for Employment Policy, 1981.

Bergmann, Barbara. *The Economic Emergence of Women*. New York: Basic Books, 1986.

Berk, Richard, and Phyllis Newton. "Does Arrest Really Deter Wife Beating?" *American Sociological Review* 50, 1985.

Beverage Industry. "Estimated Share of Market for Major Brewers." December 31, 1982.

Bianchi, Suzanne. *Household Composition and Racial Inequality*. New Brunswick, N.J.: Rutgers University Press, 1981.

Bielby, William, and James Barron. "A Woman's Place is with Other Women." In Barbara Reskin, ed., *Sex Segregation in the Workplace*. Washington, D.C.: National Academy of Sciences, 1984.

Billingsley, Andrew. "Black Families in a Changing Society." In National Urban League, *State of Black America, 1987*. Washington, D.C., 1987.

Birch, David. "Who Creates Jobs?" *Public Interest*, 1982.

Blank, Rebecca, and Emma Rothschild. "The Effect of U.S. Defense Spending on Employment and Output." *International Labour Review*, November–December 1985.

Blau, Francine D. *Equal Pay in the Office*. Lexington, Mass.: Lexington Books, 1977.

———. "The Data on Women Workers: Past, Present, and Future." In Ann H. Stromberg and Shirley Harkness, eds., *Women Working: Theories and Facts in Perspective*. Palo Alto, Calif.: Mayfield, 1978.

Blau, Judith, and Peter Blau. "The cost of Inequality: Metropolitan Structure and Violent Crime." *American Sociological Review*, February 1982.

Blaustein, Arthur I., ed. *The American Promise: Equal Justice and Economic Opportunity*. New Brunswick, N.J.: Transaction Books, 1982.

Bloch, Donald. "Discussion: Violence in the Family." In A. Green, ed., *Violence and the Family*. Boulder, Colo.: Westview Press, 1980.

Block, Richard, and Carolyn Block. "Decisions and Data: The Transformation of Robbery Incidents into Official Robbery Statistics." *Journal of Criminal Law and Criminology*, Winter 1980.

Bluestone, Barry, and Bennett Harrison. *The Deindustrialization of America*. New York: Basic Books, 1982.

Blumstein, Alfred. "On the Racial Disproportionality of U.S. Prison Populations." *Journal of Criminal Law and Criminology*, Fall 1982.

———, Jacqueline Cohen, and Daniel Nagin, eds. *Deterrence and Incapacitation*. Washington, D.C.: National Academy of Sciences, 1978.

——— and E. Graddy. "Prevalence and Recidivism in Index Arrests," *Law and Society Review* 16 (2), 1981.

Boland, Barbara. "Incapacitation of the Dangerous Offender: The Arithmetic Is Not So Simple." *Journal of Research in Crime and Delinquency*, January 1978.

Bonacich, Edna, and John Modell. *The Economic Basis of Ethnic Solidarity: Small Business in the Japanese-American Community.* Berkeley, Calif.: University of California Press, 1981.

Borjas, George. "The Demographic Determinants of the Demand For Black Labor." In Richard B. Freeman and Harry Holzer, *The Black Youth Employment Crisis.* Chicago. University of Chicago Press, 1986.

Borus, Michael. "Willingness to Work among Youth." *Journal of Human Resources,* Fall 1982.

Braithwaite, John, and Valerie Braithwaite. "The Effect of Income Inequality and Social Democracy on Homicide." *British Journal of Criminology,* January 1980.

————, and Gilbert Geis. "On Theory and Action for Corporate Crime Control." *Crime and Delinquency,* April 1982.

Braverman, Harry. *Labor and Monopoly Capital: The Degradation of Work in the Twentieth Century.* New York: Monthly Review Press, 1974.

Bredemier, Charles. "A Dent in the American Dream." *Washington Post Weekly,* September 15, 1986.

Brenner, M. Harvey. "Fetal, Infant, and Maternal Mortality during Periods of Economic Instability." *International Journal of Health Services,* Summer 1973a.

————. *Mental Illness and the Economy.* Cambridge, Mass.: Harvard University Press, 1973b.

————. *Estimating the Social Costs of National Economic Policy.* U.S. Congress, Joint Economic Committee, 1976.

Brittain, John A. *Inheritance and the Inequality of Material Wealth.* Washington, D.C.: Brookings Institution, 1978.

Brock, Horace W. "Mortgaging the Future." *San Francisco Chronicle,* April 13, 1983.

Brown, Charles, Curtis Gilroy, and Andrew Cohen. "The Effect of the Minimum Wage on Employment and Unemployment." *Journal of Economic Literature,* June 20, 1982.

Brown, Lester. "A Generation of Deficits." In Lester Brown, ed., *State of the World 1986.* New York: Norton, 1986.

Brown, Michael, and Steven Erie. "Blacks and the Legacy of the Great Society." *Public Policy,* Spring 1982.

Browning, Edgar. "How Much More Equality Can We Afford?" *Public Interest,* Spring 1976.

Budd, Edward C. Prepared statement in U.S. Congress, Joint Economic Committee, Hearings on *The 1982 Joint Economic Report of the President,* Part 2, February 1982.

Burmaster, David. "The New Pollution: Groundwater Contamination." *Environment,* March 1982.

Burnham, Walter D. *The Current Crisis in Amercian Politics.* New York: Oxford University Press, 1983.

Burr, Wesley. In U.S. Congress, Senate, Committee on Labor and Human Resources, Hearings on *Work Ethic: Materialism and the American Family,* March 1982.

Burtless, Gary. "Public Spending and the Poor." In Sheldon Danziger and Daniel Weinberg, eds., *Fighting Poverty.* Cambridge. Harvard University Press, 1986.

Business Week. The Decline of U.S. Power (and What We Can Do about It). New York: Houghton-Mifflin, 1980a.

————. "An Oil Giant's Dilemma." August 25, 1980b.

————. Special Issue on "Reindustrialization." June 14, 1980c.

————. "The Shrinking Standard of Living." April 8, 1980d.

————. "The Built-In Deficit." August 16, 1982a.

————. "Guns vs. Butter: Special Report." November 29, 1982b.

————. "The Fallout from Whoops." July 11, 1983.

————. "Corporate Women: What It Takes to Get to the Top." June 22, 1987.

Canterbury, E. R., and E. J. Nosari. "The Forbes 400: The Determinants of Superwealth." *Southern Journal of Economics,* April 1985.

Caplow, Theodore, et al. *Middletown Families: Fifty Years of Change and Continuity.* Minneapolis: University of Minnesota Press, 1982.

Carnoy, Martin, and Derek Shearer. *Economic Democracy.* White Plains, N.Y.: M. E. Sharpe, 1980.

Carter, Luther. "The Radwaste Paradox." *Science,* January 1, 1983.

Case, John. *Understanding Inflation.* New York: Penguin, 1981.

Catalano, Ralph, and David Dooley. "Economic Predictors of Depressed Mood and Stressful Life Events in a Metropolitan Community." *Journal of Health and Social Behavior,* September 1977.

———, ———, and R. Jackson. "Economic Predictors of Admissions to Mental Health Facilities in a Non-Metropolitan Community." *Journal of Health and Social Behavior,* October 1981.

Celis, William. "Drugs, Inadequate Skills Cited as Construction Deaths Rise." *Wall Street Journal,* June 17, 1987.

Center for Defense Information. "U.S. Weapons Exports Headed for Record Level." *Defense Monitor,* no. 3, 1982.

———. "The Need for a Level Military Budget." *Defense Monitor* no. 2, 1983.

———. "Militarism in America." *Defense Monitor* no. 3, 1986a.

——— "Waste in Military Procurement: The Prospects for Reform." *Defense Monitor* no. 1, 1986b.

———. "No Business Like War Business." *Defense Monitor* no. 3, 1987a.

———. "The Pentagon Prepares for Nuclear War." *Defense Monitor* no. 4, 1987b.

Cherlin, Andrew. *Marriage, Divorce, Remarriage.* Cambridge, Mass.: Harvard University Press, 1981.

———, and Pamela Walters. "Trends in United States Men's and Women's Sex-Role Attitudes, 1972-1978." *American Sociological Review,* August 1981.

Chernow, Ron. "Grey Flannel Goons: The Latest in Union Busting." *Working Papers,* January-February 1981.

Chess, Stella, et al. "Early Parental Attitudes, Divorce and Separation, and Young Adult Outcomes: Findings of a Longitudinal Study." *Journal of the American Academy of Child Psychology,* January 1983.

Children's Defense Fund. Testimony, U.S. Congress, House, Subcommittee on Health, Energy, and Commerce, October 1981.

———. *Children's Defense Budget.* Washington, D.C.: Children's Defense Fund, 1982.

Choate, Pat, and Susan Walter. *America in Ruins: Beyond the Public Works Pork Barrel.* Washington, D.C.: Council of State Planning Agencies, 1981.

Clark, Kim B., and Lawrence Summers. "Unemployment Reconsidered." Harvard Business Review, November-December 1980.

Clark, W. A. V., et al. "The Influence of Domestic Position on Health Status." *Social Science and Medicine* 24, No. 6, 1987.

Clinard, Marshall A. *Cities with Little Crime.* London: Cambridge University Press, 1978.

———, and Peter Yeager. *Corporate Crime.* New York: Free Press, 1980.

Cloward, Richard, and Lloyd Ohlin. *Delinquency and Opportunity.* New York: Free Press, 1959.

Coates, James. "Pentagon Feeling Heat from Fiscal Conservatives." *San Francisco Chronicle,* July 24, 1983.

Cobb, Sidney. "Physiological Changes in Men Whose Jobs Were Abolished." *Journal of Psychosomatic Research,* August 1974.

Cohany, Sharon. "What Happened to the High School Class of 1985?" *Monthly Labor Review,* October 1986.

Colburn, Don. "The Millions Without Health Insurance." *Washington Post Weekly,* July 21, 1986.

Cole, Robert. *Work, Mobility and Participation: A Comparative Study of American and Japanese Industry.* Berkeley: University of California Press, 1979.

Common Cause. *Gimme Shelters.* Washington, D.C.: *Common Cause,* May 1978.

———. "Throwing Money at Weapons." *Common Cause,* May–June 1983.

Congressional Quarterly. *Environment and Health.* Washington, D.C.: Congressional Quarterly, 1981.

Conrad, John, Stephan Van Dine, and Simon Dinitz. *Restraining the Wicked: The Incapacitation of the Dangerous Offender.* Lexington, Mass.: Lexington Books, 1979.

Conservation Foundation. *Siting New Industry, An Environmental Perspective.* Washington, D.C.: Conservation Foundation, 1982a.

———. *The State of the Environment—1982.* Washington, D.C.: Conservation Foundation, 1982b.

Conservation Foundation. *State of the Environment: An Assessment at Mid-Decade.* Washington, D.C., 1984.

Cook, Alice. "Collective Bargaining as a Strategy for Achieving Equal Opportunity and Equal Pay." In Ronnie Steinberg Ratner, ed., *Equal Employment Policy for Women.* Philadelphia: Temple University Press, 1980.

Cooper, David. *The Death of the Family.* New York: Vintage, 1970.

Corcoran, Mary, and Martha S. Hill. "Persistence in Unemployment among Adult Men." In Greg Duncan and James Morgan, eds., *5000 American Families, Patterns of Economic Progress,* Vol. 8. Ann Arbor: University of Michigan Institute for Social Research, 1980.

Corman, Hope, and Michael Grossman. "Determinants of Neonatal Mortality in the U.S." *Journal of Health Economics,* September 1985.

Cornelius, Wayne A. "Mexican Migration to the United States." In Jerome H. Skolnick and Elliott Currie, eds., *Crisis in American Institutions,* 5th ed. Boston: Little, Brown, 1982.

Cornell, C. P., and R. J. Gelles. "Adolescent to Parent Violence." *Urban and Social Change Review,* Winter 1982.

Council on Economic Priorities. *Jobs and Energy.* New York: Council on Economic Priorities, 1979.

———. "Occupational Safety and Health in the Chemical Industry." *Newsletter,* November 1981.

Council on Environmental Quality. *Environmental Quality, 1980.* Washington, D.C.: Government Printing Office, December 1980.

———. *The Global 2000 Report to the President.* Washington, D.C.: Government Printing Office, 1982.

Crosby, Faye, et al. "Recent Unobtrusive Studies of Black and White Discrimination and Prejudice: A Literature Review." *Psychological Bulletin,* May 1980.

Currie, Elliott. *Confronting Crime: An American Challenge.* New York: Pantheon, 1985.

———. *What Kind of Future: Violence and Public Safety in the Year 2000.* San Francisco: National Council on Crime and Delinquency, 1987.

———, Robert Dunn, and David Fogarty. "The Fading American Dream: Economic Crisis and the New Inequality." In Jerome H. Skolnick and Elliott Currie, eds., *Crisis in American Institutions,* 7th ed. Boston: Little, Brown, 1987.

———, and Paul Rosenstiel. "Six Myths about Unemployment," Third Century America Project. Berkeley: University of California, 1979.

Curtis, Lynn, ed. *American Violence and Public Policy.* New Haven, Conn.: Yale University Press, 1985.

Dam, Kenneth W. "Ensuring Security in the Nuclear Age." *Department of State Bulletin,* April 1983.

Danziger, Sheldon, and Peter Gottschalk. "Social Programs: A Partial Solution to, but Not a Cause of, Poverty." In Sara McLanahan, et al. *Losing Ground: A Critique.* Madison: University of Wisconsin, Center for Research on Poverty, 1985.

———. *How Have Families With Children Been Faring?* Washington, D.C.: U.S. Congress, Joint Economic Committee, 1986.

Danziger, Sheldon, Robert H. Haveman, and Robert Plotnick. "How Income Transfer Programs Affect Work, Savings, and the Income Distribution: A Critical Review." *Journal of Economic Literature*, September 1981.

———, and Robert Plotnick. "Demographic Change, Government Transfers, and Income Distribution." *Monthly Labor Review*, April 1977.

Danziger, Sheldon, and Daniel Weinberg. *Fighting Poverty: What Works and What Doesn't.* Cambridge. Harvard University Press, 1986.

Darity, William. "The Human Capital Approach to Black/White Earnings Inequality: Some Unsettled Questions." *Journal of Human Resources*, Spring 1982.

Darmstadter, Joel. "Intercountry Comparisons of Energy Use: Implications for U.S. Policy." In Karen Gentemann, ed., *Social and Political Perspectives on Energy Policy.* New York: Praeger, 1981.

Davis, Devra Lee. "Cancer in the Workplace: The Case for Prevention." *Environment*, July-August 1981.

Davis, J. (President of Winn-Dixie Supermarkets.) Quoted in *The Progressive*, July 1980, p. 11.

Davis, Karen, M. Gold, and Diane Makuc. "Access to Health Care for the Poor: Does the Gap Remain?" *Annual Review of Public Health*, Vol. 2, 1981.

DeGrasse, Robert. "Military Buildup Exacts Toll on Economy." *Council on Economic Priorities Newsletter*, May 1983a.

———. *Military Expansion, Economic Decline.* New York: Council on Economic Priorities, 1983b.

———, and Paul Murphy. "Impact of Reagan's Rearmament." *Council on Economic Priorities Newsletter*, May 1981.

Democratic Caucus, U.S. House of Representatives. *Rebuilding the Road to Opportunity: Turning Point for America's Economy.* Washington, D.C.: Government Printing Office, July 20, 1982.

Denton, Senator Jeremiah (D-Ala.). Statement, U.S. Congress, Senate, Committee on Labor and Human Resources, Hearings on *Work Ethic: Materialism and the American Family*, March 1982.

Derr, Patrick, et al. "Worker/Public Protection: The Double Standard." *Environment*, September 1981.

Devens, Richard. "Displaced Workers: One Year Later." *Monthly Labor Review*, July 1986.

Dobash, Russell P., and R. Emerson Dobash. "Community Response to Violence Against Wives: Charivari, Abstract Justice and Patriarchy." *Social Problems*, June 1981.

Domhoff, G. William. *The Bohemian Grove: A Study in Ruling Class Cohesiveness.* New York: Harper & Row, 1974.

———. *The Higher Circles: Governing Class in America.* New York: Vintage, 1970.

———. *Who Rules America Now?* New York: Simon and Schuster, 1986.

Dooley, Martin, and Peter Gottschalk. "Does a Younger Male Labor Force Mean Greater Earnings Inequality?" *Monthly Labor Review*, November 1982.

———. "The Increasing Proportion of Men With Low Earnings in the United States." *Demography*, February 1985.

DuBoff, Richard. "The New Economic Mythology." *Commonwealth*, July 4, 1980.

Dubos, Rene. "The Wooing of Earth." *EPA Journal*, February 1981.

Duleep, Harriet. "Measuring the Effect of Income on Adult Mortality." *Journal of Human Resources*, Spring 1986.

Dunbar, Leslie, ed. *Minority Report.* New York: Pantheon, 1984.

Duncan, Greg. *Years of Poverty, Years of Plenty.* Ann Arbor: University of Michigan Institute for Social Research, 1984.

Duncan, Greg J. and Richard Coe. *The Dynamics of Welfare.* Ann Arbor: Survey Research Center, University of Michigan, 1981.

_____ and Saul Hoffman. "A Reconsideration of the Economic Consequences of Marital Dissolution." *Demography*, November, 1985.

Duxbury, M. L., and S. J. Shelendick. "Contemporary Working Women on the Treadmill." In S. B. Day, ed., *Life Stress*. New York: Van Nostrand Reinhold, 1982.

Early, Steve, and Matt Witt. "How European Unions Cope with New Technology." *Monthly Labor Review*, September 1982.

Eberts, Randall, and Joe Stone. "Male-Female Differences in Promotions." *Journal of Human Resources*, Fall 1985.

Edelman, Marian. *Families in Peril*. Cambridge: Harvard University Press, 1987.

Ehrenreich, Barbara. "Is the Middle Class Doomed?" *New York Times Magazine*, September 7, 1986.

Ehrlich, Isaac. "The Economic Approach to Crime: A Preliminary Assessment." In Sheldon L. Messinger and Egon Bittner, eds., *Criminology Review Yearbook*. Beverly Hills, Calif.: Sage, 1979.

Eisner, Robert. "Transfers in a Total Income System of Accounts." In Marilyn Moon, ed., *Economic Transfers in the U.S.* Chicago: University of Chicago Press, 1984.

Elliott, Delbert, and David Huizinga. "Social Class and Delinquent Behavior in a National Youth Panel." *Criminology*, May 1983.

Ellwood, David, and Lawrence Summers. "Is Welfare Really the Problem?" *Public Interest*, Spring 1986.

Employment Research Associates. *The Price of the Pentagon*. Lansing, Mich.: Employment Research Associates, 1982.

Employment and Training Reporter. August 1982.

Engelhardt, Klaus. "Conversion of Military Research and Development." *International Labour Review*, March–April 1985.

Epstein, Samuel. *The Politics of Cancer*. New York: Doubleday, 1980.

Fallows, James, *National Defense*. New York: Random House, 1982.

_____. "A Parable of Automation." *New York Review of Books*, September 27, 1984.

Faux, Jeff. "Who Plans?" *Working Papers*, November-December 1982.

_____. "By Deficits Possessed." *The New Republic*, February 14, 1983.

_____. "The Post-Reagan Economy." *World Policy Journal*, Spring 1986.

Federal Bureau of Investigation. *Crime in the United States—1985*. Washington, D.C.: Government Printing Office, 1986.

Federal Bureau of Investigation. *Crime in the United States—1981*. Washington, D.C.: Government Printing Office, 1982.

Fein, Rashi. *Medical Care, Medical Costs*. Cambridge: Harvard University Press, 1985.

Feldstein, Martin. "The Economics of the New Unemployment." *The Public Interest*, Fall 1973.

_____. "The Private and Social Costs of Unemployment." *American Economic Review*, May 1978.

Fingerhut, L. A., R. W. Wilson, and J. J. Feldman, "Health and Disease in the United States." *Annual Review of Public Health, 1980*, 1981.

Flaim, Paul. "Work Schedules of Americans." *Monthly Labour Review*, November 1986.

Flavin, Christopher. "Moving Beyond Oil." In Lester Brown, ed., *State of the World, 1986*. New York: Norton, 1986a.

_____. "Reforming the Electric Power Industry." In ibid., 1986b.

_____. "Reassessing Nuclear Power: Fallout from Chernobyl." Washington, D.C.: Worldwatch Institute, 1987.

Fogarty, David. "From Saloon to Supermarket." Berkeley: University of California, Department of Urban and Regional Planning, 1985.

Forbes, "Annual Directory Issue: The *Forbes* 500's." April 29, 1985.

Forcier, Michael, and Andrew Hahn. "The Impact of Employment and Training Programs on the Work Attitudes of Disadvantaged Youth." In National Center for Research on Vocational Education, *Youth Employability: Monographs on Research and*

Policy Studies. Columbus, Ohio: National Center for Research on Vocational Education, 1982.

Fortune. "The *Fortune* Directory of the 500 Largest U.S. Industrial Corporations, 1982." May 2, 1983.

———. "The *Fortune* Directory of the 500 Largest U.S. Industrial Corporations." April 29, 1985.

———. "The Economy of the 1990s: An Introduction." February 2, 1987.

Freedman, Audrey. "Can Big Labor Rebuild Its Muscle?" *New York Times,* January 20, 1985.

Freedman, Marcia. "The Structure of the Labor Market and Associated Training Patterns." In National Society for the Study of Education, *Education and Work.* Chicago: University of Chicago Press, 1982.

Freeman, A. Myrick. *The Benefits of Environmental Improvement.* Baltimore: Johns Hopkins University Press, 1979.

Freeman, Richard B. *The Declining Economic Value of Higher Education and the American Social System.* New York: Aspen Institute for Humanistic Studies, 1976a.

———. "Black Economic Progress since 1964." *Public Interest,* Summer 1978a.

———. "Discrimination in the Academic Marketplace." In Thomas Sowell, ed., *Essays and Data on American Ethnic Groups.* Washington, D.C.: Urban Institute, 1978b.

———, and Harry Holzer. *The Black Youth Employment Crisis.* Chicago: University of Chicago Press, 1986.

———. "Troubled Workers in the Labor Market." In National Commission for Employment Policy, *7th Annual Report.* Washington, D.C.: National Commission for Employment Policy, 1981.

———, and James Medoff. *What Do Unions Do?* New York: Basic Books, 1984.

Friedan, Betty. *The Feminine Mystique.* New York: Norton, 1963.

———. *The Second Stage.* New York: Summit, 1981.

———. "Where Do We Go From Here?" *Working Woman,* November 1986.

Friedman, Milton. *Free to Choose.* New York: Harcourt Brace Jovanovich, 1980.

Friends of the Earth et al. *Ronald Reagan and the American Environment.* San Francisco: Friends of the Earth, 1982.

Fuchs, Victor. "The Economics of Health in a Post-Industrial Society." *Public Interest,* Fall 1979.

Furniss, Norman, and Timothy Tilton. *The Case for the Welfare State.* Bloomington: Indiana University Press, 1977.

Furstenburg, Frank. "Work Experience and Family Life." In James O'Toole, ed., *Work and the Quality of Life.* Cambridge, Mass.: Harvard University Press, 1974.

Galbraith, John Kenneth. *The Affluent Society.* Boston: Houghton Mifflin, 1957.

———. *The New Industrial State.* Boston: Houghton Mifflin, 1967.

———. *Economics and the Public Purpose.* Boston: Houghton Mifflin, 1973.

Gallup Poll. Cited in *Emerging Trends,* September 1982.

Garbarino, James. "An Ecological Approach to Child Maltreatment." In Leroy H. Pelton, ed., *The Social Context of Child Abuse and Neglect.* New York: Human Sciences Press, 1981.

Gartner, Timothy. "Bay Area Firms Loaded with Cash." *San Francisco Chronicle,* January 16, 1981.

Gelles, R. J., and E. F. Hargreaves. "Maternal Employment and Violence Toward Children." *Journal of Family Issues,* December 1981.

Georgiu, George. "Oil Market Instability and a New OPEC." *World Policy Journal,* Spring 1987.

Gerth, Hans H., and C. Wright Mills, eds. *From Max Weber: Essays in Sociology.* New York: Oxford University Press, 1954.

Gettys, L. D., and A. Cann. "Children's Perceptions of Occupational Sex Stereotypes." *Sex Roles,* March 1981.

Gilder, George. *Wealth and Poverty.* New York: Basic Books, 1981.

Ginzberg, Eli. "The Job Problem." *Scientific American,* November 1977.

_____, and George J. Vojta. "The Service Sector of the U.S. Economy." *Scientific American,* March 1981.

Glazer, Nathan. "Culture and Mobility." *New Republic,* July 4 and 11, 1981.

Goetting, Ann. "Divorce Outcome Research: Issues and Perspectives." In Arlene S. Skolnick and Jerome H. Skolnick, *Family in Transition,* 4th ed. Boston: Little, Brown, 1983.

Gold, David, and Geoff Quinn. "Misguided Expenditure." *Council on Economic Priorities Newsletter,* July 1981.

Goldberg, Steven. *The Inevitability of Patriarchy.* New York: Morrow, 1974.

Goodman, Paul. *Growing Up Absurd.* New York: Random House, 1960.

_____. *New Reformation: Notes of a Neolithic Conservative.* New York: Random House, 1970.

Gortmaker, Steven. "Poverty and Infant Mortality in the Unived States." *American Sociological Review,* 44, 1979.

Gough, Ian. *The Political Economy of the Welfare State.* London: Macmillan, 1979.

Gove, Walter. "Gender Differences in Mental and Physical Illness." *Social Science and Medicine* 19, No. 1, 1984.

Governor's Task Force on Civil Rights. *Report.* Sacramento, Calif.: California State Department of Fair Employment and Housing, 1982.

Green, Edward, and Russell Wakefield. "Patterns of Middle- and Upper-Class Homicide." *Journal of Criminal Law and Criminology,* Summer 1979.

Green, Mark. *Winning Back America.* New York: Bantam, 1982.

Green, Philip. *The Pursuit of Inequality.* New York: Pantheon, 1980.

Greenberg, David, and Ronald Kessler. "The Effect of Police Employment on Crime," *Criminology,* August 1983.

Greene, Richard. "Tracking Job Growth in Private Industry." *Monthly Labor Review,* September 1982.

Greenwood, Peter, and Allan Abrahamse. *Selective Incapacitation.* Santa Monica, Calif.: Rand Corporation, 1982.

Grossman, Michael. "Government and Health Outcomes." *American Economic Review,* May 1982.

Grunwald, Henry M. "American Renewal." *Fortune,* March 9, 1981.

Guzzardi, Walter. "The Right Way to Strive for Equality." *Fortune,* March 9, 1981.

Hagan, John L., and Ilene H. Nagel. "White-Collar Crime, White-Collar Time: The Sentencing of White-Collar Offenders in the Southern District of New York." *American Criminal Law Review,* Spring 1982.

Hall, Trish. "Miller Seeks to Regain Niche as Envy of Beer Industry." *Wall Street Journal,* December 3, 1986.

Hamakawa, Yoshihiro. "Photovoltaic Power." *Scientific American,* April, 1987.

Hareven, Tamara. "Themes in the Historical Development of the Family." In *Review of Child Development Research* 7, 1984.

Harrington, Michael. *Decade of Decision.* New York: Simon and Schuster, 1980.

_____. "A Path for America." *Dissent,* Fall 1982a.

_____. *The New American Poverty.* New York: Penguin, 1984.

_____. "Progressive Economics for 1988." *The Nation,* May 3, 1986.

_____, and Mark Levinson. "Are We Two Nations? The Perils of a Dual Economy." *Dissent,* Fall 1985.

Harrison, Bennett, Chris Tilly, and Barry Bluestone. "Rising Inequality." In David Obey and Paul Sarbanes, eds., *The Changing American Economy.* New York: Blackwell, 1986.

Hartman, Heidi, ed. *Comparable Worth: New Directions for Research.* Washington, D.C.: National Academy of Sciences, 1985.

Harvey, Robert E. "Can Small Business Get More Defense Contracts?" *Iron Age,* March 10, 1982.

Hatcher, Gordon. *Universal Free Health Care in Canada, 1947-1977*. Washington, D.C.: U.S. Department of Health and Human Services, 1981.

Hattis, Dale, Robert Goble, and Nicholas Ashford. "Airborne Lead: A Clearcut Case of Differential Protection." *Environment*, January-February 1982.

Haveman, Robert H. "Unemployment in Western Europe and the U.S." *American Economic Review*, May 1978.

———, and Gregory Christianson. "Environmental Regulations and Productivity Growth." In Henry Peskin, Paul Portney, and Allan Kneese, eds., *Environmental Regulation and the U.S. Economy*. Baltimore: Johns Hopkins University Press, 1981.

Hayes, Robert, and Robert Abernathy. "Managing Our Way to Decline." *Harvard Business Review*, September-October 1980.

Hayghe, Howard. "Husbands and Wives as Earners: An Analysis of Family Data." *Monthly Labor Review*, February 1981.

———. "Rise in Mothers' Labor Force Activity Includes Those with Infants." *Monthly Labor Review*, February 1986.

Hayward, Jack. *Trade Unions and Politics in Western Europe*. London: Frank Cass, 1980.

Hefferan, Colien. "Workload of Married Women." *Family Economics Review*, Summer 1982.

Heilbroner, Robert, and Lester Thurow. *Five Economic Challenges*. Englewood Cliffs, N.J.: Prentice-Hall, 1981.

Herman, Edward S. *Corporate Control, Corporate Power*. London: Cambridge University Press, 1981.

Herzog, Regula. "High School Seniors' Occupational Plans and Values: Trends in Sex Differences, 1976 through 1980." *Sociology of Education*, January 1982.

Hetherington, E. M., et al. "The Aftermath of Divorce." In J. H. Stevens and M. Mathews, eds., *Mother-Child, Father-Child Relations*. Washington, D.C.: National Association for the Education of Young Children, 1978.

Hicks, L. E., et al. "Cognitive and Health Measures Following Early Nutritional Supplementation." *American Journal of Public Health*, October 1982.

Hill, Martha S. "Authority at Work: How Men and Women Differ." In *Five Thousand American Families: Patterns of Economic Progress*, Vol. 8. Ann Arbor: Survey Research Center, University of Michigan, 1980.

———, and Mary Corcoran. "Unemployment among Family Men: A 10-Year Longitudinal Study." *Monthly Labor Review*, November 1979.

Hindelang, Michael J. "Variations in Rates of Offending." *American Sociological Review*, August 1981.

———, Travis Hirschi, and Joseph Weis. "Correlates of Delinquency: The Illusion of Discrepancy Between Self-Report and Official Measures." *American Sociological Review*, June 1979.

Hofferth, Sandra L., and Kristin Moore. "Women's Employment and Marriage." In Ralph Smith, ed., *The Subtle Revolution*. Washington, D.C.: The Urban Institute, 1979.

Hoffman, Carl, and John S. Reed. "Sex Discrimination? The XYZ Affair." *Public Interest*, Winter 1981.

Hofstadter, Richard. *Social Darwinism in American Thought*. Boston: Beacon, 1955.

Hogue, Carol, et al. "Overview of the National Infant Mortality Surveillance Project." *Public Health Reports*, March–April 1987.

Holzer, Harry. "Black Youth Nonemployment: Duration and Job Search." In Richard Freeman and Harry Holzer, eds., *The Black Youth Employment Crisis*. Chicago: University of Chicago Press, 1986.

Horowitz, Bernard, and Isabel Wolock. "Material Deprivation, Child Maltreatment, and Agency Interventions among Poor Families." In Leroy H. Pelton, ed., *The Social Context of Child Abuse and Neglect*. New York: Human Sciences Press, 1981.

Hout, Michael. "Occupational Mobility of Black Men." *American Sociological Review*, June 1984.

Howard, Robert. "Brave New Workplace." *Working Papers,* November-December, 1980.

Howe, Irving, ed. *Alternatives.* New York: Pantheon, 1984.

Humphrey, Melvin. "Minorities in the Energy Industries." In Ellis Cose, ed., *Energy and Equity: Some Social Concerns.* Washington, D.C.: Joint Center for Political Studies, 1979.

Illich, Ivan. *Medical Nemesis.* New York: Pantheon, 1978.

Jobs With Peace. *A National Budget for Jobs With Peace.* Boston: Jobs With Peace Campaign, 1986.

Joel, Billy. "Allentown." (c) CBS, Inc., 1982.

Junkerman, John. "Japan-Worship." *Working Papers,* January-February 1982.

Kagan, Jerome, Richard Kearsley, and Philip R. Zelazo. *Infancy: Its Place in Human Development.* Cambridge, Mass.: Harvard University Press, 1978.

Kaldor, Mary. *Baroque Arsenal.* New York: Hill and Wang, 1981.

Kamata, Satoshi. *Japan in the Passing Lane.* New York: Pantheon, 1982.

Kamerman, Sheila B. *Parenting in an Unresponsive Society.* New York: Free Press, 1980.

Karch, Nathan, and Marvin Schneiderman. *Explaining the Urban Factor in Lung Cancer Mortality.* Washington, D.C.: National Resources Defense Council, 1981.

Kasl, Stanislav, Susan Gore, and Sidney Cobb. "The Experience of Losing a Job: Reported Changes in Health, Symptoms, and Illness Behavior." *Psychosomatic Medicine,* March-April 1975.

Kaus, Mickey. "The Work Ethic State." *New Republic,* July 7, 1986.

Kazis, Richard, and Richard Grossman. "Environmental Protection: Job-Taker or Job-Maker?" *Environment,* November 1982.

Keithan, Charles F. *The Brewing Industry.* Washington, D.C.: Bureau of Economics, Federal Trade Commission, 1979.

Kelling, George, et al. *The Kansas City Preventive Patrol Experiment.* Washington, D.C.: Police Foundation, 1974.

———, and Mark Moore. "To Serve and Protect: Learning from Police History." *Public Interest,* Winter 1983.

Kessler-Harris, Alice. *Out to Work: A History of Wage-Earning Women in the United States.* New York: Oxford University Press, 1982.

Keyserling, Leon. "The Humphrey-Hawkins Act since Its 1978 Enactment." In David C. Colander, ed., *Solutions to Unemployment.* New York: Harcourt Brace Jovanovich, 1981.

Kilson, Martin. "Black Social Classes and Intergenerational Poverty." *Public Interest,* Summer 1981.

Kirkland, Richard. "Big Steel Recasts Itself." *Fortune,* April 6, 1981.

Kirkland, Richard. "U.S. Tax Cuts Now Go Global." *Fortune,* November 26, 1986.

Klay, William. "How Are Japanese Unions Responding to Microelectronics-Based Automation?" *Montly Labor Review,* March 1987.

Kloby, Jerry. "The Widening Rift: The Growth of Inequality in the 1970s and 1980s." New Brunswick. Department of Sociology, Rutgers University, 1986.

Knudson, Thomas. "High Housing Costs Driving the Young From Suburbs in New York Area." *New York Times,* October 6, 1986.

Kovar, Mary Grace. "Health Status of U.S. Children and Use of Medical Care." *Public Health Reports,* January-February 1982.

———, and Denise J. Meny. *Better Health for Our Children: A National Strategy,* Vol. 3, Washington, D.C.: U.S. Deparment of Health and Human Services, 1981.

Kraft, Philip, and Steven Dubnoff. "Job Content, Fragmentation, and Control in Computer Software Work." *Industrial Relations,* Spring 1986.

Kramer, Rita. *In Defense of the Family.* New York: Basic Books, 1983.

Kristol, Irving. *Two Cheers for Capitalism.* New York: New American Library, 1979.

Kuttner, Robert. "Can Labor Lead?" *New Republic,* March 12, 1984.

————. *The Economic Illusion.* Boston: Houghton-Mifflin, 1985.

LaFraniere, Sharon. "Shipyards, Asbestos, and Death." *Washington Post Weekly,* October 8, 1984.

Laird, Melvin R. *Energy—A Crisis in Public Policy.* Washington, D.C.: American Enterprise Institute, 1977.

Lasch, Christopher. *Heaven in a Heartless World: The Family Beseiged.* New York: Basic Books, 1977.

————. *The Culture of Narcissism.* New York: Warner, 1978.

Laslett, Barbara. "Family Membership, Past and Present." In Arlene S. Skolnick and Jerome H. Skonick, eds., *Family in Transition,* 4th ed. Boston: Little, Brown, 1983.

Lawrence, Robert Z. *Can America Compete?* Washington, D.C.: Brookings Institute, 1984.

Laws, Judith Long. *The Second X: Sex Role and Social Roles.* New York: Elsevier, 1979.

Lebowitz, Ann. "Overview: The Health of Working Women." In Diane Chapman Walsh and Richard H. Egdahl, eds., *Women, Work, and Health.* New York: Springer-Verlag, 1980.

Lee, Gary. "Chernobyl and the Nuclear Reaction." *Washington Post Weekly,* November 10, 1986.

Lein, Laura, and Mary C. Blehar. "Working Couples as Parents." In U.S. Department of Health and Human Services, *Families Today: A Research Sampler on Families and Children,* Vol. 1. Washington, D.C.: Government Printing Office, 1979.

Lekachman, Robert. *Greed Is Not Enough: Reaganomics.* New York: Pantheon, 1982.

Lemann, Nicholas. "The Origins of the Underclass." *Atlantic,* June 1986.

Leonard, Jonathan. "Employment and Occupational Advance Under Affirmative Action." *Review of Economics and Statistics,* August 1984.

Leontieff, Wassily. "The Distribution of Work and Income." *Scientific American,* September 1982a.

Levitan, Sar A., and Richard S. Belous. *What's Happening to the American Family.* Baltimore: Johns Hopkins University Press, 1981.

————, and Clifford Johnson. "The Future of Work: Does It Belong to Us or to the Robots?" *Monthly Labor Review,* September 1982.

Levy, Frank. "We're Running Out of Gimmicks to Sustain Our Prosperity." *Washington Post Weekly,* December 29, 1986.

————, and Richard Michel. *The Economic Future of the Baby Boom.* Washington, D.C.: U.S. Congress, Joint Economic Committee, 1985.

Lieberson, Stanley. *A Piece of the Pie.* Berkeley: University of California Press, 1981.

Liem, Ramsey, and Paula Rayman. "Health and Social Costs of Unemployment." *American Psychologist,* October 1982.

Liljestrom, Rita. "Integration of Family Policy and Labor Market Policy in Sweden." In Ronnie Steinberg Ratner, ed., *Equal Employment Policy for Women.* Philadelphia: Temple University Press, 1980.

Lindblom, Charles E. *Politics and Markets: The World's Political-Economic Systems.* New York: Basic Books, 1977.

Linsenmayer, Tadd. "ILO Examines Impact of Technology on Workers' Safety and Health." *Monthly Labor Review,* August 1985.

Lipton, Douglas, Robert Martinson, and Judith Wilks. *The Effectiveness of Correctional Treatment.* New York: Praeger, 1975.

Loftin, Colin, and David McDowall. "The Police, Crime, and Economic Theory." *American Sociological Review,* June 1982.

Loomis, Carol J. "The Madness of Executive Compensation." *Fortune,* July 12, 1982.

Loury, Glenn. "A New American Dilemma." *New Republic,* December 31, 1984.

Lovins, Amory B., and L. Hunter Lovins. *Energy/War: Breaking the Nuclear Link.* San Francisco: Friends of the Earth, 1980.

Lubar, Robert. "Why Unemployment Will Hang High." *Fortune,* June 14, 1982.

Lucy, William. "Can We Find Good Jobs in a Service Economy?" In C. Stewart Sheppard and Donald C. Carroll, *Working in the 21st Century*. New York: Wiley, 1980.

Lueptow, L. B. "Sex-Typing and Change in the Occupational Choices of High School Seniors." *Sociology of Education*, January 1981.

Lynd, Robert, and Helen M. Lynd. *Middletown*. New York: Harcourt, Brace and World, 1929.

McAdoo, Harriette P., ed. *Black Families*. Beverly Hills, Calif.: Sage, 1981.

Maccoby, Eleanor, and Carol Jacklin. *The Psychology of Sex Differences*. Stanford, Calif.: Stanford University Press, 1974.

McConnell-Condry, Sandra, and Irving Lazar. "American Values and Social Policy for Chidren." *Annals of the American Academy of Political and Social Science*, Vol. 461, May 1982.

McFadden, Dave, and Jim Wake, eds. *The Freeze Economy*. Mountain View, Calif.: Mid-Peninsula Conversion Project, 1983.

MacGraw, Onalee. Prepared statement, U.S. Congress, Senate, Committee on Labor and Human Resources, Hearings on *Work Ethic: Materialism and the American Family*, March 1982.

Magaziner, Ira, and Robert Reich. *Minding America's Business*. New York: Harcourt Brace Jovanovich, 1982.

Manpower Demonstration Research Corporation. *Summary and Findings of the National Supported Work Experiment*. Cambridge, Mass.: Ballinger, 1980.

Marcuse, Herbert. *One-Dimensional Man*. Boston: Beacon, 1964.

Mare, Robert D. "Socioeconomic Effects On Child Mortality in the United States." *American Journal of Public Health*, June 1982.

Markusen, Ann. "Military Spending and the U.S. Economy." *World Policy Journal*, Summer 1986.

Marshall, James, and Donna Funch. "Mental Illness and the Economy: A Critique and Partial Replication." *Journal of Health and Social Behavior*, September 1979.

Martin, Philip L. "Select Commission Suggests Changes in Immigration Policy." *Monthly Labor Review*, February 1982.

Maslow, Jonathan E. "Beer Wars." *Saturday Review*, July 7, 1979.

Meacham, Steve. "It's Not Just a Project, It's an Adventure." *Plowshare Press*, March-April 1983.

Mead, Lawrence M. "Social Programs and Social Obligations." *The Public Interest*, Fall 1982.

Mead, Lawrence. "The Real Crisis." *Society*, January–February 1986.

Mellor, Earl F., and George D. Stanas. "Usual Weekly Earnings: Another Look at Intergroup Differences and Basic Trends." *Monthly Labor Review*, April 1982.

Mellor, Earl. "Weekly Earnings in 1985." *Monthly Labor Review*, September 1986.

Melman, Seymour. "Looting the Means of Production." *Plowshare Press*, November-December 1982.

Meltzer, Allan. "Big Government: Democracy's Deadly Creation." Smithkline Forum for a Healthier American Society, October 1980.

Messner, Stephen. "Societal Development, Social Inequality, and Homicide." *Social Forces*, September 1982.

Meyer, Herbert E. "Jobs and Want Ads: A Look Behind the Words." *Fortune*, November 1978.

———. "The Decline of Strikes." *Fortune*, November 2, 1981.

Mills, C. Wright. *The Sociological Imagination*. New York: Oxford University Press, 1959.

Miller, Brent. Prepared Statement, U.S. Congress, Senate, Committee on Labor and Human Resources, Hearings on *Work Ethic: Materialism and the American Family*, March 1982.

Moore, Emily C. *Women and Health: United States, 1980.* Washington, D.C.: U.S. Public Health Service, 1980.

Morita, Akio. *Made in Japan.* New York: Random House, 1986.

Morrison, Ann. "Betting the Barn at Stroh." *Fortune,* May 31, 1982.

Mott, Frank, and David Shapiro. "Pregnancy, Motherhood, and Work Activity." In Frank Mott, ed., *Women, Work, and Family.* Lexington, Mass.: Lexington Books, 1978.

Mueller, Willard F. "Conglomerates: A Non-Industry." In Walter Adams, ed., *The Structure of American Industry,* 5th ed. New York: Macmillan, 1977.

Mullen, Joan, et al. *American Prisons and Jails,* Vol. I. Washington, D.C.: National Institute of Justice, 1980.

Murphy, Jim. *A Question of Race: Minority Incarceration in New York State.* Albany: Center for Justice Education, 1986.

Murray, Charles. *Losing Ground.* New York: Basic Books, 1985.

Myrdal, Gunnar. *Objectivity in Social Research.* New York: Pantheon, 1969.

Nardone, Thomas. "Part-time Workers: Who Are They?" *Monthly Labor Review,* February 1986.

Nathanson, Constance, and Marian Passannante. Johns Hopkins University Research. In *San Francisco Chronicle,* May 18, 1983.

National Academy of Sciences. *Women Scientists in Industry and Government: How Much Progress in the 1970's?* Washington, D.C.: National Academy of Sciences, 1980.

National Center for Education Statistics. "Women Outpaced Men In Faculty and Tenure Increases." *Bulletin,* June 1980.

———. "Does College Pay? Wage Rates Before and After Leaving School." *Bulletin,* November 1982.

National Commission for Employment Policy. *Hispanics and Jobs: Barriers to Progress.* Washington, D.C.: Government Printing Office, 1982.

National Commission on Employment and Unemployment Statistics. *Counting the Labor Force.* Washington, D.C.: Government Printing Office, 1979.

National Commission on Excellence in Education. *A Nation at Risk: The Imperative for Educational Reform.* Washington, D.C.: Government Printing Office, 1983.

National Research Council. *Women, Work, and Wages: Equal Pay for Jobs of Equal Value.* Washington, D.C.: National Academy Press, 1981.

Navarro, Peter. "The Politics of Air Pollution." *Public Interest,* Spring 1980.

Newsweek. "The Battle of the Beers." September 4, 1978.

———. "The Plague of Violent Crime." March 23, 1981.

———. "Defending America." December 20, 1982a.

———. "Jobs: Putting America Back to Work." October 19, 1982b.

Noble, David. *Forces of Production: A Social History of Industrial Automation.* New York: Knopf, 1984.

Nordlund, Willis, and R. Thayne Robson. *Energy and Employment.* New York: Praeger, 1980.

Novak, Michael, and Gordon Green. "Poverty Down, Inequality Up?" *Public Interest,* Spring 1986.

Nukazawa, Kazuo. "Now Japan Frets about Taxes and Deficit." *Wall Street Journal,* May 9, 1983.

Office of Management and Budget. *Special Analyses, Budget of the United States Government, Fiscal Year 1984.* Washington, D.C.: Government Printing Office, 1983.

Olsen, Marvin E. "Assessing the Social Impacts of Energy Conservation." In Karen Gentemann, ed., *Social and Political Perspectives on Energy Policy.* New York: Praeger, 1981.

Orsagh, Thomas, and Ann Dryden Witte. "Economic Status and Crime: Implications for Offender Rehabilitation." *Journal of Criminal Law and Criminology,* Fall 1981.

Osterman, Paul. "Affirmative Action and Opportunity: A Study of Female Quit Rates." *Review of Economics and Statistics,* November 1982.

Ostro, Bart, and Robert Anderson. *Morbidity, Air Pollution, and Health Statistics.* Washington, D.C.: U.S. Environmental Protection Agency, Office of Policy Analysis, 1981.

O'Toole, James. *Making America Work—Productivity and Responsibility.* New York: Continuum, 1981.

Page, Benjamin. *Who Gets What From Government.* Berkeley: University of California Press, 1983.

Paglin, Morton. "The Measurement and Trend of Inequality: A Basic Revision." *American Economic Review,* September 1975.

Passel, Jeffrey. "Estimating the Number of Undocumented Aliens." *Monthly Labor Review,* September 1986.

Paternoster, Raymond, et al. "Perceived Risk and Social Control." *Law and Society Review* 17, No. 3, 1983.

Pathirane, Leila, and Derek W. Blades. "Defining and Measuring the Public Sector: Some International Comparisons." *Review of Income and Wealth,* September 1982.

Pear, Robert. "Census Bureau Weighs Effects of Changing Poverty Criterion." *New York Times,* October 3, 1986.

Pearce, Diana. "Women in Poverty." In Arthur I. Blaustein, ed., *The American Promise: Equal Justice and Economic Opportunity.* New Brunswick, N.J.: Transaction, 1982.

Pechman, Joseph. *Who Paid the Taxes, 1966-85.* Washington, D.C.: Brookings Institute, 1985.

Pelton, Leroy H. "Child Abuse and Neglect: The Myth of Classlessness." In Leroy H. Pelton, ed., *The Social Context of Child Abuse and Neglect.* New York: Human Sciences, 1981.

Peltz, Rachael A. "The War at Home." Ph.D. diss., The Wright Institute, 1982.

Pertschuk, Michael. Quoted in Mark Green and Robert Massie, eds., *The Big Business Reader.* New York: Pilgrim, 1980.

Peskin, Janice. "Measuring Household Production for the GNP." *Family Economics Review,* Summer 1982.

Petersilia, Joan M., Peter W. Greenwood, and Marvin Lavin. *Criminal Careers of Habitual Felons.* Washington, D.C.: U.S. Department of Justice, Law Enforcement Assistance Administration, 1978.

Peterson, Mark, and Harriet Braiker. *Doing Crime: A Survey of California Prison Inmates.* Washington, D.C.: U.S. National Institute of Justice, 1980.

Peterson, William. "Chinese Americans and Japanese Americans." In Thomas Sowell, ed., *Essays and Data on American Ethnic Groups.* Washington, D.C.: The Urban Institute, 1978.

Podhoretz, Norman. *The Present Danger.* New York: Simon and Schuster, 1980.

Police Foundation. *Reducing Fear of Crime in Houston and Newark.* Washington, D.C., 1986.

Pollock, Cynthia. "Decommissioning Nuclear Power Plants." In Lester Brown, ed., *State of the World 1986.* New York: Norton, 1986.

Portney, Paul R. "The Macroeconomic Effects of Federal Environmental Legislation." In Henry Peskin, Paul Portney, and Allen Kneese, eds., *Environmental Regulation and the U.S. Economy.* Baltimore: Johns Hopkins University Press, 1981.

President's Commission on Law Enforcement and Administation of Justice. *The Challenge of Crime in a Free Society.* Washington, D.C.: Government Printing Office, 1967.

Presser, Harriett B., and Wendy Baldwin. "Child Care as a Constraint on Employment." *American Journal of Sociology,* March 1980.

Public Opinion. "Opinion Roundup." January-February 1981.

Queen, Stuart A., and Delbert M. Mann. *Social Pathology.* New York: Crowell, 1925.

Ramirez, Anthony. "America's Super Minority." *Fortune,* November 24, 1986.

Rankin, Joseph H. "The Family Context of Delinquency." *Social Problems,* April 1983.

Ratner, Ronnie S. "The Policy and Problem: Overview of Seven Countries." In Ronnie S. Ratner, ed., *Equal Employment Policy for Women.* Philadelphia: Temple University Press, 1980

Rayman, Paula, and Barry Bluestone. *The Private and Social Response to Joblessness,* Final Report. Washington, D.C.: National Institute of Mental Health, 1982.

Reagan, Ronald. *America's New Beginning: A Program for Economic Recovery.* Washington, D.C.: Government Printing Office, February 1981.

———. "Address to the Nation." March 23, 1983. Reprinted in (*Bulletin* of the U.S. Department of State), April 1983.

Reich, Michael. *Racial Inequality.* New York: Cambridge University Press, 1981.

Reich, Robert B. "The Next American Frontier." *Atlantic,* March-April 1983.

———. "The New Public Philosophy." *Atlantic,* May 1985.

———, and Ira C. Magaziner. *Minding America's Business.* New York: Harcourt Brace Jovanovich, 1982.

Reimers, Cordelia. "Why Are Hispanic Americans' Incomes So Low?" Cited in *Employment and Training Report of the President, 1983,* pp. 98-99, 1982.

Reskin, Barbara, and Heidi Hartmann, eds. *Womens' Work, Mens' Work.* Washington, D.C.: National Academy of Sciences, 1986.

Reubens, Beatrice G. "Review of Foreign Experience." In American Assembly, *Youth Unemployment and Public Policy.* Englewood Cliffs, N.J.: Prentice-Hall, 1980.

Rhodes, Steven L., and Paulette Middleton. "Acid Rain: The Complex Challenge." *Environment,* May 1983.

Rich, Spencer. "Minorities, Women Gain in Top Jobs." *Washington Post Weekly,* April 15, 1985.

———. "Are You Really Better Off Than You Were 13 Years Ago?" *Washington Post Weekly,* September 8, 1986.

Richardson, Laurel. *The Dynamics of Sex and Gender.* Boston: Houghton Mifflin, 1981.

Rice, Haynes, and LaRah Payne. "Health Issues for the Eighties." In National Urban League, *The State of Black America.* New York: National Urban League, 1981.

Rickover, Hyman. "Advice from Admiral Rickover." *New York Review of Books,* March 18, 1982.

Riesman, David. *The Lonely Crowd.* New Haven, Conn.: Yale University Press, 1955.

Ripley, Randall, and Grace Franklin. *Private Sector Involvement in Public Employment and Training Programs.* Washington, D.C.: National Commission for Employment Policy, 1981.

Rivlin, Alice. Congressional Testimony. Quoted in *Employment and Training Reporter,* August 8, 1982.

Rosen, Ellen. *Hobson's Choice: Employment and Unemployment among Women Factory Workers in New England,* Ms., Boston College. Cited in *Employment and Training Report of the President, 1983,* pp. 96-97, 1982.

Rosenbaum, Sara, and Kay Johnson. "Providing Health Care for Low-Income Children." *Milbank Quarterly* 64, No. 3, 1986.

Rosenfield, Carl. "Job Search of the Unemployed, May 1976." *Monthly Labor Review,* November 1977.

Rosenthal, Evelyn R. "Working in Mid-Life." In Ann H. Stromberg and Shirley Harkness, eds., *Women Working.* Palo Alto, Calif.: Mayfield, 1978.

Rosenthal, Neal. "The Shrinking Middle Class: Myth Or Reality?" *Monthly Labor Review,* March 1985.

Rossi, Peter, Richard Berk, and Kenneth Lenihan. *Money, Work, and Crime.* New York: Academic, 1980.

Rothschild, Emma. "Reagan and the Real America." *New York Review of Books,* February 5, 1981.

Royston, Michael. "Making Pollution Prevention Pay." *Harvard Business Review,* November-December 1980.

Rumberger, Russell W. *Overeducation in the U.S. Labor Market.* New York: Praeger, 1981.

Ruttenberg, Ruth. "Regulation Is the Mother of Invention." *Working Papers,* May-June 1981.

Rutter, Michael. *Changing Youth in a Changing Society.* Cambridge: Harvard University Press, 1980.

Safilios-Rothschild, Constantina. "Women and Work: Policy Implications and Prospects for the Future." In Ann H. Stromberg and Shirley Harkness, eds., *Women Working.* Palo Alto, Calif.: Mayfield, 1979.

Sawhill, Isabel. Testimony, U.S. Congress, Senate, Committee on Labor and Human Resources, Hearings on *The Coming Decade: American Women and Human Resources Policies and Programs,* Part I, 1979.

Sawyer, Malcolm. *Income Distribution in OECD Countries.* Paris: Organization for Economic Cooperation and Development, 1978.

Scherer, Frederick M. *Industrial Market Structure and Economic Performance,* 2nd ed. Chicago: Rand McNally, 1980.

Schipper, Lee, and A. J. Lichtenberg. "Efficient Energy and Well- Being: The Swedish Example." *Science,* December 3, 1978.

Schlozman, Kay, and Sidney Verba. "The New Unemployment: Does It Hurt? *Public Policy,* Summer 1978.

Schnaiberg, Alan. *The Environment: From Surplus to Scarcity.* New York: Oxford University Press, 1980.

Schreiner, Tim. "Americans With Extra Cash." *San Francisco Chronicle,* August 11, 1985.

Schroeder, Pat. "The Laws Must be Adapted To Today's Realities." *Washington Post Weekly,* January 5, 1987.

Schroeder, Steven A. "National Health Insurance: Always Just Around the Corner?" *American Journal of Public Health,* October 1981.

Schuman, Howard, Charlotte Steeh, and Lawrence Bobo. *Racial Attitudes in America: Trends and Interpretations.* Cambridge: Harvard University Press, 1985.

Science. April 10, 1987.

Scott, Bruce R. "Can Industry Survive the Welfare State?" *Harvard Business Review,* September-October 1982.

Shai, Donna. "Cancer Mortality, Ethnicity, and Socioeconomic Status: Two New York City Groups." *Public Health Reports,* September–October 1986.

Shaiken, Harley. *Work Transformed.* Boston: Houghton-Mifflin, 1985.

Shapiro, David. "Wage Differentials Among Black, Hispanic, and White Young Men." *Industrial and Labor Relations Review,* July 1984.

Shapiro, Sam, et al. "Prospects for Eliminating Racial Differences in Breast Cancer Survival Rates." *American Journal of Public Health,* October 1982.

Shaw, Lois B., ed. *Dual Careers: A Decade of Change in the Lives of Mature Women.* Columbus, Ohio: Center for Human Resources Research, Ohio State University, 1981.

Shepherd, William G., and Clair Wilcox. *Public Policies toward Business,* 6th ed. Homewood, Ill.: Irwin, 1979.

Sidel, Victor W., and Ruth Sidel. *A Healthy State.* New York: Pantheon, 1977.

Sidel, Victor, and Ruth Sidel. *A Healthy State.* New York: Pantheon, 1983.

Siegfried, John, ed. *The Economics of Firm Size, Market Structure, and Social Performance.* Washington, D.C.: U.S. Federal Trade Commission, 1980.

Sigal, Leon V. "Warming to the Freeze." *Foreign Policy,* Fall 1982.

Simon, Julian, and Herman Kahn. *The Resourceful Earth.* London: Basil Blackwell, 1984.

Skolnick, Jerome, and David Bayley, *The New Blue Line.* New York: Free Press, 1986.

Skolnick, Jerome H., and Elliott Currie. *Crisis in American Institutions,* 5th ed. Boston: Little, Brown, 1982.

Smith, James D. Prepared statement, U.S. Congress, Joint Economic Committee, Hearings on *The 1982 Joint Economic Report of the President,* February 1982.

Smith, Ralph E. "The Movement of Women into the Labor Force." In Ralph Smith, ed., *The Subtle Revolution: Women at Work.* Washington, D.C.: The Urban Institute, 1979.

Sorrentino, Constance. "Youth Unemployment: An International Perspective." *Monthly Labor Review,* July 1981.

Sowell, Thomas. "Myths about Minorities." *Commentary,* August 1979.

———, *Markets and Minorities.* New York: Basic Books, 1981.

———. *The Economics and Politics of Race.* New York: Morrow, 1983.

Stack, Carol B. *All Our Kin.* New York: Harper and Row, 1974.

Starr, Paul. *The Social Transformation of American Medicine.* New York: Basic Books, 1982.

Statistical Abstract of the United States, 1987. Washington, D.C.: U.S. Department of Commerce, 1986.

Stegner, Wallace. "Regress and Pillage." *New Republic,* August 31, 1982.

Stein, Herbert. "Eight Questions for Conservatives." *Fortune,* January 11, 1982a.

———. "How World War III Was Lost." *Wall Street Journal,* December 3, 1982b.

Stein, Mark. "Environment and Cancer." *San Francisco Chronicle,* October 14, 1984.

Steinberg, Stephen. *The Ethnic Myth: Race, Ethnicity, and Class in America.* Boston: Atheneum, 1980.

Steinfels, Peter. *The Neoconservatives.* New York: Simon and Schuster, 1980.

Stellman, Jeanne. *Women's Work, Women's Health.* New York Pantheon, 1979.

Stobaugh, Robert, and Daniel Yergin. *Energy Future,* rev. ed. New York: Vintage, 1982.

Straus, Murray A. "A Sociological Perspective on the Causes of Family Violence." In Maurice R. Green, ed., *Violence and the Family.* Boulder, Colo.: Westview, 1980.

———, Richard J. Gelles, and Suzanne Steinmetz. *Behind Closed Doors: Violence in the American Family.* New York: Doubleday, 1980.

Straus, Murray, and Richard Gelles. "Societal Change and Changes in Family Violence from 1975 to 1985." *Journal of Marriage and Family,* August 1986.

Sullivan, Mercer. *Youth Crime and Employment Patterns in Three Brooklyn Neighborhoods.* New York: Vera Institute, 1985.

Sutherland, Edwin. *White-Collar Crime.* New York: Holt, 1949.

Swinton, David. "Economic Status of Blacks, 1986." In National Urban League, *State of Black America, 1987.* Washington, D.C.: National Urban League, 1987.

Taeuber, Karl. "Racial Residential Segregation, 28 Cities, 1970-1980." Madison, Wis.: Center for Demography and Ecology, University of Wisconsin, 1983.

Takaki, Ronald. "Asian Successes Are Misleading." *San Francisco Chronicle,* February 9, 1985.

Thompson, James W., et al. *Employment and Crime: A Review of Theories and Research.* Washington, D.C.: Government Printing Office, 1981.

Thomson, Randall J., and Matthew T. Zingraff. "Detecting Sentencing Disparity: Some Problems and Evidence." *American Journal of Sociology,* January 1981.

Thornberry, Terence. "Sentencing Disparities in the Juvenile Justice System." *Journal of Criminal Law and Criminology,* Summer 1979.

Thornton, Arland. "The Fragile Family." *Family Planning Perspectives.* September–October 1986.

Thornton, James, Richard Agnello, and Charles Lind. "Poverty and Economic Growth: Trickle Down Peters Out." *Economic Inquiry,* July 1978.

Thurow, Lester. *The Zero-Sum Society.* New York: Penguin, 1980.

———. "Death by a Thousand Cuts." *New York Review of Books,* December 17, 1981a.

———. "How to Wreck the Economy." *New York Review of Books,* May 14, 1981b.

———. *Dangerous Currents.* New York: Random House, 1983.

———. *The Zero-Sum Solution.* New York: Simon and Schuster, 1986.

Tidwell, Billy. "A Profile of the Black Unemployed." In National Urban League, *State of Black America, 1987.* New York: National Urban League, 1987.

Tietze, Christopher. "Abortion Alarms." *American Journal of Public Health,* June 1982.

Tillman, Robert. *The Prevalence and Incidence of Arrest Among Adult Males in California."* Sacramento: California Department of Justice, 1986.

Time. "New Thrust in Antitrust." May 21, 1979.

———. "Can Capitalism Survive?" April 21, 1980.

Titmuss, Richard M. *Commitment to Welfare.* London: Allen and Unwin, 1968.

Titmuss, Richard. *The Gift of Blood.* New York: Random House, 1973.

Tittle, Charles R. *Sanctions and Social Deviance: The Question of Deterrence.* New York: Praeger, 1980.

Treas, Judith. "Trickle Down or Transfers? Postwar Determinants of Family Income Inequality." *American Sociological Review,* August 1983.

Trojanowicz, Robert. *An Evaluation of the Neighborhood Foot Patrol Program in Flint, Michigan.* East Lansing, MI: Michigan State University School of Criminal Justice, 1983.

Tsongas, Paul. *The Road from Here: Liberalism and Realities in the 1980's.* New York: Knopf, 1981.

Tucker, William. *Progress and Privilege: America in the Age of Environmentalism.* New York: Doubleday, 1982.

Union of Concerned Scientists. *Energy Strategies: Toward a Solar Future.* Cambridge, Mass.: Ballinger, 1981.

United Nations. *The Economic Role of Women in the ECE Region.* New York: U.N. Economic Commission for Europe, 1980.

———. *Transnational Corporations in the Auto Industry.* New York: U.N. Centre on Transnational Corporations, 1983.

U.S. Bureau of the Census. *Concentration Ratios in Manufacturing, 1982 Census of Manufacturers.* Washington, D.C.: Government Printing Office, 1986.

———. *Changing Family Composition and Income Differentials.* Washington, D.C.: Government Printing Office, 1982a.

———. "Trends in Child Care Arrangements of Working Mothers." *Current Population Report,* Series P-23, No. 117. Washington, D.C., 1982b.

———. "Characteristics of the Population Below the Poverty Level, 1981." *Current Population Reports,* Series P-60, No. 138. Washington, D.C., April 1983.

———. "After-School Care of School-Age Children." *Current Population Reports* Series P-23, No. 149. Washington, D.C., 1986a.

———. "Money Income and Poverty Status, 1985: Advance Report." *Current Population Reports* Series P-60, No. 152. Washington, D.C., 1986b.

———. "Child Support and Alimony, 1983." *Current Population Reports* Series P-23, No. 148. Washington, D.C., 1986c.

———. "Households, Families, Marital Status, and Living Arrangements." *Current Population Reports* Series P-20, No. 412. Washington, D.C., 1986d.

U.S. Bureau of Justice Statistics. *Survey of Prisons and Prisoners, 1979.* Washington, D.C.: Bureau of Justice Statistics, January 1982.

———. *Prisoners and Alcohol.* Washington, D.C.: Bureau of Justice Statistics, 1983a.

———. *Prisoners and Drugs.* Washington, D.C.: Bureau of Justice Statistics, 1983b.

U.S. Bureau of Labor Statistics. *One in Five Persons in Labor Force Experienced Some Unemployment in 1981.* Bulletin. Washington, D.C.: Bureau of Labor Statistics, July 20, 1982b.

U.S. Commission on Civil Rights. *Social Indicators of Equality for Minorities and Women.* Washington, D.C.: Government Printing Office, 1978.

———. *Success of Asian-Americans: Fact or Fiction?* Washington, D.C.: Government Printing Office, 1980a.

———. *Youth Unemployment.* Washington, D.C.: Government Printing Office, 1980b.

———. *Child Care and Equal Opportunity for Women.* Washington, D.C.: Government Printing Office, 1981.

————. *Unemployment and Underemployment among Blacks, Hispanics, and Women.* Washington, D.C.: Government Printing Office, 1982.

U.S. Commission on Civil Rights, Illinois Advisory Committee. *Shutdown: Economic Dislocation and Equal Opportunity.* Washington, D.C.: Government Printing Office, 1981.

U.S. Congress, House, Select Committee on Children, Youth, and Families. *Safety Net Programs: Are They Reaching Poor Children?* Washington, D.C.: Government Printing Office, 1984.

U.S. Congress, House, Committee on Small Business. *Future of Small Business in America.* Washington, D.C.: Government Printing Office, August 1979.

U.S. Congress, House, Ways and Means Committee. Data cited in *San Francisco Chronicle,* March 5, 1984.

U.S. Congress, Joint Economic Committee. *Joint Economic Report.* Washington, D.C.: Government Printing Office, January 1982a.

————. *The Concentration of Wealth in the United States.* Washington, D.C.: Government Printing Office, 1986.

U.S. Congress, Senate, Committee on Governmental Affairs. *Interlocking Directorates among the Major U.S. Corporations.* Washington, D.C.: Government Printing Office, 1978.

U.S. Congress, Senate, Committee on the Judiciary. *Hearings on Mergers and Economic Concentration.* Washington, D.C.: Government Printing Office, 1978.

U.S. Congressional Budget Office. *Federal Credit Activities: An Analysis of the President's Credit Budget for 1981.* Washington, D.C.: Government Printing Office, February 1980.

————. *Dislocated Workers: Issues and Federal Options.* Washington, D.C.: Government Printing Office, July 1982b.

————. *Defense Spending and the Economy.* Washington, D.C.: Government Printing Office, 1983b.

U.S. Congressional Budget Office. *Federal Support of the U.S. Business.* Washington, D.C.: Government Printing Office, 1984.

U.S. Department of Health and Human Services. *Health—United States, 1986.* Washington, D.C.: Government Printing Office, 1986.

————. *National Study of the Incidence and Severity of Child Abuse and Neglect.* Executive Summary. Washington, D.C.: National Center on Child Abuse and Neglect, 1982b.

U.S. Department of Labor. *Interim Report to Congress on Occupational Diseases.* Washington, D.C.: Government Printing Office, June 1980.

U.S. Department of Labor, Women's Bureau. *Employment Goals of the World Plan of Action: Developments and Issues in the United States.* Washington, D.C.: Government Printing Office, 1980.

U.S. General Accounting Office. *Advances in Automation Prompt Concern over Increased U.S. Unemployment.* Washington, D.C.: Government Printing Office, 1982a.

————. *Labor Market Problems of Teenagers.* Washington, D.C.: Government Printing Office, 1982b.

U.S. News and World Report. "How to Get the Country Moving Again: Advice from Six Nobel Prize Economists." January 31, 1983.

U.S. Office of Management and Budget. *Budget of the United States Government, Fiscal Year 1988,* Supplement. Washington, D.C.: Government Printing Office, 1987.

Urquhart, Michael, and Marilyn A. Hewson. "Unemployment Continued to Rise in 1982 as Recession Deepened." *Monthly Labor Review,* February 1983.

Van den Haag, Ernest, "Could Successful Rehabilitation Reduce the Crime Rate?" *Journal of Criminal Law and Criminology,* Fall 1982.

Vedder, Richard K. *Robotics and the Economy.* Washington, D.C.: Government Printing Office, March 1982.

Vera Institute of Justice. *Felony Arrests: Their Prosecution and Disposition in New York City's Courts.* New York: Longman, 1981.

Vera Institute. *Employment and Crime: A Summary Report.* New York: Vera Institute of Justice, 1984.

Vernon, Raymond. "Gone Are the Cash Cows of Yesteryear." *Harvard Business Review,* November-December 1980.

Vickery, Claire. "Women's Economic Contribution to the Family." In Ralph Smith, ed., *The Subtle Revolution,* Washington, D.C.: The Urban Institute, 1979.

Vigderhous, Gideon, and Gideon Fishman. "The Impact of Unemployment and Familial Integration on Changing Suicide Rates in the USA." *Social Psychiatry,* Spring 1978.

Waite, Linda. *Women in Nontraditional Occupations: Choice and Turnover.* Santa Monica: Rand Corporation, 1985.

Wallace, Michael, and Arne L. Kalleberg. "Industrial Transformation and the Decline of Craft: The Decomposition of Skill in the Printing Industry." *American Sociological Review,* June 1982.

Waller, Willard. "Social Problems and the Mores." *American Sociological Review,* December 1936.

Wallerstein, Judith, and Joan Kelly. *Surviving the Breakup.* New York: Basic Books, 1980.

Wanniski, Jude. *The Way the World Works.* New York: Simon and Schuster, 1979.

Weinberger, Caspar. Quoted in Center for Defense Information, "The Need for a Level Military Budget." *Defense Monitor,* 1983.

Weiskopf, Michael. "California's Subterranean Toxic Blob." *Washington Post Weekly,* December 1, 1986.

Weitzman, Lenore. *The Divorce Revolution.* New York: Free Press, 1985.

Westcott, Diane Nilsen. "Blacks in the 1970's: Did They Scale the Job Ladder?" *Monthly Labor Review,* June 1982.

Whelan, Elizabeth M. "Chemicals and Cancerphobia." *Society,* March-April 1981.

White, Lynn K., and David B. Brinkerhoff. "The Sexual Division of Labor: Evidence from Childhood." *Social Forces,* September 1981.

Wildavsky, Aaron. "Richer Is Safer." *The Public Interest,* Winter 1980.

Will, George. "In Defense of the Welfare State." *New Republic,* May 9, 1983.

Williams, Walter. "The State Against Blacks." In Manhattan Institute for Policy Research, *Manhattan Report on Economic Policy.* New York: Manhattan Institute for Policy Research, November 1982.

Williams, Winston. "White-Collar Crime: Booming Again." *New York Times,* June 9, 1985.

Williamson, Jeffrey, and Peter Lindert. "Long-Term Trends in American Wealth Inequality." In James D. Smith, ed., *Modeling the Distribution and Intergenerational Transmission of Wealth.* Chicago: University of Chicago Press, 1980.

Wilson, James Q. *Thinking about Crime.* New York: Basic Books, 1975.

——. *Thinking About Crime,* Revised Edition. New York: Random House, 1983.

——, and Richard Herrnstein. *Crime and Human Nature.* New York: Simon and Schuster, 1985.

Wilson, William J. *The Declining Significance of Race.* Chicago: University of Chicago Press, 1978.

——, and Kathryn Neckerman. "Poverty Status and Family Structure." In Sheldon Danziger and Daniel Weinberg, *Fighting Poverty.* Cambridge: Harvard University Press, 1986.

Wirtz, Willard, Testimony. In U.S. Congress, Senate, Committee on Labor and Human Resources, Hearings on *The Coming Decade: American Women and Human Resources Programs,* 1979.

Wolfe, Alan. *America's Impasse.* New York: Pantheon, 1981.

Wolfgang, Marvin. Testimony, U.S. Congress, Senate, Committee on the Judiciary, Hearings on *Violent Juvenile Crime*, 1981.

———, Robert Figlio, and Thorsten Sellin. *Delinquency in a Birth Cohort.* Chicago: University of Chicago Press, 1972.

Wolfgang, Marvin, and Neil Alan Weiner. "Violent Crime in America, 1969–1982." In Lynn A. Curtis, ed., *American Violence and Public Policy.* New Haven: Yale University Press, 1985.

Womens' Economic Agenda Working Group. *Toward Economic Justice for Women.* Washington, D.C.: Institute for Policy Studies, 1985.

Working Women. *In Defense of Affirmative Action: Taking the Profit Out of Discrimination.* Cleveland: Working Women, June 1981.

World Health Organization. *World Health Statistics Annual.* Geneva: World Health Organization, 1986.

Wrigley, Julia. "A Message of Marginality: Black Youth, Alienation, and Unemployment." In National Society for the Study of Education, *Education and Work,* 81st yearbook. Chicago: University of Chicago Press, 1982.

Yeager, Matthew. "Unemployment and Imprisonment." *Journal of Criminal Law and Criminology,* Winter 1979.

Yudken, Joel, and Andrew Goldenkranz. "There's More than One Way to Run a Factory." *Plowshare Press,* March-April 1983.

Zacharias, Jerrold, George Rathjens, and Myles Gordon. "The Arms Race." *Bulletin of the Atomic Scientists,* January 1983.

Zeitlin, Maurice. "Industry Is Ducking the Issue." *San Jose Mercury-News,* October 14, 1984.

Name Index

Subject Index

Arrests for crimes
  of minorities, 372–373
  rate of, 355, 367
    compared to number of
      crimes, 367
    and rearrest rates, 377–378
Arsenic, health and environmental effects of, 342
Asian-Americans, achievements
  of, 159–161
Assault, aggravated, yearly
  number of, 352, 354
Authority, women employed in
  positions of, 190–191
Automation of workplace, 46,
  267–272, 273
  in foreign countries, 435
  job skills in, 268–269
  occupations affected by, 270,
    271
  unemployment in, 254,
    269–272
  workers displaced by, 254
Automobile industry
  automation of, 270
  and energy consumption,
    325
  government bailouts for, 48,
    51, 130
  and lead in automobile ex-
    hausts, 344

Baby boom generation in labor
  force, affecting income
  distribution, 100
Bailouts of corporations, 48,
  51, 130
Banking system
  congressional recommenda-
    tions on, 441
  interlocking directorates in,
    35
Beer industry, economic concentration in, 31–34
  social costs of, 33–34
Benzene, health and environmental effects of, 342

Biases
  in crime rate statistics,
    353–355, 372–373,
    375–378
  in study of social problems,
    12–13
Birth control and family planning, 298–299
Blacks, and racial inequality,
  136–167. *See also* Minorities
Blood pressure, and hypertension in minorities, 294
Blue-collar jobs, 265, 266
  automation affecting, 270
Breweries, and economic concentration in beer
  industry, 31–34
Bridges, repairs needed to,
  398, 399, 443
Budget of government, 42
  affecting economic growth,
    77–80
  alternative energy expendi-
    tures in, 443
  balancing of, 79
  compared to gross domestic
    product, 42, 43
  deficit in
    active and passive types of,
      80
    affecting economic growth,
      79–80
    definition of, 92
  direction of expenditures in
    hidden welfare system,
    132
  environmental protection ex-
    penditures in, 338–340
  general funds in, 390, 391,
    392
  international differences in,
    77, 79, 80
  military expenditures in,
    386–419. *See also* Military
    expenditures
  public attitude on, 440
  trust funds in, 390–391

unemployment affecting, 78
welfare expenditures in,
  10–11, 117, 118, 121,
  389, 390–392, 410
Burglaries, yearly number of,
  352, 354
Businesses. *See also* Corporations
  economic cycles of, 92
  external costs of, government
    aid for, 50
  private enterprises, 23–24.
    See also Private enter-
    prise
  public enterprises, govern-
    ment sponsored, 42–44.
    See also Public enterprise,
    government sponsored
  small, decreasing activity of,
    36–38

Cadmium, health and environmental effects of, 342
Cancer
  environmental factors in,
    337, 338, 341, 342–343
  mortality rates in, 284, 287,
    301
    gender differences in, 297
    of low-income persons, 289
    of minorities, 292
    work-related, 301–302, 303
Capacity utilization rate, as
  measure of productivity,
  65
Capital, 92
  and capital-intensive pro-
    cesses, 92
    in defense industries,
      394–395
    in energy production, 328
  human resources as, 88, 93
    returns to, 93
    in social reconstruction
      strategy, 439–444
  income from gains in, 98,
    100–101
  for investment, 92

shortage of, affecting economic growth, 82–84
Carbon tetrachloride, health and environmental effects of, 342
Cerebrovascular disease, mortality rate in, 283, 284
Chemicals, toxic, 332–338. *See also* Toxic wastes
Chemical industry, government health and safety regulations on, 304–305, 306
Chernobyl nuclear accident, 7, 321
Childbirth, work leaves for, 231–232
Children
  abuse of, 233–234
    death of child in, 235
    and economic problems, 234–236
    and gender inequality, 237–238
    and lack of social supports, 236
    reporting of, 353
    sexual exploitation in, 234
    statistics on, 233–234
    and unemployment, 76
  and Aid to Families with Dependent Children, 118–119, 120, 125, 129
  delinquent behavior of, 383
  divorce affecting, 221
  household responsibilities of, 227–228
  and infant mortality rates, 284, 285–286, 289, 291–292
  lead poisoning in, 341, 344
  in low-income families, 107, 110
    health status of, 288, 289, 291
    of minority groups, 140, 142
  responsibilities for care of, 229–232

affecting employment, 182, 183, 229–232
  in day care programs, 229–231
  international differences in, 229–231, 232
  as private or social responsibility, 231
  in single-parent families, 223
  in single-parent families, 214, 215, 223
  delinquent behavior of, 383
  problems of, 221–222
  and violence against parents, 233
Chromium, health and environmental effects of, 342
Cigarette smoking, 307
Cities. *See* Urban areas
Civil Rights Act of 1964, 9, 136, 139, 168
Civil Rights movement, 5, 108
Climate, and greenhouse effect from coal burning, 318
Coal
  burning of
    acid rain from, 318, 331–332
    environmental problems in, 318–319, 331–332
    reduction of emissions in, 332
  mining of
    employment in, 329
    safety standards and productivity in, 91
  as nonrenewable energy source, 316, 318–319
  reserves of, 318
Collective bargaining on wages, 203
College education. *See* Education
Competition
  definition of, 92

in international economy
  changing position of United States in, 60–62
  government trade restrictions in protection from, 49
  as limit to economic expansion, 3
  in revitalization strategy, 429–430, 432
  and unemployment, 254
in military-industrial complex, 50, 404
and price fixing and price leadership of corporations, 86
Comprehensive Employment and Training Act, 165
Computer industry, as symbol of revitalization, 431
Concentration of economic power, 27–38, 52–53
  aggregation concentration ratio on, 28
  in beer industry, 31–34
  concentration ratio on, 92
  and concentration of wealth, 102–105
  in corporate mergers and takeovers, 30–31, 92
  decentralization of, in social reconstruction strategy, 445
  and decreasing activity of small businesses, 36–37
  definition of, 92
  and income distribution, 98–99
  in interlocking directorates of corporations, 34–35
  market concentration in, 28–30, 92, 93
  measurement of, 27–30
  in private sector, 52–53
  in world economy, 35–36
Conglomerate corporations, 30–31
  definition of, 92

recent trends in structure of, 211–218

role of women in, 10, 223–228, 240
  affecting employment, 181–184, 223–224, 225–226, 228
  and violence, 236–239

satisfaction in, 217–218, 241

single-parent. *See* Single-parent families

in social reconstruction strategy, 439–440

and stress in unemployment, 76

structure of, and poverty, 133–134
  of minorities, 147–149, 165

violence in, 232–239
  against children, 233–234. *See also* Children, abuse of
  against parents by children, 233
  against spouse, 233, 234, 236–237, 353, 371
  deterrence of, 371
  in economic problems, 234–236
  in gender inequality, 236–239
  in lack of social supports, 236
  rate of, 232–234
  reporting of, 353
  in unemployment, 76

as "vital center," 215–218

Family planning, 298–299

Foreign countries
  anti-American feelings in, 10
  child care in, 229–231, 232
  in competitive international economy. *See* Competition, in international economy
  crime in, 361, 371, 373–374, 377
  decline of American influence in, 3, 10

energy consumption in, 314, 324–325

gender inequality in, 202–203

government expenditures in, 77, 79, 80
  compared to gross domestic product, 42, 43
  on welfare programs, 121

gross domestic product in, 42, 43, 59, 60

gross national products of, compared to corporate sales, 25, 26

income in, 86, 114–115, 203

labor unions in, 47

military assistance to, 415–416

military budget in, 392–393
  compared to investments, 399–400
  compared to productivity growth, 400, 401

mortality rates in, 285–287

national health insurance programs in, 294–295

nuclear weapons of, 413–414

occupational exposure to chemicals in, 305

oil producing, 3

police in, 368

pollution control measures in, 345–346

public enterprises in, 42–44

questions on U.S. policies in, 9

reinvestment of corporate profits in, 84

rights of workers in, 89–91, 434–435

taxes in, 41, 81

technological advances in workplace in, 434–435

trade with. *See* Trade

unemployment in, 63–64, 250, 251, 258, 260
  of youth, 250, 251, 258

Fossil fuels, limits of, 316–319

Free enterprise system, 23–24

Gas, natural
  cost of exploration for, 317–318
  as nonrenewable energy source, 316
  reserves of, 316–317

Gender inequality of women, 168–205. *See also* Women

Gini index on income distribution, 99

Global 2000 report on ecological trends, 3–4

Government
  and congressional recommendations on economic reconstruction, 441–443
  employment in. *See* Employment, in government
  employment and training programs of, 274–277
  environmental protection regulations of, 311, 312, 329
    corporate violations of, 379, 380
    costs and benefits of, 338–346, 347–348
  expenditures of. *See* Budget of government
  health and safety regulations of, 280, 304–306
    costs and benefits of, 280, 304, 306
    and economic growth, 280, 304, 306
  intervention in economy, 6, 24, 47–52, 77–80
  public attitudes toward role of, 423
  in public enterprises, 42–44
  regulations affecting productivity, 91
  in reprivatization strategy, 422–429
  responsibility for social problems, 9

Household responsibilities
  changing attitudes towards, 226–228
  for child care, 229–232
  of children, 227–228
  and displaced housewives, 248
  economic value of work in, 224–225
  and employment of women, 181–184, 223–224, 225–226, 228
  gender inequality in, 223–228
  time required for, 224–225
Housing
  and racial segregation in urban areas, 143
  rising cost of, 70
    and generation of exiles, 68–69
  solar energy applications in, 326–327, 328
Hypertension, of minorities, 294

Illness. *See also* Health
  in divorce, 220
  incidence in population, 283
  mortality rates in, 283–284, 287
  occupational, 301–306
  stress-related, of women, 297, 300
  in unemployment, 75–76
Immigrants, as undocumented workers, 262–264
Imports of United States
  increase in, 61
  of oil, 312, 315
Incapacitation, in prevention of crime, 362–363, 365–368
  selective, 367–368
Incarceration rates, 360–362
  and crime rate, 361–362
  in foreign countries, 360, 361
  of minorities, 360–361, 373, 375
  and prison population, 362

Income
  adjusted for inflation, 66–70, 85, 86
  capital gains in, 98, 100–101
  comparison of earnings and transfer payments in, 93
  of crime victims, 356–357
  definition of, 98
  discretionary, 70
  disposable, 66, 93
  distribution of, 98–99
    and concentration of wealth, 102–105
    demographic changes affecting, 99–100
    and earnings of executives, 108–109
    inequality of, 98–102, 137–142, 147
    international differences in, 114–115
    measurement of, 98–99
    and tax system, 129–130
    trends in, 98–99, 101–102
  and economic inequality, 96–135
  and Gini index on income concentration, 99
  and guaranteed income plans, 259
  and health status, 287–291
  international differences in, 86, 114–115, 203
  minimum wages in, 259–261
  of minority groups, 138–140, 151–155
    of Asian-Americans, 161
    of native Americans, 162, 163
  real disposable, 66–67
  and relationship of high wages to slow economic growth, 85–86
  service industry wages in, 266–267
  and standard of living, 66–70
  statistics on, problems with, 98, 99–101
  in underemployment, 248, 252

and wage replacement ratio of unemployment benefits, 258, 259
  of women, 173–178, 184–185, 192–193, 201
    and health, 290–291
    international differences in, 203
    and level of education, 177–178
    and life-cycle earnings, 176
    at poverty level, 194–197, 201–202
    and solidary wage policy, 203
    and undervaluing of work, 185–186
Industries
  automation of. *See* Automation of workplace
  defense-related
    capital-intensive, 394–395
    kinds of jobs in, 395–397
    in military-industrial complex, 403–406
    number of jobs in, 394–395
    regional concentration of, 397–398
  and deindustrialization of economy, 65, 252–254
  productivity of, environmental regulations affecting, 340, 341
  and reindustrialization in New England, 272
  revitalization of, 430, 431–432
  in service sector. *See* Service industries
  in social reconstruction strategy, 435, 436
  toxic wastes of, by sectors, 334, 335
  women workers in, 192–193
Inequality, 96–205
  and crime, 350–351, 371, 372–378, 383–384
  economic, 96–135. *See also* Economic inequality

Women (continued)
labor-force participation rates on, 170–173, 179
life expectancy of, 296–297, 300
myths and realities on, 178–185
poverty of, 148–149, 169, 194–197, 202
public policies affecting, 199–204
rape of, 352, 353, 354, 357
reprivatization strategy affecting, 428
revitalization strategy affecting, 432
social reconstruction strategy affecting, 437–439
stress-related diseases of, 297, 300
in underclass, 196
underemployment of, 252
unemployment of, 196, 247
in child care problems, 229
in welfare programs, 123, 124, 197, 199, 201–203, 238–239
Women, Infants, and Children (WIC) program, 291, 308, 309
Wood, as alternative energy source, 326
Work ethic
decline of, affecting economic growth, 87–91
and productivity, 87–88
public opinion on, 243, 244
Workplace, 243–278. *See also* Employment

health problems related to, 301–308
technological advances in, in foreign countries, 434–435
World War II, employment of women during, 172

Youth, unemployment of, 244–245, 249–251, 255, 256, 258, 260
in foreign countries, 250, 251, 258, 260
in growth of labor force, 261, 262
minimum wage affecting, 259, 260–261